The Open University
Faculties of Social Sciences and
Educational Studies

WITHDRAWN

Welfare in Action

edited by

Mike Fitzgerald,
Paul Halmos,
John Muncie
and David Zeldin
at the Open University

London and Henley
Routledge & Kegan Paul
in association with The Open University Press

First published in 1977
by Routledge & Kegan Paul Ltd
39 Store Street,
London WC1E 7DD and
Broadway House,
Newtown Road,
Henley-on-Thames,
Oxon RG9 1EN
Set in 9 on 10pt Times by
Kelly & Wright, Bradford-on-Avon, Wiltshire
and printed in Great Britain by
Lowe & Brydone Printers Ltd, Thetford, Norfolk

British Library Cataloguing in Publication Data

Welfare in Action.

1. Social service—Great Britain—Addresses, essays,
lectures
I. Fitzgerald, Mike II. Open University
361'.941   HV245

ISBN 0 7100 8738 1
ISBN 0 7100 8739 X Pbk

Contents

Acknowledgments

The Open University and the publishers would like to thank the following for permission to reproduce copyright material. All possible care has been taken to trace ownership of the selections included and to make full acknowledgment for their use.

Reading I. 1   © Professor John Saville, 1958.

I. 2   By permission of the National Association of Social Workers, *Social Work*, 1974.

I. 3   By permission of Professor Marshall and Cambridge University Press, 1972.

I. 4   By permission of the editor, *New Left Review*, 1975.

I. 5   Copyright © J. C. Kincaid, 1973; reprinted by permission of Penguin Books Ltd.

II. 1   Reprinted by permission of Oxford University Press, 1972.

II. 2   By permission of *Social Problems*, the Society for the Study of Social Problems, and the author, 1972.

II. 3   By permission of the editor, *The British Journal of Psychiatry*, 1975.

II. 4   By permission of Souvenir Press Ltd, 1973.

II. 5, III. 9 and V. 3   These articles first appeared in *New Society*, London, the weekly review of the Social Sciences.

II. 6   By permission of Coventry Workshop, 1975.

III. 1 and IV. 2   By permission of the editor, *Social Work Today*, 1973.

III. 2   By permission of the editor, *Case Conference*, 1964.

III. 3   By permission of Mrs Helen Harris Perlman and Jossey-Bass Inc., 1972.

III. 4   By permission of the Family Service Association of America, 1970.

III. 5   Copyright © 1965 by the Free Press, a Division of The Macmillan Company.

III. 6   By permission of George Allen & Unwin (Publishers) Ltd, 1975.

III. 7   By permission of the editor, *British Journal of Social Work*, 1974.

III. 8   By permission of Tavistock Publications, 1972.

III. 10, IV. 3 and V. 1   By permission of the editor, *British Journal of Social Work*, and the authors, 1973, 1971, 1973.

IV. 1   By permission of Anthony S. Hall, 1971.

IV. 4   By permission of Tony F. Marshall and the executrix of the late Dr Gordon Rose, 1975.

IV. 5   By permission of the National Council for Special Education, 1966.

IV. 6   By permission of the Controller of Her Majesty's Stationery Office, 1974.

V. 2   By permission of The Merlin Press Ltd, 1973.

V. 4   By permission of the Editorial Board, *Sociological Review*, 1975.

V. 5   © Stanley Cohen, 1977.

Introduction

This book of readings has been designed as an integral part of the Open University second-level undergraduate course, 'Social Work, Community Work and Society', offered jointly by the Faculties of Social Sciences and Educational Studies. At the time of writing, the course is not designed to be part of a social work training programme.

Although the contents are best understood in the light of the objectives and content of the course, the volume will be found useful for all those who are interested in the general issues surrounding social work and community work practices within the modern welfare state.

Our attempt throughout has been to gain a general overview of present-day welfare provisions, and the selected readings are designed to illustrate the many controversies that presently surround the adequacy and nature of such provisions. The course in general, and this volume in particular, does not include a comparative element other than occasional reference to the USA, although it has been argued that many of the problems and issues discussed in this Reader are paralleled in socialist societies.

Our main objective is thus to give some understanding of the nature and implications of the theoretical and political debates surrounding 'welfare', and in particular social work and community work in contemporary Britain.

We have been particularly concerned to situate accounts of social work role and practice in the wider context of the economic and political structures of the welfare state, of which the so-called 'helping professions' are just one part. Part I illustrates some of the wider constraints—legal, material, economic— which are placed on any attempt to apply widespread welfare measures in contemporary society.

The social worker's role is thus inevitably limited to a certain extent, as a result of having to work within this wider context. While social welfare can be seen as a well-established institution in modern society,

social work is best described as an emerging profession within that institution. Both are designed to try and cope with the many social problems that occur in modern society—problems arising from social change and urban industrial life. Part II highlights some of the controversies inherent in both the analysis of issues such as deviancy, delinquency, poverty, urban decay and unemployment, and the various attempts which have been made to resolve them. It is only to be expected, then, that the development of state welfare provisions has been neither smooth nor uncontested.

The specific tasks, and the orientations of social work in helping to solve some of these problems, are discussed in Part III. Social work and community work are largely concerned with intervening in the lives of others in order to produce personal or political change. The nature of these changes is itself a highly controversial subject. How is intervention justified? Are social workers truly part of a caring profession or are their efforts better seen in the light of their social control function? Do they really 'help', or are they more concerned with persuading clients to accept already existing living conditions which may or may not be decisive causes of their predicament?

Since its emergence in the late nineteenth century, social work has been concerned with both the emotional and the material implications of human suffering, and has concentrated its attentions on solving individual, family or group problems. More recently, community work has expanded this focus by understanding and approaching individual problems in the context of wider community, political or structural change. Whatever the method of intervention, social work has long been criticised for not being able to help enough. Social workers are usually of middle-class status and thus viewed by some as being incapable of understanding and relating to the needs of many of their working-class clients. Sometimes their efforts are seen as attempts to pry into people's lives and to place

1

blame for many social problems on certain individual deficiencies. This issue is often referred to as the subject of the so-called 'care : control' debate.

Perhaps for this more than any other reason, the effects of social work are constantly being researched and evaluated. Part IV illustrates some types of research that are presently being undertaken into certain aspects of social work, ranging from the clients' own evaluation of social work success to the views of the practitioners themselves. At the basis of a good deal of such research also are attempts to raise the practice of social work to that of an applied social science, rather than an art, and to establish social work firmly as a clearly defined profession, similar to that of medicine and law. This, however, may well be an unrealistic goal; social problems can never be seen in the same light as physiological deficiencies. A consensus of opinion on diagnosis and problem resolution is peculiarly difficult to reach, given the political and economic background against which such decisions are made.

This is illustrated by the fact that existing welfare provisions have come under much criticism from many quarters, not least the welfare recipients themselves. Part V looks at some of the areas to which criticism has been directed, including those of the Claimants' Unions and the Mental Patients' Unions, and the search for a more equitable distribution of wealth and economic power. But are all social problems reducible to material factors—poverty and the like? Would social work, as an identifiable profession, be redundant in a more humane society? These questions are hard to answer, but important to bear in mind when looking at the issues raised by a state welfare system which is increasingly coming to dominate all our lives.

It is hoped that this selection of readings will go some way in alerting the students, teachers and practitioners involved in the whole industry of welfare to the wide range of differing perspectives and approaches that are prevalent in this field. Resolution of the problems and issues raised through this Reader will not be easy to find, but we should all be wary of ignoring the implications of the diverse opinions that spring out of any discussion of welfare provision.

The Reader is but one component of a guided course of study which includes correspondence texts, BBC radio and television programmes and other set reading, including the following specific texts which deal with a host of issues raised by the implementation of welfare provisions: Family Welfare Association, *Guide to the Social Services*; *Paul Halmos* (1976), *The Faith of the Counsellors*; Bill Jordan (1974), *Poor Parents*; George Konrad (1975), *The Case Worker*; Howard J. Parker (1974), *View from the Boys*; Geoffrey Pearson (1975), *The Deviant Imagination*; Richard M. Titmuss (1974), *Social Policy*.

Items for this Reader have not been selected from these books, which are complementary to it.

Part I Welfare state or welfare society?

Explanations of the role of welfare provision in contemporary British society have been characterised by Richard Titmuss as involving a distinction between a welfare state and a welfare society.

The term 'welfare society' implies a recognition that in Britain a system of welfare provision has been created which is egalitarian and humanitarian in its effects. The term 'welfare state' implies that this vast development of provision has been introduced only against a backcloth of state control and conflict between state and private interests.

The readings in this Part have been chosen to indicate various views on the historical development and contemporary role played by welfare provision. It is directed towards asking questions about the viability of securing a 'true' welfare society within capitalism, where state political interests and private economic interests may often clash; about the effect the expansion of social welfare has had in the reduction of poverty and inequality; and about the values and nature of a society which attempts to satisfy many of the needs of its members by a highly centralised state machinery.

Saville introduces these themes by looking at the relationship between welfare provision and social inequality; giving a historical analysis of the development of social welfare from the nineteenth century to the present day. He focuses primarily on two factors: the effect of a labour movement actively attempting to secure wider provisions; and the general limitations of the effects such provisions will have within a capitalist society, where 'the central interests of private property have never seriously been challenged'.

The view that welfare also essentially has a controlling function rather than providing a more open and freer society is taken up by Cowger and Atherton, who view social workers as agents of social control in addition to the more repressive agents of 'police power'. Above all, they indicate how we are all con-

strained and controlled in order that society can attain some essential functional cohesiveness.

This in turn raises questions concerning the values of what Marshall terms 'welfare-capitalism'. He isolates a major 'value problem' in the seemingly contradictory situation where policy decisions on welfare may be taken by a democratically elected government, only to be confronted by economic constraints emanating from the market sector.

The extent of state expenditure on social services as a percentage of the Gross National Product is discussed by Gough, and illustrates how 'real state consumption expenditure has fallen as a share of GNP over the last two decades', and that this in part explains the current (mid-1970s) cutbacks in social service resources.

Kincaid concludes this Part and provides a general overview of the effect the welfare state has had in solving problems of poverty, inequality and income distribution by looking at the distribution of wealth—and in particular pension schemes and social security payments. He is able to conclude that the welfare state has not made any fundamental change in the order of society. In conjunction with Saville, he feels justified in asking whether welfare provisions in Britain were ever in fact designed to achieve this objective, and whether welfare can be distributed equally to all in a capitalist society that is necessarily economically constrained by private and market interests.

Part I thus gives a critical analysis of the concept of 'welfare', highlighting its piecemeal effects, its role as an element of control and its anomalous nature within a capitalist society, where values are generated which are diametrically opposed to the very value of welfare.

The readings have been selected to give a firm critical base to enable the reader to evaluate the practice and role of social and community work more closely within this wider setting.

I. 1 The Welfare State: an historical approach
J. Saville

[. . .] This conviction that the Welfare State is, if not a halfway, then a part-way house to socialism, and that the same road will lead to socialism, is based upon three main premises:

(1) that the managerial revolution, among other things, has resulted in the owners of capital no longer having a decisive influence over business decisions, and in their political power being much weakened;

(2) that the techniques of full employment are of such a character, and are so well understood, that prolonged mass unemployment is not likely to reappear; and the Labour movement is now so strong that in this, as in other matters, there is no likelihood of the clock being put back;

(3) that the growth of the Welfare State—and in particular the levelling up of incomes and the extension of social services have largely abolished primary poverty.

Given these circumstances, the Labour movement must continue to push hard for social reform and for further economic changes; and on past evidence there is no reason to believe that the political problems, against the background of a more mature and greatly strengthened working-class movement, will in any way prove insuperable.

The arguments developed in the present essay are concerned to deny certain of these propositions. The Welfare State, it will be suggested, has come about as a result of the interaction of three main factors: (1) the struggle of the working class against their exploitation; (2) the requirements of industrial capitalism (a convenient abstraction) for a more efficient environment in which to operate and in particular the need for a highly productive labour force; (3) recognition by the property owners of the price that has to be paid for political security. In the last analysis, as the Labour movement

has always recognized, the pace and tempo of social reform have been determined by the struggle of working-class groups and organizations; but it would be historically incorrect and politically an error to underestimate the importance of either of the other factors in the situation. To do so would be to accept the illusion that the changes are of greater significance than in fact they are, as well as to misread the essential character of contemporary capitalism.

The political problems associated with social reform became immensely complicated with the rise of the modern Labour movement. The intelligent bourgeois—Mrs Webb's 'great employer'—was confronted with a complete programme of radical reform put forward in the name of those who were now the majority of the electorate. In the 1860s the demands of the politically articulate sections of the working class were largely those which the rare enlightened entrepreneur or the liberal humanitarian were already advocating but within two or three decades large parts of the working-class programme had become specifically socialist, and on paper at least went beyond the boundaries of existing society. The new political problem for the propertied classes was a two-fold one: on the one hand to accept those economic and social demands which made no serious inroad into property rights (an acceptance which always involved conflict with the simple-minded traditional conservatives who always fail to appreciate the new territory they are moving through) and on the other, to recognize those claims which, implicitly or explicitly, were concerned with fundamentals and which must either be sidestepped or smothered. As Cardinal Manning so nicely put the problem, in 1888, in a letter to his friend J. E. C. Bodley: 'If the Landlords, Householders and Capitalists will "engineer a slope" we may avert disastrous collisions. If they will not, I am afraid you will see a rough time.'

The question of timing was, and is, crucial; for what may be a major victory for the working class at one

Source: *New Reasoner*, 3, winter 1957–8, pp. 5, 6, 11, 12–17, 20–4 (reprinted in Butterworth and Holman (eds), *Social Welfare in Modern Britain*, Fontana, 1975, pp. 57–70).

point in time and which may well lead to significant changes in the internal balance of political forces in the country, is not necessarily of the same importance when it has been long delayed. From the standpoint of property, delay must always be supported: for delay gives opportunity for the vested interests to mobilize themselves, and on the other side it has often a marked centrifugal effect upon the forces of reform, who can rarely agree about the relationship of short-term with long-term aims. Coal nationalization is an excellent case in point. The first serious demand for coal nationalization came in 1919, a year when the desire for change was immensely strong among large sections of the people. Of all the years in the twentieth century, not excluding 1926, 1919 had probably the greatest potential for radical reform. The 'passion of Labour' to remake the world was echoed by many outside the movement. The Labour Party's new programme 'Labour and the New Social Order', adopted in the middle of 1918, called for the common ownership of land, the railways, coal, electric power and among other industries 'the manufacture and retailing of alcoholic drink'. The opening months of 1919 were a time when a political explosion seemed inevitable. There were mutinies in the Army by soldiers who wanted quicker demobilization; Clydeside saw the 40-hour week strike (Jan. 27–Feb. 11); there was the threat of a national coal strike backed by the other members of the Triple Alliance (railwaymen and transport workers). Among large sections of the people there was not only an immense war weariness but a widespread rejection of the old order; and it was to be expected that politicians and publicists alike, following this mood, would go on record for change. So we find Winston Churchill, during his election campaign in Dundee in December 1918, advocating railway nationalization; and J. L. Garvin, editor of the *Observer*, noting that nationalization of coal, electricity and transport was 'inevitable'. But the situation never seriously got out of hand, for the leadership of the Labour Party and the trade unions were easily fooled, and in Lloyd George the ruling class had a politician of genius. Lloyd George played for time—the Sankey Coal Commission and the National Industrial Conference were his principal instruments, and by a judicious mixture of lies, half-truths, evasion and deceit Lloyd George saw the year through to tame conclusions. A combination of an extension of social insurance in 1919 with the beginning of mass unemployment in the spring of 1920 completed his efforts on behalf of the propertied classes. But had coal nationalization been achieved in 1919 the political consequences would have been immense, for among other things it would have meant that Lloyd George's major aim would have been defeated and the position of Labour would have been tremendously strengthened. In the event, coal nationalization, the pivot of the whole situation in the years immediately after 1918, was delayed for over two decades; and when it came it was a matter of the State taking over a bankrupt indus-

try from the incompetent mine owners who could congratulate themselves only on the compensation they successfully extorted from the Labour Government. As a political act coal nationalization in 1945 was of minor significance.

The British political situation has always contained certain special and difficult features that have demanded much subtlety of manoeuvre on the part of the bourgeois politicians. Compared with America, Britain was a closed and less dynamic economy with vertical movements for the working class severely restricted and with emigration as the main avenue of escape; while compared with France, Britain was overwhelmingly proletarian. It was this fact of a predominantly working-class society that occasioned Lloyd George's famous comment, quoted by Lenin in *Left Wing Communism* (Lenin dedicating his pamphlet 'to the Right Honourable Mr Lloyd George as a token of my gratitude for his speech of March 18, 1920, which was almost Marxist and, in any case, exceedingly useful for Communists and Bolsheviks throughout the world'). The passage quoted by Lenin reads:

> If you go to the agricultural areas I agree that you have the old party divisions as strong as ever: they are far removed from the danger [of Socialism]. It does not walk in their lanes. But when they see it, they will be as strong as some of these industrial constituencies now are. Four-fifths of this country is industrial and commercial; hardly one-fifth is agricultural. It is one of the things I have constantly in mind when I think of the dangers of the future here. In France the population is agricultural, and you have a solid body of opinions which does not move very rapidly, and which is not very easily excited by revolutionary movements. That is not the case here. This country is more top heavy than any country in the world, and if it begins to rock, the crash here, for that reason, will be greater than in any land.

It was not numbers only—although the working-class majority in the nation certainly worried the Victorians—but political cohesiveness that presented the dangers. The working class had been kept outside the civic pale for two decades after 1848—one of the payments made in return for the hysteria that Chartism generated. Despite the absence of political democracy after 1850 there took place the great development of skilled trade unionism and a growing political sense of unity and solidarity among the working people. It was these developments that produced the widespread anxiety over 'the leap in the dark' when the vote was given for the first time to sections of the urban workers in 1867. In many towns this made the working-class the majority of the voters, and the many correctives and brakes upon full democracy are an indication of the fears that were aroused. Universal suffrage was introduced only by stages, and it was not until 1884 that most of the miners and the agricultural labourers received the vote. Even then many workers remained outside the franchise. But delaying tactics of this kind (in addition to plural voting for property owners and the many tiresome difficulties put in the way of the working-class voter recording his vote) could work effectively only for a few decades; and in the long run, given the working-class majority among the electorate, both Tories and Liberals were forced to adapt themselves to the political demands of this new audience. Both parties made careful and sustained appeals; but while the Tories, with their record on factory legislation and their anti-bourgeois bias, were never without working-class support in the towns, and for different reasons in the countryside, most workers attached themselves to the Liberal Party and the politically conscious among them became part of its left wing. To lead the left wing in the 1870s and 1880s were a group of Radical leaders—Bradlaugh, Dilke and Chamberlain—whose historical role was to delay for several decades the emergence of an independent Labour Party representing the industrial workers. Given the facts of British society, an independent workers' party was historically inevitable; but compared with similar situations elsewhere—Germany for example—the development of an independent working-class political force was extraordinarily slow; and among the reasons for the long period of gestation was the vigour and the liveliness, as well as the personal courage and ability, of the Radical leaders. The crux of the Radical position—and it states the central assumptions of the Welfare State of the twentieth century—was summed up in a famous phrase which Joseph Chamberlain used in 1885. His speech on this occasion marked the opening of the campaign for the Unauthorized programme, an early blue-print of the Welfare State of today. 'I ask', said Chamberlain, 'what ransom will property pay for the security which it enjoys?'

Now ransom, as Chamberlain's biographer sorrowfully noted, is an 'ugly' word. It went, explained Garvin, far beyond Chamberlain's real intention which was only that 'private property must pay to be tolerated'. Chamberlain himself immediately recognized his error, and anxious to correct what he appreciated was a serious mistake, substituted for ransom in all his later speeches, the less explosive word 'insurance'. This, said Garvin, was what he was henceforth to 'speak and think'. The programme that Chamberlain was explaining to his audiences, and which because of his use of such an ungentlemanly word as ransom was to appear much more radical than in fact it was, has provided the framework within which the modern Welfare State has been built. Chamberlain and his colleagues recognized that State intervention was developing at an accelerated rate, and it was further accepted that much of the intervention must be on behalf of labour against the predatory claims of capital. The division between classes was too great for the political health of society; and new positions must be built as a result of which confidence between employers and workers could grow.

Not, of course, that Chamberlain in any way accepted the idea of displacing private enterprise; his concern was always, wrote Garvin, 'to supplement it [private enterprise] powerfully where it was no longer adequate for social justice and national needs'. As the last phrase shows, Chamberlain was fully aware of the relationship between welfare and economic efficiency, although his primary concern was with political stability.

Chamberlain pioneered within the old established parties and those who followed him did no more than enlarge upon the foundations he had laid. Among these the Fabians are by far the most important, and in many fields of social policy it was the Fabians, directed by the Webbs, who provided the detailed blue-prints for the legislation of the twentieth century. Believing in the inevitability of gradualness, the Fabians emphasized the ways in which collectivist practices and legislation had been increasing steadily throughout the second half of the nineteenth century; and how what we have come to call the Welfare State developed naturally and inevitably, despite intensive political opposition, out of the individualism of the early years of Victorian England. As Sidney Webb wrote in 1889:

> The 'practical man', oblivious or contemptuous of any theory of the Social Organism or general principles of social organization, has been forced by the necessities of the time, into an ever deepening collectivist channel. Socialism, of course, he still rejects and despises. The individualist Town Councillor will walk along the municipal pavement, lit by municipal gas and cleansed by municipal brooms with municipal water, and seeing by the municipal clock in the municipal market that he is too early to meet his children coming from the municipal school hard by the county lunatic asylum and municipal hospital, will use the national telegraph system to tell them not to walk through the municipal park but to come by the municipal tramway, to meet him in the municipal reading room by the municipal art gallery, museum and library, where he intends to consult some of the national publications in order to prepare his next speech in the municipal town hall, in favour of the nationalization of the canals and the increase of the government control over the railway system. 'Socialism, sir', he will say, 'don't waste the time of a practical man by your fantastic absurdities. Self-help sir, individual self-help, that's what's made our city what it is.'

Like the Benthamites, their predecessors, the Fabians were primarily concerned with efficiency and social justice; like Chamberlain, they sought to influence the traditional parties. In practical terms what they have done is vastly to enlarge the meaning of 'supplement' to private enterprise; and the twentieth century has witnessed a most striking growth of State intervention. It is this change in the role of the State that has confused so many as to the essential characteristics of contemporary society; but what has not changed is that State intervention still 'supplements' private enterprise, in Chamberlain's meaning of the terms. After more than half a century of overt socialist thought and agitation and majority Labour Governments the fundamental structure of society remains unaltered.

As the quotation from Sidney Webb indicated, the growth of municipal and State enterprise in social and economic affairs had already proceeded a long way by the end of the nineteenth century. Sidney Webb's list of collectivist measures is by no means complete; and among those omitted were factory legislation and the establishment of a factory inspectorate, the elementary beginnings of a housing policy, and the introduction of workmen's compensation. This last achievement began an important new stage in the relationships between capital and labour and represents one of the pillars of the Welfare State.

In the twentieth century the legislative structure of the Welfare State, erected upon Radical-Fabian foundations, was carried through in three main periods of social reform. These were:

(1) The Liberal Governments of 1906–1914; and among the major social reforms of the successive Liberal Governments may be noted the following:

1906 meals for necessitous school children
1907 medical inspection for school children
1908 the first Old Age Pensions
1909 the first Trade Boards Act and the establishment of a minimum wage in selected industries
1911 the beginnings of national health and unemployment insurance.

(2) The second main period of reform, not as spectacular or as concentrated in time as that of the Liberal Governments after 1906, was the years of the First World War and the inter-war years. The pace of change was uneven and slower, but the Conservative administrations—the minority Labour Governments, in this as in all other matters, making a poor showing —continued to extend social security benefits. Among the reforms of this second period, the most important were the 1918 Maternity and Child Welfare Act; the 1919 Housing and Town Planning Act (which introduced subsidies on a considerable scale and took the Government into the business of housing); the 1920 Unemployment Insurance Act, which brought nearly all workers earning below £250 a year into the scheme; the 1926 Hadow report on education and the slow improvement in educational structure and organization in the years which followed; the 1927 Widows, Orphans and Old Age Contributory Pensions Act; and the 1934 Unemployment Act.

(3) The Labour Government, 1945–1950. In general this short period after the Second World War may be compared with that of the Liberal Government after 1906, although in terms of social policy the Labour Government showed much less originality and initiative and were more in the stream of tradition than were the Liberals before 1914. Hence the relative ease with which social legislation was passed after 1945, largely because the proposals represented a minimum which the Tories had already accepted in principle. The main contribution of these years was to make an extended range of social security benefits available to the whole population. Among these were the raising of the school leaving age, a comprehensive health service, retirement pensions and family allowances. It was a modest programme, and a couple of decades overdue by the standards of the previous half century and its achievement was followed by a partial retreat in 1950 with the imposition of charges for certain health services.

This growth in social security benefits in the twentieth century has involved an increase in expenditure per head of population of about twelve times between 1900 and 1950 (allowing for changes in the value of money). But the starting point was from a very low level, and for an economy as industrially advanced and as economically wealthy as that of Britain, the pace of change has been surprisingly slow. It is the success of the determined opposition to reform that merits attention—not the social legislation that has been achieved. The range and distribution of social security in Britain represents no more than elementary social justice for the mass of the people; and from the side of industry it can be reckoned as a sound economic investment. The struggle for any particular reform has always in this country aroused so much opposition that when it is achieved it is at least understandable that those who have spent half a lifetime on its behalf too easily believe that with its enactment a new period in social history is beginning. Members of Parliament in particular are cautious individuals (if not by temperament and training then certainly by adaptation to the Parliamentary scene) and they are especially liable to emphasize the difficulties of legislative change. When it comes, its results are usually exaggerated and its significance grossly over-estimated.

A main reason why public opinion in general, and the Labour movement in particular, have become confused as to the essentially bourgeois nature of the Welfare State is that both in the propaganda of the Labour Party and in the criticisms of its opponents, the legislation of the 1945 Labour Government was labelled 'socialist'. The melancholy business of making a collection of the idiotic and wildly unrealistic statements of Labour's intellectual leaders concerning the 'social revolution' of the post-war years must be left to others; but it must be noted that given the attribution of 'socialist' to the measures of nationalization and 'free' social security benefits, even the rank and file of the Labour movement began to believe this propaganda which came as much from those who purport to be its friends as from its enemies. With most of the Labour 'New Thinkers' the changes in the last twenty years have been elevated to a radical transformation in the character of society. Mr Crosland, one of the more articulate of the Labour Party's economists, has argued that with the legislative achievements of the 1945 Government we have all been involved in 'a major historical change'. This revolution, it is no less, Mr Crosland used to call 'statism' (although he has since discarded the term).

> With its arrival, the most characteristic features of capitalism have all disappeared: the absolute rule of private property, the subjection of the whole of economic life to market influences, the domination of the profit motive, the neutrality of government, the typical *laissez faire* division of income, the ideology of individual rights. This is no minor modification; it is a major historical change.

It should be remarked, fi st of all, that nowhere, except in the more remote parts of Scandinavia and among Labour publicists in Britain, is this sort of viewpoint seriously argued. As for the claim that the Welfare State is an early form of a socialist society, it must be emphasized that both in Western Europe and the United States social security schemes are placed firmly within the framework of a free enterprise economy and no one suggests that what is a natural development within a mature capitalist economy should be given new names. In Britain the socialists before 1914 did not make this mistake, and it is worth-while to look again at the discussions in which they considered the relationship between social reform and socialism.

The general proposition that most socialists accepted before 1914 was that the State, from the proceeds of a progressive system of taxation, should pay for social reform. When, in 1911, Lloyd George introduced the principle of compulsory contributions into the new insurance schemes, the left wing socialists Lansbury, Snowden, Keir Hardie and a few others went into vigorous opposition, with MacDonald and the majority of the Labour Party supporting Lloyd George. In the Commons George Lansbury and Snowden were the most vehement opponents of the new measures (Lloyd George much annoying the Tories by taunting them that 'Lansbury had taken the position of leader of the Opposition'). Their main arguments can be summed up as follows:

(1) that social reform must at all times be paid for by those best able to bear the burden and not by those whose economic and social condition the reform was intended to benefit;

(2) that the principle of compulsory contribution not only placed at least a part of the financial burden upon the poor but by avoiding the necessity of having to raise the whole financial amount by taxation it thereby side-stepped the political problem involved in a drastic redistribution of wealth;

(3) that it was a retrograde measure. As Snowden said in the House of Commons, 6 July, 1911; '. . . the principle of State financial responsibility is embodied in nearly all recent legislation—in the Workmen's

Compensation Act, in Public Health Acts and even in the Old Age Pensions legislation.'

Fortunately for Mr Crossman these arguments have for the most part been forgotten by the Labour movement; and the latest Labour Party proposals are based firmly upon the contributory principle which Mr Crossman, following Beveridge, has elevated into a virtue. The increasing acceptance of the principle by successive Governments in the twentieth century has meant that the social services have developed in such a way that the financial burden upon the rich has been very largely cushioned. Even more striking however—and it is a matter on which there has been virtually no hostile comment from Labour theoreticians—is the growth of direct and indirect taxation upon working-class incomes to the point where much of the expenditure upon social services is no more than a transfer of income by taxation within the working class. Or, to put the matter more simply, to a very considerable extent the working class pay for their own social security benefits by compulsory contributions and a high level of indirect taxation.

One study of this problem was made by an American scholar, Findley Weaver, in *The Review of Economics and Statistics* (August 1950). His main conclusions are given below, and they deserve to be widely known. His study relates to the years 1948 and 1949.

> The outstanding feature of the post-war growth in redistribution is not that of taking from the 'classes', and giving to the 'masses'. The main feature is that the benefits of redistribution cut across income groups and are largely related to consumption. As a general proposition, the working class pays enough additional in beer, tobacco, and purchase taxes, and other indirect levies to meet the increased cost of the food subsidies and health and education expenditures, while the increase in the direct taxes they pay covers the rise in their transfer money receipts. . . . Most of the post-war increase in personal taxes has been levied indirectly on consumption and has fallen on those who smoke and drink or consume non-utility clothing and household goods. The incidence of these regressive taxes is mainly on the working class who are also the chief recipients of the benefits of redistributive governmental expenditures. Generally, the low income group pays for its benefits, the redistribution being within the group based largely on considerations as to the most socially desirable forms of consumption.

All this has a good deal of bearing upon the much disputed matter of the levelling up of incomes in the years since 1940; and while this question must be left to another occasion for a detailed analysis, there are some points that can be made here. There is, in the first place, no doubt that there has been some levelling up of incomes in favour of the working class. The figures are widely known and have been used by

Labour commentators such as Mr Strachey and Mr Crosland to indicate the magnitude of the social changes which they believe have taken place. There are three points to be made in this connection. The first is that at least part of the additional share of the national income accruing to the working class in the post-war years has been absorbed by higher indirect taxation to pay for the increased social services. Secondly, the major redistribution occurred during the war years; and since then, the official calculations show a slow but persistent trend towards greater inequality. This is, of course, what must always be expected of capitalism, for it continuously generates inequality. Thirdly, the official calculations of income distribution, the basis for many sweeping generalizations made by those who are convinced they have been living through major historical changes in Britain since 1945, omit three factors whose individual and collective effect is to increase sharply the inequality of incomes. These are (1) capital gains, (2) expense allowances, and (3) tax evasion; and only the politically innocent really believe that the official figures of taxable income for the upper income brackets represent the true position.

Concerning the distribution of property in the country there is no dispute. The Welfare State, with its higher death duties and its supposedly crippling and burdensome taxation upon the rich, has effected practically no change in the distribution of private capital.

The Welfare State is the twentieth-century version of the Victorian ideal of self-help; and since this involves, in addition to benefits, high taxation on alcohol and tobacco, it must be said that these aspects of the Welfare State, taken by themselves, cannot be objected to by socialists. The State now 'saves' for the working class and translates the savings into social services. As the *Economist* remarked in 1950 of the social services: 'It is still true that nobody—or practically nobody—gets anything for nothing.' Since the Welfare State in Britain developed within a mature capitalist society, with a ruling class long experienced and much skilled in the handling of public affairs, its growth and development has been slow and controlled; and the central interests of private property have never seriously been challenged. Britain remains a society in which the distribution of capital wealth is no more equal than it was half a century ago; and although income distribution has proved more amenable to political pressure from the Labour movement, there exists within any capitalist society strong and powerful tendencies offsetting egalitarian measures.

I. 2 Social control: a rationale for social welfare

Charles D. Cowger and Charles R. Atherton

From a functional sociological perspective social control is the primary function of social welfare. Is this a legitimate rationale or an inappropriate one? Social workers have tended to view it as inappropriate. Part of the problem lies in the term *social control*, which to many has become equated with the arbitrary exercise of power by an elitist group. This view is unfortunate because, sociologically, it does not necessarily have this meaning. An obvious solution is to use a less loaded term. Parsons, for example, uses 'boundary maintenance', but such semantic substitution avoids the issue.[1]

As a sociological term, *social control* refers to those processes in a society that support a level of social cohesiveness sufficient for the survival of the society as a recognizable functional unit.[2] Basically, social control takes three forms:

Socialization. As children grow, the family, the educational system, and the religious institutions in the society teach them the ways of their culture. The norms or standards that are inculcated help regulate social behavior within culturally desirable patterns.

Direct behavior control. The formal laws of the society backed by the police power of the state define and enforce the limits of behavior.

Resocialization. Social welfare agencies, mental health facilities, and other psychological and social services help solve social problems for those having difficulty in coping with life situations.

Although it is possible to separate these three forms of social control for the purpose of analysis, they are closely intertwined. Each has preventive as well as corrective aspects.

Misgivings of social workers

Because of their orientation to humanistic values, social workers may view social control as antithetical to social work practice although they must concede

Source: *Social Work*, 19, July 1974, pp. 456–62.

that social control is a necessary and important element of any culture. [. . .]

Although social control is inherent in organized social life and is necessary if a society is to survive, it does not follow that any specific control mechanism is part of the process. Different societies go about the business of maintaining their boundaries in characteristic ways. No society has absolute boundaries. Even totalitarian societies allow some leeway. It is true that the limits in a totalitarian society are much more narrow, but such a society often plays a reasonably fair game within its rules and may provide significant 'payoff' for its citizens. Failing to do so requires an enormous investment in repression, which in the long run of history has been counterproductive. Easton's comments on the necessity of government support this position:[3]

> Whatever the form of government it must also possess some moral authority and be acceptable either to a majority of the people or to a minority that commands enough moral or material resources to enable it to coerce the majority. No government, whether by one man or by many, can survive without some support and acceptance.
>
> A government, to ensure its acceptance by any of the people, cannot behave in an arbitrary and unpredictable manner. It must make clear what its policy is in matters of daily concern to the people. This need for certainty is satisfied by the establishment of law, which explains to the people what is expected of them and decrees penalties for the behavior it defines as unacceptable. Law is essentially the regulation of the public behavior of human beings in an organized society and it is enforced by the power of the government as long as the government is able to maintain its authority.

Such discussion regarding the regulation of behavior is not characteristic of social work. Social workers do not like to entertain the idea of social demands on behavior. Nor do they like to think that their work is part of a process to produce social competence for the good of the society. Nevertheless, whenever a social worker, parent, educator, physician—anyone—engages in an activity to modify or set boundaries on human conduct according to valued norms, that person is engaging in social control. When, for example, a mother teaches a child manners, arithmetic, or health habits, she is engaging in social control as she passes on through the socialization-education process a set of rules or values that are part of our civilization.

Psychotherapy is a form of social control to the extent that it encourages a patient to give up one set of behaviors (for example, delusions, compulsions) for another set considered more appropriate in the society. Family counseling is a form of social control in that it encourages family members to temper certain interactions that are judged faulty in favor of more normative behavior that will enable them to get along with each other with less friction and pain. When social workers assist clients to find a job, apply for public aid, or manage the use of alcohol or other drugs, they are engaging in the process of social control. The objective in all these instances is to enable clients to get along better within the social order.

The concept of social action is not antithetical to this rationale of social welfare. Social action involves strategies and tactics that individuals or groups in society may undertake to change norms. When people embark on social action, they are not denying the reality of normative behavior. Those who seek to change society (with the exception of anarchists) do not seek to end all norms, but to substitute different ones.

Criticism of social control

Miller has argued that, to protect the dignity of man, social casework should deal only with the voluntary client.[4] He is markedly uncomfortable with the control aspects of practice in child welfare and corrections.

Piven and Cloward criticize the control aspects of public assistance as follows:[5]

> Historical evidence suggests that relief arrangements are initiated or expanded during the occasional outbreaks of civil disorder produced by mass unemployment, and are then abolished or contracted when political stability is restored. We shall argue that expansive relief policies are designed to mute civil disorder, and restrictive ones to reinforce work norms. In other words, relief policies are cyclical—liberal or restrictive depending on the problems of regulation in the larger society with which government must contend.

To Piven and Cloward, the use of public welfare to dampen civil disorder is questionable social policy.

Gyarfas questions using the knowledge of social science in social work practice. She holds that there is

a possibility, particularly in behaviorism, that the use of such knowledge would limit individual freedom and self-determination. However, her argument for the 'self-determined client' asks for social control over certain processes that she considers inimical to the interests of citizens and indirectly inimical to society.[6]

Confusion arises in that these writers actually support social control as legitimate while they are seemingly writing *against* the idea of control. They do not maintain that social control is objectionable, but rather they protest who is doing the controlling and according to what value system.

In his stance of advocacy, Miller suggests that social workers should influence society to conform to certain moral norms that he considers of value. He contends that social workers should challenge social institutions on behalf of clients, should try to persuade institutions to change the rules—but change to another set of rules, not to a system of no rules.[7]

Piven and Cloward urge that society deal with the problem of poverty. They espouse social action designed to get society to live up to certain values. They insist that harmful deviance from these values (deviance by institutions, but still deviance) should be controlled so that the poor are not excluded. In their view, excluding the poor from equal access to the benefits of society results in harmful consequences to the society as well as to the poor.[8]

Miller, Piven and Cloward, and Gyarfas do not reject social control as such. They do reject one set of rules or values in favor of others. They prefer that society live up to the values that they themselves espouse, and they naturally want these values to prevail. They propose that the moral authority of government and the force of law support the values they promote. In supporting justice—ephemeral as this concept is—over special privilege, these writers are engaging in social control.

Who decides values?

The real issue, then, is not whether social workers engage in social control. Clearly they are engaging in it, as the term is defined sociologically. The questions are to decide what values to support and how to support them.

Who decides which behaviors are the norm? How do social workers guard against the danger that an elite will decide what behavior is to be controlled? These questions are not affected by defining social welfare in the context of social control. They exist now as legitimate concerns regardless of how social welfare and social work are defined.

Callahan's concern for normative ethics grows out of his observations of the variety of bases on which scientists and physicians make ethical decisions. His discussion that follows is important:[9]

> A number of schools of popular ethical thought can be distinguished. In the 'religious' school,

ethical decisions are made out of the context of a tradition of religious morality. If asked for a reason why he thinks some particular act is 'right' or 'good', a person in this school is likely to reply, 'because I am a Christian,' or 'because I am an Orthodox Jew,' and so on. The 'emotive' school believes that certain acts are right or wrong because they 'feel' they are. 'Gut reactions' are taken to be normative. The 'conventionalist' judges acts to be right or wrong on the basis of accepted conventions or mores. An acceptable reason for a certain type of behavior is, for instance, because 'that's what everyone does,' or 'it's always been done that way.' Another school might be called 'empirical conventionalism,' which relies on the results of public opinion surveys. If a majority of persons thinks something is right, then it must be right. 'Simple utilitarians' believe that acts are good because they are conducive to the greatest good for the greatest number.

If these are representative of the kinds of reasons given for personal behavior, another related cluster of schools can be found to classify judgments about public behavior and social conflicts. For example, the 'barefoot civil liberties' school allows everyone to be free to 'do his own thing' or to 'make up his own mind.' It is not necessary for people to justify their conduct; it is enough if they are honest, sincere, or authentic. Another school, 'gross majoritarianism,' judges public acts and laws as right if they command majority support. If it is legal, then it must be morally acceptable. Still another criterion of judgment is 'primitive cost-benefit analysis,' which says that if the public will save x dollars by carrying out a certain policy, then that must be the ethically correct policy.

Finally, there are some expressions that are variants of 'professional ethics'; 'That's not our responsibility'; 'If we don't do it, then someone else will'; 'I'm not a philosopher or theologian'; 'That's a political (or ethical, or social, or theological) question.'

Callahan traces the rise of this diversity to the liberal movements of the past—'individualism, libertarianism, affluence and all forms of liberation.' He offers the following recommendation:[10]

In handling the ethical problem of the life sciences, it is quite possible that the democratic political method is the best we have and all that we should aspire to. It does provide a procedure for resolving public disputes and, together with the courts, ways of adjudicating conflicting values. If that is the case, then the best path to follow would be to attempt to maximize public information and debate, submit vexing issues to the courts and legislators, and hope for the best.

Kurtz recognizes the diversity of ethical positions and echoes Callahan's faith in the democratic process.

He rejects, as follows, normative decisions made by various categories of the elite, but renders his insistence on democracy less convincing by putting his trust in other elitists:[11]

I would resist entrusting our destiny to a group of behavioral scientists, Pentagon experts, party bureaucrats, or philosopher kings who claim to know what is best for individuals without their consent. . . .
In the last analysis the best guarantee against abuse [of sciences] is full initial discussion by the community of scientists and the educated public.

Clark has perhaps the most startling answer to the question of who decides and who ought to decide normative behaviors. His conclusion, recommendation, and explanation of his position, are as follows:[12]

It is a fact that a few men in the leadership position in the industrialized nations of the world now have the power to determine among themselves, through collaboration or competition, the survival or extinction of human civilization. . . .
Given these contemporary facts, it would seem logical that a requirement imposed on all power-controlling leaders—and those who aspire to such leadership—would be that they accept and use the earliest perfected form of psychotechnological, biochemical intervention which would assure their positive use of power and reduce or block the possibility of their using power destructively. . . .
In medicine, physical diseases are controlled through medication. Medicines are prescribed by doctors to help the body overcome the detrimental effects of bacteria or viruses—or to help the organism restore that balance of internal biochemical environment necessary for health and effectiveness. Medicines are not only used to treat the diseases of individuals, but are also used preventively in the form of vaccines. All medicines are drugs—and all drugs used therapeutically are forms of intervention to influence and control the natural process of disease. Selective and appropriate medication to assure psychological health and moral integrity is now imperative for the survival of human society.

Clark does not say how he would persuade the leaders who control power to try his remedy. Fortunately for human society it is unlikely that his recommendation will be carried out. Any power strong enough to force us to take our medicine would not need to give it.

A provocative forecast for the future is offered by Bell, chairman of the Commission on the Year 2000 of the American Academy of Arts and Sciences. He expects the emergence of a 'knowledge class' composed of scientific, technological, administrative, and cultural professionals as the highest and most powerful class in the post-industrial society. He foresees the following complexities with respect to power in determining normative behavior:[13]

> If one turns, then, to the societal structure of the post-industrial society . . . two conclusions are evident. First, the major class of the emerging new society is primarily a professional class, based on knowledge rather than property. But second, the control system of the society is lodged not in a successor-occupational class but in the political order, and the question of who manages the political order is an open one.

Bell thinks that (1) contending political parties, (2) various mobilized groups such as labor unions, ethnic minorities and the poor; and (3) elites in science, the academic world, business, and the military will make the decision through contest and conflict in the political arena.

What is normative? Clearly, the question is still open. The strong hopes for its resolution expressed by Callahan, Kurtz, and Clark indicate that this is an uncomfortable situation. The diversity of their proposals shows that it cannot be easily resolved. Bell's forecast of a fluid pluralism, if correct, does not suggest any immediate relief.

Accountability

In exploring social control as an explicit rationale for social services, one is confronted with this problem: What is the appropriate relationship between the social services and society? To whom are the providers of social services accountable?

The authors' answer is that those who provide social services are accountable to their constituency—the legislators, the donors and the citizens who support agencies and programs, and the consumers who use the services. The providers of services are responsible for helping people resolve the problems of their lives in ways that permit them to get along better in society. This concept is not revolutionary, nor does it need to be. But as soon as one takes this position one returns to the original theme: The primary function of social welfare is social control. Social workers—and others in the helping professions—are free, in most societies at least, to define normative behavior compassionately but are less free to espouse values independent of their constituency. The answer to the question 'Who decides normative behavior?' is thus answered as best it can be within the framework of the constituency concerned.

Social agencies are funded and chartered to achieve certain ends. Social programs are funded and designed to attain specific objectives. For example, family agencies are expected to strengthen family life. This expectation does not impose such a severe limit that the family agency cannot be innovative or accepting toward changes that have taken place in relations between men and women. However, it is doubtful whether a family agency could continue to operate if the staff decided that elimination of family life was their mission.

What would be the advantages if social workers openly embraced the concept of social control as a primary rationale of social welfare? The authors believe that their constituency would better understand what social workers are trying to do. Social control has more honesty and integrity than the notion that social services are based on simple altruism and good will. It is not enough to tell people that social workers' hearts are pure. People are now asking embarrassing questions about the benefits that social services provide and for whom they are provided. No longer are social workers automatically seen as the 'good guys in the white hats.'

In today's cynical society, altruistic rationales are not marketable. Good intentions are not enough to earn sanction for social welfare programs. Dependence on altruistic rationales rather than concrete contributions to society may have helped social workers win the sarcastic sobriquets of 'do-gooder' and 'bleeding heart.'

The concept that social control is the primary function of welfare and that social control involves providing constructive services—this is a marketable idea. People can understand being responsible to a constituency. Such a rationale is realistic in the contemporary sociopolitical arena. Social work could move from idealistic, well-intentioned moralism about the nature of man to rational and pragmatic provision of evidence that social services contribute significantly to society in terms of desired outcomes—for example, less child abuse, fewer family breakdowns, and less class and racial discrimination. Unless the social worker thinks in terms of such specific accomplishments, social work will no longer be sanctioned and funded even at present levels.

Pincus and Minahan have suggested that 'the credibility of the profession of social work rests on its ability to demonstrate that it can bring about the changes it claims to be able to make.'[14] This is good advice. Can it best be followed in the context of social control?

Social services versus police power

In an advanced industrial society, social and economic situations are constantly changing, with new social and economic needs continually appearing. Rapid technical changes, discrimination against minorities, relocation of industries, and governmental anti-inflation programs that accept 6 per cent unemployment as a situation not requiring rectification—all these increase social and economic inequality. If society does not meet the needs of the people who are adversely affected by these factors, deviance is likely to continue and multiply, and greater social unrest and disorder are probable.

Societies have attempted to exercise social control in a variety of ways as a response to deviance, social unrest, and disorder. Some societies have relied heavily on the perpetual threat or use of police power.

Some have relied on elaborate systems of social welfare. Most have relied on both. It would appear that our society is not firmly convinced that the development of social welfare services is a satisfactory means of social control in some problem areas. Therefore, when dealing with these areas it fluctuates between police power and the provision of social services. This is the current response to drug abuse. Is there a trade-off between social welfare services and police power as two of the predominant mechanisms for the control of deviance? Is it not true that the primary options available for attaining social control in our society are often either police power or social services? This seems most obvious in problem areas such as drug abuse, alcoholism, mental illness, and juvenile delinquency.

Social workers can contribute significantly to an orderly society by helping to seek and provide remedies or solutions for the dysfunctions in the social and economic system. Their contribution would include helping the poor, minorities, and other disfranchised people participate actively in the social and economic system of the society. This is not to suggest a new thrust for social welfare services. The task of the social services should involve the provision of evidence that the best way to control disorder and deviance in the society is by responsive, universal, and flexible social services focused on (1) alleviation of individual problematic behavior, and (2) intervention in the ongoing process of the society. This may be done by direct service to individuals and groups, social change strategies, and planning. As the social services are able to demonstrate that their approach to disorder and deviance is effective, the approach will be more universally sanctioned and provide a viable alternative to the direct behavior control of police power.

References

1 Talcott Parsons, *The Social System*, Chicago, Free Press, 1951, pp. 482–3.
2 For a full exposition of this point, see John W. Bennett and Melvin M. Tumin, 'Some cultural imperatives', in Peter B. Hammond, ed., *Cultural and Social Anthropology*, New York, Macmillan, 1964.
3 Stewart Easton, *The Heritage of the Past*, New York, Holt, Rinehart & Winston, 1964, p. 4.
4 Henry Miller, 'Value dilemmas in social casework', *Social Work*, 13, January 1968, pp. 27–33.
5 Frances Piven and Richard A. Cloward, *Regulating the Poor*, New York, Pantheon Books, 1971, p. xiii.
6 Mary Gyarfas, 'Social science, technology and social work: a caseworker's view', *Social Service Review*, 43, September 1969, pp. 259–72.
7 Miller, op. cit.
8 Piven and Cloward, op. cit.
9 Daniel Callahan, 'Normative ethics and public morality in the life sciences', *Humanist*, 32, September–October 1972, p. 5.
10 ibid., pp. 6–7.
11 Paul Kurtz, 'The uses and abuses of science', *Humanist*, 32, September–October 1972, p. 8.
12 Kenneth Clark, 'The pathos of power: a psychological perspective', *American Psychologist*, 26, December 1971, pp. 1056, 1057.
13 Daniel Bell, *The Coming of Post-Industrial Society*, New York, Basic Books, 1973, p. 374.
14 Allen Pincus and Anne Minahan, *Social Work Practice: Model and Method*, Itasca, Ill., Peacock, 1973, p. 273.

I. 3 Value problems of welfare-capitalism

T. H. Marshall

[. . .] I shall begin at the macro-political level, and consider how the three components of the hyphenated democratic-welfare-capitalist social system approach the task of taking policy decisions. Kenneth Arrow has said that 'in a capitalist democracy there are essentially two methods by which social choices can be made: voting, typically used to make "political" decisions, and the market mechanism, typically used to make "economic" decisions'. And a little later he defines the central problem of welfare economics as that of 'achieving a social maximum derived from individual desires'.[1] The democratic and the economic process are alike in that they both take a mass of individuals, process them through institutions—the ballot and the market—which register and react to their desires, and produce a single body of answers, a set of prices or a Houseful of Members. But, whereas the market gets its result by combination, by discovering the combined effect of the expressed wishes of everyone and so arriving at what Arrow calls the 'social maximum', the ballot reaches its conclusion by division, by sorting out the expressed wishes so as to identify the majority, and then accepting *their* wish as the decision. The case of welfare is different again. Although it must take careful note of expressed desires, it does not simply react to or obey them. Its responsibility is to satisfy needs, which is a different undertaking.

In contrast to the economic process, it is a fundamental principle of the Welfare State that the market value of an individual cannot be the measure of his right to welfare. The central function of welfare, in fact, is to supersede the market by taking goods and services out of it, or in some way to control and modify its operations so as to produce a result which it would not have produced of itself. The life-history of a policy decision in welfare, as in any other sphere of democratic government, begins in a general election and is

marked at various stages by the use of the political instrument of the majority vote. But this in all cases is only a part of the process by which vital choices are made, and in some cases it is less in tune with the true nature of those choices than in others. Some political decisions, that is to say, could more appropriately be submitted to a plebiscite than others. The relation between majority voting and policy decisions in welfare is very equivocal. Democratic voting is egotistic; most voters voice what they believe to be their own interests. The more comprehensive the franchise, the more legitimate this seems to be, because everybody can speak for himself. Welfare decisions depend on altruism—both concern for others and mutual concern for one another. In Victorian bourgeois democracy this was obvious, because the enfranchised were persons of property and the needy were voteless. Not that the former were conspicuously altruistic, but it was only to their social conscience that reformers could appeal in support of measures which were not vote-catchers. Dicey was convinced that if pensioners were allowed to vote—if, that is, the beneficiaries could put pressure on their benefactors—government would be corrupted and the foundations of democracy undermined.

That idea no longer holds, and the appeals of politicians to the self-interests of voters are frank and loud. Is it possible that the legitimacy of democratic egotism partly, at least, accounts for the obstinate blindness of total democracy to the urgent needs of minorities which, for various reasons, are not psephologically significant? When everybody is represented, it is easy to assume that everybody has been taken care of. This myopic inability to focus on things outside one's own circle can be, and to an important extent is, counteracted by the mass media, which are an integral part of the political apparatus of mass democracy. Television has had some remarkable successes, but it has its limitations. A case can rarely be argued to its conclusion, a subject run for too long

Source: *Journal of Social Policy*, 1 (1), January 1972, pp. 18–19, 20–4, 25, 26–32.

becomes boring, and shock tactics may only produce the familiar sequence—distortion, sensation, oblivion. [. . .]

Welfare decisions, then, are essentially altruistic, and they must draw on standards of value embodied in an autonomous ethical system which, though an intrinsic part of the contemporary civilization, is not the product either of the summation of individual preferences (as in a market) or of a hypothetical majority vote. It is impossible to say exactly how these ethical standards arise in a society or are recognized by its members. Total consensus with regard to them is unthinkable, outside a devout religious community, but without a foundation of near-consensus, no general social welfare policy would be possible. [. . .] It would be dishonest to pretend that there is not about welfare policy decisions something intrinsically authoritarian or, to use a less loaded but rather horrible word, paternalistic. Dahrendorf, for example, writes that 'in a certain sense the authoritarian State is always a Welfare State, just as, the other way round, the Welfare State always contains authoritarian elements'.[2] For one thing, welfare policy would be of little use if it did not actively help to create standards of value in its field and promote consensus on them. It is by nature educational, not only in schools and colleges, but in its health service and welfare centres, and in everything it does to impress upon the public and the politicians the true significance, in real terms, of the disabilities under which many categories of citizen suffer. In all this it is creating and, quite frankly, inculcating concepts and standards of welfare which are not yet universally accepted. This, no doubt, is what Gunnar Myrdal is referring to when, looking ahead to the 'next phase', he speaks of 'the coming into existence of a "Welfare Culture" within the structure of the Welfare State.'[3]

The three components of my hyphenated social system differ also as to the agencies through which basic policy decisions are translated into operational programmes and put into effect. Each has, I suggest, one type of agent particularly associated with its characteristic methods of procedure, though all of them make some use of all three. They are, for economic policy (the 'capitalist' component) the social scientist and technician, for welfare the professional, and for general political administration the bureaucrat. Many students of social policy are suspicious of those who think progress lies in making more use of scientific methods, such as cost-benefit analysis and model-building. 'We tend,' says Martin Rein, 'to over-estimate the contribution of social science disciplines, and to accept "technical decisions" in place of value judgements and political choices.'[4] The same point was made more recently by critics of the Roskill Committee Report on the third London airport. This is one source of potential conflict within the hyphenated social structure. Comparison of professionalism with bureaucracy reveals another.

The professional is in a special position with regard both to public policy and to its execution at the level of the individual case. When on the job he (or she) enjoys a certain autonomy which is the complement of the personal responsibility of which, at that stage, he cannot be relieved. Within the limits set by his professional skills and his official function he takes personal, that is to say original, decisions in the light of the character of the case. The bureaucrat has much less freedom and is much more tightly bound by rules; he must apply them equally and impartially; he must be fair. The professional, on the job, does not have to think of being fair, but only of doing what is best. Impartiality for him does not consist in treating all cases in the same way, but in treating them with equal devotion. But at the same time the professional has the right and the duty to criticize policy and contribute to its improvement, and his association has the right and the duty to act as a pressure group in national and local politics. The bureaucrat cannot do this either. Social policy must make use both of the professional and of the bureaucrat, and they do not always run happily in double harness. The severest test of their compatibility occurs in those hybrid cases where a cut-and-dried official decision must be given on a welfare claim in an area not governed by rules. A discretionary judgement must be given which is at least as much a bureaucratic as a professional one. Obvious examples are the administration of non-contractual benefits in cash and in kind and the allocation of housing—and especially, perhaps, the handling of appeals against such decisions. The findings of recent research on appeal tribunals are disquieting, but the very fact that one uses that word implies that, once the fact are fully understood, the problem should be soluble. For 'disquiet' signifies awareness that a value is being violated.

In passing from this general comparison of the three components of democratic-welfare-capitalism to look at some specific areas in which incompatibilities might be expected to reveal themselves I can do no more than take a few examples, and I shall begin with that authoritarian or paternal character of welfare of which I have already spoken. Its potentialities as a creator of conflicts with both the democratic and the capitalist principles are obvious. These may involve either the producers or the consumers of welfare services. Beginning with the former, let us look first at the question of the respective roles of public and private enterprise in the welfare field. As things are now, we have a spectrum extending from those services in which a large or even a dominant part is played by voluntary organizations or private enterprise to those in which the State has a near-monopoly, as in the running of hospitals, or a total monopoly, as in probation. This seems to indicate that the Gaitskell view on the nationalization issue, namely that to treat it as a battle between good and evil is ideological nonsense, applies as much to welfare services as to industries. There is room for both public and private enterprise, and the criterion on which to determine their respective roles is efficiency in achieving the desired result. But this is too simple; there are some important qualifications to be made.

First, the responsibility of government in the field of welfare is more immediate and compelling than it is, generally speaking, in economic affairs. One of the virtues claimed for capitalist private enterprise is that it can take risks, and it earns a considerable part of its substantial rewards by doing so. But a government cannot allow risk-taking in welfare—or only minimally. It cannot leave any important part of its overall responsibilities in the hands of private agencies unless it takes steps to limit risk by regulation, supervision, inspection or safety-nets, as when a basic State pension underpins private ones. It was, in fact, the disastrous effects of the frequent failure of private savings and pension schemes that forced European governments to intervene in this field in the nineteenth century. Thus the distinction between public and private enterprise in welfare is not as sharp as one might imagine; it is a matter of degree.

My second qualification starts from this and leads on to a new point. Where there is in a major service like health or education a division or, if you like, a partnership between the public and the private sectors, with the State taking very much the larger share, the public service must be potentially comprehensive. By this I mean that it must make its service accessible to all by spreading it nation-wide, and it must be ready to provide for anybody who comes back to it from the private sector (for financial or other reasons), and also to cater for a possible shift of the balance of demand in its direction in the rising generation. The larger the private sector, the more difficult it is to meet this responsibility, especially in the case of personal service. On this rests one objection to the proposal to allow people to 'opt out' of the national health and education services, taking with them part of their contribution to their cost. In the circumstances I have described 'fair competition' between the public and the private sectors is not possible, since the transfer of clients from the former to the latter would reduce the income of the public service without permitting a corresponding economy of expenditure, and, by splitting resources, would lower the standard of efficiency attainable in it.

But it is not only a question of efficiency. Two major issues of value are involved. First, quantitative change would inevitably lead, very rapidly, to qualitative change. A point would soon be reached at which the whole conception of a community dedicated to providing for the vital needs of its members by systems of mutual aid would be lost, and the balance between the elements constituting the democratic-welfare-capitalist society destroyed. Secondly, it is beyond dispute that medical care and education, which enter into the lives of all citizens, are areas in which differences of opportunity and experience, and particularly an institutionalized dual standard (which would inevitably follow), do more to create and sustain class distinctions

than any other. It proved possible to establish a democratic Welfare State in this country without abolishing or drastically altering the status of the Public Schools, but the two cannot coexist indefinitely in their present form. Any deliberate enlargement or extension of this kind of social distinction by a democratic policy decision would signify not so much a conflict between the elements of the hyphenated society as an abandonment by the majority of the very concept itself.

But without envisaging such a debacle, it is easy to see that disputes and conflicts over the design and administration of the personal social services will be continuous and they will not all be technical, value-free disputes about the best means of achieving agreed ends. It is, I think, true that a very high degree of consensus exists about the aims of the welfare services; without this there could be no Welfare State. But two things must be remembered. First, while in the case of a health service ends and means can be fairly clearly distinguished, this is not true of a service like education. Whereas in medicine one may be able to test alternative treatments and eliminate those that are least successful, the relative value of different educational systems or methods may be matters of opinion which are not testable in that way. It is therefore all the more important that room for variety be provided both within the public system and in a private sector of acceptable size and scope. Secondly, means, as well as ends, raise value problems. A system which could be shown to make the optimum use of scarce resources could be rejected because it involved a means-test of a kind that is offensive to human dignity, just as a policy deemed likely to bring economic prosperity in the long run might be rejected because it would cause an unacceptable level of unemployment on the way. [. . .]

[. . .] From the point of view of the consumer of welfare services, there are two main ways in which it may be thought that the authoritarian, or paternal, character of welfare must do him injury, namely by limiting his scope for the exercise of choice, and by weakening his initiative and self-reliance. Obviously there are values at stake here, the values of freedom and independence, both of which have a crucial role to play in the democratic and the 'capitalist' components of the composite society. So there is bound to be conflict, but at what level? It is not, as I see it, in the nature of a head-on clash between irreconcilable beliefs or of a contest seen by each side as a battle between good and evil. Welfare recognizes the values of freedom and independence, not only in the abstract but in its daily work, and the champions of these values know that without some curtailment of them welfare could not meet its responsibilities. You cannot make the optimum use of scarce skills and resources in a nation-wide service open to all if you allow every applicant for its help to pick and choose as he pleases. In some cases, like primary schools, choice is geographically limited; in others the knowledge on which a rational choice can be made is lacking. So the issue is one of balance and proportion, of deciding how much freedom of choice can be provided for, both by arrangements within the public services and by the operation of a private sector in co-operation, or at least in harmony, with the public one. As to the exercise of the faculty of choice itself, there is probably more scope for this in our contemporary civilization than there has ever been before. It is not likely to atrophy. [. . .]

I want to turn now to an aspect of welfare at the micro-level of the individual case, and again I start by quoting an economist, this time Adam Smith. He began his discussion of value by distinguishing between 'value in use' and 'value in exchange', and then devoted his whole attention to the latter, because it was the only kind with which an economist was concerned. But for welfare, value in use is vital. Smith referred to it also as 'utility', but not in the modern sense (to quote Jacob Viner) of 'an attempt to explain price-determination in psychological terms'.[5] It was not subjective in this individual sense. For, in his famous illustration he said that, in contrast to water, diamonds had 'scarce any value in use'. This must refer, not to their value in the eyes of those who wear them, which is great, but to some common estimation of their capacity to satisfy a real human need, which is negligible. Welfare, as I have already said, must base its action on value of this kind, and cannot simply react directly to individual, subjective desires. When the discrepancy between these two kinds of value is insuperable and the consequences intolerable, welfare steps in and takes over from the market. My example is housing. A house is a commodity to the landlord but to the occupant it is a home, and these are two quite different objects. When houses are scarce and incomes low, governments of all countries have stepped in to assert what we might call the welfare value of a home over the market value of a house, by controlling or freezing rents and by suspending the normal rights of property and contract so as to guarantee security of tenure. The methods were crude, devoid of any principle of valuation, subjective or objective, and operated unilaterally for tenant against landlord. The result was a mess.

The invention by the Labour government of the 'fair rent' standard of value is extraordinarily interesting. [. . .] It provides a means of arriving at a bilaterally conceived evaluation through which the different types of value can be reduced to a common denominator. What it does is to strike an acceptable balance between 'value in use', or welfare value and 'value in exchange', or market value through the intermediary concept of the value and the thing itself seen in terms of its physical properties—size, structure, accommodation, equipment, etc.—estimated, not objectively as a commodity in the market nor subjectively as a home in use, but as a thing *for* use, which can be classified and valued in relation to others of its kind. The formula took account of the interests of both parties,

as must be done if the State continues to depend in part on a private housing sector to meet its responsibilities towards its citizens and their families.

For my last illustration I take the subject of poverty and inequality. There has been evident for some time past a reaction against the idea of the 'poverty line' in favour of the view that the concept 'poverty' has no meaning except in a relative sense, whereas the 'poverty line' implies that it can be conceived in absolute terms. This has been accompanied by the contention that the real problem is not poverty, but inequality. If this means that poverty is relative to the standard of civilization of the country concerned, it is beyond dispute. If it means that I may not say that *A* is poor, but only that he is poorer than *B*, I cannot accept it. If it means that inequality is a major social issue of which poverty is a part, that is beyond dispute. But if it means that the problems of poverty and inequality are identical and inseparable, so that one could not eradicate poverty without solving the problem of inequality, then I cannot accept that either. What I said above about welfare value and welfare standards implies the belief that it is possible and necessary, in the present state of society, to envisage a state of destitution or deprivation which must be condemned as intolerable and, even though no exact measurement or definition of this condition can be given, we may refer to it as 'poverty'. The poor remain a category, and the fact that its boundaries would be different in another place or age does not make it any the less absolute for the country in which it exists. Nor does the recognition of poverty as a problem and the poor as a category imply that all forms of poverty are the same; on the contrary, it emphasizes the value of making subtle studies of its distinguishing features. The common factor in the state of the poor is the urgency of their need.

At this point the complexity of the subject obliges me to adopt an 'ideal type' approach and ask what place poverty and inequality would occupy in a democratic-welfare-capitalist society which had, so to speak, fulfilled itself. The simple answer is that in such a society poverty is a disease, but inequality is an essential structural feature. We, who are now enmeshed in this composite social system, have long ago rejected the theory of the necessity of poverty, as expressed by Patrick Colquhoun when he described poverty as 'a most necessary and indispensable ingredient in society', because 'it is the source of wealth'.[6] We have abandoned belief in the evolutionary benefits of poverty, as a weeder-out of the unfit. We no longer accept poverty as the inevitable and perpetual deposit of personal failures in the competitive struggle, and we do not even rely greatly on the fear of poverty as an incentive to work, as witness unemployment benefits and redundancy payments. It has no logical place in the system, but it obstinately remains with us, so we relieve it—when we notice it. Not very long ago it became almost invisible, but now it has reappeared. The invisibility of poverty has been a recurrent phenomenon in the western world.

The task of banishing poverty from our 'ideal type' society must be undertaken jointly by welfare and capitalism; there is no other way. Not only is there no evidence in history or in contemporary affairs to suggest that conflict between these two components must frustrate any effort at a joint solution but, on the contrary, it is clear that our particular type of social system has got nearer to achieving this objective than any that has gone before or now exists—unless one takes a totally relative view and asserts that poverty has been abolished in societies in which everybody is poor. Furthermore, the mechanics of the process are understood, the instruments have been forged or are on the drawing-board, and all that is needed is the will to use them and a period of economic calm and stability long enough to allow the complexities of the problem to be mastered and the large variety of exceptional and abnormal cases to be brought within the scope of the operation. It is not necessary for me, nor have I the space, to give an exposition of these mechanics and instruments, the range and potentialities of which are well known in this country, thanks to the writings of Peter Townsend and others. So I will press on to my final problem, that of inequality, an area in which the different principles and pressures of the three components of the hyphenated society are most difficult to reconcile with one another.

Democracy stands for equality of citizenship rights. The aim of welfare services it to give equal care to similar cases. 'Capitalism'—or the market—lives by recognizing and rewarding inequalities, and depends on them to provide the motive force that makes it work. When this process was given free rein and welfare picked up the casualties, there was no problem. The shape of inequality was rough-hewn by the market. But two things have happened since then. Democracy took a hand. First, it made collective bargaining possible and this led in turn to the formal recognition of differentials, both within and between units of labour. Then it developed, somewhere in the socio-economic atmosphere, the notion that, by correctly reading the cultural signs, one could tell what a certain sort of man ought to be paid, especially if he was in the civil service or one of the professions. Differentials were given an ethical flavour. Thirdly it made a show of cutting inequalities down to the ethical scale, as far as money incomes were concerned, by heavy progressive taxation. Democracy, one might say, legitimized inequality (since you do not tax stolen goods), with the help of the trade unions.

The second thing that happened was that social security in the typical affluent western countries tied itself to the inequalities of the market by relating its whole system of contributions and benefits to differences in earnings, up to a limiting ceiling. Since social security contains, as I have said, a welfare element and forms the bridge between 'capitalism' and welfare, one may say that welfare, like democracy, legitimized inequality. There was nothing conspiratorial in all this. It represents the convergence without which the com-

posite social system would have had little chance of stabilizing itself, and there could have been no 'end of ideology'. It certainly does not imply approval of any particular scale of inequality.

So we have a position where all three components accept inequality, but without agreement as to its pattern in any detail. Obviously there could not be any fixed pattern, or the whole economic system would be ossified. But there is no agreement even about the principle to apply in drawing a pattern, or any clear idea where to look for such a principle. A high growth-rate can cover a multitude of sins, but with our low rate, the confusion is patent and the disruption of life serious. Prestige, politics and bargaining-power overlay the simpler facts of relative productivity, creating a state of uncertainty in which jealousy and 'relative deprivation' flourish—not only at the bottom, but right up the scale, and probably least of all among the poor. That is why I said that poverty and inequality were different problems, when viewed structurally. Poverty is a tumour which should be cut out, and theoretically could be; inequality is a vital organ which is functioning badly.

This malfunctioning of the system of legitimate inequality is probably the most deeply-rooted threat to the viability of the hybrid or hyphenated social structure. This is not just another way of saying that the most disturbing factor in society is the class struggle. Of course the reaction to economic differentials is coloured by the power structure of industry and, in British society, by the peculiar persistence of historic forms of class-consciousness. But these are not indispensable features, as Dr Samuelsson argues in the case of Sweden. The trouble is that no way has been found of equating a man's value in the market (capitalist value), his value as a citizen (democratic value), and his value for himself (welfare value). But that is not all. The democratic and welfare components have each its own internal, unsolved problem—how to find a balance, so perfect as to silence all discontent, between equality of persons and their circumstances on the one hand and equality of opportunity, that great architect of inequality on the other. Militating against a resolution of this dilemma is the ebullience of that subjective and wholly individual assessment of social injustice which sociologists call 'relative deprivation', but which our ancestors classed (under a simpler name) among the seven deadly sins. In these circumstances it is futile to imagine that differentials can be made acceptable simply by scaling them down, however necessary this may be. It can be done only by changing the attitude towards them. The problem is structural in origin, but there is no purely structural solution to it.

The failure to solve the problem of economic inequality is evidence of the weakness of contemporary democracy. Since the task of maintaining the balance between the component elements of the system falls on democracy, this weakness is dangerous, but it is not critical nor, one hopes, irremediable. The outstanding needs are for better two-way communication to remedy the lack of contact and understanding between politicians, bureaucrats and the public, and for a reconciliation of the roles of the two competing democracies, the political and the industrial, in the power structure. [. . .]

[. . .] Even the most cursory glance at the history of western Europe during the last ten or fifteen years shows that [. . .] the disturbances of those years did not arise, in my view, from the incompatibility of the three components I have been examining. Of course there was conflict between them. But conflict is a normal feature of every healthy society. The unrest which struck a new note in recent years was something other than this. It was in part a fulfilment of a prophecy made by Shils in 1955 when he wrote that, if you ban ideology altogether, it 'will creep in through the back door, or more particularly, through a rebellious younger generation'.[7] And it was in part an expression of the disillusionment of many people in the older generations with the dominant values of their societies. But, though the principles and practices of democracy, capitalism, and welfare were the objects of much criticism, this did not reflect battles being waged between them, but dissatisfaction with the whole of which they were the parts. Materialism, profit-seeking, quantity-worship and growth-mania are not characteristics of capitalism alone, but permeate the whole of modern technological mass society. Bureaucratic excesses and rigidities are not a political malady only but are found also in the economy, the universities and even in welfare. The transformation sought by the more purposeful and less destructive sections of those voicing our present discontents is one of attitudes and values rather than of basic structure, though institutional changes are sought as a means to this end, as is also the protection of the physical environment. I see no reason why their aims should not be achieved— if they can be achieved at all—within a social framework that includes representative government, a mixed economy and a Welfare State. The only alternative is something more totalitarian and bureaucratic, and that is not at all what the more novel and significant elements in the movement of protest are seeking.

References

1 Kenneth Arrow, *Social Choice and Individual Values*, Chapman & Hall, 1951, pp. 1, 3.
2 Ralf Dahrendorf, *Gesellschaft und Freiheit*, Munich, Piper, 1964, p. 238.
3 *Beyond the Welfare State*, Duckworth, 1960, p. 53.
4 Martin Rein, *Social Policy: Issues of Choice and Change*, New York, Random House, 1970, p. 10.
5 Quoted in Alfred N. Page, *Utility Theory: a Book of Readings*, New York, Wiley, 1968, p. 123.
6 Patrick Colquhoun, *A Treatise of Indigence*, Hatchard, 1806, pp. 7–8.
7 E. A. Shils, 'The end of ideology', *Encounter*, 5, November 1955, p. 57.

I. 4 State expenditure in advanced capitalism

Ian Gough

[. . .] Tables 1 and 2 summarize the structure and trends of total state expenditure in the UK and the five other major OECD countries.[1] In 1972 it amounted to 37–40 per cent of GDP in the major European economies, 34 per cent in the USA and perhaps 20 per cent in Japan. Since the war, state spending has grown faster than GDP in every OECD country. From 1955 to 1969 it rose 23 per cent faster in all countries taken together, with only France and Japan among the major economies exhibiting a slower relative growth (see bottom half of Table 1). This trend has continued up to 1972. Of course the divergent rates of growth of these economies has meant that the *absolute* growth of state spending has varied enormously. On this count it has grown most rapidly in Japan: 50 per cent faster than the EEC and twice as fast as the UK.[2] Taking the growth of public expenditure in the UK over a longer time period, it can be seen there have been three major periods of expansion. The first occurred during the First World War when its share of GNP (at factor cost) doubled to between 25 per cent and 30 per cent in the inter-war period. During the Second World War, the economic role of the state rose to record levels (three-quarters of GNP in 1943), but at the end of hostilities it settled down to a much higher plateau than before, accounting for about two-fifths of GNP. The third period of expansion did not begin in the UK until the early 1960s (during the 1950s its share fell somewhat), but since then it has proceeded without interruption to take the share of total public expenditure over 50 per cent of GNP in the late 1960s.

This rapid expansion since the Second World War has *not* been financed by a secular increase in state borrowing, with the crucial exception of the USA. From the mid 1950s to the late 1960s taxation in all OECD countries combined rose by 4·7 per cent of

GNP—faster than the rise in all *current* expenditure if the USA is excluded, and not much below the rise in *total* expenditure including capital investment.[3] In this context it should be remembered that some state capital expenditure provides assets which yield a trading income, for which therefore loan finance is not necessarily inflationary: hence, it is reasonable to expect taxation to cover only part of capital spending. Data for the UK in Table 2 shows that up to 1971 taxation plus trading surpluses rose roughly in line with expenditure. Since 1971 deficits have mushroomed in the UK, Italy and several other countries but this in no way disturbs our conclusions on the long run trend in state finance: there are specific conjunctural explanations of this new 'fiscal crisis of the state'.[4] Alongside this long-run growth in tax revenues there has been a marked shift in their burden away from corporations and onto households in all countries:[5] an important point to which we return later.

Trends

Turning to the composition of state expenditure, certain trends are clearly discernible in all advanced capitalist countries. These are: the growth in expenditure on the social services, certain infra-structure items and aid to private industry, and the decline in the share absorbed by armaments. Of these 'the most striking feature is the extent to which education, health and social security were responsible for the rising share of government expenditure over this period' according to an OECD report.[6] In the UK the social services (including housing) have expanded continuously since the beginning of the century, with the exception of the 1930s, and today account for one half of public expenditure. In the US they increased from 9 per cent of GNP in 1955 to 15 per cent in 1969. In the EEC social expenditure rose as a percentage of private consumption from 1962–70; in the Netherlands

Source: *New Left Review*, no. 92, July–August 1975, pp. 58–60.

Table 1   State expenditure[a] in major OECD countries

	UK	France	West Germany	Italy	USA	Japan
Per cent of GDP[b] in 1972						
Military	4·9	3·5	3·0	2·4	6·7	
+Health and education	7·7 ⎫	8·8	14·7	⎰ 5·7	7·1	
+Other civilian	6·1 ⎭			⎱ 6·7	7·0	
=Current real expenditure	18·7	12·3	17·7	14·8	20·8	9·1
+Capital expenditure	4·7	3·1	3·7	2·6	3·2	
=Total real expenditure	23·4	15·4	21·4	17·4	24·0	
+Social security	8·9	17·2	13·0	14·6	8·0	4·7
+Debt interest	3·8	0·8	1·0	2·9	1·9	0·8
+Other transfers and subsidies	3·7	3·3	2·6	5·1	0·4	
=TOTAL EXPENDITURE[c]	39·8	36·7	38·0	40·0	34·3	
TOTAL REVENUE[d]	37·9	38·0	39·0	34·7	31·4	22·6
State borrowing[e]	1·8	−0·5	0·1	6·5	0·3	
Ratio of growth rates to growth of GNP, 1955–69[f]						
Military	0·62	0·44	0·84	1·22	0·80	
All civilian	1·36	1·20	1·34	1·13	1·65	
Current real expenditure	1·09	0·92	1·22	1·15	1·23	0·92
Capital expenditure	1·41	1·51	1·22	0·71	1·15	
Social security	1·59	1·32	1·19	1·37	1·47	1·10
TOTAL EXPENDITURE	1·24	1·14	1·24	1·20	1·23	
Current expenditure at *constant* prices	0·62	0·58	0·85	0·74	1·06	0·55

Sources: OECD, *National Accounts 1961–1972*, 1974; OECD, *Expenditure Trends in OECD Countries, 1960–1980*, 1972.
Notes: [a] Excluding state productive enterprises.
[b] At market prices.
[c] Excluding capital transfers.
[d] All taxation, including social security contributions and local taxes, government trading income and current transfers.
[e] Equals expenditure − revenue % capital transfers.
[f] France 1959–69, West Germany 1960–69.

Table 2   State expenditure[a] in the UK, 1910–73

	1910	1937	1951	1961	1971	1973
Per cent of GNP[b] in each year						
Social security		5·2	5·3	6·7	8·9	8·7
Health and welfare		1·8	4·5	4·4	5·8	5·9
Education		2·6	3·2	4·2	6·5	6·8
Housing		1·4	3·1	2·3	2·6	3·5
Total social services	4·2	10·9	16·1	17·6	23·8	24·9
Environment[c]	⎫ 0·7	⎫ 1·0	⎰ 1·5	1·6	2·4	2·5
Transport and communications	⎭	⎭	⎱ 2·1	3·2	3·9	3·9
Commerce and industry[d]	1·8	2·8	6·9	4·9	6·5	5·6
Justice and law[e]	0·6	0·7	0·6	0·8	1·3	1·4
Military and external	3·5	5·0	10·8	7·6	6·6	6·4
Debt interest and other	1·9	5·2	6·9	6·3	5·9	5·8
TOTAL PUBLIC EXPENDITURE	12·7	25·7	44·9	42·1	50·3	50·5
Total taxation	11·0	22·5	37·5	32·8	41·8	37·7
Trading surpluses, rent, interest		1·3	5·2	5·7	6·8	6·9
TOTAL REVENUE	11·0	23·8	42·7	38·5	48·6	44·6
Borrowing requirement[f]	1·7	1·9	2·2	3·6	1·7	5·9

Sources: A. Peacock and D. Wiseman, *The Growth of Public Expenditure in the UK*, London, 1961; London and Cambridge Economic Service, *The British Economy: Key Statistics 1900–1970*; CSO, *National Income and Expenditure* and *Social Trends*.
Notes: [a] Including capital expenditure of public corporations.
[b] At factor cost.
[c] Water, sewerage and refuse disposal; public health, clean air, parks, town and country planning etc.
[d] Employment services, research and development, investment grants, agricultural support, and certain public corporations' investment.
[e] Police, prisons, law courts and Parliament.
[f] Plus other financial transactions (a residual item).

a huge increase from 22 per cent to 35 per cent.[7] Parallel with this expansion has been the ubiquitous decline in military spending relative to GNP. From the mid 1950s to the late 1960s its share fell from 7·1 per cent to 6·2 per cent of GNP in all OECD countries combined; from 4·1 per cent to 3·2 per cent if the US is excluded.[8] Since then this tendency has if anything intensified with a major drop in the US from 9 per cent to below 7 per cent in 1972 and in Italy, from 4 per cent to 2½ per cent. Other major developments since the Second World War have been a growth in 'environmental' and infra-structure expenses, transport and roads, and a relative decline in agricultural support. Comparable data on these and other items is harder to come by but the trends in the UK revealed in Table 2 are probably common to all advanced capitalist economies.[9] Two further notable increases also occurred in the 1960s: a growth in state economic aid to the private sector and a growth in state expenditure on its legal and coercive apparatus. The decline in expenditure on 'commerce and industry' since 1971 does not represent a real decline in the former item. Instead direct investment grants have been replaced by tax allowances to corporations, a change which leaves unaltered the impact on total state finances, and which reveals the pitfalls in extrapolating figures on expenditure to reveal the total economic impact of the modern state.

By no means does all state spending pre-empt resources and reduce the total available for the private sector. This is only the case with real (current and capital) spending, such as on arms or education services. The remaining money transfers do just that: they merely transfer the ability to purchase resources to other groups, whether individual households (e.g. pensions or family allowances) or private firms (e.g. investment grants). They thus add to private purchasing power, just as the taxes to finance them subtract from it. Table 1 shows that for the major OECD countries real expenditure accounted for between 42 per cent of total spending in Italy and 70 per cent in the USA. In most OECD countries it was transfer expenditure which rose most rapidly between 1955 and 1969. For all OECD countries combined it grew 42 per cent faster than GNP, whereas real state expenditure rose only 16 per cent faster (8 per cent faster if the US is excluded) and total state spending 23 per cent faster.[10] Almost everywhere this has been due to the decline in arms spending, since real civilian expenditure continued to grow throughout this period. In the UK, total real expenditures actually fell as a share of GNP in the 1950s, and this trend has continued since then in France and Japan (see bottom half of Table 1). So the rapid growth of the state since the Second World War has not significantly reduced the share of growing resources available for private consumption, investment or exports. Rather it has been utilized to raise the share of the last two in particular—noticeably so in the last few years as profit rates have been squeezed.

Structures

Of course, despite the similarity in *trends*, the *structures* of state expenditure still differ substantially between the major OECD countries. In general one can distinguish three groups of countries: the US and UK, the EEC countries and Japan. The US and UK are characterized by higher military and lower social security spending than the EEC. Partly because of this the share of public expenditure which pre-empts real resources is higher in the US and UK, accounting for almost one quarter of GDP (Table 1). Since interest on the National Debt is also more burdensome there, the total of 'war related expenditure' is also higher than in the EEC, and total social spending is markedly lower (especially in the USA until recent years).[11] Japan is in a category of its own, the state spending less than any other OECD country with the exception of Spain and Portugal. These differences are matched by variations in the structure of state revenues. Not suprisingly the high social security benefits in the EEC are matched by higher social security contributions, though in France especially these are mostly paid by employers. In the UK and US personal income taxation is higher and in the US corporation tax is still significant; social security contributions are much lower. In Japan taxes of all kinds are very low: less than two-thirds of the OECD average.[12] These different patterns of expenditure and revenue reflect of course the very different historical antecedents and processes in each nation state (the high war-related expenditures of the UK even today reminding us of its past global role). On the other hand the similarity in *trends* mean that these differences are diminishing and the structures of expenditure are 'converging' in all advanced capitalist countries.

Two further points should be emphasized when interpreting data on state spending. First, part, even of real expenditure, consists of purchases of goods and services from the capitalist sector, for example arms, drugs, books, building construction etc. In the UK at the present time this amounts to one third of current real expenditure, the remaining two thirds representing the wages of state employees, whether soldiers, teachers or doctors. Ten per cent of the output of UK manufacturing industry (and a much higher proportion in certain sectors, e.g. aerospace) is purchased by the central government alone.[13] Not all state *expenditure* represents state *production*.

Secondly, trends in productivity in the state sector must also be considered, for it is well known that this rises less fast than in the capitalist sector, due to the predominance of low productivity, labour-intensive services in the former, particularly the social services. As a result the cost index of state services has risen faster than the average and a greater level of expenditure is required year by year in all countries just to maintain the level of services in real terms. Thus state consumption expenditure, which in *money* terms has risen faster than GNP in the OECD as a whole has in constant price terms risen more slowly (see Table 1, last line). Excluding the USA (where it was boosted by military spending in the 1960s) state consumption rose by 3·9 per cent p.a. in real terms in all OECD countries from 1955–69, whilst GNP rose by 5·7 per cent.[14] In other words *real* state consumption expenditure has fallen as a share of GNP over the last two decades. Admittedly this is more than accounted

for by the decline in military spending, and social transfers have continued to rise, but the point remains. For slow growing economies such as the British, it can mean that a rising proportion of GNP must be expanded each year in order merely to protect the social services against the inflation in their costs.[15] [. . .] This phenomenon has contributed to the recent crisis of social expenditure in the UK and elsewhere. [. . .]

Notes

1 The two tables are not comparable. Table 1 excludes capital expenditure of state productive enterprises, i.e. it measures total government rather than public expenditure. It also excludes capital transfers. In Table 1 the items are expressed as a percentage of GDP at purchasers' values, in Table 2 of GNP at factor cost. The purchasers' values/factor cost distinction is crucial since the latter excludes the artificial inflation of national output brought about by the imposition of indirect taxes, notably on consumer items, which raises their market price. Since the burden of indirect taxes on government expenditure is small, the procedure in Table 2 gives a more accurate impression of the relative weight of state expenditure. Gross National Product differs from Gross Domestic Product by including net property income paid or received from abroad; but the difference is slight.

2 OECD, 'Public expenditure trends' (by M. Garin-Painter) in *Occasional Studies*, July 1970, Table 1, p. 45.

3 Current spending rose by 4·4 per cent of GNP (4·9 per cent including the USA) and total spending by 5·0 per cent (5.5 per cent including the USA). OECD, *Expenditure Trends in OECD Countries 1960–1980*, 1972, Tables 16, 19. In these and subsequent calculations, countries are weighted by their aggregate GNPs at current exchange rates. In 1967–9 this gave the USA a weight of

51 per cent and the other five major countries a weight of 34 per cent of the OECD total.

4 And for the aberrant behaviour of the US. J. O'Connor (*The Fiscal Crisis of the States*, New York, 1973, p. 43) attributes the growing government deficit in the 1960s to the unpopularity of the war in South East Asia which prevented the imposition of tax increases to finance it.

5 OECD, 1972, p. 56.

6 OECD, 1970, p. 48.

7 OECD, 1972, pp. 72–81 for a detailed comparative analysis.

8 ibid., Table 16.

9 See OECD, 1970, p. 53.

10 OECD, 1973, Table 17.

11 T. Hill, 'Too much consumption', *National Westminster Bank Review*, November 1969.

12 OECD, 1972, Table 19, and CSO, *Social Trends*, no. 5, 1974, Table 210.

13 T. Chester, 'Public money in the private sector', *National Westminster Bank Review*, May 1973, p. 24.

14 OECD, 1972, Tables 2, 3. 'State consumption' refers to current real expenditure in Table 1.

15 For example, expenditure on the National Health Service in the UK which rose as a share of GNP at current prices (see Table 2) actually fell at constant prices from 3·9 per cent in 1951 to 3·4 per cent in 1971.

I. 5 Poverty and equality

J. C. Kincaid

Each week, under the national-insurance scheme, more than eight million separate payments are made to individuals or families, to old-age pensioners, widows, the unemployed and to people unable to work because of sickness or industrial injury. At any one time as many as one in four of the households in Britain are dependent on national-insurance benefits as their major source of income. In addition, each week nearly three million supplementary pensions and allowances are paid out to people qualifying for them after a means test. And, finally, there are seven million children for whom a family allowance is paid.

Although social security benefits are anything but generous for the individual recipient, in terms of national finance the sums passing through the system are enormous. Government expenditure on social security currently equals about 8 per cent of gross national product, by far the largest single item in the Government's annual budget.

In 1973–4, over £5,200 million was paid out in social security benefits, more than 23 per cent of central Government expenditure. By comparison, the next biggest item was spending on education at just under £4,000 million. Defence cost £3,400 million, and the entire National Health Service less than £3,000 million.

Expressed in these broad terms, State provision for social security appears to be quite impressive. But behind the figures lies a familiar and depressing reality. For millions of people the social security system provides their sole, or at least their major, source of financial support. Yet, for many of the groups who depend on the system for an income, the level of benefits provided is quite inadequate to maintain a decent standard of living. Widespread poverty is a direct consequence of the limited effectiveness of social security provision. Whatever may have been the case

in the immediate post-war period, the social security schemes in Britain now fail to match the standard of those which operate in comparable industrial societies on the Continent. British entry into the Common Market does not, of itself, commit the British Government to effecting improvements in the social security system to bring it up to European standards. The Common Market treaty obligations are concerned only with the rights to welfare services of people moving from one country to another within the Community, and not with the level of welfare services available to people within their own country.

Radical improvements in social security provision in Britain are urgently needed and long overdue. This book is mostly concerned with one central question. How far does the present social security system operate to reduce inequality in British society? Huge sums of money are raised in taxation and by national-insurance contributions and are transferred in the form of social security benefits to millions of recipients. The sheer size of these income flows—equivalent to nearly one eighth of the total income provided by all wages and salaries—means that the social security system could have a major impact on the pattern of social class inequality in Britain. Certainly the common assumption is that social security, along with the other major components of the Welfare State, is substantially egalitarian in its effects. Such a view is carefully sustained within the political establishment and given wide currency by the mass media. It is usually accepted that the Welfare State operates as a gigantic funnel which transfers resources and purchasing power from the higher to the lower income groups in society. My argument is, on the contrary, that the social security system as established by the Labour Government in the late 1940s was much less egalitarian in its effects than was widely supposed at the time, and, more important, that over the past twenty years the modifications to the social security system which have been introduced by successive Governments have on

Source: *Poverty and Equality in Britain*, Penguin, rev. ed. 1975, pp. 9–21.

the whole made it less and less egalitarian in its consequences.

If this view can be successfully established it undercuts most of the assumptions about welfare which are current within the major political parties. We are continually told that poverty can only be reduced, and social security provision improved, by modest steps and by a process of gradual reform. It is commonly accepted by the leadership of the Labour Party, as well as universally within the Conservative Party, that the present tax system and the Welfare State have made British society pretty well as egalitarian as it could reasonably become. For nearly fifteen years now, Labour's overriding objective has been to present itself to the electorate as the party of industrial efficiency and rapid economic growth. The Labour movement's traditional preoccupation with social justice has been completely subordinated to this end. In 1969, the late Richard Crossman, then Minister of Social Security, delivered an elaborate lecture to the Fabian Society on the problems of social security finance. He discussed at length the continuing necessity of effecting a shift in resources away from private spending and into the social services. But, in the very first paragraph of his lecture, redistributive taxation as a source for extra welfare finance is curtly dismissed. 'That the working class can achieve this shift painlessly by taxing the rich in order to pay for the social services is a fallacy . . .'[1] The point is made flatly and without supporting argument; Crossman obviously assumes that the proposition will be accepted as completely self-evident by his audience. Later I shall document in some detail the ways in which inequalities in income and wealth have been allowed to multiply during Labour's recent terms of office.

My basic proposition is that no adequate system of social security can be created without a serious redistribution of income. Most of the deficiencies of existing schemes for social security have arisen as a result of efforts by politicians and administrators to deal with poverty as if it were an isolated social problem, which could be attacked by diverting small flows of extra income to the poorest and by minimizing more radical changes in the overall distribution of privilege in society. The attempt to reduce poverty by multiplying inexpensive means-tested schemes has been largely self-defeating. The result has been to create a Welfare State of such bewildering complexity that comparatively few working-class people on low incomes could possibly find out what they might be entitled to, or how to apply and to whom, for all of the benefits to which they might in theory be entitled.

The whole system is becoming increasingly irrational. Large numbers of people dependent on social security for an income are reduced to desperate poverty. Meanwhile the Government spends larger and larger sums of money on advertising campaigns to guide possible claimants through the maze of schemes, qualifying conditions, exceptions, application forms, means tests etc., which the attempt to run a Welfare State on the cheap has generated. An increasing array of social workers is employed, one of whose main functions is to offer guidance to citizens lost in the welfare jungle. In many cases the social workers themselves, despite expensive training, have a less than adequate grasp of the complexities of social security entitlement. Increasing amounts of money are devoted to the employment of highly paid administrators to organize the social workers into large, bureaucratic empires. Underlying all of these developments is a refusal to see poverty and social equality as issues which are, in reality, quite inseparable.

Poverty and old age

Two thirds of the total expenditure on national-insurance benefits goes to meet the cost of retirement pensions. The simplest test of the adequacy of the pension is to compare the level of the basic State pension with average earnings for full-time work. As illustrated in Table 1, the record is not inspiring.

Table 1 Old-age pensions as proportion of average wages

	Single-person pension (per week)	Average weekly earnings for manual work	Pension as % of earnings
1937	£ 0·50	£ 3·00	17
1948	£ 1·30	£ 7·05	18
1964	£ 3·37	£18·95	18
1966	£ 4·00	£20·65	19
1968	£ 4·50	£23·60	19
1970	£ 5·00	£28·90	17
1971	£ 6·00	£30·93	19
1972	£ 6·75	£36·20	19
1973	£ 7·75	£41·52	19
1974	£10·00	£49·12	20

For more than three decades, the relative purchasing power of the single-person pension has not risen above one fifth of the average industrial wage and the pension rate for a married couple has been continuously less than one third of the average wage. Thus increases in pension have barely matched improvements in working-class living standards. Since the mid 1930s, very approximately, the real purchasing power of the average wage has doubled. So too with the old-age pension. But *in relative terms* the purchasing power of the basic pension has improved only very marginally.

Even the small gains registered during the 1970s are immensely vulnerable in a context of rapidly rising inflation. Until recently improvements in the cash value of pensions were made at irregular and widely spaced intervals. In 1971, 1972 and 1973 a pattern was established of pension increases each autumn. At the time of writing the practice is for pension increases to come roughly at nine-month intervals—i.e. there were increases in July 1974 and April 1975; a further review is promised for December 1975.

But already—and until the rate of inflation slows down—a shift to more frequent increases in all social security benefits has become very urgent. The improvement in benefits which the Wilson Government made in April 1975 left those dependent on national insurance worse off than they had been in July 1974. The April increase was 15·5 per cent for pensioners, 14 per cent for the sick and the unemployed. Yet retail prices rose by 17 per cent in the nine-month period ending in April 1975. More serious still, the Government were promising no further rise until December 1975, by which time on current trends pensions and benefits will have fallen more than 25 per cent behind the standard set in July 1974. Pensioners and other national-insurance dependants are going to be in severe financial difficulties in the month or two before benefits are increased.

Since pre-war days old-age pensions have been continuously below the official poverty line, as currently defined by the Supplementary Benefit scale. This scale takes the form of a payment to cover rent and rates, and an additional payment in cash of 30–40p a week.

The official poverty line is one of the key elements in the whole structure of social security and will be discussed a good deal in this book—both the way it is operated and how it originated and developed historically. This minimum income system is now administered by the Supplementary Benefits Commission (SBC), which was created in 1966 to take over the functions of the old National Assistance Board.

Since the autumn of 1973, the SBC has run a two-tier system of rates. The long-term scale, which is higher, is paid to old-age pensioners and to those under retirement age who have been continuously dependent on supplementary benefit income for more than two years. However, the extra long-term benefit is restricted to adults; only the short-term rate is paid in respect of children, no matter how long their family has been on supplementary benefit. It should be noted that family allowances are *included* in the supplementary scales, not paid in addition. Of claimants under retirement age, over 60 per cent get only the

short-term level of benefit, and a special regulation lays down that the unemployed and their families get only the short-term rate, however long they have been out of work.

The basic rates of supplementary benefit have been raised at roughly the same time as pensions. The kind of living standards available to people on supplementary benefit are indicated by Table 2.

The figures given in Table 2 were those operating in the autumn of 1974. The pattern shown is typical of the relationship between wages and supplementary benefits in the 1970s. Since supplementary benefit rates are changed no more frequently than pensions, it follows that the degree of poverty involved deepens considerably in the month or two before the new scales come into operation.

Not just retirement pensions, but most other long-term national-insurance benefits are currently so low that, if a person has no other income beyond the insurance benefit, he or she is automatically below the poverty line. Ever since the present system was set up in 1948 it has been the case that the main national-insurance benefits have provided less than a subsistence income to those dependent on them. As originally planned in 1948, national assistance was to be no more than the final safety net for a limited number of people who might slip through the fine meshes of the contributory national-insurance sector. It was expected and hoped by the Attlee Government that improvements in national-insurance would eventually allow the means-tested supplementary

Table 3 Dependent on national insurance and also getting supplementary benefit (%)

Old-age pensioners	26
Widows	13
Sick and disabled	9
Unemployed	21

Source: DHSS, *Annual Report for* 1973, HMSO. 1974.

system to be abolished altogether. But the outcome has been exactly the opposite. Year by year the number of people qualifying for supplementary assistance has increased. At the end of 1949 1·1 million weekly payments were being made by the National Assistance Board and the total of men and women provided for was 1·8 million. By the 1970s the corresponding number of supplementary pensions and allowances had risen to more than 2·7 million and the number of people catered for was over 4 million. The money handed out by the SBC goes overwhelmingly to supplement deficiencies in the level of benefits operating in the national-insurance scheme. Three out of four of all SBC allowances go to people with a pension or national-insurance benefit that has left them below the official poverty line. As Table 3 shows, a substantial proportion of people dependent on national insurance benefits are also obliged to apply for supplementary income.

Table 2 SBC payments as proportion of average wages[a]

	Short term %	Long term %
Single person	22	26
Married couple	33	38
Married couple+2 children	46	—
Married couple+3 children	50	—

[a] Average rent payments are included in these rates. Assumed that 2 children are 5–10 years of age, and where 3 children the youngest is under 5. Family allowances added to wages, and are included anyway in SBC scales for children.

The Supplementary Benefits Commission is one of the most controversial institutions in the whole machinery of British Government. As portrayed in the more reactionary of the mass-circulation newspapers, its officers are sentimental fools, over-ready to fall for the plausible story and the soft touch. Correspondingly the typical claimant is assumed to be an unemployed man, feckless, disinclined to work, and with a large family for the State to support.

In fact the major function of the SBC is to supplement the inadequate State pensions of the elderly. In 1972, for example, 70 per cent of all allowances paid out by the SBC went to people over retirement age; of the remainder 10 per cent went to the sick and disabled, a further 11 per cent mainly to women with children to look after, widows, separated or deserted wives and unmarried women. Only 9 per cent of SBC allowances went to families where the bread-winner was unemployed.

Under the poverty line

Only very sketchy and out-of-date information is available about what sorts of individuals and families are below the poverty line, and why. Probably the largest group in poverty are those who, though entitled by the Ministry rules to supplementary assistance, nevertheless do not apply for it. The SBC does not go knocking on doors to find unmet need. It can advertise its willingness to help in newspapers, leaflets, and by posters on Post Office notice boards. The administrative rules allow its officers to go no further. The initiative to approach the Ministry must be taken by the prospective claimant.

Despite the importance of non-application as an immediate cause of poverty, only very limited information is available about the numbers and circumstances of those involved. It is, however, clear that non-application is partly common among old-age pensioners. The only detailed official investigation was carried out as long ago as 1965 and indicated that some 850,000 pensioners could have received assistance had they applied.[2] One in ten of this group were living on an income more than 25 per cent below the poverty line. The main reasons given by pensioners for not applying were that they felt they could manage on what they had, or that they were not willing to accept charity, or that they did not realize they might be entitled to benefit.

More recently the Department of Health and Social Security has publicly conceded that non-application among the elderly is now even more extensive than in the mid 1960s. The Department estimates that at December 1972 there were 980,000 pensioners (in 760,000 households) whose incomes were below the supplementary benefit level, and who were not claiming a supplementary pension.[3]

A Government survey, *Circumstances of Families*,[4] carried out in 1966, had confirmed that non-application is by no means confined to the elderly. It was found, for example, that of the 135,000 men on unemployment or sickness benefit who had a family of at least two children, some 30,000 had incomes below the poverty line, but were not getting assistance from the Supplementary Benefits Commission. Some allowance must be made for income being understated in the interview, but over 19,000 of these families were more than £2 below the official poverty line. The same survey found that 7,000 fatherless families (7 per cent of this group) were also below the poverty line. It remained quite unclear whether such groups had in fact not applied, or whether a claim had been made and wrongly rejected.

In December 1972, it was officially estimated that there were 800,000 people (in 460,000 households) under retirement age whose incomes were below supplementary benefit level. Table 4 gives the details.

Table 4   Numbers with income below supplementary benefit level

Family head of single person	Families	Persons
(a) normally in full-time work (including those sick and disabled for less than 3 months)	80,000	250,000
(b) sick and disabled for more than 3 months	70,000	110,000
(c) unemployed for more than 3 months	120,000	190,000
(d) others	190,000	250,000
	460,000	800,000

Source: Ruth Lister, *Take Up of Means Tested Benefits*, Child Poverty Action Group, 1974.

The SBC is not allowed by statute to give general financial assistance to individuals in full-time employment, or to their dependants. Yet the wages paid for a large number of jobs are so low as to leave many families below the poverty line, particularly if they have one or more children. In April 1974, nearly 1¼ million men were earning less than £30 a week from full-time work, including overtime.[5] Around 800,000 women in full-time work were earning less than £17 a week. At that time a worker with under £30 a week, after deduction of tax and national insurance, would be taking home less than the poverty line standard for a married couple with two children.

To try to fill the gap between low wages and the poverty line, the Conservative Government in 1971 introduced the Family Income Supplement (FIS), a special means-tested family allowance payable on application by parents in full-time work, and with exceptionally low wages. This benefit has been exceptionally ineffective in meeting its purpose. Although in its first two years of operation, £783,000 was spent in advertising the existence of FIS, one half of the families estimated to be eligible did not claim the money to which they were theoretically entitled.[6] Nor has there been any subsequent improvement in take-up.

Thus, in summary, the immediate causes of poverty in Britain can be reduced to three sorts of reasons. (1) That although the national insurance system provides benefits as of right, in most cases those benefits leave an individual or family well below the poverty line, unless they happen to have some other source of income. (2) That the supplementary benefits system—which exists in theory to fill out the gaps and correct the inadequacies of national insurance—does not do an effective job. The SBC has no responsibility for actively seeking out cases of poverty. The nature of the 'help' offered by the SBC, and the terms on which it is given, are such as to deter many potential claimants from coming forward. (3) That for a substantial number of jobs the wages paid are so low that the family, especially where there are children, is automatically in poverty.

Exactly how many people are currently under the poverty line can only be a matter of guesswork—making projections from fragmentary and out-of-date evidence. The necessary large scale investigations could be carried out only by the Government, and in this critical area of policy recent Governments have preferred to let obscurity reign. In a study published in 1969 based on a careful assessment of the evidence, Professor Tony Atkinson concluded that 'around 5 million people are living below the income standard which the government feels to be the national minimum'.[7] It is unlikely that the position has greatly changed since this estimate was made.

In addition it is surely clear that the present SBC scale rate is too low to be acceptable as the line which defines poverty. In far too much current research it is assumed without question that as soon as income is above the SBC scale rate the family is no longer in poverty. That the problems of the poorest should take precedence over those of the less poor is reasonable enough. But it would be intolerably complacent to imply that the distribution of income in Britain would be quite satisfactory, provided that no one fell below what the SBC regards as a reasonable minimum income. The official minimum is far too low. In any case it is a curious definition of poverty which suggests that a family is not in poverty, although its income may be dependent on excessive hours of overtime work, or on the full-time work of a wife who has responsibility for young children, or on a husband working permanently away from home, or on bonuses earned by shiftwork systems which disrupt family relationships.

Certainly the SBC scale rates can be used to define the poorest—if not all of the poor—so that a start could be made by some radical reorganization of the social security system to ensure that no one falls below what the Government at present regards as a minimum tolerable income. From the point of view of the politician or the Government planner this need not appear as a completely impossible achievement—so long as the problem is posed only in strictly financial terms. The number of households living under the poverty line might be around two million. The average short-fall in their income might be of the order of £5 a week per household. A Government spending, in all, about £25,000 million a year should not be too pushed to find £500 million a year to eliminate the worst problems of financial poverty. Why is it not done?

For a great many reasons, some of which are strictly practical. It is one thing to use sample surveys to estimate the numbers of people whose incomes fall below some tolerable minimum, and by how much—although even that task has yet to be systematically carried out. It is quite another matter to identify and contact all of the actual families living throughout the country and to assess how much extra cash they should be paid. It should be remembered also that the two million households in question are not a fixed group of people who could be identified once and for all. It is a characteristic of life on the poverty line that household income tends to be irregular and fluctuating. The sums required to bring a family up to the poverty line will tend to vary, perhaps even from week to week. Any estimate of the numbers of people in poverty at a given time in fact conceals the real situation, which is of a much larger group of individuals or families, all of whom are under the minimum income line for some of the time. Thus the substantial costs of keeping millions of people under some kind of administrative surveillance would have to be added to the £500 million of additional benefit.

It has to be recognized that any serious attempt by the authorities to eliminate financial poverty would mean abandoning those assumptions and procedures which, in the present system, have the effect of penalizing and deterring so-called 'misuse' of the Welfare State. In practice this would mean the abolition of the Supplementary Benefits Commission, since there would seem to be no way of reorganizing such a complex means-testing apparatus so as to ensure that people had not only formal rights, but the information and the power to enforce those rights. The gradual abandonment of the means-tested part of the social security system was a key objective of the Beveridge Plan, which formed the basis of the present social security system. And yet now—thirty years after the Beveridge Report—the abolition of means-testing is scarcely even mentioned in public discussion about welfare questions.

It is a quite widely held opinion that many of those dependent on social security are layabouts, who prefer a life of ease at public expense to doing an honest day's work. There is precious little evidence to support the layabout thesis. But that such doctrines should be generally accepted is convenient to any social group or Government which aims to defend the prevailing degree of social inequality. For people doing well out of the present social and economic system it is advantageous that inadequacies in the Welfare State should be blamed on the poor rather than on the privileged. Any serious attempt to abolish poverty endangers the whole structure of inequality in society—partly because money must then be found for the poor at the expense of the rich, but also because such an attempt threatens the values which underwrite social inequality and the whole existing structure of privilege. So long as society is organized on a deeply competitive basis, it appears indispensable that social failure should exist for individuals as a visible and possible fate.

Poverty is such a fate, just as mental illness is another. Poverty cannot be considered as a residual, historically determined defect of an otherwise fair society, but as an integral element that helps support a competitive social order. It follows therefore that proposals to reduce poverty often involve very much more than technical and administrative problems. They tend rather to raise issues of principle about the whole structure of society.

Notes

1 R. H. S. Crossman, *Paying for the Social Services*, Fabian Society, 1969, p. 1.
2 Ministry of Pensions, *Financial and Other Circumstances of Retirement Pensioners*, HMSO, 1966.
3 In a letter from DHSS to Brian Sedgemore MP, 13 May 1974. Reported in a useful survey by Ruth Lister, *Take Up of Means Tested Benefits*, Child Poverty Action Group, 1974.

4 Ministry of Social Security, *Circumstances of Families*, 1967.
5 *Low Pay Bulletin*, no. 1, January 1975.
6 Lister, op. cit.
7 A. B. Atkinson, *Poverty in Britain and the Reform of Social Security*, Cambridge University Press, 1969, p. 38.

Part II Perspectives on social problems

The second Part of the Reader reviews a range of theories about social problems. The articles included represent markedly different theoretical standpoints, arrived at by very different routes, and advocating divergent views of what needs to be done. What this Part shows is that not only can there be no single 'objectively correct' definition of a social problem, but that there is much conceptual and intellectual confusion surrounding different uses of the term.

It is in an attempt to clear some of this cloudiness that Bradshaw seeks to classify social needs. He begins from the premiss that 'the history of the social services is the story of the recognition of social needs and the organisation of society to meet them.' Although numerous reports, such as Seebohm, have been deeply concerned with needs, he argues that there have rarely been attempts to define what those needs are. If we are to resolve social problems, Bradshaw believes that we must develop some way of identifying more precisely different areas of need. To this end, he puts forward a taxonomy of social need based on four separate definitions used by administrators and research workers. Without such a classification, he concludes, much social policy will continue to be determined by hunches and guesses.

Liazos is more sceptical of the assumption that social problems are defined in order that situations may be understood and resolved. His article is based on an examination of sixteen textbooks in the field of deviance. He concludes that, although they may be concerned to 'normalise' the deviant's behaviour, the authors, particularly those writing from a labelling approach, have in fact done the opposite. First, he argues that the books have served to raise and reinforce the popular prejudices which the authors wanted to dispel; the net effect has been to emphasise that the deviant is indeed different. Second, by their overwhelming concentration on the 'dramatic' nature of those types of deviance that are usually discussed (prostitution, homosexuality, marijuana-smoking),

sociologists have neglected to examine other more serious and more harmful forms of what Liazos calls 'covert institutional violence', such as poverty, exploitation, war and racism. Third, although premissed on the assumption that power is a crucial concept in the definition of a situation, activity or person as a problem, Liazos argues that there has been little discussion of 'the powerful' and the means they use to maintain and intensify their position. He concludes that the concept of deviance should be banished, and replaced by a discussion of oppression, conflict, control and suffering.

In sharp contradistinction, the Sheffield study was designed to evaluate the contribution of psychiatric illness and personality disorder in social maladjustment. It was a study of thirty-three 'problem families' from one postal area of Sheffield. A 'problem family' was taken to mean 'one which was currently involved with several social agencies'. It is based upon a particular theory of social problems—maladjustment. The authors pay careful attention to what they perceive as the 'demoralisation' and 'self-condemnation' of the families studied, arguing that one of the most important consequences is the decline in their morale which serves to reinforce their desperate situation. Problem families are to be distinguished neither by their poverty, nor by their psychiatric pathology, but rather by 'the fact that they can no longer struggle with their failure'.

To enable the poor overcome their demoralised situation, and to help them to cope with what are perceived to be their failures, the study suggests that the school might play a crucial role, particularly in supporting the children. Schools, it is argued, 'have an opportunity to promote an integrated and accepting community' around the children. Ivan Illich presents a fundamental critique of this conclusion. Far from supporting the child, the school has become one of the chief agents of repression. For Illich, then, the 'disestablishment' of the school as an institution has become inevitable. Far from liberating the pupil, schools have functioned to restrict children's learning.

We must distinguish learning from schooling; that is, we must separate the 'humanistic goal of the teacher' from the controlling structure of the school. It is this structure which is crucial to the legitimisation of the role of schooling in education. For Illich, it constitutes the 'hidden curriculum', the 'unalterable framework of the system within which all changes in the curriculum are made'.

Power *et al.* also take on the Sheffield study's conclusions by exploring the relationship between the school and delinquency. They argue against the belief that difficulties in the family are the primary cause of delinquency, and examine the role played by the school in creating and reinforcing delinquent behaviour. The research team gathered evidence from the six school years 1958–64 in the Tower Hamlets area of London. They try to show that while some schools may help the kids to stay out of trouble, others actively encourage delinquency. Thus, they conclude that any preventive and treatment work must be focused on both the school and the home.

The final article in this section is an extract from the Final Report of the Coventry Community Development Project. Again, the CDP presents a markedly different type of explanation of social problems to the 'Families Without Hope' study, and comes up with opposing proposals for intervention.

The report is particularly interesting because the authors acknowledge that 'we did not hold our current views when we started the Project in 1970'. The experience of working in the area brought about a fundamental shift in their understanding of both the nature and causes of the problems they faced. By the beginning of 1973, they had begun to undertake a political economy of Coventry in general, and of Hillfields in particular, and to try to work out a fresh political initiative in the struggle for change. The sections of the Report reproduced here detail the questions they asked and the types of responses they evoked. Most significantly, the Report represents an attempt to understand social problems in structural rather than in individual terms.

II. 1 The concept of social need

Jonathan Bradshaw

The concept of social need is inherent in the idea of social service. The history of the social services is the story of the recognition of social needs and the organisation of society to meet them. The Seebohm report was deeply concerned with the concept of need, though it never succeeded in defining it. It saw that 'the personal social services are large-scale experiments in ways of helping those in need.'

Despite this interest, it is often not clear in a particular situation what is meant by social need. When a statement is made to the effect that a person or group of persons are in need of a given service, what is the quality that differentiates them what definition of social need is being used?

The concept of social need is of particular interest to economists. They have a clearcut measure of 'effective demand': demand is 'effective' when people are prepared to back it financially and ineffective or non-existent when they are not. This measure will not do for the social services, because there is normally no link between service and payment (though some economists think there ought to be). If the social services are trying to cope with need without limiting it by the ability to pay, how is it actually assessed?

In practice, four separate definitions are used by administrators and research workers:

1. *Normative need.* This is what the expert or professional, administrator or social scientist defines as need in any given situation. A 'desirable' standard is laid down and is compared with the standard that actually exists—if an individual or group falls short of the desirable standard then they are identified as being in need. Thus the British Medical Association's nutritional standard is used as a normative measure of the adequacy of a diet (see Royston Lambert's *Nutrition in Britain*). The incapacity scale developed

Source: 'The taxonomy of social need', *Problems and Progress in Medical Care*, 7th ser., 1972, ed. G. McLachlan, Nuffield Provincial Hospitals Trust, OUP; as reprinted in *New Society*, 30.3.72.

by Peter Townsend and the measure of social isolation used by Jeremy Tunstall are also examples of normative standards used as a basis of need.

A normative definition of need is in no sense absolute. It may not correspond with need established by other definitions. It may be tainted with a charge of paternalism—i e., the use of middle-class norms to assess need in a working-class context—though where the aspirations are to middle-class standards, this may be reasonable. A further difficulty with the normative definition of need is that there may well be different and possibly conflicting standards laid down by different experts. The decision about what is desirable is not made in a vacuum. As Ronald Walton has pointed out, the statement 'x is in need' is often taken as an empirical fact. This is not so. It is a value-judgment entailing the following propositions: x is in a state y, y is incompatible with the values held in society z. Therefore y state should be changed. So the normative definition of need may be different according to the value orientation of the expert—on his judgments about the amount of resources that should be devoted to meeting the need, or whether or not the available skills can solve the problem. Normative standards change in time both as a result of developments in knowledge, and the changing values of society.

2. *Felt need.* Here need is equated with want. When assessing need for a service, people are asked whether they feel they need it. In a democracy, it could be imagined that felt need would be an important component of and definition of need, but a felt need measure seems to only be used regularly in studies of the elderly and in community development. Felt need is, by itself, an inadequate measure of 'real need'. It is limited by the perceptions of the individual—whether they know there is a service available, as well as a reluctance in many situations to confess a loss of independence. On the other hand, it is thought to be inflated by those who ask for help without really needing it.

3. *Expressed need* or demand is felt need turned into action. Under this definition, total need is defined as those people who demand a service. One does not demand a service unless one feels a need but, on the other hand, it is common for felt need not to be expressed by demand. Expressed need is commonly used in the health services where waiting-lists are taken as a measure of unmet need. Waiting-lists are generally accepted as a poor definition of 'real need'—especially for pre-symptomatic cases.

4. *Comparative need.* By this definition, a measure of need is found by studying the characteristics of those in receipt of a service. If people with similar characteristics are not in receipt of a service, then they are in need. This definition has been used to assess needs both of individuals and areas. Bleddyn Davies has identified the community-wide factors which indicate a high incidence of pathology in one area which are not present in another. Need established by this method is the gap between what services exist in one area and what services exist in another, weighted to take account of the difference in pathology. This is an attempt to standardise provision, but provision may still not correspond with need. The question still has to be asked—supply at what level? The statement that one area, A, is in need in comparison with another area, B, does not necessarily imply that area B is still not in need.

Comparative need used to define individuals in need can be illustrated by the following statements: 'This person *x* is in receipt of a service because he has the characteristics A–N. This person *z* has also the characteristics A–N but is not receiving the service. Therefore *z* is in need.' The difficulty in this situation is to define the significant characteristics. The method has been used by some local health authorities to compile a risk register of babies in need of special attention from the preventive services. Conditions which in the past have been associated with handicaps like forceps delivery, birth trauma, birth to older mothers, and so on, are used as indicators to babies in special need. The definition is more commonly used in an ad hoc way—a crude rule of precedence to assess eligibility for selective services provided by the personal social services.

The chart demonstrates diagrammatically the inter-relation of the four definitions. Plus (+) and minus (−) denote the presence or absence of need by each of the foregoing definitions—i.e., + − − + is a need that is accepted as such by the experts, but which is neither felt nor demanded by the individual, despite the fact that he has the same characteristics as those already being supplied with the service. Other examples of the twelve possible combinations are given. It will be noted that none of the squares is coterminous and the problem that the policymaker has to face is deciding exactly what part of the total is 'real need' —that is, need it is appropriate to try to meet.

1.   + + + +
This is the area where all definitions overlap, or (using an analogy from intelligence test studies) the 'g' factor of need. An individual is in need by all definitions, so this is the least controversial part of need.

2.   + + − +
Demand is limited by difficulties of access to a service. Although the individual is in need by all other definitions, he has not wanted to, or been able to, express his need. Difficulties of access may be due to a stigma attached to the receipt of a service; geographical distances that make it difficult to claim; charges which are a disincentive to take up; administrative procedures that deter claimants; or merely ignorance about the availability of the service. Demand must also vary according to how intense is the felt need. Two examples of need of this type are the non-take-up of means-tested benefits, and the under-use of fair rent machinery.

3.   + + − −
Here need is accepted as such by the expert and is felt by the individual, but there is no demand as well as, and possibly because of, the absence of supply. Examples may be need for family planning facilities for unmarried girls, free nursery education, and need for chiropody services for the elderly.

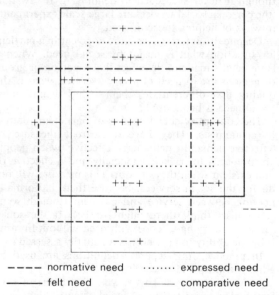

---- normative need   ········ expressed need
——— felt need   ——— comparative need

Figure 1   A taxonomy of social need

4.   − + + +
Here the need is not postulated by the pundits, but is felt, demanded, and supplied. The less essential types of cosmetic surgery are examples. Also some of the work of the GP, it is often thought, could come into this category—for example, the prescribing of 'clinically unnecessary' drugs. The pundits may suggest that a compassionate label for this category could be 'inappropriate need'. On the other hand, the pundits may be exercising inappropriate value-judgments.

5. $+ + + -$

A need that is postulated, felt, and demanded but not supplied. These needs represent likely growth areas in the social services. An example would be the need for a fatherless families allowance or adequate wage-related pensions. Resources are usually the limiting factor in this category.

6. $+ - - +$

Here the need is postulated by the experts and similar persons are being supplied with the service, but the need is neither felt nor demanded by the individual. Some of the work of the probation officer, or the health visitors' postnatal visits (when they are not wanted), are examples of meeting this kind of need. Another example is the unwanted supply of expensive central-heating plant in public sector housing.

7. $+ - - -$

Here need is postulated by the pundits or professionals. Examples could be found in the area of preventive medicine. To the layman, the need is probably obscure, technical and new. The need to provide fluoride in the water supplies was accepted as such by the public health experts long before it was felt, demanded, or supplied.

8. $- - - +$

Here a service is supplied despite the absence of need as assessed by the other definitions. This could be called a service-oriented service. Examples can be found in the many small and outdated charities to which the charity commissioners are striving to apply the doctrine of *cy près* for example, paying electricity bills instead of buying farthing candles for old ladies at Michaelmas.

9. $- + + -$

This is need which is not appreciated by the experts and is not supplied, but which is felt and demanded. Prescriptions for bandages requested from the GP may be an example of this. Another example is the need for improved services—the need for improved educational maintenance allowances.

10. $- + - -$

This represents felt needs which are not within the ambit of the social services to meet. Perhaps loneliness —or the need for love/company is an example of this. A need for wealth or fame are certainly examples.

11. $- + - +$

A need that is not postulated by the experts but is felt, not expressed, but supplied. People feel a need to make contributions for social benefits and the need is met by insurance stamps, but many experts feel it would be simpler to finance these benefits wholly through taxation.

12. $- - - -$

Absence of need by all definitions.

To illustrate how this could be used by research workers and policymakers, it might be useful to outline a hypothetical situation.

A local housing authority has become concerned about the housing position of the elderly in its area. It wishes to have assessment of the need for public sector housing for this age group. A research worker is therefore commissioned to do a study of the housing need. The first problem the research worker has to face is the question of what constitutes housing need? He can either make a decision as to what he himself believes housing need to be, or he can produce information on the amount of need under each section of the taxonomy and allow the policymakers to decide what part of the total they regard as 'real need'. The research worker decides to take the latter course of action. This will provide the maximum information with the minimum number of value-judgments. In order to produce a figure for each section of the taxonomy, he must first decide on the amount of need under each of the four separate definitions.

Normative need. It has already been pointed out that there is no one definition of normative need. Let us assume that the local housing authority is laying down the norms in this situation, and that it would agree that old persons living in homes lacking any of the basic amenities, and old persons living in overcrowded accommodation, are in need by its standards. An estimate of the number of persons who are in this situation could be obtained by means of a sample survey.

Felt need. An estimate of the degree of felt need can be obtained by means of the same sample survey by asking the respondents whether they are satisfied with their present housing and, if not, whether they would like to move. Ignoring the problems inherent in exploring people's attitudes on such a delicate question and remembering that their attitudes will be affected by their knowledge of alternative housing opportunities, as well as their fears about the upheaval of the move, another measure of need is obtained.

Expressed need. The local housing authority's waiting-lists provide the measure of expressed need in this context. It is, at the same time, the easiest measure of need to obtain and the most inadequate. On the one hand, the list may be inflated by persons who have resolved their housing problem since they applied for the housing and yet who have not withdrawn their application; and, on the other hand, the list may under-estimate expressed need if certain categories are excluded from the waiting list. There may be a residence qualification, applications from owner-occupiers may not be accepted unless they are overcrowded, and persons who have refused the first offer may also be excluded. All these exclusions mean that the waiting list is not an adequate measure of expressed need but, because it is the only one available, it is used as another measure of need.

Comparative need. The measure of comparative need is more difficult to obtain. It would entail investigating the characteristics of elderly persons already in public sector housing and then, through a sample survey, obtaining an estimate of the number of persons in the community (not in public sector housing) who have similar characteristics. As the local housing authority's norms have been taken for the measure of normative need, and as the local housing authority is responsible for choosing their tenants, it is likely that in this example the characteristics of tenants will be similar to those norms and thus the measure of comparative need will be very similar (though not necessarily identical) to the measure of normative need.

The research worker has now produced four separate but interrelated measures of need. By sorting, he is able to put a figure against each of the permutations of the four measures. For instance:

$+ + - +$ This will consist of persons whose houses are overcrowded or lack basic amenities, who want to move but who are not on the council waiting-list and yet who are 'as deserving as' other residents in council accommodation.

$- + - -$ This will consist of persons whose housing is considered satisfactory by local authority standards, who are not on the council waiting-list, and are not in need when compared with other residents in council property and yet who want to move.

So now the policymaker is presented with a picture of total need for public sector housing in his area. He is now able to use the taxonomy to clarify his decisions. Instead of housing being allocated on the basis of either first come first served, or whether the old person is articulate, energetic, and knowledgeable enough to get on the housing waiting-list, it can now be allocated on the basis of explicit priorities. No longer is the local authority providing houses to meet need, but, rather, providing houses to meet certain specific conditions of need.

Thus the policymaker can do one of two things. Either he can decide that certain categories of the total (say, $+ + + +$, $+ + - +$, $+ - - +$, $- + + +$,

$+ + + -$) constitute 'real need' and plan to provide enough housing for the numbers in these groups, or secondly if it is found that need is very large and his resources are limited, he can decide that certain categories of need should be given priority. For instance, he may decide that category $+ + - +$: those in need who have not applied for help (the iceberg below the waterline) should be given priority over category $- + + +$: those in need on all bases except that they are already adequately housed on a normative measure.

The policymaker can now return to the research worker. Having made his priorities explicit, he could ask the research worker to carry out a detailed study of the 'real need' categories to ascertain their aetiology so that, in future, they may be more easily identified and the services explicitly designed to get at and help them. The research worker could also use the taxonomy as a framework for monitoring the effects on need of technical advances, demographic change, changes in the standard of living, and improvements in the services.

This taxonomy may provide a way forward in an area where precise thinking is needed for both theoretical and practical reasons. Without some further classification, much social policy must remain a matter of political hunches and academic guesswork. The taxonomy provides no easy solutions either for the research worker or the policymaker. The research worker is still faced with difficult methodological problems and the policymaker has still to make complex decisions about those categories of need which should be given priority. But the taxonomy may help to clarify and make explicit what is being done when those concerned with the social services are studying or planning to meet social need.

References

Royston Lambert, *Nutrition in Britain 1950–60*, Occasional Papers in Social Administration no. 6, Bell, 1964.

Peter Townsend and Dorothy Wedderburn, *The Aged in the Welfare State*, Occasional Papers in Social Administration no. 14, Bell, 1965.

J. Tunstall, *Old and Alone*, Routledge & Kegan Paul, 1966.

Ronald Walton, 'Need: a central concept', *Social Service Quarterly*, 43 (1), 1969.

Bleddyn Davies, *Social Needs and Resources in Local Services*, Michael Joseph, 1968.

II. 2 The poverty of the sociology of deviance: nuts, sluts and prerverts[1]

Alexander Liazos

C. Wright Mills left a rich legacy to sociology. One of his earliest, and best, contributions was 'The Professional Ideology of Social Pathologists' (1943). In it, Mills argues that the small-town, middle-class background of writers of social problems textbooks blinded them to basic problems of social structure and power, and led them to emphasize melioristic, patchwork types of solutions to America's 'problems,' 'ranging from rape in rural districts to public housing'; they conceived as orderly the structure of small-town America; anything else was pathology and disorganization. Moreover, these 'problems,' 'ranging from rape in rural districts to public housing,' were not explored systematically and theoretically; they were not placed in some larger political, historical, and social context. They were merely listed and decried.[2]

Since Mills wrote his paper, however, the field of social problems, social disorganization, and social pathology has undergone considerable changes. Beginning in the late 1940s and the 1950s, and culminating in the 1960s, the field of 'deviance' has largely replaced the social problems orientation. This new field is characterized by a number of features which distinguish it from the older approach.[3]

First, there is some theoretical framework, even though it is often absent in edited collections (the Rubington and Weinberg [1968] edited book is an outstanding exception). Second, the small-town morality is largely gone. Writers claim they will examine the phenomena at hand—prostitution, juvenile delinquency, mental illness, crime and others —objectively, not considering them as necessarily harmful and immoral. Third, the statements and theories of the field are based on much more extensive, detailed, and theoretically-oriented research than were those of the 1920s and 1930s. Fourth,

writers attempt to fit their theories to some central theories, concerns, and problems found in the general field of sociology; they try to transcend mere moralizing.

The 'deviant' has been humanized; the moralistic tone is no longer ever-present (although it still lurks underneath the explicit disavowals); and theoretical perspectives have been developed. Nevertheless, all is not well with the field of 'deviance.' Close examination reveals that writers of this field still do not try to relate the phenomena of 'deviance' to larger social, historical, political, and economic contexts. The emphasis is still on the 'deviant' and the 'problems' he presents to himself and others, not on the society within which he emerges and operates.

I examined sixteen textbooks in the field of 'deviance,' eight of them readers, to determine the state of the field. (They are preceded by an asterisk in the bibliography.) Theoretically, eight take the labelling-interactionist approach; three more tend to lean to that approach; four others argue for other orientations (anomie, structural-functional, etc.) or, among the readers, have an 'eclectic' approach; and one (McCaghy et al., 1968) is a collection of biographical and other statements by 'deviants' themselves, and thus may not be said to have a theoretical approach (although, as we shall see, the section of the types of statements and 'deviants' still implies an orientation and viewpoint). A careful examination of these textbooks revealed a number of ideological biases. These biases became apparent as much from what these books leave unsaid and unexamined, as from what they do say. The field of the sociology of deviance, as exemplified in these books, contains three important theoretical and political biases.

1. All writers, especially those of the labelling school, either state explicitly or imply that one of their main concerns is to *humanize* and *normalize* the 'deviant', to show that he is essentially no different from us. But by the very emphasis on the 'deviant' and

Source: *Social Problems*, 20 (1), summer 1972, pp. 103–20 (reprinted in Rose and Giallombardo (eds), *Contemporary Social Issues*, Hamilton, 1975, pp. 13–31).

his identity problems and sub-culture, the opposite effect may have been achieved. The persisting use of the label 'deviant' to refer to the people we are considering is an indication of the feeling that these people are indeed different.

2. By the overwhelming emphasis on the 'dramatic' nature of the usual types of 'deviance'—prostitution, homosexuality, juvenile delinquency, and others—we have neglected to examine other, more serious and harmful forms of 'deviance.' I refer to *covert institutional violence* (defined and discussed below) which leads to such things as poverty and exploitation, the war in Vietnam, unjust tax laws, racism and sexism, and so on, which cause psychic and material suffering for many Americans, black and white, men and women.

3. Despite explicit statements by these authors of the importance of *power* in the designation of what is 'deviant,' in their substantive analyses they show a profound unconcern with power and its implications. The really powerful, the upper classes and the power elite, those Gouldner (1968) calls the 'top dogs,' are left essentially unexamined by these sociologists of deviance.

Always implicit, and frequently explicit, is the aim of the labelling school to humanize and normalize the 'deviant.' Two statements by Becker and Matza are representative of this sentiment.

In the course of our work and for who knows what private reasons, we fall into deep sympathy with the people we are studying, so that while the rest of society views them as unfit in one or another respect for the deference ordinarily accorded a fellow citizen, we believe that they are at least as good as anyone else, more sinned against than sinning (Becker, 1967: 100–101).

The growth of the sociological view of deviant phenomena involved, as major phases, the replacement of a correctional stance by an *appreciation* of the deviant subject, the tacit purging of a conception of pathology by a new stress on human *diversity*, and the erosion of a simple distinction between deviant and conventional phenomena, resulting from intimate familiarity of the world as it is, which yielded a more sophisticated view stressing *complexity* (Matza, 1969: 10).

For a number of reasons, however, the opposite effect may have been achieved; and 'deviants' still seem different. I began to suspect this reverse effect from the many essays and papers I read while teaching the 'deviance' course. The clearest example is the repeated use of the word 'tolerate.' Students would write that we must not persecute homosexuals, prostitutes, mental patients, and others, that we must be 'tolerant' of them. But one tolerates only those one considers less than equal, morally inferior, and weak; those equal to oneself, one accepts and respects; one

does not merely allow them to exist, one does not 'tolerate' them.

The repeated assertion that 'deviants' are 'at least as good as anyone else' may raise doubts that this is in fact the case, or that we believe it. A young woman who grew up in the South in the 1940s and 1950s told Quinn (1954: 146): ' "You know, I think from the fact that I was told so often that I must treat colored people with consideration, I got the feeling that I could mistreat them if I wanted to." ' Thus with 'deviants'; if in fact they are as good as we are, we would not need to remind everyone of this fact; we would take it for granted and proceed from there. But our assertions that 'deviants' are not different may raise the very doubts we want to dispel. Moreover, why would we create a separate field of sociology for 'deviants' if there were not something different about them? May it be that even we do not believe our statements and protestations?

The continued use of the word 'deviant' (and its variants), despite its invidious distinctions and connotations, also belies our explicit statements on the equality of the people under consideration. To be sure, some of the authors express uneasiness over the term. For example, we are told:

In our use of this term for the purpose of sociological investigation, we emphasize that we do not attach any value judgment, explicitly or implicitly, either to the word 'deviance' or to those describing their behavior or beliefs in this book (McCaghy *et al.*, 1968: v).

Lofland (1969: 2, 9–10) expresses even stronger reservations about the use of the term, and sees clearly the sociological, ethical, and political problems raised by its continued use. Yet, the title of his book is *Deviance and Identity*.

Szasz (1970: xxv–xxvi) has urged that we abandon use of the term:

Words have lives of their own. However much sociologists insist that the term 'deviant' does not diminish the worth of the person or group so categorized, the implication of inferiority adheres to the word. Indeed, sociologists are not wholly exempt from blame: they describe addicts and homosexuals as deviants, but never Olympic champions or Nobel Prize winners. In fact, the term is rarely applied to people with admired characteristics, such as great wealth, superior skills, or fame—whereas it is often applied to those with despised characteristics, such as poverty, lack of marketable skills, or infamy.

The term 'social deviants' . . . does not make sufficiently explicit—as the terms 'scapegoat' or 'victim' do—that majorities usually categorize persons or groups as 'deviant' in order to set them apart as inferior beings and to justify their social control, oppression, persecution, or even complete destruction.

Terms like victimization, persecution, and oppression are more accurate descriptions of what is really happening. But even Gouldner (1968), in a masterful critique of the labelling school, while describing social conflict, calls civil-rights and anti-war protesters 'political deviants.' He points out clearly that these protesters are resisting openly, not slyly, conditions they abhor. Gouldner is discussing political struggles; oppression and resistance to oppression; conflicts over values, morals, interests, and power; and victimization. Naming such protesters 'deviants,' even if *political* deviants, is an indication of the deep penetration within our minds of certain prejudices and orientations.

Given the use of the term, the definition and examples of 'deviant' reveal underlying sentiments and views. Therefore, it is important that we redefine drastically the entire field, especially since it is a flourishing one: 'Because younger sociologists have found deviance such a fertile and exciting field for their own work, and because students share these feelings, deviance promises to become an even more important area of sociological research and theory in the coming years' (Douglas, 1970a: 3).

The lists and discussions of 'deviant' acts and persons reveal the writers' biases and sentiments. These are acts which, 'like robbery, burglary or rape [are] of a simple and dramatic predatory nature . . .' (The President's Commission on Law Enforcement and the Administration of Justice, in Dinitz *et al.*, 1969: 105). All sixteen texts, without exception, concentrate on actions and persons of a 'dramatic predatory nature', on 'preverts'. This is true of both the labelling and other schools. The following are examples from the latter:

> Ten different types of deviant behavior are considered: juvenile delinquency, adult crime, prison sub-cultures, homosexuality, prostitution, suicide, homicide, alcoholism, drug addiction and mental illness (Rushing, 1969: preface).

> Traditionally, in American sociology the study of deviance has focused on criminals, juvenile delinquents, prostitutes, suicides, the mentally ill, drug users and drug addicts, homosexuals, and political and religious radicals (Lefton *et al.*, 1968: v).

> Deviant behavior is essentially violation of certain types of group norms; a deviant act is behavior which is proscribed in a certain way. [It must be] in a disapproved direction, and of sufficient degree to exceed the tolerance limit of the community. . . . [such as] delinquency and crime, prostitution, homosexual behavior, drug addiction, alcoholism, mental disorders, suicide, marital and family maladjustment, discrimination against minority groups, and, to a lesser degree, role problems in old age (Clinard, 1968: 28).

Finally, we are told that these are some examples of

deviance every society must deal with: 'mental illness, violence, theft, and sexual misconduct, as well as . . . other similarly difficult behavior' (Dinitz *et al.*, 1969: 3).

The list stays unchanged with the authors of the labelling school:

> in Part I, 'The Deviant Act,' I draw rather heavily on certain studies of homicide, embezzlement, 'naive' check forgery, suicide and a few other acts . . . in discussing the assumption of deviant identity (Part II) and the assumption of normal identity (Part III), there is heavy reference to certain studies of paranoia, 'mental illness' more generally, and Alcoholics Anonymous and Synanon (Lofland, 1969: 34).

> Homicide, suicide, alcoholism, mental illness, prostitution, and homosexuality are among the forms of behavior typically called deviant, and they are among the kinds of behavior that will be analyzed (Lofland, 1969: 1). Included among my respondents were political radicals of the far left and the far right, homosexuals, militant blacks, convicts and mental hospital patients, mystics, narcotic addicts, LSD and marijuana users, illicit drug dealers, delinquent boys, racially mixed couples, hippies, health-food users, and bohemian artists and village eccentrics (Simmons, 1969: 10).

Simmons (1969: 27, 29, 31) also informs us that in his study of stereotypes of 'deviants' held by the public, these are the types he gave to people: homosexuals, beatniks, adulterers, marijuana smokers, political radicals, alcoholics, prostitutes, lesbians, ex-mental patients, atheists, ex-convicts, intellectuals, and gamblers. In Lemert (1967) we find that except for the three introductory (theoretical) chapters, the substantive chapters cover the following topics: alcohol drinking, four; check forgers, three; stuttering, two; and mental illness, two. Matza (1969) offers the following list of 'deviants' and their actions that 'must be appreciated if one adheres to a naturalistic perspective': paupers, robbers, motorcycle gangs, prostitutes, drug addicts, promiscuous homosexuals, thieving Gypsies, and 'free love' Bohemians (1969: 16). Finally, Douglas' collection (1970a) covers these forms of 'deviance': abortion, nudism, topless barmaids, prostitutes, homosexuals, violence (motorcycle and juvenile gangs), shoplifting, and drugs.

The omissions from these lists are staggering. The covert, institutional forms of 'deviance' are nowhere to be found. Reading these authors, one would not know that the most destructive use of violence in the last decade has been the war in Vietnam, in which the US has heaped unprecedented suffering on the people and their land; more bombs have been dropped in Vietnam than in the entire World War II. Moreover, the robbery of the corporate world—through tax breaks, fixed prices, low wages, pollution of the environment, shoddy goods, etc.—is passed over in our fascination with 'dramatic and predatory' actions. Therefore, we are told that 'while they certainly are of no greater social importance to us than such subjects as banking and accounting [or military violence], subjects such as marijuana use and motorcycle gangs are of far greater interest to most of us. While it is only a coincidence that our scientific interests correspond with the emotional interest in deviants, it is a happy coincidence and, I believe, one that should be encouraged' (Douglas, 1970a: 5). And Matza (1969: 17), in commenting on the 'appreciative sentiments' of the 'naturalistic spirit,' elaborates on the same theme: 'We do not for a moment wish that we could rid ourselves of deviant phenomena. We are intrigued by them. They are an intrinsic, ineradicable, and vital part of human society.'

An effort is made to transcend this limited view and substantive concern with dramatic and predatory forms of 'deviance.' Becker (1964: 3) claims that the new (labelling) deviance no longer studies only 'delinquents and drug addicts, though these classical kinds of deviance are still kept under observation.' It increases its knowledge 'of the processes of deviance by studying physicians, people with physical handicaps, the mentally deficient, and others whose doings were formerly not included in the area.' The powerful 'deviants' are still left untouched, however. This is still true with another aspect of the new deviance. Becker (1964: 4) claims that in the labelling perspective 'we focus attention on the other people involved in the process. We pay attention to the role of the non-deviant as well as that of the deviant.' But we see that it is the ordinary non-deviants and the low-level agents of social control who receive attention, not the powerful ones (Gouldner, 1968).

In fact, the emphasis is more on the *subculture* and *identity* of the 'deviants' themselves rather than on their oppressors and persecutors. To be sure, in varying degrees all authors discuss the agents of social control, but the fascination and emphasis are on the 'deviant' himself. Studies of prisons and prisoners, for example, focus on prison subcultures and prisoner rehabilitation; there is little or no consideration of the social, political, economic, and power conditions which consign people to prisons. Only now are we beginning to realize that most prisoners are *political prisoners*—that their 'criminal' actions (whether against individuals, such as robbery, or conscious political acts against the state) result largely from current social and political conditions, and are not the work of 'disturbed' and 'psychopathic' personalities. This realization came about largely because of the writings of political prisoners themselves: Malcolm X (1965), Eldridge Cleaver (1968), and George Jackson (1970), among others.[4]

In all these books, notably those of the labelling school, the concern is with the 'deviant's' subculture and identity: his problems, motives, fellow victims, etc. The collection of memoirs and apologies of 'deviants' in their own words (McCaghy *et al.*, 1968)

covers the lives and identities of 'prevert deviants': prostitutes, nudists, abortionists, criminals, drug users, homosexuals, the mentally ill, alcoholics, and suicides. For good measure, some 'militant deviants' are thrown in: Black Muslims, the SDS, and a conscientious objector. But one wonders about other types of 'deviants': how do those who perpetrate the covert institutional violence in our society view themselves? Do they have identity problems? How do they justify their actions? How did the robber barons of the late 19th century steal, fix laws, and buy politicians six days of the week and go to church on Sunday? By what process can people speak of body counts and kill ratios with cool objectivity? On these and similar questions, this book (and all others)[5] provides no answers; indeed, the editors seem unaware that such questions should or could be raised.

Becker (1964), Rubington and Weinberg (1968), Matza (1969), and Bell (1971) also focus on the identity and subculture of 'prevert deviants.' Matza, in discussing the assumption of 'deviant identity,' uses as examples, and elaborates upon, thieves and marijuana users. In all these books, there are occasional references to and questions about the larger social and political structure, but these are not explored in any depth; and the emphasis remains on the behavior, identity, and rehabilitation of the 'deviant' himself. This bias continues in the latest book which, following the fashions of the times, has chapters on hippies and militant protesters (Bell, 1971).

Even the best of these books, Simmons' *Deviants* (1969), is not free of the overwhelming concentration of the 'deviant' and his identity. It is the most sympathetic and balanced presentation of the lives of 'deviants': their joys, sorrows, and problems with the straight world and fellow victims. Simmons demystifies the processes of becoming 'deviant' and overcoming 'deviance.' He shows, as well as anyone does, that these victims *are* just like us; and the differences they possess and the suffering they endure are imposed upon them. Ultimately, however, Simmons too falls prey to the three biases shown in the work of others: (a) the 'deviants' he considers are only of the 'prevert' types; (b) he focuses mostly on the victim and his identity, not on the persecutors; and (c) the persecutors he does discuss are of the middle-level variety, the agents of more powerful others and institutions.

Because of these biases, there is an implicit, but very clear, acceptance by these authors of the current definitions of 'deviance.' It comes about because they concentrate their attention on those who have been *successfully labelled as* '*deviant*,' and not on those who break laws, fix laws, violate ethical and moral standards, harm individuals and groups, etc., but who either are able to hide their actions, or, when known, can deflect criticism, labelling, and punishment. The following are typical statements which reveal this bias.

'. . . no act committed by members of occupational

groups [such as white-collar crimes], however unethical, should be considered as crime unless it is
punishable by the state in some way' (Clinard, 1968:
269). Thus, if some people can manipulate laws so
that their unethical and destructive acts are not 'crimes,'
we should cater to their power and agree that they are
not criminals.

Furthermore, the essence of the labelling school
encourages this bias, despite Becker's (1963: 14)
assertion that 'insofar as a scientist uses "deviant" to
refer to any rule-breaking behavior and takes as his
subjects of study only those who have been *labelled*
deviant, he will be hampered by the disparities
between the two categories.' But as the following
statements from Becker and others show, this is in
fact what the labelling school does do.

Deviance is 'created by society . . . *social groups
create deviance by making the rules whose infraction
constitutes deviance*, and by applying those rules to
particular people and labelling them as outsiders'
(Becker, 1963: 8–9). Clearly, according to this view, in
cases where no group has labelled another, no matter
what the other group or individuals have done, there
is nothing for the sociologist to study and dissect.

> Rules are not made automatically. Even though a
> practice may be harmful in an objective sense to
> the group in which it occurs, the harm needs to
> be discovered and pointed out. People must be
> made to feel that something ought to be done
> about it (Becker, 1963: 162).

> What is important for the social analyst is not
> what people are by his lights or by his standards,
> but what it is that people construe one another
> and themselves to be for what reasons and with
> what consequences (Lofland, 1969: 35).

> . . . deviance is in the eyes of the beholder. For
> deviance to become a social fact, somebody must
> perceive an act, person, situation, or event as a
> departure from social norms, must categorize that
> perception, must report the perception to others,
> must get them to accept this definition of the
> situation, and must obtain a response that
> conforms to this definition. Unless all these
> requirements are met, deviance as a social fact
> does not come into being (Rubington and
> Weinberg, 1968: v).

The implication of these statements is that the
sociologist accepts current, successful definitions of
what is 'deviant' as the only ones worthy of his attention. To be sure, he may argue that those labelled
'deviant' are not really different from the rest of us, or
that there is no act intrinsically 'deviant,' etc. By concentrating on cases of successful labelling, however, he
will not penetrate beneath the surface to look for other
forms of 'deviance'—undetected stealing, violence,
and destruction. When people are not powerful
enough to make the 'deviant' label stick on others, we
overlook these cases. But is it not as much a *social*

fact, even though few of us pay much attention to it,
that the corporate economy kills and maims more, is
more violent, than any violence committed by the
poor (the usual subjects of studies of violence)? By
what reasoning and necessity is the 'violence' of the
poor in the ghettoes more worthy of our attention
than the military bootcamps which numb recruits
from the horrors of killing the 'enemy' ('Oriental
human beings,' as we learned during the Calley trial)?
But because these acts are not labelled 'deviant,'
because they are covert, institutional, and normal,
their 'deviant' qualities are overlooked and they do
not become part of the province of the sociology of
deviance. Despite their best liberal intentions, these
sociologists seem to perpetuate the very notions they
think they debunk, and others of which they are
unaware.

As a result of the fascination with 'nuts, sluts, and
preverts,' and their identities and subcultures, little
attention has been paid to the unethical, illegal, and
destructive actions of powerful individuals, groups,
and institutions in our society. Because these actions
are carried out quietly in the normal course of events,
the sociology of deviance does not consider them as
part of its subject matter. This bias is rooted in the
very conception and definition of the field. It is
obvious when one examines the treatment, or, just as
often, lack of it, of the issues of violence, crime, and
white-collar crime.

Discussions of violence treat only one type: the
'dramatic and predatory' violence committed by individuals (usually the poor and minorities) against
persons and property. For example, we read, 'crimes
involving violence, such as criminal homicide, assault,
and forcible rape, are concentrated in the slums'
(Clinard, 1968: 123). Wolfgang, an expert on violence,
has developed a whole theory on the 'subculture of
violence' found among the lower classes (e.g., in
Rushing, 1969: 233–40). And Douglas (1970a: part 4,
on violence) includes readings on street gangs and the
Hell's Angels. Thompson (1966), in his book on the
Hell's Angels, devotes many pages to an exploration of
the Angels' social background. In addition, throughout the book, and especially in his concluding chapter,
he places the Angels' violence in the perspective of a
violent, raping, and destructive society, which refuses
to confront the reality of the Angels by distorting,
exaggerating, and romanticizing their actions. But
Douglas reprints none of these pages; rather, he offers
us the chapter where, during a 4 July weekend, the
Angels were restricted by the police within a lakeside
area, had a drunken weekend, and became a tourist
sideshow and circus.

In short, violence is presented as the exclusive
property of the poor in the slums, the minorities,
street gangs, and motorcycle beasts. But if we take the
concept *violence* seriously, we see that much of our
political and economic system thrives on it. In violence,
a person is *violated*—there is harm done to his person,

his psyche, his body, his dignity, his ability to govern himself (Garver, in Rose, 1969: 6). Seen in this way, a person can be violated in many ways; physical force is only one of them. As the readings in Rose (1969) show, a person can be violated by a system that denies him a decent job, or consigns him to a slum, or causes him brain damage by near-starvation during childhood, or manipulates him through the mass media, and so on endlessly.

Moreover, we must see that *covert institutional violence* is much more destructive than overt individual violence. We must recognize that people's lives are violated by the very normal and everyday workings of institutions. We do not see such events and situations as violent because they are not dramatic and predatory; they do not make for fascinating reading on the lives of preverts; but they kill, maim, and destroy many more lives than do violent individuals.

Here are some examples. Carmichael and Hamilton (1967: 4), in distinguishing between *individual* and *institutional* racism, offer examples of each:

When white terrorists bomb a black church and kill five black children, that is an act of individual racism, widely deplored by most segments of the society. But when in that same city— Birmingham, Alabama—500 black babies die each year because of lack of proper food, shelter and medical facilities, and thousands more are destroyed and maimed physically, emotionally and intellectually because of conditions of poverty and discrimination in the black community, that is a function of institutional racism.

Surely this is violence; it is caused by the normal, quiet workings of institutions run by respectable members of the community. Many whites also suffer from the institutional workings of a profit-oriented society and economy; poor health, dead-end jobs, slum housing, hunger in rural areas, and so on, are daily realities in their lives. This is surely much worse violence than any committed by the Hell's Angels or street gangs. Only these groups get stigmatized and analyzed by sociologists of deviance, however, while those good people who live in luxurious homes (fixing tax laws for their benefit) off profits derived from an exploitative economic system—they are the pillars of their community.

Violence is committed daily by the government, very often by lack of action. The same system that enriches businessmen farmers with billions of dollars through farm subsidies cannot be bothered to appropriate a few millions to deal with lead poisoning in the slums. Young children

get it by eating the sweet-tasting chips of peeling tenement walls, painted a generation ago with leaded paint.

According to the Department of Health, Education, and Welfare, 400,000 children are poisoned each year, about 30,000 in New York City alone. About 3,200 suffer permanent brain damage, 800 go blind or become so mentally retarded that they require hospitalization for the rest of their lives, and approximately 200 die.

The tragedy is that lead poisoning is totally man-made and totally preventable. It is caused by slum housing. And there are now blood tests that can detect the disease, and medicines to cure it. Only a lack of purpose sentences 200 black children to die each year (Newfield, 1971).[6]

Newfield goes on to report that on 20 May 1971, a Senate-House conference eliminated $5 million from an appropriations budget. In fact, 200 children had been sentenced to death and thousands more to maiming and suffering.

Similar actions of violence are committed daily by the government and corporations; but in these days of misplaced emphasis, ignorance, and manipulation we do not see the destruction inherent in these actions. Instead, we get fascinated, angry, and misled by the violence of the poor and the powerless. We see the violence committed during political rebellions in the ghettoes (called 'riots' in order to dismiss them), but all along we ignored the daily violence committed against the ghetto residents by the institutions of the society: schools, hospitals, corporations, the government. Check any of these books on deviance, and see how much of this type of violence is even mentioned, much less explored and described.

It may be argued that some of this violence is (implicitly) recognized in discussions of 'white-collar' crime. This is not the case, however. Of the sixteen books under consideration, only three pay some attention to white-collar crime (Cohen, 1966; Clinard, 1968; Dinitz *et al.*, 1969); and of these, only the last covers the issue at some length. Even in these few discussions, however, the focus remains on the *individuals* who commit the actions (on their greediness, lack of morality, etc.), not on the economic and political institutions within which they operate. The selection in Dinitz *et al.* (1969: 99–109), from the President's Commission on Law Enforcement and the Administration of Justice, at least three times (pp. 101, 103, 108) argues that white-collar crime is 'pervasive,' causes 'financial burdens' ('probably far greater than those produced by traditional common law theft offenses'), and is generally harmful. At least in these pages, however, there is no investigation of the social, political, and economic conditions which make the pervasiveness, and lenient treatment, of white-collar crime possible.

The bias against examining the structural conditions behind white-collar crime is further revealed in Clinard's suggestions on how to deal with it (in his chapter on 'The Prevention of Deviant Behavior'). The only recommendation in three pages of discussion (704–7) is to teach everyone more 'respect' for the law. This is a purely moralistic device; it pays no attention to the structural aspects of the problem, to the fact that even deeper than white-collar crime is ingrained a whole network of laws, especially tax laws, administrative policies, and institutions which systematically favor a small minority. More generally, discussions on the prevention of 'deviance' and crime do not deal with institutional violence, and what we need to do to stop it.[7]

But there is an obvious explanation for this oversight. The people committing serious white-collar crimes and executing the policies of violent institutions are respectable and responsible individuals, not 'deviants'; this is the view of the President's Commission on Law Enforcement and the Administration of Justice.

> Significantly, the Antitrust Division does not feel that lengthy prison sentences are ordinarily called for [for white-collar crimes]. It 'rarely recommends jail sentences greater than 6 months— recommendations of 30-day imprisonment are most frequent.' (Dinitz *et al.*, 1969: 105.)

> Persons who have standing and roots in a community, and are prepared for and engaged in legitimate occupations, can be expected to be particularly susceptible to the threat of criminal prosecution. Criminal proceedings and the imposition of sanctions have a much sharper impact upon those who have not been hardened by previous contact with the criminal justice system (in Dinitz *et al.*, 1969: 104).

At the same time, we are told elsewhere by the Commission that white-collar crime is pervasive and widespread; 'criminal proceedings and the imposition of sanctions' do not appear to deter it much.

The executives convicted in the Electrical Equipment case were respectable citizens. 'Several were deacons or vestrymen of their churches.' The rest also held prestigious positions: president of the Chamber of Commerce, bank director, little-league organizer, and so on (Dinitz *et al.*, 1969: 107). Moreover, 'generally . . . in cases of white-collar crime, neither the corporations as entities nor their responsible officers are invested with deviant characters . . .' (Cohen, 1966: 30). Once more, there is quiet acquiescence to this state of affairs. There is no attempt to find out why those who steal millions and whose actions violate lives are not 'invested with deviant characters.' There is no consideration given to the possibility that, as responsible intellectuals, it is our duty to explore and expose the structural causes for corporate and other serious crimes, which make for much more suffering than does armed robbery. We seem satisfied merely to observe what is, and leave the causes unexamined.

In conclusion, let us look at another form of institutional 'deviance.' The partial publication of the Pentagon papers (June 1971) made public the conscious lying and manipulation by the government to quiet opposition to the Vietnam war. But lying pervades both government and economy. Deceptions and outright lies abound in advertising (see Henry, 1966). During the 1968 campaign, Presidential candidate Nixon blessed us with an ingenious form of deception. McGinniss (1969: 149–50) is recording a discussion that took place before Nixon was to appear on live TV (to show spontaneity) the day before the election and answer, unrehearsed, questions phoned in by the viewing audience.

> 'I understand Paul Keyes has been sitting up for two days writing questions,' Roger Ailes said.
>   'Well, not quite,' Jack Rourke said. He seemed a little embarrassed.
>   'What is going to happen?'
>   'Oh . . .'
>   'It's sort of semiforgery, isn't it?' Ailes said. 'Keyes has a bunch of questions Nixon wants to answer. He's written them in advance to make sure they're properly worded. When someone calls in with something similar, they'll use Keyes' question and attribute it to the person who called. Isn't that it?'
>   'More or less,' Jack Rourke said.

In short, despite the supposedly central position of *social structure* in the sociological enterprise, there is general neglect of it in the field of 'deviance.' Larger questions, especially if they deal with political and economic issues, are either passed over briefly or overlooked completely. The focus on the actions of 'nuts, sluts, and preverts' and the related slight of the criminal and destructive actions of the powerful, are instances of this avoidance.

Most of the authors under discussion mention the importance of *power* in labelling people 'deviant.' They state that those who label (the victimizers) are more powerful than those they label (the victims). Writers of the labelling school make this point explicitly. According to Becker (1963: 17), 'who can . . . force others to accept their rules and what are the causes of their success? This is, of course, a question of political and economic power.' Simmons (1969: 131) comments that historically, 'those in power have used their positions largely to perpetuate and enhance their own advantages through coercing and manipulating the rest of the populace.' And Lofland (1969: 19) makes the same observation in his opening pages:

> It is in the situation of a very powerful party opposing a very weak one that the powerful party sponsors the *idea* that the weak party is breaking the rules of society. The very concepts of 'society' and its 'rules' are appropriated by powerful parties and made synonymous with their interests (and, of course, believed in by the naive, e.g., the undergraduate penchant for the phrases 'society says . . .,' 'society expects . . .,' 'society does . . .').

But this insight is not developed. In none of the sixteen

books is there an extensive discussion of how power operates in the designation of deviance. Instead of a study of power, of its concrete uses in modern, corporate America, we are offered rather fascinating explorations into the identities and subcultures of 'deviants,' and misplaced emphasis on the middle-level agents of social control. Only Szasz (1961, 1963, and notably 1970) has shown consistently the role of power in one area of 'deviance,' 'mental illness.' Through historical and contemporary studies, he has shown that those labelled 'mentally ill' (crazy, insane, mad, lunatic) and institutionalized have always been the powerless: women, the poor, peasants, the aged, and others. Moreover, he has exposed repeatedly the means used by powerful individuals and institutions in employing the 'mental illness' label to discredit, persecute, and eliminate opponents. In short, he has shown the political element in the 'mental illness' game.

In addition, except for Szasz, none of the authors seems to realize that the stigma of prostitution, abortion, and other 'deviant' acts unique to women comes about in large part from the powerlessness of women and their status in society. Moreover, to my knowledge, no one has bothered to ask why there have always been women prostitutes for men to satisfy their sexual desires, but very few men prostitutes for women to patronize. The very word *prostitute* we associate with women only, not men. Both men and women have been involved in this 'immoral' act, but the stigma has been carried by the women alone.

All sixteen books, some more extensively than others, discuss the ideology, modes of operation, and views of *agents of social control*, the people who designate what is to be 'deviant' and those who handle the people so designated. As Gouldner (1968) has shown, however, these are the lower and middle level officials, not those who make basic policy and decisions. This bias becomes obvious when we look at the specific agents discussed.

For example, Simmons (1969: 18) tells us that some of 'those in charge at every level' are the following: 'university administrators, patrolmen, schoolmasters, and similar public employees.' Do university administrators and teachers run the schools alone? Are they teaching and enforcing their own unique values? Do teachers alone create the horrible schools in the slums? Are the uniformity, punctuality, and conformity teachers inculcate their own psychological hang-ups, or do they represent the interests of an industrial-technological-corporate order? In another sphere, do the police enforce their own laws?

Becker (1963: 14) has shown consistent interest in agents of social control. However, a close examination reveals limitations. He discusses 'moral crusaders' like those who passed the laws against marijuana. The moral crusader, 'the prototype of the rule creator,' finds that 'the existing rules do not satisfy him because there is some evil which profoundly disturbs him.' But the only type of rule creator Becker dis-

cusses is the moral crusader, no other. The political manipulators who pass laws to defend their interests and persecute dissenters are not studied. The 'unconventional sentimentality,' the debunking motif Becker (1964: 4-5) sees in the 'new deviance' is directed toward the police, the prison officials, the mental hospital personnel, the 'average' person and his prejudices. The basic social, political, and economic structure, and those commanding it who guide the labelling and persecution, are left untouched. We have become so accustomed to debunking these low-level agents that we do not even know how to begin to direct our attention to the ruling institutions and groups (for an attempt at such an analysis, see Liazos, 1970).

In a later paper, Becker (1967) poses an apparently insoluble dilemma. He argues that, in studying agents of social control, we are always forced to study subordinates. We can never really get to the top, to those who 'really' run the show, for if we study X's superior Y, we find Z above him, and so on endlessly. Everyone has somebody over him, so there is no one at the top. But this is a clever point without substance. In this hierarchy some have more power than others and some are at the top; they may disclaim their position, of course, but it is our job to show otherwise. Some people in this society do have more power than others: parents over children, men over women; some have considerable power over others: top administrators of institutions, for one; and some have a great deal of power, those Domhoff (1967) and others have shown to be the ruling class. It should be our task to explore and describe this hierarchy, its bases of strength, its uses of the 'deviant' label to discredit its opponents in order to silence them, and to find ways to eliminate this hierarchy.

Discussions of the police reveal the same misplaced emphasis on lower and middle level agents of social control. In three of the books (Matza, 1969: 182–95; Rubington and Weinberg, 1968: ch. 7; Dinitz *et al.*, 1969: 40–7), we are presented with the biases and prejudices of policemen; their modes of operation in confronting delinquents and others; the pressures on them from various quarters; etc. In short, the focus is on the role and psychology of the policeman.

All these issues about the policeman's situation need to be discussed, of course; but there is an even more important issue which these authors avoid. We must ask, who passes the laws the police enforce? Whose agents are they? Why do the police exist? Three excellent papers (Cook, 1968; A. Silver, in Bordua, 1967; T. Hayden, in Rose, 1969) offer some answers to these questions. They show, through a historical description of the origins of police forces, that they have always been used to defend the status quo, the interests of the ruling powers. When the police force was created in England in the early 1800s, it was meant to defend the propertied classes from the 'dangerous classes' and the 'mob.'[8] With the rise of capitalism and industrialism, there was much unrest from the suffering underclass; the professional police were meant to act as a buffer zone for the capitalist elite. Similarly, in America during the early part of this century, especially in the 1930s, police were used repeatedly to attack striking workers and break their strikes. During the Chicago 'police riot' of 1968, the police were not merely acting out their aggressions and frustrations; as Hayden shows, they acted with the consent, direction, and blessing of Mayor Daley and the Democratic party (which party represents the 'liberal' wing of the American upper class).

It must be stressed that the police, like all agents of social control, are doing someone else's work. Sometimes they enforce laws, and prejudices of 'society,' the much maligned middle class (on sex, marijuana, etc.); but at other times it is not 'society' which gives them their directives, but specific interested groups, even though, often, 'society' is manipulated to express its approval of such actions. Above all, we must remember that '*in a fundamentally unjust society, even the most impartial, professional, efficient enforcement of the laws by the police cannot result in justice*' (Cook, 1968: 2). More generally, in an unjust and exploitative society, no matter how 'humane' agents of social control are, their actions necessarily result in repression.

Broad generalization is another device used by some of these authors to avoid concrete examination of the uses of power in the creation and labelling of 'deviance.' Clairborne (1971) has called such generalization '*schlock.*' The following are some of the tactics he thinks are commonly used in writing popular *schlock* sociology (some sociologists of deviance use similar tactics, as we shall see).

The Plausible Passive:
'New scientific discoveries are being made every day. . . . These new ideas are being put to work more quickly . . .' [Toffler, in *Future Shock*, is] thereby rather neatly obscuring the fact that scientists and engineers (mostly paid by industry) are making the discoveries and industrialists (often with the aid of public funds) are putting them to work. An alternative to the Plausible Passive is the Elusive Impersonal: 'Buildings in New York literally disappear overnight.' What Toffler is trying to avoid saying is that contractors and real estate speculators *destroy* buildings overnight (Clairborne, 1971: 118).

Rampant Reification, by which 'conceptual abstractions are transformed into causal realities,' also abounds. Toffler

speaks of the 'roaring current of change' as 'an elemental force' and of 'that great, growling engine of change—technology.' Which of course completely begs the question of what fuels the engine and whose hand is on the throttle. One does not cross-examine an elemental force, let alone suggest that it may have been engendered by monopoly profits (especially in defense and aerospace) or accelerated by government incentives (e.g., open or concealed subsidies, low capital gains tax, accelerated depreciation— which Nixon is now seeking to reinstitute) (Clairborne, 1971: 118).

There are parallels in the sociology of deviance. Clinard (1968: ch. 4) argues that urbanization and the slum are breeding grounds for 'deviant behavior.' But these conditions are reified, not examined concretely. He says about urbanization and social change:

Rapid social and cultural change, disregard for the importance of stability of generations, and untempered loyalties also generally characterize urban life. New ideas are generally welcome, inventions and mechanical gadgets are encouraged, and new styles in such arts as painting, literature, and music are often approved (1968: 90).

But the slum, urbanization, and change are not reified entities working out their independent wills. For example, competition, capitalism, and the profit motive— all encouraged by a government controlled by the upper classes—have had something to do with the rise of slums. There is a general process of urbanization, but at given points in history it is fed by, and gives profits to, specific groups. The following are a few historical examples: the land enclosure policies and practices of the English ruling classes in the 17th and 18th centuries; the building of cheap housing in the 19th century by the owners of factory towns; and the profits derived from 'urban renewal' (which has destroyed neighbourhoods, created even more crowded slums, etc.) by the building of highways, luxury apartments, and stores.

Another favorite theme of *schlock* sociology is that 'All Men Are Guilty.' That means nothing can be done to change things. There is a variation of this theme in the sociology of deviance when we are told that (a) all of us are deviant in some way, (b) all of us label some others deviant, and (c) 'society' labels. Such statements preclude asking concrete questions: does the 'deviance' of each of us have equal consequences for others? Does the labelling of each of us stick, and with what results?

For example, Simmons (1969: 124) says:

I strongly suspect that officials now further alienate more culprits than they recruit back into conventional society, and I think they imprison at least as many people in deviance as they rehabilitate. We must remember that, with a sprinkling of exceptions, officials come from, are hired by, and belong to the dominant majority.

Who is that dominant majority? Are they always the numerical majority? Do they control the labelling and correctional process all by themselves? These questions are not raised.

Another case of *schlock* is found in Matza's discussion (lack of it, really) of 'Leviathan' (1969, especially ch. 7). It is mentioned as a potent force in the labelling and handling of 'deviance'. But, vainly, one keeps looking for some exploration into the workings of 'Leviathan.' It remains a reified, aloof creature. What is it? Who controls it? How does it label? Why? Matza seems content to try to mesmerize us by mentioning it constantly (Leviathan is capitalized throughout); but we are never shown how it operates. It hovers in the background, it punishes, and its presence somehow cowers us into submission. But it remains a reified force whose presence is accepted without close examination.

The preceding examples typify much of what is wrong with the sociology of deviance: the lack of specific analysis of the role of power in the labelling process; the generalizations which, even when true, explain little; the fascination with 'deviants'; the reluctance to study the 'deviance' of the powerful.

I want to start my concluding comments with two disclaimers.
(a) I have tried to provide some balance and perspective in the field of 'deviance,' and in doing so I have argued against the exclusive emphasis on *nuts*, *sluts*, and *preverts* and their identities and subcultures. I do not mean, however, that the usually considered forms of 'deviance' are unworthy of our attention. Suicide, prostitution, madness, juvenile delinquency, and others *are* with us; we cannot ignore them. People do suffer when labelled and treated as 'deviant' (in *this* sense, 'deviants' *are* different from conformists). Rather I want to draw attention to phenomena which also belong to the field of 'deviance.'[9]

(b) It is because the sociology of deviance, especially the labelling approach, contains important, exciting, and revealing insights, because it tries to humanize the 'deviant,' and because it is popular, that it is easy to overlook some of the basic ideological biases still pervading the field. For this reason, I have tried to explore and detail some of these biases. At the same time, however, I do not mean to dismiss the contributions of the field as totally negative and useless.

The argument can be summarized briefly. (1) We should not study only, or predominantly, the popular and dramatic forms of 'deviance.' Indeed, we should banish the concept of 'deviance' and speak of oppression, conflict, persecution, and suffering. By focusing on the dramatic forms, as we do now, we perpetuate most people's beliefs and impressions that such 'deviance' is the basic cause of many of our troubles, that these people (criminals, drug addicts, political dissenters, and others) are the real 'troublemakers'; and, necessarily, we neglect conditions of inequality, powerlessness, institutional violence, and so on, which lie at the bases of our tortured society. (2) Even when we do study the popular forms of 'deviance,' we do not avoid blaming the victim for his fate; the continued use of the term 'deviant' is one clue to this blame. Nor have we succeeded in normalizing him; the focus on the 'deviant' himself, on his identity and subculture, has tended to confirm the popular prejudice that he is different.

Notes

1 The subtitle of this paper came from two sources. (a) A Yale undergraduate once told me that the deviance course was known among Yale students as 'nuts and sluts.' (b) A former colleague of mine at Quinnipiac College, John Bancroft, often told me that the deviance course was 'all about those preverts.' When I came to write this paper, I discovered that these descriptions were correct, and concise summaries of my argument. I thank both of them. I also want to thank Gordon Fellman for a very careful reading of the first draft of the manuscript, and for discussing with me the general and specific issues I raise here.

2 Bend and Vogenfanger (1964) examined social problems textbooks of the early 1960s; they found there was little theory or emphasis on social structure in them.

3 What I say below applies to the 'labelling-interactionist' school of deviance of Becker, Lemert, Erikson, Matza, and others: to a large degree, however, most of my comments also apply to the other schools.

4 The first draft of this paper was completed in July 1971. The killing of George Jackson at San Quentin on 21 August 1971, which many people see as a political murder, and the Attica prisoner rebellion of early September 1971, only strengthen the argument about political prisoners. Two things became clear: (a) Not only a few 'radicals,' but many prisoners (if not a majority) see their fate as the outcome of political forces

and decisions, and themselves as political prisoners (see Fraser, 1971). Robert Chrisman's argument (in Fraser, 1971) points to such a conclusion clearly: 'To maintain that all black offenders are, by their actions, politically correct, is dangerous romanticism. Black antisocial behavior must be seen in and of its own terms and corrected for enhancement of the black community.' But there is a political aspect, for black prisoners' condition 'derives from the political inequity of black people in America. A black prisoner's crime may or not have been a political action against the state, but the state's action against him is always political.' I would stress that the same is true of most white prisoners, for they come mostly from the exploited poorer classes and groups. (b) The state authorities, the political rulers, by their deeds if not their words, see such prisoners as political men and threats. The death of George Jackson, and the brutal crushing of the Attica rebellion, attest to the authorities' realization, and fear, that here were no mere riots with prisoners letting off steam, but authentic political actions, involving groups and individuals conscious of their social position and exploitation.

5 With the exception of E. C. Hughes, in Becker (1964).

6 As Gittlin and Hollander (1970) show, the children of poor whites also suffer from lead poisoning.

7 Investigation of the causes and prevention of institutional violence would probably be biting the hand that feeds

the sociologist, for we read that the government and foundations (whose money comes from corporate profits) have supported research on 'deviant behavior,' especially its prevention. 'This has meant particularly that the application of sociological theory to research has increased markedly in such areas as delinquency, crime, mental disorder, alcoholism, drug addiction, and discrimination' (Clinard, 1968:742). That's where the action is, not on white-collar crime, nor on the covert institutional violence of the government and economy.

8 See Rude (1966) on the role of mobs of poor workers and peasants in 18th and 19th century England and France.

9 The question of 'what deviance is to the deviant' (Gordon Fellman, private communication), not what the labelling, anomie, and other schools, or the present radical viewpoint say *about* such a person, is not dealt with here. I avoid this issue not because I think it unimportant, rather because I want to concentrate on the political, moral, and social issues raised by the biases of those presently writing about the 'deviant.'

References

Becker, Howard S., 1963, *Outsiders* New York, Free Press.

Becker, Howard S., *1964 (ed.), *The Other Side*, New York, Free Press.

Becker, Howard S., 1967, 'Whose side are we on?', *Social Problems*, 14, 239–47 (reprinted in Douglas, 1970a, 99–111; references are to this reprint).

Bell, Robert R., *1971, *Social Deviance: a Substantive Analysis*, Homewood, Ill., Dorsey.

Bend, Emil and Martin Vogenfanger, 1964, 'A new look at Mills' critique', in *Mass Society in Crisis*, Bernard Rosenberg, Israel Gerver, F. William Howton (eds), New York, Macmillan, 1964, 111–22.

Bordua, David (ed.), 1967, *The Police*, New York, Wiley.

Carmichael, Stokeley and Charles V. Hamilton, 1967, *Black Power*, New York, Random House.

Clairborne, Robert, 1971, 'Future schlock', *Nation*, 25 January, 117–20.

Cleaver, Eldridge, 1968, *Soul On Ice*, New York, McGraw-Hill.

Clinard, Marshall B., *1968, *Sociology of Deviant Behavior* (3rd ed.), New York, Holt, Rinehart & Winston.

Cohen, Albert K., *1966, *Deviance and Control*, Englewood Cliffs, N.J., Prentice-Hall.

Cook, Robert M., 1968, 'The police', *Bulletin of the American Independent Movement* (New Haven, Conn.), 3(6), 1–6.

Dinitz, Simon, Russell R. Dynes, and Alfred C. Clarke (eds), *1969, *Deviance*, New York, Oxford University Press.

Domhoff, William G., 1967, *Who Rules America?*, Englewood Cliffs, N.J., Prentice-Hall.

Douglas, Jack D., *1970a (ed.), *Observations of Deviance*, New York, Random House.

Douglas, Jack D., *1970b (ed.), *Deviance and Respectability: the Social Construction of Moral Meanings*, New York, Basic Books.

Fraser, C. Gerald, 1971, 'Black prisoners finding new view of themselves as political prisoners', *New York Times*, 16 September.

Gittlin, Todd and Nanci Hollander, 1970, *Uptown: Poor Whites in Chicago*, New York, Harper & Row.

Gouldner, Alvin W., 1968, 'The sociologists as partisan: sociology and the welfare state', *American Sociologist*, 3(2), 103–16.

Henry, Jules, 1966, *Culture Against Man*, London, Tavistock.

Jackson, George, 1970, *Soledad Brother*, New York, Bantam Books.

Lefton, Mark, J. K. Skipper, and C. H. McCaghy (eds), *1968, *Approaches to Deviance*, New York, Appleton-Century-Crofts.

Lemert, Edwin M., *1967, *Human Deviance, Social Problems, and Social Control*, Englewood Cliffs, N.J., Prentice-Hall.

Liazos, Alexander, 1970, 'Processing for unfitness: socialization of "emotionally disturbed" lower-class boys into the mass society', Ph.D. dissertation, Brandeis University.

Lofland, John, *1969, *Deviance and Identity*, Englewood Cliffs, N.J., Prentice-Hall.

McCaghy, Charles H., J. K. Skipper, and M. Lefton (eds), *1968, *In Their Own Behalf: Voices from the Margin*, New York, Appleton-Century-Crofts.

McGinniss, Joe, 1969, *The Selling of the President, 1968*, New York, Trident.

Malcolm X, 1965, *The Autobiography of Malcolm X*, New York, Grove.

Matza, David, *1969, *Becoming Deviant*, Englewood Cliffs, N.J., Prentice-Hall.

Mills, C. Wright, 1943, 'The professional ideology of social pathologists', *American Journal of Sociology*, 49, 165–80.

Newfield, Jack, 1971, 'Let them eat lead', *New York Times*, 16 June, p. 45.

Quinn, Olive W., 1954, 'The transmission of racial attitudes among white southerners', *Social Forces* 33(1), 41–7 (reprinted in E. Schuler *et al.*, eds, *Readings in Sociology*, 2nd ed., New York, Crowell, 1960, 140–50).

Rose, Thomas (ed.), 1969, *Violence in America*, New York, Random House.

Rubington, Earl and M. S. Weinberg (eds), *1968, *Deviance: the Interactionist Perspective*, New York, Macmillan.

Rude, George, 1966, *The Crowd in History*, New York and London, Wiley.

Rushing, William A. (ed.), *1969, *Deviant Behavior and Social Processes*, Chicago, Rand McNally.

Simmons, J. L., *1969, *Deviants*, Berkeley, Cal., Glendessary.

Szasz, Thomas S., 1961, *The Myth of Mental Illness*, New York, Harper & Row.

Szasz, Thomas S., 1963, *Law, Liberty, and Psychiatry*, New York, Macmillan (Routledge & Kegan Paul, 1974).

Szasz, Thomas S., 1970, *The Manufacture of Madness*, New York, Harper & Row (Routledge & Kegan Paul, 1971).

Thompson, Hunter S., 1966, *Hell's Angels*, New York, Ballantine.

II. 3 Families without hope: a controlled study of thirty-three problem families

W. L. Tonge, D. S. James and S. M. Hillam

The anatomy of despair

Problem families are not very common. Only one in every 600 households on the estate fell into the multi-agency category. They are important for two reasons.

In the first place such families present a costly challenge to the health, welfare and law-enforcing agencies out of all proportion to their numbers. Secondly, they raise crucial issues concerning the relationship between psychological pathology, sub-cultural deviation and poverty which must be clearly grasped if preventive action is to be effective, either in their case or possibly in other types of social mal-adjustment.

Typology of problem families

Can problem families be classified into types? Inghe (in Klanfer,[1]) distinguished the apathetic slum dweller from the pathological antisocial family. Buell, Beisser and Wedemeyer[2] described four types of abnormal families, but only two of these types (parentally irresponsible and non-conforming hostile) appeared to apply to problem families. Philp[3] could not demonstrate any regular pattern or types of disorder: 'They were in fact individual families with different personalities among the parents and children . . .'

If different types of problem families exist, it should be possible to demonstrate that two or more patterns of social maladjustment are mutually exclusive, and that each have characteristic associations with other factors such as psychiatric pathology, poverty or overcrowding. To test this hypothesis, a list was made of 23 variables which appeared to be the most important in distinguishing the problem from the comparison families. A phi matrix of the inter-correlations between these variables was then computed, and was examined

Source: *British Journal of Psychiatry*, Special Publication no. 11, Headley Bros, Ashford, 1975, pp. 115–21, 125.

by the method of Elementary Linkage Analysis as described by Philip and McCulloch.[4] Elementary Linkage Analysis, which was devised by McQuitty, 'defines the linkage between two items as being the largest index of association which a variable has with any of the other variables', and yields clusters of associated variables. There was only one cluster in which two items of social performance were associated: defective household hygiene and poor child care. In all other clusters an item of social performance was linked with medical or social characteristics of the family. [. . .] We were not dealing with different types of abnormal families but with a mosaic of social and individual pathology. Although the repertoire of social deviation is not unlimited, each family provided a unique selection from it. It is possible that an examination of a much larger group of problem families would have yielded a different conclusion, but our findings are in support of Philp's opinion.

Perhaps there is no such thing as a problem family, only families with different degrees of disorganization, and only an arbitrary line separates designated problem families from those who are not in such great difficulties. There is much to commend this point of view. There is no single pattern of maladjustment which is pathognomonic, nor are there any handicaps or disadvantages which are specific to problem families. It can be argued that any definition of a problem family is bound to be arbitrary, including the one we used of multi-agency involvement. The difference between the designated families and others is finally only one of the quantity of the difficulties and not the nature of them.

Although this seems to be a reasonable point of view, a nagging doubt remains. 'Hard to define but easy to recognize' was the comment of Philp and Timms. When identifying a problem family social workers could be responding intuitively to clues which are too subtle to be measured in indices of social performance and mental health.

The effect of psychiatric pathology

This study was undertaken in an attempt to find the extent of psychiatric pathology in problem families and to observe its effect on their social maladjustment. It was obvious to Philp that problems of mental health or personality disorder affected almost all the families he studied, and our direct observations have amply confirmed his view. The details of the effect of psychiatric pathology on the families and their adjustment are [. . .] summarized [in Table 1].

Two conclusions emerge from this table: psychiatric disorder has more effect on social adjustment when it occurs in women; secondly, its effects are greater on family relationships than on other aspects of adjustment.

Can we not conclude that our task is finished? The problem family husbands and wives had an overwhelming excess of psychiatric disorder which has been shown to affect every field of social performance we could observe: ability to secure an adequate income,

Table 1 Summary of findings: psychiatric pathology and social adjustment

	Men	Women
Psychiatric illness	Absence from work	
	Low earnings	
	Estrangement from relatives	Estrangement from relatives
Low intelligence	Estrangement from relatives	
Personality disorder	Conspicuous marital maladjustment	Debt
	Psychiatric illness of children	
	Juvenile convictions and adult recidivism	

to care for children and the home, and to keep on the right side of the Law. [. . .] We are in agreement with the eugenists if we believe the propensities for normal personality development and mental health to be inherited, or with the caseworkers and dynamic psychiatrists if we believe the anomalies in mental health are engendered by environment, early or late. Support for this argument comes from studies which have traced the later career of unstable children. Lee Robins[5] followed up 524 children seen thirty years previously in a child guidance clinic; 77 per cent had originally been referred for antisocial behaviour, the remainder for other reasons. These were compared with 100 children living in the same area, who served as a control group. She concluded:

Antisocial behaviour in childhood not only predicts the full-blown picture of antisocial behaviour that is diagnosed sociopathic personality, it also predicts the level of antisocial behaviour in adults whose psychiatric picture is pre-empted by psychosis or who have less antisocial behaviour than that required for a diagnosis of sociopathic personality.

In addition to discovering that antisocial behaviour in childhood persists into adult life, Robins found associations between sociopathy of fathers, low socioeconomic status and antisocial behaviour in children. She states: 'No measure of social status was found to operate independently of the child's and his father's antisocial behaviour'. It was assumed that the child was influenced by the father's behaviour patterns. As low social status did not always predict antisocial behaviour in fathers and children, Robins also concluded that it was the conduct of the father which often led to degradation in his status.

Values and choices in problem families

Robins' careful study carries authority, and her findings must be respected. But all facts must be respected, and there are a few which, uncomfortably, do not fit the hypothesis being advanced. One example is the criminal behaviour which we called non-payment offences (failure to pay for a TV licence, fines or maintenance). These offences were not related to other offences, nor were they particularly common in the records of problem family men who had both a history of juvenile offences and repeated offences of larceny. We have already drawn attention to the association of this latter group with personality disorder. Neither were non-payment offences associated with poverty, so there is no evidence that this type of offending is determined either by external economic pressure or internally by personality pathology. It appears to represent a choice on the part of the offender. Another example can be given in the care of the home. In 27 of the problem family homes either beds or bedding, or both, were inadequate, and we were unable to relate this either to poverty or to psychiatric pathology. This too must have represented a choice on the part of the families because they preferred to spend their money on other things. This behaviour is closely identified with the group of problem families, but is not directly linked with psychiatric abnormalities.

As Handel[6] has pointed out, the choice of how we spend our money 'is not random but reflects underlying choices of values'. We are suggesting that certain types of criminal activity, as well as certain aspects of household management in these families, reflect their system of values. It is difficult to be sure in how many areas these families had real choices to make, because so much of their behaviour was either dictated by economic necessity or was symptomatic of their psychiatric state. It seems likely that their attitudes to education are also an expression of their values. The link between preferring a lower school-leaving age and not paying for the TV licence immediately acquires greater significance.

The important effect of the values held by these families on their social behaviour was not recognized during the planning of this investigation, so our information is not as full as we would now wish. The choices open to problem families which were not directly controlled by economic necessity or by psychiatric disturbance were as follows:

1. Rules were ignored;
2. Discomfort was ignored;
3. Long-term consequences of actions were ignored;
4. Education was distrusted.

This is a curious set of values. It adds up to a complete failure to plan for long-term action. It takes forethought to do all that these families failed to do: to take out motor insurance and TV licence, to accumulate household comforts, to limit family size; and education is above all a long-term endowment insurance. This is a style of life which shuts its eyes to the future. The only amenity universally provided was the television, and possibly the value of this medium lay more in its capacity to distract than to inform or stimulate.

In view of the doubts expressed in the first chapter, can this set of values be called a subculture? Handel, in the passage already referred to, remarks:

We are perhaps justified in saying that a family is not so much a carrier of the culture as the *mediator* of the culture. In some meaningful sense, a family is aware of and cognizes larger portions of the culture than it uses. Some portions it adopts and some it rejects or ignores.

Problem families are only too well aware of the culture which surrounds them. Baldamus and Timms[7] distinguished between the nominal values of the larger society (to which the problem families paid lip service) and the real values which were displayed in problem family living.

The problem families which we studied lived close to their comparison neighbours and were exposed to the same general cultural influences of the area. Yet they adopted a more isolated and radically different style of living, a situation which Sprott, Jephcott and Carter[8] had already described as existing between Dyke Street and Gladstone Road in Radby. It is possible that, being rejected by their neighbours, the problem families got to know each other in an underground way. We did not study all social contacts, but some families certainly knew each other at different ends of the estate. Unwanted people tend to accept each other, and their mutual acceptance lends stability to deviant styles of living. Despite these arguments, our judgment was that their way of life was largely idiosyncratic and relatively free from influence by other families. Their situation was fundamentally different from that of a family in the sociopathic culture of 'Branch Street'.[9]

The collapse of morale

This way of living might be understood as a reaction against the time-ridden, over-controlled middle-class mores of the larger society. It has something in common with the culture of poverty: 'The reality of the moment . . . which the culture of poverty experiences as natural, everyday phenomenon' (Lewis,[10]). However true this may be of Puerto Rico, it does not do justice to at least one important aspect of the way of life of the problem families we studied. One of their most striking features was their refusal to notice discomfort. For a subculture which has sometimes been called hedonistic, this is a most curious omission. A similar characteristic has been noted of men with asthenic personality disorder,[11] but this explanation would apply only to a proportion of our subjects.

We have tried to establish that the characteristic choices in living exhibited by our subjects cannot be fully accounted for in terms of either mental pathology, poverty or participation in a subcultural network. It is even doubtful if they were of any help to the families, in the sense of social survival of the individual or family group (what is the point in being uncomfortable in bed?), yet these choices were widespread in the families. One possible interpretation of this way of living is that it is a sign of living without hope. In any group in which morale has been shattered, whether it is the forgotten poor or a defeated army, the effort to maintain standards wavers, flags and ultimately lapses.

Hope of what? Certainly not money. Some of the problem families were better off than some of their comparison neighbours.

Hope of escaping from being in the wrong or being an object of censure and criticism might be nearer the mark. We have [. . .] noted [. . .] how the exclusion of these families from their working-class neighbours was a result of behaviour which was blameworthy in the eyes of these neighbours (and no doubt in their own eyes too); how their dislike of teachers contrasted with the readiness of the families to accept help from the non-judgmental professions of social work and medicine; and finally the preoccupation of many families with attempts to justify themselves. One woman's attempt at self-justification went so far as to insist on each occasion on which her husband shouted or swore at her that he should sign a confession: 'I, A . . . B . . ., tell you M . . . B . . . to fuck off; signed A . . . B . . .'. She collected these 'pieces of evidence' (as she called them) in an Oxo tin. A number of families asked for the support of the social investigator's opinion in their struggles with each other and the authorities.

Wilson[12] suggested that these families fail to respond to social services because of the authoritative appearance of the latter and their power to apply official sanctions. It was noted [earlier] that, contrary to the expectations of some, most families were very accepting of the social worker. The social workers who visited probably seemed very different to the families from the officers of agencies who had the discretion to grant or withhold material help such as supplementary benefit. Hilary Rose comments on the conflict between client and agency:[13]

> We have to understand this process, not as a culture of poverty—as a social pathology of the poor, but as the culture of the *interface*, where the potential provider and the potential receiver of social services meet.

The process with which Rose was concerned ('the diminution of their sense of identity') takes place, we believe, at other and more important 'interfaces' than between the families and local authority agencies. It occurs between themselves and their neighbours, and, we suspect, between the actuality of their social performance and their knowledge of how other people manage better.

We are now approaching the heart of the argument. The problem families which we studied had many problems of which poverty and psychiatric disorder were perhaps the most important. These problems are found in many families and lead to certain consequences: marital conflict, certain types of crime, debt, etc. If these problems accumulate, the family will begin to experience difficulties with neighbours, friends and relatives. After a certain point the family finds it progressively difficult to maintain the fiction of its 'respectability' in its own eyes and in those of its neighbours. Morale is broken, hope is lost.

This is our interpretation of Lemert's concept of secondary deviation. Faced by a spectrum of negative responses ranging from criticism to avoidance and outright rejection, the families withdraw into alternative choices of living, including crime. An unbridgeable gap develops between the actual way of life of the family and the 'nominal' standards of the neighbourhood which are left far behind.

Psychological disorganization

We have reason to believe that in this process of demoralization, the self-condemnation of these families may be a more important factor than their rejection by the neighbours. Indeed the social isolation is likely to be in part a self-fulfilling prophecy of a family which believes itself to be already estranged.

The evidence on this point is the remarkable way in which the families do not seem to perceive the squalor and general discomfort in which they live. This fact has already been advanced as an argument against the theory of a hedonistic subculture, but its significance goes deeper. In one example [. . .], the social investigator was invited to deny the evidence of her eyes regarding the state of the bedroom. Was the family simply making a fool of her in the course of their conflict with the housing welfare officer, or did the woman not see her own squalor? The latter was the frequent impression of both investigators in many of the homes.

There are many different types of squalor apart from those in which the carpet sticks to one's shoes, and it is probably true that none of us have a particularly clear insight into our own private brand. We are all tempted to deny what we cannot accept, and problem families are no different.

Most of us can cope with failure provided it is restricted to only part of our lives or to a single field of endeavour. For many problem families the failure is nearly total. They have to face the accumulating effects of inadequate performance. Social failure, like debt, can breed a type of compound interest. In some cases the emergence of ego defence mechanisms such as denial are an indication of the massive anxiety which is provoked by the overwhelming stress to which these families are subjected. Anxiety disrupts performance in families as in individuals, and their behaviour becomes random, disorganized and of little effect. The qualities of 'crisis-living' appear: apathy, impulsiveness, aggression; decisions are made for that moment only.

This we believe to be an important point of breakdown in some problem families. They are to be distinguished not by reason of poverty, psychiatric pathology or any other 'problem'; they are to be distinguished by the fact that they can no longer struggle with their failure. The evidence of lapsed standards is no longer clearly seen by them, and the unconscious mechanism of denial takes over. The meaning of hopelessness is that one no longer cares and no longer takes note. This process is not fixed, absolute and final. Families varied in their insight into the situation (perhaps that is why so many of the wives were depressed) and made sporadic efforts at recovery. But it is this situation of no longer being able to respond effectively to the true depth of their social failure that is expressed in the values they live by, and is also the basis, we suspect, of the intuitive recognition of problem families by social workers.

The frustrations with which these families struggle go a lot deeper, therefore, than the obvious ones of poverty, ill health and friendlessness. They are, above all, frustrated by their utter failure.

It is in vulnerable personalities that this type of psychological disorganization is especially liable to occur, and many reports witness to the child-like nature of many members of problem families:[14]

> 'The most striking characteristic of these families is that they are *families of children*', and later, 'You could hardly distinguish the adults from the children except for the fact that the former were taller.'

[Earlier in this report we] pointed out that the concept of immaturity, in the sense of delayed development, hardly did justice to the personality difficulties of these subjects. Some of the most characteristic problems occurred with their own children, especially over infant feeding. For nearly half of them, the expert help of the doctor was called for any difficulty in feeding. Equally important is the way in which the mother appeared to derive vicarious satisfaction in providing instant comfort for her young children and her ignoring of their real needs.

Reiner and Kaufman define this type of mothering with a psychoanalytic label:[15]

An example of such confusion of identities is the oral erotic mother who regards her children as part of herself. She makes a close knit group of her family for the main purpose of meeting its members' mutual needs for mothering. The children meet the mother's needs and vice versa; they live together as in a nest . . .

They go on to point out that inquiries about sleeping arrangements result 'in a confused account', and that handling of finances presents an especial problem, observations which accord well with our own findings.

These were not all abnormal women, although a few of them had a frank personality disorder; but it is believed by psychoanalytic observers that for this type of subject the experience of love and the dangers that cling to it are akin to those of the very young child. We have all lived through this stage, and traces of it still flavour our adult emotional relationships. Under stress, such as that of psychoanalytic treatment, the unremembered residues of these experiences may come to life again in the transference relationship. 'I want to be the cuckoo in your nest' was a remark made to one of the writers by a patient in psychotherapy. That patient was not from a problem family, but the need she expressed is acted out in some of the scenes from problem family life.

Without doubt, frustration is potent in bringing about a regression of the ability to love to such an infantile level. But constitutional factors cannot be ignored:[16]

Nor can we call regression of the libido a purely psychical process . . . for though it may exert the most powerful influence upon mental life, the organic factor in it is nevertheless the most important.

The frustrations which can bring about such regressions in vulnerable, predisposed individuals are of two kinds. In the first place there are the emotional traumata in development. The problem family parents did not show an excess of the crude trauma of separation, but it is impossible to believe that they entirely escaped the less visible deprivations of inconsistency of affection and under-protectiveness which we could record in their dealings with their own children. Malone provides a vivid and detailed account of the hazards encountered by the children of such families.[17]

It is our view that the children's premature ability to compensate for deficiencies in themselves and others and to defend themselves leads to early closure of their development whereby flexible adaptability and genuine mastery are forfeited.

With such inbuilt disadvantages, many of our subjects were unable to deal with the later frustrations of adult life. For the women especially, the advent of motherhood revives the conflicts over feeding and loving that had persisted unresolved from their own childhood. For both men and women the unbearable conflict engendered by their total failure is, we believe, the final frustration which forces their feelings to return to a child-like or (more accurately) infantile level of experience.

Apathy, impulsiveness and aggression were characteristics of most of the men. This type of behaviour is a sign of instability of personality even when not so marked as to amount to personality disorder. In analytical terms this behaviour can be an expression of emotional regression to an oral level. It may not be coincidence that such behaviour was associated with marital disharmony and with difficulties in bringing up the children. It is safe to regress only in the most intimate relationships. The mothers themselves often reported anxiety over infant feeding, and the way in which food was served could be interpreted as anxiety-disrupted behaviour. Similarly, an aggressive style of behaviour was associated more clearly with the marital relationship than with any external aspect of the families social performance.

Wilson[18] said that the squalor of the home might be unconsciously created by the women 'as a justification of the self'. We would prefer to say that the squalor is more likely to be an expression of the emotional regression of a woman in the grip of an intolerable internal conflict.

Wilson was not far wrong in describing traits of immaturity as a regressive response to continuous frustrating situations, but such conclusions need to be understood in the light of the organically determined vulnerability of these personalities, and the lifelong pressure of deprivation. Much of the emotional life of those individuals is fixated at the earliest stage of development, and such fixations are hardly if ever undone. It is this inner lack of development that leaves the individual so ill defended against the hazards of necessity, and so prone to regression when under stress.

This understanding of the significance and quality of the emotional responses of our subjects, which owes much to psychoanalytic observations, must not be confused with the phenomenological insight into personality discussed [earlier in this report]. Personality disorder was associated with the inability of the subject to develop meaning and purpose in his life. The vicissitudes in the development of the instincts, from which none of us are free, are part of the material from which personality is fashioned. It is impossible to define the strength which in one personality will sublimate a complex of oral feelings into the role of a gifted chef (albeit with a prima donna temperament!), while in another person the lack of a similar strength will result in a problem family life. Both approaches are needed if the personality problems of our subjects are to be understood.

Living without hope

We suggested [earlier in this report] that a similar way of life might be found in shanty towns and slums as well as in isolated problem families. The findings of this study suggest that this might be so. When families are faced with a problem of social adjustment which is beyond their resources the members regress to an infantile mode of experiencing and relating to people and events. Part of this maladjustment consists in ignoring (the unconscious mechanism of denial) all that they cannot deal with—the squalor, the rules imposed by society and the long-term planning needed for a comfortable existence in contemporary society. This pattern of living is easily identified, especially in the way a mother deals with her children. When it occurs it is not because they catch it from each other (as would be the case of a true subculture) and not because all members of problem families have the same type of personality, but because the dissolution under stress of the more mature functions of personality tends to follow the same path.

The amount of stress required for regression to occur and the vulnerability of the personality are presumably in inverse proportion. In the worst areas, the slums of San Juan for example, it may be impossible to maintain a mature and well ordered existence. Leighton[19] has demonstrated that in a similarly demoralized and disorganized group, the building up of an integrated community had beneficial results. Fifteen years later there was a marked change in the pattern of living and a drop in the prevalence of psychiatric disorders. The psychological changes were reversible.

In our problem families, the collapse of morale could not be attributed to the socio-cultural environment alone. For each problem family there were 599 others living in the same area with radically different standards. Our subjects must have been predisposed to respond with failure and regression, to a climate in which other families could exist satisfactorily. Their proneness to regression may well be due to the constitutional organic factor to which Freud[20] referred, and the high prevalence of personality disorders supports this view.

Intermediate between these two extremes lie the families of Marienthal.[21] All were exposed to unemployment and poverty, and although the majority were affected in some way only a minority responded with a problem-family style of living.

To summarize, a possible interpretation of the characteristic style of problem-family life is that it is the end state of living without hope. It is mediated by changes in the level of functioning of the personality. Few who live in a disintegrative anomic society like a shanty town can be expected to escape this regression. In a society with well developed welfare and community institutions it is mainly the vulnerable and damaged personalities who are changed by despair. (. . .)

Not as simple as we thought

Charles Booth wrote of the submerged *tenth* of the population who lived in vice, squalor and poverty; the families we studied constituted 0·17 per cent of a working-class area. This sixty-fold reduction in the size of the social problem group is testimony enough to the work of reclamation which has been going on in this country since the early years of the century. Policies of rehousing and the untiring efforts of social welfare agencies have dispersed in many areas (there are exceptions) the culture expressive of disorganization which was described in 'Branch Street'. What has happened to the families who lived in those former ghettos of social maladjustment? Many have been rehoused and assimilated into areas with a stable working class culture. A minority of families have failed in this task. In seeking out these families we believed that psychiatric illness and personality disorder could be identified as important factors disturbing their social adjustment.

This project was started in an attempt to elucidate the part played by psychiatric pathology in the social maladjustment of problem families. Starting from the viewpoint of the psychiatrist, the material forced us (painfully!) to develop an overall point of view. We became more interested in the social pathology which could *not* be ascribed to psychiatric disorder, and in the inter-relationships of the different types of social disorder.

There was no single discipline or field of study that would adequately account for the social pathology of problem families. Instead we found an interlocking mosaic, in which each piece of socially deviant behaviour was linked with a characteristic stress or handicap. Remedies consequently will be piecemeal.

References

1 Klanfer, J., 1965, *L'Exclusion sociale*, Cahiers Science and Service, vol. 2, Paris, Bureau de Recherches Sociales.

2 Buell, B., Beisser, P. T., and Wedemeyer, J. L., 1958, 'Reorganizing to prevent and control disordered behaviour', *Mental Hygiene*, 42(2), 155–94.

3 Philp, A. F., 1963, *Family Failure*, Faber.

4 Philip, A. E., and MCulloch, J. W., 1966, 'Use of social indices in psychiatric epidemiology', *British Journal of Preventive and Social Medicine*, 20, 122–6.

5 Robins, L. N., 1966, *Deviant Children Grown Up*, Livingstone.

6 Handel, G. (ed.), 1968, *The Psychosocial Interior of the Family*, George Allen & Unwin.

7 Baldamus, W. and Timms, N., 1955, 'The problem family: a sociological approach', *British Journal of Sociology*, 6(4), 318–26.

8 Sprott, W. J. H., Jephcott, P. and Carter, M. R., 1954, *The Social Background of Delinquency*, University of Nottingham.

9 Klein, J., 1965, *Samples from English Cultures*, vol. I, Routledge & Kegan Paul.

10 Lewis, O., 1968, *La Vida*, Secker & Warburg and Panther.

11 Tonge, W. L., 1955, 'The neurasthenic psychopath', *British Medical Journal*, 1, 1066–73.

12 Wilson, H. C., 1962, *Delinquency and Child Neglect*, George Allen & Unwin.

13 Rose, H. (undated), 'Rights, participation and conflict', *Poverty Pamphlet* no. 5, Child Poverty Action Group.

14 Pavenstedt, E. (ed.), 1967, *The Drifters*, Churchill.

15 Reiner, B. S. and Kaufman, I., 1959, *Character Disorders in Parents of Delinquents*, New York, Family Service Association of America.

16 Freud, S., 1949, *Introductory Lectures on Psychoanalysis*, trans. J. Rivière, George Allen & Unwin.

17 Malone, C. A., 1967, 'Developmental deviations and environmental forces', in Pavenstedt, E. (ed.), *The Drifters*.

18 Wilson, op. cit.

19 Leighton, A. H., 1967, 'Some notes on preventive psychiatry'. *Canadian Psychiatric Association Journal*, 12, S43–S50.

20 Freud, op. cit.

21 Jahoda, M., Lazarsfield, P. K. and Zeisel, H., 1966, 'Attitudes under conditions of unemployment', in *Attitudes*, Jahoda, M. and Warren, N. (eds), Penguin Books.

II. 4 The deschooled society

Ivan Illich

For generations we have tried to make the world a better place by providing more and more schooling, but so far the endeavour has failed. What we have learned instead is that forcing all children to climb an open-ended education ladder cannot enhance equality but must favour the individual who starts out earlier, healthier, or better prepared; that enforced instruction deadens for most people the will for independent learning; and that knowledge treated as a commodity, delivered in packages, and accepted as private property once it is acquired, must always be scarce.

I believe that the disestablishment of the school has become inevitable and that this end of an illusion should fill us with hope. But I also believe that the end of the 'age of schooling' could usher in the epoch of the global schoolhouse that would be distinguishable only in name from a global madhouse or global prison in which education, correction, and adjustment become synonymous. I therefore believe that the breakdown of the school forces us to look beyond its imminent demise and to face fundamental alternatives in education. Either we can work for fearsome and new educational devices that teach about a world which progressively becomes more opaque and forbidding for man, or we can set the conditions for a new era in which technology would be used to make society more simple and transparent, so that all men can once again know the facts and use the tools that shape their lives. In short, we can disestablish schools or we can deschool culture.

The hidden curriculum of schools

In order to see clearly the alternatives we face, we must first distinguish learning from schooling, which means separating the humanistic goal of the teacher from the impact of the invariant structure of the school. This hidden structure constitutes a course of instruction

Source: P. Buckman (ed.), *Education without Schools*, Souvenir Press, 1973, pp. 9–19.

that stays for ever beyond the control of the teacher or of his school board. It conveys indelibly the message that only through schooling can an individual prepare himself for adulthood in society, that what is not taught in school is of little value, and that what is learned outside of school is not worth knowing. I call it the hidden curriculum of schooling because it constitutes the unalterable framework of the system, within which all changes in the curriculum are made.

The hidden curriculum is always the same regardless of school or place. It requires all children of a certain age to assemble in groups of about thirty, under the authority of a certified teacher, for some 500 or 1,000 or more hours per year. It does not matter whether the curriculum is designed to teach the principles of Fascism, liberalism, Catholicism, socialism, or liberation, so long as the institution claims the authority to define which activities are legitimate 'education'. It does not matter whether the purpose of the school is to produce Soviet or United States citizens, mechanics, or doctors, as long as you cannot be a legitimate citizen or doctor *unless* you are a graduate. It makes no difference whether all meetings occur in the same place so long as they are somehow understood as attendance: cane-cutting is work for cane-cutters, correction for prisoners, and part of the curriculum for students.

What is important in the hidden curriculum is that students learn that education is valuable when it is acquired in the school through a gradual process of consumption; that the degree of success the individual will enjoy in society depends on the amount of learning he consumes; and that learning *about* the world is more valuable than learning *from* the world. The imposition of *this* hidden curriculum within an educational programme distinguishes schooling from other forms of planned education. All the world's school systems have common characteristics in relation to their institutional output, and these are the result of the common hidden curriculum of all schools.

55

Educational reformers who accept the idea that schools have failed fall into three groups. The most respectable are certainly the great masters of alchemy who promise better schools—alchemists being those who sought to refine base elements by leading their distilled spirits through twelve stages of successive enlightenment, so that for their own good and for all the world's benefit they might be transmuted into gold. The most seductive reformers are those popular magicians who promise to make every kitchen into an alchemic lab. The most sinister are the new Masons of the Universe who want to transform the entire world into one huge temple of learning.

Notable among today's masters of alchemy are certain research directors employed or sponsored by the large foundations who believe that schools if they could somehow be improved, could also become economically more feasible than those that are now in trouble, and simultaneously could sell a larger package of services. Those who are concerned mainly with the curriculum claim that it is outdated or irrelevant. So the curriculum is filled with new packaged courses on African Culture, North American Imperialism, Women's Lib, Pollution, or the Consumer Society. Passive learning is wrong—it is indeed—so we graciously allow students to decide what and how they want to be taught. Schools are prison houses. Therefore principals are authorized to approve touch-outs, moving the school desks to a roped-off Harlem street. Sensitivity training becomes fashionable. So we import group therapy into the classroom. School, which was supposed to teach everybody everything, now becomes all things to all children.

Other critics emphasize that schools make inefficient use of modern science. Some would administer drugs to make it easier for the instructor to change the child's behaviour. Others would transform school into a stadium for educational gaming. Still others would electrify the classroom. If they are simplistic disciples of McLuhan, they replace blackboards and textbooks with multimedia happenings; if they follow Skinner, they claim to be able to modify behaviour more efficiently than old-fashioned classroom practitioners can.

Most of these changes have, of course, some good effects. The experimental schools have fewer truants. Parents do have a greater feeling of participation in a decentralized district. Pupils, assigned by their teacher to an apprenticeship, do often turn out more competent than those who stay in the classroom. Some children do improve their knowledge of Spanish in the language lab because they prefer playing with the knobs of a tape recorder to conversation with their Puerto Rican peers. Yet all these improvements operate within predictably narrow limits, since they leave the hidden curriculum of school intact. Some reformers would like to shake loose from the hidden curriculum of public schools, but they rarely succeed. Free schools that lead to further free schools produce a mirage of freedom, even though the chain of attendance is often

interrupted by long stretches of loafing. Attendance through seduction inculcates the need for educational treatment more persuasively than the reluctant attendance enforced by a truant officer. Permissive teachers in a padded classroom can easily render their pupils impotent to survive once they leave.

Learning in these schools often remains nothing more than the acquisition of socially valued skills defined, in this instance, by the consensus of a commune rather than by the decree of a school board. New presbyter is but old priest write large.

Free schools, to be truly free, must meet two conditions: first, they must be run in a way to prevent the introduction of the hidden curriculum of graded attendance and certified students studying at the feet of certified teachers. And more importantly, they must provide a framework in which all participants, staff and pupils, can free themselves from the hidden foundations of a schooled society. The first condition is frequently stated in the aims of a free school. The second condition is only rarely recognized and is difficult to state as the goal of a free school.

To go beyond the simple reform of the classroom, a free school must avoid incorporating the hidden curriculum of schooling. An ideal free school tries to provide education and at the same time tries to prevent that education from being used to establish or justify a class structure, from becoming a rationale for measuring the pupil against some abstract scale, and from repressing, controlling, and cutting him down to size. But as long as the free school tries to provide 'general education', it cannot move beyond the hidden assumptions of school. Among these assumptions is that which impels us to treat all people as if they were newcomers who had to go through a naturalization process. Only certified consumers of knowledge are admitted to citizenship. Another assumption is that man is born immature and must 'mature' before he can fit into civilized society. Man must be guided away from his natural environment and pass through a social womb in which he hardens sufficiently to fit into everyday life. Free schools can perform this function often better than schools of a less seductive kind.

Free educational establishments share with less free establishments another characteristic. They de-personalize the responsibility for 'education'. They place an institution *in loco parentis*. They perpetuate the idea that 'teaching', if done outside the family, ought to be done by an agency, for which the individual teacher is but an agent. In a schooled society even the family is reduced to an 'agency of acculturation'. Educational agencies which employ teachers to perform the corporate intent of their board are instruments for the de-personalization of intimate relations.

Recovery of responsibility for teaching and learning

A revolution against those forms of privilege and power which are based on claims to professional knowledge must start with a transformation of consciousness about the nature of learning. This means, above all, a shift of responsibility for teaching and learning. Knowledge can be defined as a commodity only as long as it is viewed as the result of institutional enterprise or as the fulfillment of institutional objectives. Only when a man recovers the sense of personal responsibility for what he learns and teaches can this spell be broken and the alienation of learning from living be overcome.

The recovery of the power to learn or to teach means that the teacher who takes the risk of interfering in somebody else's private affairs also assumes responsibility for the results. Similarly, the student who exposes himself to the influence of a teacher must take responsibility for his own education. For such purposes educational institutions—if they are needed at all—ideally take the form of facility centers where one can get a roof of the right size over his head, access to a piano or a kiln, and to records, books, or slides. Schools, TV stations, theatres, and the like are designed primarily for use by professionals. Deschooling society means above all the denial of professional status for the second-oldest profession, namely teaching. The certification of teachers now constitutes an undue restriction on the right to free speech; the corporate structure and professional pretensions of journalism an undue restriction on the right to free press. Compulsory attendance rules interfere with free assembly. The deschooling of society is nothing less than a cultural mutation by which a people recovers the effective use of its Constitutional freedoms: learning and teaching by men who know they are born free rather than treated to freedom. Most people learn most of the time when they do whatever they enjoy; most people are curious and want to give meaning to whatever they come in contact with; and most people are capable of personal intimate intercourse with others unless they are stupefied by inhuman work or turned off by schooling.

The fact that people in rich countries do not learn much on their own constitutes no proof to the contrary. Rather it is a consequence of life in an environment from which, paradoxically, they cannot learn much, precisely because it is so highly programmed. They are constantly frustrated by the structure of contemporary society in which the facts on which decisions can be made have become more elusive. They live in an environment in which tools that can be used for creative purposes have become luxuries, an environment in which the channels of communication serve a few to talk to many.

A new technology rather than a new education

A modern myth would make us believe that the sense of impotence with which most men live today is a consequence of technology that cannot but create huge systems. But it is not technology that makes systems huge, tools immensely powerful, channels of communication one-directional. Quite the contrary: properly controlled, technology could provide each man with the ability to understand his environment better, to shape it powerfully with his own hands, and to permit him full intercommunication to a degree never before possible. Such an alternative use of technology constitutes the central alternative in education.

If a person is to grow up he needs, first of all, access to things, to places, and to processes, to events and to records. He needs to see, to touch, to tinker with, to grasp whatever there is in a meaningful setting. This access is now largely denied. When knowledge became a commodity, it acquired the protections of private property, and thus a principle designed to guard personal intimacy became a rationale for declaring facts off limits for people without proper credentials. In schools teachers keep knowledge of themselves unless it fits into the day's programme. The media inform, but exclude those things they regard as unfit to print. Information is locked into special languages, and specialized teachers live off its retranslation. Patents are protected by corporations, secrets are guarded by bureaucracies, and the power to keep others out of private preserves—be they cockpits, law offices, junkyards, or clinics—is jealously guarded by professions, institutions, and nations. Neither the political nor the professional structure of our societies, East and West, could withstand the elimination of the power to keep entire classes of people from facts that could serve them. The access to facts that I advocate goes far beyond truth in labelling. Access must be built into reality, while all we ask of advertising is a guarantee that it does not mislead. Access to reality constitutes a fundamental alternative in education to a system that only purports to teach *about* it.

Abolishing the right to corporate secrecy—even when professional opinion holds that this secrecy serves the common good—is, as shall presently appear, a much more radical political goal than the traditional demand for public ownership or control of the tools of production. The socialization of tools without the effective socialization of know-how in their use tends to put the knowledge-capitalist into the position formerly held by the financier. The technocrat's only claim to power is the stock he holds in some class of scarce and secret knowledge, and the best means to protect its value is a large and capital-intensive organization that renders access to know-how formidable and forbidding.

It does not take much time for the interested learner to acquire almost any skill that he wants to use. We tend to forget this in a society where professional teachers monopolize entrance into all fields and thereby stamp teaching by uncertified individuals as quackery. There are few mechanical skills used in industry or research that are as demanding, complex, and dangerous as driving cars, a skill that most people acquire quickly from a peer. Not all people are suited for advanced logic, yet those who are make rapid progress if they are challenged to play mathematical games at an early stage. One out of twenty kids in Cuernavaca can beat me at Wiff 'n' Poof after a couple of weeks' training. In four months all but a small percentage of motivated adults at our CIDOC centre learn Spanish well enough to conduct academic business in the new language.

A first step towards opening up access to skills would be to provide various incentives for skilled individuals to share their knowledge. Inevitably, this would run counter to the interests of guilds and professions and unions. Yet multiple apprenticeship is attractive. It provides everybody with an opportunity to learn something about almost anything. There is no reason why a person should not combine the ability to drive a car, repair telephones and toilets, act as a midwife, and function as an architectural draftsman. Special interest groups and their disciplined consumers would, of course, claim that the public needs the protection of a professional guarantee. But this argument is now steadily being challenged by consumer protection associations. We have to take much more seriously the objection that economists raise to the radical socialization of skills: that 'progress' will be impeded if knowledge—patents, skills, and all the rest —is democratized. Their arguments can be faced only if we demonstrate to them the growth rate of futile dis-economies generated by an existing educational system.

Access to people willing to share their skills is no guarantee of learning. Such access is restricted not only by the monopoly of educational programs over learning and of unions over licensing but also by a technology of scarcity. The skills that count today are know-how in the use of tools that were designed to be scarce. These tools produce goods or render services that everybody wants but only a few can enjoy, and which only a limited number of people know how to use. Only a few privileged individuals out of the total number of people who have a given disease ever benefit from the results of sophisticated medical technology, and even fewer doctors develop the skill to use it.

The same results of medical research have, however, also been employed to create a basic tool kit that permits Army and Navy medics, with only a few months of training, to obtain results under battlefield conditions that would have been beyond the expectations of full-fledged doctors during World War II. On an even simpler level any peasant girl could learn how to diagnose and treat most infections if medical scientists prepared dosages and instructions specifically for a given geographic area.

All these examples illustrate the fact that educational considerations alone suffice to demand a radical reduction of the professional structure that now impedes the mutual relationship between the scientist and the majority of people who want access to science. If this demand were heeded, all men could learn to use yesterday's tools, rendered more effective and durable by modern science, to create tomorrow's world.

Unfortunately, precisely the contrary trend prevails at present. I know a coastal area in South America where most people support themselves by fishing from small boats. The outboard motor is certainly the tool that has changed most dramatically the lives of these coastal fishermen. But in the area I have surveyed, half of all outboard motors that were purchased between 1945 and 1950 are still kept running by constant tinkering, while half the motors purchased in 1965 no longer run because they were not built to be repaired. Technological progress provides the majority of people with gadgets they cannot afford and deprives them of the simpler tools they need.

Metals, plastics, and ferro cement used in building have greatly improved since the 1940s and ought to provide more people with the opportunity to create their own homes. But in the United States, while in 1948 more than 30 per cent of all one-family homes were owner-built, by the end of the 1960s the percentage of those who acted as their own contractors had dropped to less than 20 per cent.

The lowering of the skill level through so-called economic development becomes even more visible in Latin America. Here most people still build their own homes from floor to roof. Often they use mud in the form of adobe and thatchwork of unsurpassed utility in the moist, hot, and windy climate. In other places they make their dwellings out of cardboard, oildrums, and other industrial refuse. Instead of providing people with simple tools and highly standardized, durable, and easily repaired components, all governments have gone in for the mass production of low-cost buildings. It is clear that not one single country can afford to provide satisfactory modern dwelling units for the majority of its people. Yet everywhere this policy makes it progressively more difficult for the majority to acquire the knowledge and skills they need to build better houses for themselves.

Self-chosen 'poverty'

Educational considerations permit us to formulate a second fundamental characteristic that any post-industrial society must possess: a basic tool kit that by its very nature counteracts technocratic control. For educational reasons we must work toward a society in which scientific knowledge is incorporated in tools and components that can be used meaningfully in units small enough to be within the reach of all. Only such tools can socialize access to skills. Only such tools favour temporary associations among those who want to use them for specific occasions. Only such tools allow specific goals to emerge in the process of their use, as any tinkerer knows. Only the combination of guaranteed access to facts and of limited power in most tools renders it possible to envisage a subsistence economy capable of incorporating the fruits of modern science.

The development of such a scientific subsistence economy is unquestionably to the advantage of the overwhelming majority of the people in poor countries. It is also the only alternative to progressive pollution, exploitation, and opaqueness in rich countries. But as we have seen the dethroning of the GNP cannot be achieved without simultaneously subverting GNE (Gross National Education—usually conceived as manpower capitalization). An egalitarian economy cannot exist in a society in which the right to produce is conferred by schools.

The feasibility of a modern subsistence economy does not depend on new scientific inventions. It depends primarily on the ability of a society to agree on fundamental, self-chosen, anti-bureaucratic and anti-technocratic restraints.

These restraints can take many forms, but they will not work unless they touch the basic dimensions of life. The substance of these voluntary social restraints would be very simple matters that can be fully understood and judged by any prudent man. All such restraints would be chosen to promote stable and equal enjoyment of scientific know-how. The French say that it takes a thousand years to educate a peasant to deal with a cow. It would not take two generations to help all people in Latin America or Africa to use and repair outboard motors, simple cars, pumps, medicine kits, and ferro cement machines if their design does not change every few years. And since a joyful life is one of constant meaningful intercourse with others in a meaningful environment, equal enjoyment does translate into education.

At present a consensus on austerity is difficult to imagine. The reason usually given for the impotence of the majority is stated in terms of political or economic class. What is not usually understood is that the new class structure of a schooled society is even more powerfully controlled by vested interests. No doubt an imperialist and capitalist organization of society provides the social structure within which a minority can have disproportionate influence over the effective opinion of the majority. But in a technocratic society the power of a minority of knowledge capitalists can prevent the formation of true public opinion through control of scientific know-how and the media of communication. Constitutional guarantees of free speech, free press, and free assembly were meant to ensure government by the people. Modern electronics, photo-offset presses, time-sharing computers, and telephones have in principle provided the hardware that could give an entirely new meaning to these freedoms. Unfortunately these things are used in modern media to increase the power of knowledge bankers to funnel their programme-packages through international chains to more people, instead of being used to increase true networks that provide equal opportunity for the encounter among the members of the majority.

Deschooling the culture and social structure requires the use of technology to make participatory politics possible. Only on the basis of a majority coalition can limits to secrecy and growing power be determined without dictatorship. We need a new environment in which growing up can be classless, or we will get a brave new world in which Big Brother educates us all.

II. 5 Delinquent schools?

M. J. Power et al.

The government white paper on the treatment of young delinquents proposed a 'family service'. The assumption in it is that difficulties in the family are the primary cause of delinquency, perhaps the sole cause. But there is no evidence that this is so. Proper studies have never been undertaken in this country and much that goes for fact is more in the nature of faith. Delinquent children in child guidance clinics or approved schools are naturally likely to show the characteristics which made them be selected for such institutions—i.e., individual emotional disturbances and disrupted families. So it is wrong to generalise from studies based just on such selected samples of children.

As part of a study of juvenile delinquency in the London borough of Tower Hamlets (formerly the boroughs of Stepney, Bethnal Green and Poplar) the Social Medicine Research Unit has been collecting information on all children and young people under seventeen—juveniles in law—who live in this borough and have made a court appearance since 1958.

We chose Tower Hamlets partly because it is in the 'parish' of the London Hospital (which has served east London for over two centuries and, as Barnardo showed, has a special concern for its children), and partly because the borough has unusually clear boundaries (which is very helpful for a community study). Another reason for our choice was the concern expressed by the local community. Many official and voluntary agencies have helped us; so have local families who are concerned about delinquency as it affects their children. In choosing Tower Hamlets we do not suggest that it has more delinquency than other comparable urban areas.

One of our findings is that it is not enough to consider the children themselves, their families and the neighbourhood when one tries to understand delin-

quency. One must also look at the secondary schools the children attend.

Evidence for the six school years 1958–64 suggests that delinquency varies widely among Tower Hamlets schools. It seems, too, as if some schools may be successful in protecting children from the risk of delinquency, though they live in neighbourhoods where many children come before the courts. Conversely, other schools may be exposing children who live in delinquency-free neighbourhoods to just such a risk.

In the strictest confidence, the local office of the former London County Council children's department let us have information on all Tower Hamlets children coming before a court in 1958–64. The education authority told us the total numbers and ages of boys attending local schools. From these we calculated, for all of the twenty 'secondary modern' schools then serving the area, rates of court appearances by boys where the case was proven. (Far fewer girls come before the courts, so they are omitted from this particular analysis. We are studying them but in another context.) These twenty schools between them took 85 per cent of all the Tower Hamlets boys aged 11–14 years (inclusive). The other 15 per cent went to grammar schools, where official delinquency was negligible, or special schools; very few attended schools not in the borough. The offences were almost always committed locally and out of school. About 90 per cent were stealing and about 5 per cent truancy. Many were minor offences, but some were more serious.

Table 1 shows the incidence rate. It gives an annual average of boys making a first court appearance over the six years, expressed as a proportion of the boys of the same age in each school during each year. The range is very wide. During the six years the school population had, of course, turned over completely.

We have examined various simple explanations of the remarkable variation in incidence between schools. It cannot be disposed of by difference in school size;

Source: *New Society*, 19 October 1967, pp. 542–3.

Table 1 First appearance before the courts (cases proven), 1958–64

Secondary schools in Tower Hamlets	Annual average 'delinquency rate' per 100 boys aged 11–14
J	0·7
B	1·2
R	1·5
N	1·9
D	2·1
P	2·3
G	2·8
L	3·3
F	3·5
S	3·6
E	3·8
C	4·0
T	4·1
H	4·3
U	4·4
O	4·4
W	4·8
A	5·7
Q	6·4
M	7·8
all	3·4

by the age and type of the school buildings; by the sex or ethnic composition of the school; by whether the schools are 'voluntary' or 'county'; by the overall ability gradings of the entry to each school at eleven; or by other selection processes that we have studied. It is rare for boys to make court appearances during primary schools, so their selection for particular secondary schools cannot be much influenced because they are known delinquents. Another part of our study suggests that the majority of the boys before the courts are quite normal boys from ordinary homes. It is difficult to believe that such children, who are of average intelligence and attainment in their primary schools, are selected for particular secondary schools on the basis of future delinquency. Only a very few boys are transferred from one secondary school to another after a court appearance. Finally, so far as we have been able to discover, there are no variations in local police practice that would account for these differences in school delinquency rates.

In Tower Hamlets, as elsewhere, about half the boys who made a first appearance as juveniles later reappear in court. So schools with high rates for first appearances tend to be the same schools that have high rates of boys coming before the courts a number of times. Table 2 is, for simplicity, an annual average for the six years of all court appearances, where the case was proved. (Some boys appeared several times in a single year, or in more than one year.) The gap between the schools at the top and bottom of the Table is now wider, as might be feared. The same

schools appear low in both the tables, a finding unlikely to be due to chance. The persistent juvenile offenders in the four or five schools at the bottom of Table 2 must represent part of the beginning of the problem of the adult offender.

The variation has been remarkably consistent over the years. The low-rate schools have hardly changed position: year after year they have only a few boys, if any, before the courts. The high-rate schools have also shown little change over the years. Recently there has been much educational reorganisation in the borough; new schools have been opened, others closed and yet others amalgamated. Despite these changes, data for the year 1965 alone give the same picture of gross variation in school delinquency rates.

One of the few established facts about crime comes from ecological studies which have shown the unequal distribution in different parts of cities. We have examined the rates in Tower Hamlets, and found huge differences between neighbourhoods within this almost exclusively working-class borough.

At the 1961 census, Tower Hamlets was divided into 301 enumeration districts with an average population of 600 each. We found out the number of boys living in each of these districts, divided according to their age in years. We could then calculate the local rates of delinquency (as we had done for the schools), using the home addresses of the boys. Over the eight years 1958–65, some districts had an annual average rate of boys making a first court appearance as high

Table 2 Annual average of all cases proven before the courts, 1958–64

Secondary schools in Tower Hamlets	Annual average 'delinquency rate' per 100 boys aged 11–14
J	0·9
B	1·9
R	2·1
N	2·6
D	3·2
G	5·2
P	5·7
S	6·1
E	7·2
T	7·7
F	7·8
H	8·5
U	8·8
O	9·2
W	9·8
C	10·0
L	10·4
A	13·8
Q	16·6
M	19·0
all	7·2

as 12 per cent. Others had fewer than 1 per cent of their boys before the courts each year.

With this information we began testing whether the schools with high rates served neighbourhoods where many children made court appearances while the delinquency-free schools drew their pupils from other districts. This means separating, to some extent, the effects of neighbourhood and school.

We ranked the delinquency rates for the enumeration districts and grouped them into two: high and low. We also chose five schools which covered the full range of sizes—and of delinquency. We then classified all the boys in these schools according to whether they lived in 'high' or 'low' districts.

Table 3 Relation of delinquency rates to districts served by the schools

Secondary schools in Tower Hamlets	'Delinquency rate' (%) prevalence in 1964–5 per 100 boys aged 11–14 resident in		
	all districts	'high' delinquency districts	'low' delinquency districts
B	3	3	4
D	4	6	3
K	7	9	5
C	11	13	9
Q	25	25	25
Average in these schools	8	10	6

No. of boys in these schools = 1,717
No. of the boys 'ever delinquent' = 141

Table 3 shows, for each of the five schools, the overall proportion of boys who had ever been delinquent—the 'total prevalence' (column 2). It then gives this proportion among boys living in high and low delinquency districts (columns 3 and 4). Within any one school, there is little difference in the delinquency rates of boys coming from 'high' or 'low' districts. Thus, school Q, a small one, had six boys delinquent out of 24 living in low-rate districts, and 13 out of 52 living in high; while school B, also small, had only two boys delinquent out of 66 living in high-rate districts, and one out of 23 living in low-rate districts.

The other three (considerably larger) schools showed differences in rates between pupils living in low and high delinquency districts. But these differences were not significant, and they were nowhere near as big as one would expect if district delinquency was the only or main explanation for the differences between school rates. For example, school C had 22 delinquents out of 233 boys living in low-rate districts and 30 delinquents out of 229 living in high-rate districts.

Schools like the 3 per cent and 6 per cent in column 3 may be protecting their pupils from the risk of delinquency. Those like the 9 per cent and 25 per cent in column 4 may put them at risk.

This has both practical and theoretical implications. If prevention and treatment were based on schools as well as on homes and courts, they could be more effective than the present programmes. The social services might find an easier way into the community than by continuing the work only with delinquent pupils and their families. The part that schools may play was foreshadowed by the Newsom report's recommendations on the development of a 'school community'. In Britain, education is concerned not only with academic achievement but also with social behaviour. So it is perhaps not surprising that some schools seem to exert a positive and beneficent influence on the conduct of their pupils as well as on their attainment.

There are no comparable published studies, but we would be exceedingly surprised if the kind of picture found is limited to one London borough. In fact, our study arose out of an impression in quite another area that some of its schools seemed to be contributing far more than their share of offenders.

Meanwhile, we have explained nothing. Besides continuing the type and analysis shown in Table 3, we need detailed studies in schools with different rates of delinquency to investigate such factors as: the social education provided; the kind of social relationships within the school and between school, parents and the local community; the personalities and attitudes involved; and, of course, the selective processes of admission to various schools.

References

The Child, the Family and the Young Offender, HMSO, Cmd 2742, 1965.

Bennett, I. *Delinquent and Neurotic Children*, Tavistock, 1960.

Scott, D., *Delinquency and Human Nature*, Carnegie, 1950.

Morris, J. N., *Uses of Epidemiology*, Livingstone, 1964.

The Sentence of the Court, HMSO, 1964.

Taylor, R. S., 'The habitual criminal', *British Journal of Criminology*, 1 (21), 1960.

Gibbens, T. C. N., *Psychiatric Studies of Borstal Lads*, Oxford University Press, 1963.

Shaw, C. R. and McKay, H. D., *Social Factors in Juvenile Delinquency: report on the causes of crime*, United States Government Printing Office, 1931.

Central Advisory Council for Education, *Half our Future*, (Newsom Report), HMSO, 1963.

II. 6 CDP Final Report, part 1: Coventry and Hillfields: prosperity and the persistence of inequality (extracts)

City of Coventry CDP

Towards a political economy of Hillfields and fresh political initiatives

By the beginning of 1973 we had decided that in order to understand better why Hillfields had become run-down and under-developed in a prosperous and progressive city; and in order to explore more fully where one could expect to find hopeful initiatives to break the apparent deadlock of the situation; we needed, in the final phase of the Project:

(i) to investigate more fully the political economy of Coventry in general, and of Hillfields and the poorer working-class areas in particular;

(ii) to test out what potential for change could be mobilised by organised groups of residents taking initiatives to tackle their own problems when supported with clear information about their situation and serviced by 'hard' technical skills.

After a number of attempts to get help with the first category of work, we eventually commissioned a small team of economists and sociologists from Warwick University to begin an analysis of:

(i) The patterns of private industrial investment (particularly capital concentration and techno-logical change) in the four main industries in Coventry and their consequences for different sections of the workforce (particularly the un-skilled, working women and the immigrant) and hence for different geographical areas of the city.

(ii) The pressures and constraints imposed by central government, private industry and the wider money markets upon the overall level and pattern of investment (particularly the capital programme) in Coventry.

Source: Home Office and City of Coventry Community Development Project (CDP) in association with the Institute of Local Government Studies, March 1975, pp. 41–62, 83–5.

Part of this work was to be carried out in collaboration with the City Treasurer's Department and with the Department of Architecture and Planning. The pro-gramme did not get under way until mid-1974, and a variety of problems prevented us from getting access to all the necessary data. This means that our con-clusions in this field have to remain fairly tentative at this stage. However, the change in perspective that even preliminary work has opened up for us suggests the value of painting a bold canvas here, even though the detail may still be sketchy, or inaccurate, in places. [. . .]

Industry in Coventry and the decline of Hillfields[1]

Our study suggests that the fortunes of Hillfields have been tied to the life-cycle of two main products—its period of development in the mid-19th century was related to the rise and fall in the ribbon-weav-ing industry while its under-development in the 20th century is related to the needs of the car in-dustry. Both are aspects of exactly the same economic processes.

Hillfields was built between 1820 and 1860 as the city's first suburb and was not joined to the city centre until about 1850. It was known as New Town—a boom community of prosperous ribbon-weavers. The ribbon trade fluctuated markedly, mostly in response to the whims of European fashion. During times of prosperity the trade spread among the wives of colliers in the villages to the north and north-east of Coventry. Hillfields journeymen were cushioned from trade fluctuations as these villages would be given work mainly when the city could not handle the load, and during a recession the village workers would be the first out of work.

During the 1840s and 1850s the ribbon factories in the city centre gradually converted to steam-power, and Hillfields felt the pressure of competition through technological innovation. By the early 1850s factory weavers were earning slightly more than Hillfields journeymen and a drift of Hillfields journeymen to ribbon factories and to the watch trade began. In 1860 the protective tariff on foreign ribbons was removed and further competition came from the cotton industries in the north. The ribbon-weaving trade slumped, and the Hillfields boom town was hit particularly hard. However, the immediate effects of the ribbon-weaving slump on the outlying areas were far greater. Their contracts were the first to be cancelled and the immediate depopulation of the weaving villages was much greater than for Coventry.

For the next twenty to thirty years Coventry as a whole was a depressed area and the population of the city fell considerably. Then during the 1880s and 1890s people began moving into Coventry and Hillfields again with the emergence of the new bicycle and sewing machine industries. The 'manufacturers' of the bicycle and the sewing machine were at this stage little more than assemblers of components. However, the new markets for bicycles, then motor cycles, and finally cars created opportunities for middle-class entrepreneurs from outside the city to come to invest their capital and their engineering skills. The city teemed with men grouping and re-grouping to exploit the demand, but the ribbon-weavers of Hillfields had inappropriate skills for the new industries which were all based on engineering and metal-working.

People who moved into Coventry after the 1880s moved to the newer suburbs if they could afford it. As public transport, bicycles and, later, cars allowed workers to live further from the factories, Hillfields' central location no longer represented an attraction in itself. The wealthier people who worked in Coventry began to move to the outlying villages to the south. Furthermore, during the 1920s and 1930s new housing estates were built in suburbs close to the motor-car factories.

Hillfields with its large stock of older and cheaper housing increasingly came, therefore, to attract the poorer, unskilled immigrants. Some of these and some of the native Hillfields population managed to increase their earnings to the point where they were able to move out of Hillfields to one of the more attractive newer suburbs. This was relatively easy during the 1940s and 1950s because of the tremendous post-war demand for labour in Coventry. Since then the highest-paying jobs in the highest-paying industries (cars and aircraft) have not expanded.

Hillfields has thus come to house a heavy concentration of the least well-paid sections of the labour force (the unskilled; semi-skilled; manual public service workers; coloured immigrants) side by side with a residue of the economically dependent (the sick, the unemployed, unsupported mothers and the elderly) who cannot afford to move to more expensive areas. The economic fortunes of Hillfields now depend upon the functions which these sections of the population perform within the present labour market in Coventry (which, as shown above, is heavily dominated by the motor and engineering industries) and on the way the non-productive members of the community are treated by the central and local state.

End of the boom for the car industry?

Coventry's boom this century has been bound up with the growth of the motor vehicles industry, just as that of Hillfields was tied to the rise and fall of the ribbon-weaving industry.

Our studies suggest that the peak period in the market for cars in the UK began in the early 1930s and (although interrupted by the war) lasted until the mid-1960s when new car registrations in the UK reached their peak. At the end of the war the backlog of demand for cars, and the coincidence of the peak period in home demand with the absence of foreign competition in export markets, resulted in a long period of prosperity for UK car firms.

However, although car production has grown very rapidly since the war, short-term fluctuations have always been great. Declines in production have become more severe and more prolonged. The UK has been steadily losing its share of the world market for cars, falling from over 50 per cent in the early 1950s to 13 per cent in 1970 and even lower since. Furthermore, UK producers' share of the home market has also fallen dramatically since the 1950s; over 25 per cent of cars now bought in the UK are imported.

It appears that the growth in ownership of cars in the UK has now begun to decline and that the UK car industry is past the peak of its product-cycle. We would argue that this is not a temporary symptom of the oil crisis or world inflation but a predictable and 'normal' phase of capitalist development. The product-cycle for cars in Coventry is following exactly the same logic as that described for ribbons in Hillfields—with similar consequences for firms, the labour force and the wider community.

Concentration and centralisation of capital

The main response by car firms to fluctuations in their product markets has been to increase their size, thereby reducing competition and also cutting costs through economies of scale and the introduction of labour-saving technology.

The UK car industry began with the setting up of the Daimler plant in Coventry in 1896. Between then and the early 1920s hundreds of small manufacturers entered the market. In 1920 alone fifty-nine new car firms entered the market in Coventry but by 1931 there were only eleven separate firms left. By 1971 there were only two.

In the world context, UK car firms are still not concentrated and centralised enough to take advantage of the economies of scale possible with modern technology and organisation. Compared with the American and European giants, British Leyland is still not producing a sufficient volume of cars in each model to be viable. It is still a collection of fairly independently organised plants. Further concentration and rationalisation is likely to take place, either through state intervention or within the context of the European Common Market.

Production in the car industry has been subject to violent short-term fluctuations in demand, resulting in the need to cut production back quickly. The major car firms have achieved this by maintaining a multitude of subcontracting arrangements with smaller engineering firms. British car firms have traditionally purchased a higher proportion of parts and components from outside suppliers than have overseas firms (50 to 65 per cent of the value of a British mass-produced car is bought from outside suppliers compared with 25 to 40 per cent in Japan, Italy, West Germany, France and the USA). In a slump it is relatively costless for large firms to cut back on subcontracts.

What about the workers?

The pattern of the product-cycle for cars has had its consequences not just for the firms but also for the labour force and the wider community. In the early stages of development of a product, firms are likely to require highly skilled labour. As production becomes standardised and routinised, the skill content of jobs generally falls, but the degree of supervision and inspection rises. As automation proceeds, the workforce may be split into skilled supervisors and unskilled machine minders.

In Coventry, the proportion of skilled manual workers in the labour force fell by 13·1 per cent between 1931 and 1951 (compared with 1·7 per cent in England and Wales). This drastic decline was balanced by a rise in the Coventry proportion of semi-skilled manual workers by 6·0 per cent (compared with a fall of 3·0 per cent in England and Wales), a rise in the proportion of clerical workers by 2·8 per cent (3·5 per cent in England and Wales) and a rise in the Coventry proportion of foremen, supervisors and inspectors by 3·7 per cent (1·6 per cent in England and Wales).

Although since the war the motor industry has expanded enormously, the expansion has not been steady. Although Coventry's level of unemployment through the post-war period was well below the national average, the rate of unemployment has in fact shown a cyclical pattern with 1956, 1958 and 1962–3 as well-defined troughs; unemployment rose to high plateaux in both 1967 and 1971 without fully recovering.

Although the cyclical pattern in Coventry unemployment is relatively mild when compared with the overall country pattern, there are indicators that the stability from 1953 to 1967 in the unemployment figures have masked significant changes in the distribution of employment among different industries. It would seem that the short-term changes in demand for labour in the motor industry have resulted partly in fluctuations in the overall level of unemployment in the city and partly in shifts in employment between the motor industry, the construction industry and, to a lesser extent, the local authority.

Those workers who are thrown out of their regular employment into less well paying industries or into complete unemployment when the motor industry is experiencing a short-term slump are primarily manual workers and especially unskilled manual workers. This is reflected by the fact that in Coventry in 1971 the unemployment rate among unskilled workers was nearly three times higher than the overall level of unemployment.[2]

Hillfields as a reserve tank of labour

Hillfields is directly or indirectly related to the fortunes and behaviour of industry in the city in two main ways:

1. 40 per cent of the economically active in Hillfields are employed by the fifteen largest firms in the city. All but two of these firms are involved in motor vehicle, vehicle component manufacture or machine tools. The proportion of Hillfields workers in these firms (40 per cent) is less than the proportion for Coventry as a whole (54 per cent). However, as a high proportion (41 per cent) of the economically active in Hillfields are classified as unskilled or semi-skilled, and as this represents the heaviest concentration in the city of those sections of the workforce (one-sixth of all Coventry unskilled male manual workers), it is likely that the area will be particularly responsive to fluctuations in the demand for such labour by the manufacturing industries.

2. 12 per cent of the economically active in Hillfields, compared with only 7 per cent for Coventry as a whole, are employed by metal and engineering firms other than the fifteen largest firms. The links between the smaller engineering firms and the large manufacturers are particularly close and strong in Coventry. Although many of these smaller firms also supply firms outside Coventry, they are closely tied to the fortunes of the major manufacturing firms in the city. The fortunes of Hillfields are thus closely tied up with the changing relationship between the larger firms and the smaller subcontracting firms in Coventry.

There is a general trend within manufacturing industry for the proportion of skilled technical and administrative staff to increase at the expense of the less skilled.[3] This will be accentuated by the substitution of capital-intensive for labour-intensive processes. Manual workers and particularly unskilled manual workers are more at risk of unemployment during periods of general recession than other sections of the workforce. In October 1971 it was estimated that the national unemployment rate for unskilled men was 13·4 per cent when the overall male unemployment rate was 5·2 per cent. However, the differential was even more acute in the engineering industry in Coventry: in December 1971 the ratio of unemployed men to vacancies was 26 : 1 for skilled engineering workers, but 528 : 1 for labourers in engineering and allied trades.[4]

Although unskilled workers are relatively expendable to engineering firms, it is essential to be able to re-employ such labour in great quantities very quickly when the market re-expands. It is therefore vital to the firm for such labour to be available in the location where the firms needs it (particularly in view of the short-term immobility of unskilled labour). Our hypothesis is that in Coventry, Hillfields provides that pool of unskilled labour.

The smaller engineering firms are at the mercy of the larger firms in a very similar way to the unskilled, since during a recession it is easier for a large producer to cut back on subcontracting work than to lay-off its own workforce. Smaller firms are also generally less able to take advantage of expensive technological advances or modern organisational methods. Thus they are less efficient than larger firms and more likely at periods of competition or slump in the market to go out of business or to be taken over by larger firms. The first alternative means certain unemployment for the workforce; the second also often results in redundancies, as take-overs by larger firms are usually accompanied by redundancies in the smaller firms being merged. Coventry's economic history has been one of continuous take-over and merger from the bicycle boom onwards. In addition to the three periods of merger in the car industry, there have been the BLMC mergers of the 1950s and 1960s which produced 14,000 redundancies; contraction of the aircraft industry during the 1960s with a loss of 11,000 jobs; the GEC/AEI/English Electric mergers in 1967 and 1968 which created 1,650 redundancies; and finally the prospect of further redundancies in British Leyland following public control.

The profitability of Coventry's industries has depended upon maintaining a reservoir of labour to be siphoned off or into as the market expands or contracts. In Coventry, as in any growth area based around a single industry, there will be competition for labour with the specialised skills necessary. Thus firms will attempt to retain their skilled labour at difficult times and will cut back instead on their unskilled labour and on their subcontractors. It is essential for industry to be able to take on such labour and such contracts quickly again when the market expands. The unskilled and semi-skilled workers of Hillfields provide a pool of low-paid labour which local firms hire and fire at will as they take up opportunities for expansion or cushion themselves against cut-backs in demands. Its high proportion of workers in smaller engineering firms also provide the same kind of regulating value for the larger firms.

Hillfields thus plays an active role in alleviating the difficulties of local firms as they adjust to the normal fluctuations of economic development.

The consequences for the public sector

The boom industry in Coventry has had mixed consequences, not just for the workforce but for the local authority and the community as a whole. The rapid expansion of the car industry created heavy pressures both on the city's land and on its finances.

The Klondyke growth of the motor and engineering industry in Coventry this century created a massive demand for labour in the city. This was recruited from the depressed areas of the British Isles and later of the New Commonwealth. The growth of the engineering industry was accelerated further by munitions production in both world wars and this created a further demand for labour. The population of the city almost doubled between 1901 and 1921 and again between 1921 and 1940. Between 1921 and 1937 it rose at a rate seven times that of the country as a whole.

This large-scale recruitment of labour put enormous pressure on the city's housing and basic services, particularly in the older areas like Greater Hillfields. Until sufficient new accommodation could be provided, central government had to help finance cottages and hostels near the new factories in the north of the city, but the main costs fell on the local authority. In 1927 it was estimated that 15,000 houses would be needed over the next ten years if Coventry's supply of housing was to be adequate to cope with population expansion. In addition, it was estimated that 1,000 slum houses would have to be demolished before 1938, but by 1937 it was found that in fact the city was having to meet a demand for about 4,000 houses a year and the rate was still increasing.

Although the private sector could help to meet the urgent demand for housing, the burden of providing other basic services (roads, sewerage, water, gas, electricity, fire and refuse collection) and community facilities (schools, transport, etc.) largely fell on the local authority.

Bomb damage during the war imposed massive further costs upon the city. With the loss of homes and the further expansion of the population expected after the war, the city had an immense problem of reconstruction. It was estimated that two out of every three properties had been affected and 8,500 houses had been destroyed or irreparably damaged. By 1951 there were still 13,600 on the Corporation's waiting list and further expansion of the city's population was expected with the continued growth of the engineering industry. The rapid growth in population and the scale of bomb devastation together confronted the local authority with impossible choices about priorities. The eventual pattern of investment was determined partly by the continued pressure for expansion from private industry, partly by the level of rate income, partly by the availability of central government grants for particular purposes, and partly by local political choice.

The raising of resources

Of course the rateable value of the city had increased with the growth of population and employment but the demand for services outpaced the resources available. Furthermore, the resources available to meet these heavy costs had been seriously reduced by the de-rating of industrial property in the 1930s. During this period the better-off section of the ratepaying population increasingly moved out to the surrounding dormitory villages of Warwickshire (Kenilworth, Warwick, Leamington, Stratford) which had escaped the negative effects of the intrusion of industry. The less well-off working population left behind not only had to meet the high costs of their own needs and those of industry, but also the commuting needs (e.g. car-parking, policing, etc.) of the managerial and professional classes getting their livelihood from the city but not contributing to its rates. Coventry's financial base was further weakened by the wartime destruction of property. The rateable value of the city slumped to one-third of its original figure before the Blitz. In order to try to improve its rate-base Coventry asked the 1963 Local Government Boundary Commission to extend its boundaries into the surrounding commuter area. This was not successful. Although Coventry's rateable value increased with the new building development, this did not directly benefit the Council in cash terms, as increases are automatically deducted from the rate deficiency grant received from central government to bring resources up to the national average. In any case new capital building normally brings with it extra calls on supporting services, and therefore revenue costs. In Coventry in the 1960s the basis of rates increased at the rate of $2\frac{1}{2}$ per cent p.a., whereas local authority expenditure on services rose at 8 per cent p.a.[5] In 1973 revaluation of the rates shifted the burden of costs carried within Coventry further on to domestic ratepayers and away from industry and commerce. The swing to the domestic sector in Coventry was 4·0 per cent compared with the national average of 0·3 per cent. The domestic multiplier for Coventry (2·9) was much higher than the national average (2·56). Even within the domestic sector, the highest average increases in Coventry fell on the least desirable Council property compared with the most desirable private property.[6]

Capital borrowing

The massive job of reconstruction which faced the city after the war has meant that a high proportion of Coventry's fixed capital investment (compared with other local authorities of a similar size) has been concentrated in the post-war period. The sums to be borrowed have, therefore, been large and the interest rates higher. Interest rates on loans have increased significantly since 1945 and this has had a profound effect on the cost of the whole rebuilding operation. (It has been estimated that between 1945 and 1966 approximately £195 m, at 1966 building costs, was spent on reconstruction.)

In the 1950s the Conservative Government removed the protection of the Public Works Loan Board rates of interest on loans, which left local authorities little choice but to turn to the City of London finance market and the international money markets. This has meant that the City Council has had to borrow in the market at interest rates which are increasing continuously due to inflation. For example, in 1973–4 the rate of interest on the Consolidated Loans Fund rose from 7 per cent to an estimated 8·13 per cent, costing the City Council an extra £0·5 m in one year. Interest charges now account for about one-fifth of the local authority's total expenditure each year. The net loan debt per head of population has increased seven-fold over the last 50 years.[7] The fastest rate of increase was between 1926 and 1931 when it doubled.

The distribution of available resources

Thus the framework for public investment in Coventry since the war has been set by:
  (i) the pressures of need arising first from the rapid immigration into the city of a young working population (with a high proportion of dependants, especially children) and, second, from the scale of post-war reconstruction;
  (ii) the level of resources available from rates and government grants.
The city's first development plan after the war reveals not only the scale of the problem but the choice of priorities facing the city. The plan designated three areas of the city for comprehensive development: the central area, Spon End and Hillfields. It also allocated expenditure for major building works as shown in Table 1. The allocation for Spon End and Hillfields

Table 1

	First 5 years (£m)	Following 15 years (£m)	Total (£m)
New housing including cost of roads and services	10	40	50
Central area reconstruction	3·5	12	15·5
Industrial development	2·5	10	12·5
Schools	4	6	10

CDAs was much less specific than for the central area. Separate amounts were included for the compulsory purchase of small sites, but the costs of new development were now shown separately from the general city-wide allocation for housing, schools, etc.

In the event, investment in the Hillfields comprehensive development area has not been either comprehensive or sustained. Instead it has been piecemeal and sporadic. The renewal of the area has been reaffirmed as a priority in successive plans (1966 Review Plan, 1973 Structure Plan) but the publication of paper plans without a confident timetable for action on the ground has set in motion a vicious spiral of planning blight, eroding certainty in the area and contributing to its physical, social and economic decline.

Our work suggests a number of factors contributing to this stop-go rhythm of investment in Hillfields:

1. *Central government constraints on urban renewal and redevelopment*. Successive economic crises since the 1947 devaluation have led to restraint on public expenditure. In each crisis central government has insisted upon limiting the involvement of local authorities in the purchase of land and property development generally and urban renewal in particular. At each cut-back the Hillfields CDA programme has been 'rephased' by the local authority. This caused particularly serious stops, starts and delays throughout the 1960s. The withdrawal in 1958 of a specific grant for dealing with blight also impeded urban renewal.

2. *Central government constraints on house building*. Central government has tended to use local government expenditure as a whole and housing expenditure in particular as a short-term regulator within the economy.[8] Coventry's housing programme has been turned on and off with each switch of government policy on housing throughout the economic crises of the 1940s, 1950s and 1960s.

3. *The uncertain political priority given to council housing in Coventry*. Over the last thirty years Coventry has consistently spent a lower proportion of its budget on housing than is the average for local authorities in England and Wales. When capital expenditure per head is compared, Coventry is found to have exceeded the national average from 1951 to 1958, but to have spent below the average in every year since, with only one exception (1966). This may be partly a reflection of the high levels of capital expenditure in other fields (e.g. schools, city centre, roads) in Coventry since the war. It may partly reflect the preference in Coventry for owner-occupation and the high level of activity of the private sector in this field. But it also must indicate the relatively low priority which the Council (of both parties) has given to investment in housing compared with other fields of activity.

The consequences for land use and land values in the older areas. The consequences for Hillfields and the older areas of Coventry are clear. In spite of repeated plans, the actual programme of investment in the area has not been sufficiently large or rapid or sustained to counteract the scale, the pace, or the cumulative effect of the pressures assaulting the community. These can be summarised as:

1. The intrusion of industry and commerce. The Railway Triangle contains a quarter of the city's housing stock and more than one-third of the industry in the city. The 1966 Review Plan substantially increases the acreage allocated to industry, warehousing and roads in the area. Plum sites in the area have already been allocated for office buildings, warehouses and wholesale firms, and there are plans to demolish more houses near to the ring road to provide for light industry.

2. The successive waves of immigration into the city. The Railway Triangle area has functioned as the main reception area for newcomers to the city, providing the only large supply of cheap accommodation to rent or buy.

3. The utilisation of land for a number of city-wide and public services, e.g. football ground, bus depot, central hospital and the ring road. This pattern is continuing at an increasing pace now that land is scarce in the city, involving smaller-scale public and private uses, e.g. hostel for hotel staff, proposed postgraduate student hostel, leisure and night-life facilities (bingo, cinema, social clubs).

4. Planning blight, which has led to economic uncertainty, loss of property values and deterioration in the condition of both housing and the environment. Public labelling then helped to set in motion a self-fulfilling prophecy in which the area gradually came to be defined as a 'black spot'.

The programme of investment in Hillfields and other redevelopment areas has been hit particularly badly at times of national economic squeeze or central government cut-backs in local authority finance. The comprehensive development area programme seems to have functioned as a kind of valve, opening and shutting in response to fluctuations in the finance available to the local authority. The combination of these pressures and the fluctuations in the programme of investment together mean that important changes in land use and land value are taking place and the social composition and function of the area is being changed. Some parts of Hillfields are gradually becoming incorporated as an extension of the city centre, while others like housing and shopping are being pushed up-market. The original reception area functions (housing newcomers to the city) and residual area functions (housing long-standing less well-off families) are gradually being transferred to adjoining areas which are themselves now afflicted by the kind of uncertainty and blight that has affected Hillfields over the last twenty years.

It is arguable that land has now become the city's scarcest resource, and future development is likely to take place not by expansion of boundaries but by changes in ownership and function within existing boundaries. Hillfields and the rest of the older areas occupy prime land near the centre of the city and the inner-ring road and so take on a new scarcity value. The delays and changes in redevelopment since the war have kept Hillfields as a fluid pool of land, able to accommodate a variety of demands from both the private and public sector. The 'value' of Hillfields to Coventry now lies not so much in its labour as in its land.

Private capital, the local state and the councillor

Up till now this section has largely concentrated on the pressures and constraints imposed on the local authority by external forces outside its direct control. However, local government is not simply a passive victim of such pressures; it performs a number of active functions within the political economy of the city. There have been a number of theoretical studies[9] of the role of the national state within advanced capitalist economies. One school of argument is that the state functions to create the conditions in which capital accumulation is possible and profitable by maintaining the 'calculability' of the economic environment (e.g. reducing the risks of investment, cushioning the effects of business fluctuations). One of the most straightforward ways in which the state is able to achieve this is through changes in the overall levels and categories of public expenditure. This stimulates or regulates demand, creates or expands markets, and thus stabilises the consumption and investment outlets required by the private sector for the absorption of surplus. There is persuasive evidence[10] that since the 1950s British capitalism has had a crisis of falling profitability, as a result of increasing international competition and pressure from wages. In this situation state expenditure is particularly important in providing private capital with a predictable market for its products.

Public authorities spend about £1,500 million a year on construction alone. These contracts account for about 60 per cent of the output of the construction industry and 90 per cent of the output of the civil engineering industry.[11] In the UK the contracts for building schools, council housing, many roads, children's and old people's homes and many other public buildings are all placed by local government. Capital expenditure represents nearly 30 per cent of total local government expenditure nationally, compared with 5 per cent for central government. It is also far greater in absolute terms—£3,100 m for local government in 1973–4 compared with £834 m for central government.[12] Local government thus involves large-scale capital investment and one of its effects is to provide the construction industry with expanded and more predictable markets. Although the construction industry is better protected from international competition than most, it is an industry which is highly vulnerable to fluctuations in market conditions. A firm market is needed before funds are committed. Corporate planning has spurred local authorities into producing forward plans, and ten-year rolling capital programmes, which thus enhance the 'calculability' of the market for private building firms, providing them with a firmer agenda of forward work.

The heavy programme of capital works which has been necessary in Coventry, because of the rapid growth in population and the scale of bomb devastation, has obviously had direct outputs for the local community, and for industry, but indirectly it has also provided big business for a limited number of building and civil engineering firms. The local authority's comprehensive forward plans for land-use and for capital expenditure have thus helped to contribute to the 'calculability' of the economic environment for private developers and the building industry.

The local authority has also performed a number of active functions on behalf of the engineering industry. In addition to the provision of infrastructure already noted, it has also supported and serviced the search for new markets and new contracts for the car and machine tool industries, directly through trade missions, and indirectly through criticism of central government's Industrial Development Certificate policy. Presumably the assumption is that what is good for industry in this respect must be good for the city as a whole. However, our study suggests that the contraction in jobs in Coventry has taken place not because of government regional policy but as part of the 'normal' process of concentration and rationalisation of industrial capital and that this has not been equally good for all sections of the city.

In their role as workers and trade unionists, many Coventry councillors (of both parties) have seen the need to challenge the 'logic' which governs these processes and to demand that the workforce has a say in the decisions which have consequences for their pay and conditions. It is paradoxical that in their role as managers of the local authority the same councillors often appear to accept a very different stance in relation to industry and the requirements of the private sector. Yet our tentative analysis of the political economy of Hillfields suggests that the same free market 'logic' has had severe consequences for the conditions and quality of life outside the workplace, and for the older working-class areas in particular. The challenge to those forces has tended to come most visibly from those groups in the community who suffer their consequences most directly and acutely.

Possibilities for fresh political initiatives at the local level

While we have been trying in the last phase of the Project to reach a better theoretical understanding of the creation, maintenance and decline of Hillfields in relation to the political economy of the city and the role of the local state, at the same time we have been exploring the potential for change that lies in the hands of the residents of such areas.

Our work with residents' groups has been focused around two key issues: (1) legal and income rights; and (2) housing and environment.

Legal and income rights

In addition to advice and advocacy on specific problems this programme has attempted to disseminate information about, and understanding of, the issues underlying our income maintenance system, through information leaflets and teach-ins aimed at both community groups and the trade unions. We have offered the services of a solicitor and a welfare rights expert in the following ways:

(a) to individuals who call at weekly surgeries in four neighbourhoods;
(b) to community groups who are helping claimants and others with legal and income problems;
(c) to pensioners' rights groups in the city;
(d) to trade union groups, helping their members to claim their full rights at times of short-time working or strike.

Housing and environment

We have been able to offer the services of a housing team containing a planner, a public health inspector, a solicitor and a community worker. This has enabled groups to prepare reports on collective demands, alternative plans for general improvement areas and action areas, and has helped other groups collect data about their areas to inform and support their particular campaigns. This has involved work with neighbourhood groups concerned about the following range of issues:

(a) the effects of the Local Authority's Comprehensive Development Area and Action Area plans for particular small areas;[13]
(b) campaigns to get streets declared as General Improvement Areas or to influence the kind of improvements which take place once such areas are declared for GIA treatment;[14]
(c) action to achieve the scrapping of a major road proposal for the city which had blighted an area of 600 houses for the last ten years;
(d) groups concerned with more general problems affecting their housing, e.g. spiralling house prices through speculative dealings in the area, the intrusion of industry and other non-conforming uses into residential areas, homelessness and the loss of family houses as a result of change of use by landlords; and environmental nuisances such as derelict buildings and land;
(e) this work has led to the setting up of a tenant-controlled housing co-operative and a feasibility study for a Common-Ownership House Improvement Company.[15]

In each of these two programmes we have tried to offer five inter-related services:

1. Information and intelligence—help to residents in the gathering of information about their own situation (e.g. household surveys, census analyses) and about how decisions affecting their lives are made (e.g. housing finance; local government structures and procedures).

2. Hard technical skills—a pool of expertise to be drawn upon by residents and their representatives on a 'hire or fire' basis; the range of skills include those of a solicitor, planner, public health inspector and income and welfare rights specialist. The aim is to present the knowledge which such specialists have in a clear and understandable form and to share it as openly and widely as possible, to reduce the dependency of groups on outside experts.

3. Community organisation—helping groups and individuals to identify and define the problems they wish to tackle, to organise and develop a constituency, to keep their supporters informed and involved throughout the course of a campaign, and to draw on the experience of other organised groups, both nationally and locally, who are involved with similar issues.

4. Adult education—encouraging mutual learning, by reflecting on the experience of action, and by sharing our own analysis of the concrete issues around which the groups are working.

5. Administrative support and practical resources—help in the preparation and presentation of newsletters, reports and campaign material plus access to typing, photographic and other resources.

The lessons we drew from this work with groups are as follows:

1. Groups of ordinary men and women who have organised collectively to try to improve the circumstances in their local community have been able to gain small but valuable changes. In many cases the collective experience has sharpened their understanding of the nature of their situation and allowed further initiatives to be attempted. However, it has become clear that there are limits to the possibilities for effective change from the neighbourhood base on its own. If the problems experienced in the residential community have the same fundamental sources as those experienced in the workplace, then effective action must bridge the gap between community politics and industrial politics. Although we have only very limited experience of such divisions being bridged, where we have seen this beginning to take place the results seem to have been particularly fruitful both for action and for understanding of the issues.

2. In addition to the need for broader based alliances and stronger organisation it appears that groups trying to tackle problem issues can be helped by having access to hard information and technical skills. Our experience suggests that it is possible for groups to make effective use of the services of planners, lawyers, public health inspectors, research workers and so on. We have been able to begin to explore various ways in which such skills can be made not only available but accountable to the group tackling a particular issue. Our aim has been to demystify professional knowledge and to try to share it as widely as possible within a local community. The best examples have been where the technical service has not simply suggested some new solution to a group's problem

but also provided new information and material for learning about the situation.

3. There seem to be few if any agencies which are geared up to providing such a systematic technical and educational service to groups at the local level. The trade unions have traditionally aimed to protect working-class interests at the workplace, while the Labour Party has traditionally sought to achieve this in the wider community through the local authorities and through the machinery of the welfare state. Yet the issues which confront many of the groups we have been working with seem to strain the capacity of the traditional machinery. While the local authorities develop increasingly sophisticated methods of planning and managing their available resources, there seems to have been much less success in making available the local authority's manpower to disadvantaged groups to help them tackle problems they perceive as important in ways which they find helpful. Similarly while the trade unions develop increasingly effective means of improving pay and conditions at the workplace, they seem to be much less effective in servicing their members when retired, redundant or on strike, or members' families in their home environment. More fundamentally, there seem to be few if any agencies at the local level providing the kind of relevant adult education to support groups as they act to take greater responsibility over their local situation and as they face wider questions about the kind of society they want. Members of the action team are proposing to explore these possibilities further through two new organisations which aim to build on the work begun in Hillfields.[16]
(a) A Legal and Income Rights Trust, supported by the Home Office and the City Council, through the Urban Programme, but managed by an independent committee involving councillors, trade unionists and residents.
(b) A new kind of community development and adult education agency to be funded by Trusts in the first place, but aiming to operate in association with labour movement. and offering a range of specific services (research; technical skills. e.g. planning, public health, accountancy; adult education and community organisation) to working-class groups.

[. . .]

Examples of work with community groups towards fresh political initiatives?

Hartlepool, Redcar and Stockton Roads Residents' Association

The HRS Residents' Association was formed in 1970 around general environmental and amenity issues in the three streets covered by the Association (140 homes). Shortly afterwards the area was promised General Improvement Area (GIA) status by the City Council, which would secure the life of the houses for at least thirty years and would include substantial environmental improvements. The residents' committee were delighted, but for two years nothing more was heard. In 1972 the committee asked the team for help in pursuing this promise. A new approach was made to the Council, which responded by declaring a new, far less attractive and cheaper Repair Area policy which would reduce the security of life for the houses and cut out all environmental work. The committee examined both policies carefully, with technical help from the team, and decided they needed to involve the other residents of the area in any decision. A survey was designed and carried out by the group, which involved all the residents; the information gathered was sufficient to allow the group to produce a declaration report for the City Council, demanding GIA status. The focus then shifted from assimilating and applying technical information to political action which would represent residents' views to the Council. The CDP housing team was asked to supply a variety of technical information (on, for example, rates, legislation) which was used by residents to support their campaign in bargaining situations. Finally, the area was accorded GIA status. This example shows how residents and professionals can and did learn together to mount a campaign relevant to the specific needs of an area. All came to understand the political nature of technical information, and residents were able to use their new knowledge to press their demands.

The Five Ways Residents' Association

The Five Ways area is one of old, war-damaged, working-class housing near the city centre (1,100 homes). For twenty years the local authority's intention has been to demolish and redevelop the area, but no specific moves were made until December 1973 when a consultative plan was published calling for the demolition of the majority of the houses, enlargement of an industrial site and expansion of school grounds. This plan, which used supposedly technical evaluations of house conditions, demonstrated the Council's commitment to industry and its need to meet statutory educational requirements. It can be seen as a technical solution to issues lying outside the local democratic arena. The local residents' group—poorly organised and unrepresentative—opposed the plan and asked for help from the CDP housing team. The latter was able to offer advice and technical expertise (including house condition surveys, the results of which contrasted strongly with the local authority's findings) and organisational help, to enable residents to develop both a representative organisation and an alternative technical plan. Working together, the group drew up questionnaires and organised a 100 per cent survey of an area of 750 houses. Facts and opinions were collected and correlated. The results were compared with a charter of demands finalised earlier in a series of mass meetings. From this combined base an alternative plan for the area was drawn up and presented to the Council. The business of the residents' association was carried out through weekly meetings, attended by sixty to seventy people, which saw one of its major tasks as keeping all the residents informed of progress. The meetings allowed them to take new initiatives, using the facts and technical information at their disposal. The housing team was asked to interpret the responses from the Council and the implications of legislation and national policy. They were also able to provide a commentary describing the local political and economic situation within which groups were working, the activities of other campaigning groups, and the structure and operation of the local authority—all of which were discussed in depth with residents. A large number of houses have been saved from demolition, but the campaign will continue until all the fit houses are saved. Solidarity has been maintained and strengthened through the activity of the representative group. The demands on time and input from the team of three workers have been considerable, and it has been realised that such a team can effectively service only a small number of groups of this kind if it is to fulfil adequately its contract with the groups and a realistic commitment to adult educational aims.

Wickmans Limited

When 120 workers from Wickmans (a machine-tool firm) went on strike in March 1974, our solicitor and welfare rights workers were contacted by a member of the strike committee for advice on strikers' rights to supplementary benefit. At their suggestion, a small committee of strikers was rapidly formed to advise and assist the other strikers on claiming supplementary benefit. They met this committee at the home of one of the members within a few days of first being approached. At this meeting they provided the committee with leaflets they had prepared on strikers' rights to supplementary benefit and were able to explain these rights and point out some of the commonly-held myths about the supplementary benefits system and the importance of an active strikers' committee to ensure that all strikers received their rights in full. At this meeting the committee drafted a short leaflet to give to their fellow-strikers, encouraging them to claim, and giving the names of the committee members to be contacted in case of difficulty. They produced and distributed this leaflet the following day. Over the next couple of weeks we had several telephone conversations with committee members over snags that had arisen over individual claims and were able to clarify the legal questions involved. The committee organised themselves so that one or other members was able to be in attendance at the supplementary benefits office most days to deal with individual problems and where necessary they represented their colleagues in negotiations with the SBC management. The combination of their trade union approach to bargaining and their rapidly acquired expertise in the law relating to supplementary benefits made them formidable negotiators. For example, the first week that claimants were due to claim benefit they were told that no special arrangements were being made by the SBC and that all 120 men would have to make individual appointments. They replied that they were bringing down 100 men to claim the next day, and that unless the SBC co-operated they would all be asking for form A124 to be given to them. (This is the form explaining how each individual's SBC entitlement is calculated. Every claimant has a right to one if he requests it, but the overwhelming majority of claimants are unaware of this right. Its compilation involves a certain amount of extra work by the SBC staff.) The SBC agreed to make special arrangements and opened the office half an hour early the next day to deal with claims from Wickmans. The committee also took up and won cases of hardship where supplementary benefit had been refused to single strikers and applied for and obtained exceptional needs payments to prevent hardship in other cases. They also successfully represented their colleagues at two supplementary benefits appeal tribunals and complained to their MP over the treatment one of their members received from the SBC. They have since agreed to attend any 'teach-ins' on strikers' rights to supplementary benefits that we give to other trade unionists to explain the bargaining techniques they developed for ensuring that their colleagues received their rights in full.

Note

The CDP housing team are working with nine residents' action groups covering 3,000 houses in and around Hillfields. This involves the team in an intensive working relationship with some 200 men and women who form the organised committees for the nine areas. Most action groups meet at least once a fortnight, the result being that the housing team are working to capacity most evenings of the week.

References

1 The material on industry and on public investment in this section is largely drawn from the work of Andy Friedman, Lisa Carter and Norman Ginsburg, summarised in Background Working Papers 6 and 2. Full sources and references are given there.

2 M. J. Hill *et al.*, *Men Out of Work* (a study of unemployment in three English towns, including Coventry), Cambridge University Press, 1973.
3 Background Working Paper 6.
4 Hill, op. cit.

5 J. K. Friend and W. N. Jessop, *Local Government and Strategic Choice*, Tavistock, 1969, chapter 1.

6 N. Bond and L. Carter. 'Revaluing the rates: who gains, who loses?', *Municipal Review*, January 1974.

7 City of Coventry Accounts 1973.

8 'Rates of Decline' (National CDP Submission to the Layfield Committee on Local Government Finance, January 1975). Also Association of Municipal Authorities Evidence to the Layfield Committee, January 1975; and CDP Occasional Paper 11.

9 Occasional Paper 11.

10 A. Glyn and B. Sutcliffe, *British Capitalism, Workers and the Profits Squeeze*, Penguin, 1972.

11 C. Hood, 'The rise and rise of the British quango', *New Society*, 16 August 1973.

12 Association of Municipal Authorities, Evidence to the Committee of Enquiry into Local Government Finance, January 1975.

13 A Future for Five Ways (petition report presented to Coventry City Council by the Five Ways Residents' Association).

14 The HRS Residents' Association Report.

15 Triangle Tenants' Union.

16 Occasional Papers 12 and 13 give the background of the Legal and Income Rights work in Coventry.

Current Occasional Papers

1(a) John Benington, *Coventry Community Development Project: Background and Progress.*

1(b) CDP Team, *Coventry Community Development Project: Report to the Home Secretary.*

2 Nick Bond, *The Hillfields Information and Opinion Centre: the Evolution of a Social Agency Controlled by Local Residents.*

3 Rev. Harry Salmon, *The Hillfields Community Association: a Case Study.*

4 Nick Bond, *Knowledge of Rights and Extent of Unmet Need Among Recipients of Supplementary Benefit.*

5 Report of Steering Committee, *Homeless Men in Hillfields.*

6 K. R. Carter, J. K. Friend, G. M. Luck, C. J. L. Yewlett (Institute for Operational Research), *Area Improvement Policies for the Inner City.*

7 Research Team, *Tax Credits: Some Notes on the Green Paper.*

8 Helen Brown, *Transition from School to Work.*

9 Linda Forbes, *A Review of Research on the Relocation of the Elderly.*

10 Brian Gearing and Geoffrey Sharp, *Exceptional Needs Payments and the Elderly.*

11 John Benington, *Local Government Becomes Big Business.*

12 Nick Bond and Robert Zara, *CDP Legal and Income Rights Programme: Casework, Campaigns and Adult Education.*

13 Martin Partington (London School of Economics), *Recent Developments in Legal Services for the Poor: Some Reflections on Experience in Coventry.*

14 Stephen Humble and Jennifer Talbot (Institute of Local Government Studies, Birmingham University), *A Community Forum in Coventry? A Case Study.*

Fuller and more up to date examples are included in the October 1976 Progress Report, available from John Benington, Coventry Workshop, 40 Binley Road, Coventry.

Part III Looking at social work practice

This volume of readings now attends to social work practice. The guiding principle in selecting the papers for this part was not so much to get an all-round view of what social workers do but to present the more general issues of their practice and theory. Social work is an intervention in social life with a view to helping individuals and their families, one by one, to pursue their own aims more successfully, so long as neither the pursuit, nor the aims violate the laws of the state or the major conventions of the most influential groups in society.

Such a proviso as this must, to a certain extent, move social work in a politically conservative direction. But this is not inevitable, nor is it so prescribed by the principles of its practice. Indeed many social workers believe that the wisdom necessary for the effective advancement of radical policies in society is unlikely to be weakened, let alone emasculated, by social work. Nor is it firmly held that conservative policies will benefit by those habits of self-searching and self-criticism that the social work regimen encourages.

It is hoped that the paper by Brown will not only illustrate this interaction very suitably, but will also serve as a backcloth for the rest of the papers in this Part.

The view that a radical change in society at large is necessary, and that a certain violation of laws or conventions is also inevitable, is held by a number of theorists and practitioners of social work today. Those social workers whose thinking about these matters has been influenced by an earlier generation's ideas now come up against the substantially logical tenet that the real enemy of those who set out to help people is, as H. H. Perlman puts it, 'the social conditions that pollute social living'. According to this view, the preoccupation with individual unhappiness and failure is a distraction and a regrettable indulgence. Perlman acknowledges, not too soon, that social casework with the individual or his family is no substitute for social reform and social change. She stresses, however, that care for and concern with the individual will survive into even a radically reformed society. Her point is that just as doctors, nurses, lawyers and teachers must go on working for individuals—no matter what the social order is—so do social workers. Their services are to be rendered not *instead of*, but *alongside*, the work carried out by political workers in the community and the state. She also stresses that social casework comprises help to secure material resources and services, and that it is not a blinkered preoccupation with the client's inner perception of himself and of his problems.

Probably it has been the narrow clinical and psychiatric interpretation of social work which fostered a rigid defensiveness about the professional status of social work and thus held off a serious consideration of the employment of paraprofessionals, non-professionals and untrained people in general in social work and social helping. But today, the inclusion of the volunteer and of the indigenous non-professional in social work tasks is not only a growing practice but also a source of new insights into, and appreciation of, those tasks. It is not just that there are not, and could not be, enough trained and professionalised workers to meet the great need for guidance, support and friendship, but that these non-professional personnel are in fact more appropriate to be involved in the intimate helping of others than the professional, who is more often than not an intruder from another social class or race. Also, the volunteer and the non-professional find a personal enrichment in being involved in this way—which we cannot but welcome as another return on our investment into sharing the helping task with them. From G. Goldberg's paper we gain a vivid and most encouraging impression about the effortless warmth of black women workers when meeting their black clients. And from a paper by Roger Hadley *et al.* we can see and be persuaded to appreciate the value of the volunteer visitors. The volunteer here is employed to break through the loneliness of some old people and is not only more generously available than the professionals but is also less in need of professional achievements. In both the Goldberg and Hadley papers we can still see that a hierarchical structure survives, for in both cases there is an organising and supervisory trained staff which continue to exercise control over the indigenous and the volunteer.

So as to bring up to date theoretical thinking about social work, the older caseworker's model of the client as a whole person, with his intrapsychic divisions such as his conscious–unconscious and the like, has had to be replaced. If social work's emphasis is no longer to be on the individual alone, but must be on the group, the community and beyond, a new conceptual system was required to cover all sorts of different interventions by social workers. A so-called 'unitary' conception has gained currency which stopped talking about 'persons' and 'communities' and bracketed them together under the all-embracing concept of 'client-systems'. This concept came in handy for those contemporary social work courses and teachers who have had to combine the teaching of social work with community work. It is as yet difficult to see what, if any, benefits will come from the new concepts and terminology. Certainly the 'system theories', as they are called, are more viable, but aren't they less vital? To talk about a client system instead of persons or communities may be economical when one wishes to say something about both at the same time; but the mechanical image of 'systems' is unlikely to yield new insights in this area. Just the same, A. Vickery's exercise, in the wake of people such as Pincus, Minahan and Goldstein, is necessary at this stage to keep up our efforts for a renewal of our conceptual scheme for social work today. One must not allow reverential talk about 'persons' and 'communities' to become an enquiry-stopping device.

To include a discussion on residential work here is to allow a somewhat wider interpretation of social work and social helping. The staffs of residential institutions are not often referred to as 'social workers'. They are often doctors, nurses, teachers, domestic staff and so on. Nevertheless their intimate connection with social workers at all levels, and the social workers' own deep concern with this link, attaches this subject to our present area of interest. E. J. Miller and G. V. Gwynne treat the subject from a point of view which underlines the social work involvement in residential work. The institutionalised defective is rejected by parents and by the community, and these rejecting areas are where social workers work. They encounter the rejecting values and attitudes even before rejection matures and occurs. Without these values and attitudes, the 'warehousing' of humanity would not take place. It is sadly not an exaggeration to say, as these authors do, that the institutionalisation of many defectives is a social death which continues until physical death takes over. To a painfully large extent the problems have no total solution, medical or social. Man is vulnerable and the consequences of this can be mitigated only by medical and social measures. The social worker's role when encountering such values and attitudes is unenviably difficult, nor does that role end with facing up to a rejecting world. Social workers must continue to act as an intermediary between the residential worker and the outside world: they have to interpret the latter to the former. And equally important: they have to provide support for residential staff who are now carrying on with a difficult and often interminable task.

But, as we said in the beginning of this introductory note, the personal intervention of social workers and their commitment to personal helping may conceal other and more pressing needs of clients which cannot be met by the use of person-to-person relationships. G. Parkinson's paper announces that 'I give most of my clients money'. This admission does make at least one salutary point about the relative urgency of the material needs of clients and the occasionally crass irrelevance of psychologising about the client. There is no place for embarrassment about replacing instant interpretation with instant cash. However, to adopt this model of social work holds some hazards. Some of these are less obvious than the insolvency of the underpaid social worker or of the underendowed agency. The climate of opinion in which ideas such as Parkinson's are generated would be severely against the proposal that charity should replace social work, no matter how briskly and unlady-bountifully it is dispensed. Even so, this paper is an appropriate document to use to illustrate the contemporary disenchantment with psychologistic and psychoanalytic thinking about the tasks of social work.

G. Pearson's paper, the last in this Part, pursues an absorbing theme: why do people want to be social workers? What are these people's motives? Pearson believes that for most of them the work and the vocation is a means whereby they can generate some meaning and purposefulness in life and even secure opportunities to transcend the limitation of their personalities: limitations imposed upon them by an alienating society and its culture. So it would seem that social work students, and later social work practitioners are in business to solve their personal problems by doing social work. Pearson says this is a privatised solution to problems which are political in an 'advanced capitalist society'. Instead of being a political protest, doing social work is contracting out of making political protests. One wonders how one would have to interpret the motives of those people who in the 'advanced societies' today are increasingly seeking and finding employment of a caseworker nature. What cultural alienation makes them seek these privatised solutions of social problems? Are they too contracting out of political protest? Or is their privatisation itself a political protest? And are they too propelled by a desire to escape from an alienating culture and society? It is a pity that we have no access to reliable answers to these questions.

III. 1 The inalienable element in social work

British Association of Social Workers

1. We have sought to identify the quintessence of social work in order to be able to show what relevance it has in our culture and what contribution it makes to the life of the community. We have tried to describe as concisely as possible what social work is. We have deliberately not couched our definition in terms of what social workers do because this varies greatly with the agency and with the worker. Moreover other people—teachers, clergymen, politicians, civil servants and many more—do things which are very similar to those which social workers may do.

2. Social work is an evolutionary phenomenon. It has its roots in social philosophies and ethical values and its antecedents have existed in a relatively unorganised state for centuries. The industrial revolution profoundly transformed society, broke up long-established support groups and exposed everyone to rapidly accelerating change on different fronts simultaneously. In the last hundred years social work has developed dramatically in response to the needs arising from the interaction of demographic change, industrialisation, mechanisation and technology.

3. Such interaction brought with it profound changes which have both benefited and burdened the individual. Material standards are higher, opportunities of all sorts are wider, but at the same time the penalties for inadequacy or failure, whatever their causes, are harsh and inescapable. Moreover, as social structures, whole industries, services and businesses are reorganised in response to modern developments, people are increasingly being affected by changes which are fundamental and far reaching in their effects. Factors which profoundly affect the lives of individuals are increasingly difficult for them to influence or control; the systems created to meet people's needs are sometimes in danger of taking precedence over the individuals they should serve.

Source: Discussion paper no. 3 adopted by the Council of BASW on 9 February 1973 (reprinted in BASW News, in *Social Work Today*, 4 (1), 5 April 1973, p. 17).

4. Professional social work can be regarded as a spontaneous development, a manifestation of awareness of the need to create a means of protecting and helping those individuals adversely affected by changes which are reshaping society.

5. Social work aims to harness the potential in society towards solving its own problems. It is concerned with helping people to realise their potential to the maximum, whilst ensuring that the facilities which already exist to assist them are fully used and with supplementing these where they are lacking. The focus of the work done will shift as society adjusts itself to cultural and technological changes which alter the pattern of living. It is concerned with bridging the gap between the individual and society, with supporting him when he is vulnerable and with striving to improve the quality of life by ensuring that human needs are not overlooked or over-ridden in this industrial society. The tasks of showing the community what conditions are necessary for the protection and promotion of the needs of individuals, and of pressing for changes in legislation and in regulations are as much a part of social work as the tasks of dealing with individual's problems.

6. One expression of the concern in society for its disadvantaged members is the provision of resources without which social work would be largely ineffective.

7. These resources are deployed through social work, which is carried out through agencies within the social structure, some statutory, some voluntary. Responsibility for caring for individuals in need is vested in these social work agencies and the way the work is carried out is influenced by the agency and by the need to account for the way resources are used.

8. Since social work exists for the good of the individual in society, it must influence and seek to adjust the social care structure as well as carry out agency policy and function. This dual responsibility, to the individual and to the agencies which have been

established to serve him, may draw social work into situations of conflict.

9. All social work activity and methods seek to contribute to helping people to function to their maximum capacity and to securing conditions favourable to their development.

10. All social work is based upon respect for the value of the individual. Knowledge about the individual and about the environment and material conditions necessary for him to fulfil himself, is derived from many other disciplines, as well as from social work itself.

11. The special function of social work, and its inalienable element, is to project and promote the interests of the individual client or clients and to ensure that social technological changes serve and do not enslave the individual as a person in his own right. The community's concern to safeguard and promote the welfare of the individual within society manifests itself in part through social work.

III. 2 A review of casework methods
Margaret A. G. Brown

In 1915 Mary Richmond, speaking at the American National Conference of Charities and Correction, defined social casework as: 'The art of doing different things for and with different people by cooperating with them to achieve at one and the same time their own and society's betterment.'[1] Although many definitions have been published since 1915 and Mary Richmond herself produced two others, which have perhaps been more frequently quoted, this still seems to express simply and succinctly the essence of casework. Father Swithun Bowers, in his thesis on The Nature of Social Casework, suggested that Mary Richmond's definition was defective as a definition because it could be applied to endeavours beyond the scope of casework.[2] This is true, but here I am concerned less with semantics than with emphasizing again that skill in casework lies in the understanding of the different needs of different people in various social circumstances and in the provision of different, appropriate kinds of help.

Despite the fact that casework was defined in these terms forty-eight years ago and that much has subsequently been written on differential assessment and treatment methods, there is still a good deal of confusion about the nature of casework and the range of caseworkers' activities. For example, in a foreword to a recent publication on casework in the child care service, the following statement occurred:[3] 'True casework occupies only a very small fraction of a child care officer's working hours. It is of course fortunate that this is so, both for the officer concerned, and for the authority with a large caseload and too few child care officers. But situations do continually arise when a child care officer must take the initiative and deliberately introduce a casework approach.'

During two refresher courses and a conference for experienced case-workers and student supervisors held during 1962, these comments were made in discussion. 'Casework is only part of the social worker's job. At other times he has to be authoritarian.' 'The caseworker has to do many things that are not pure casework—implementing the law, for instance.' 'We kid ourselves if we think that authority and casework are compatible.'

In an article entitled 'The probation officer as caseworker', S. R. Eshelby states:[4]

To-day's probation officer would have no difficulty in defining his work to fit most definitions of casework, for example, (Bowers') 'Social casework is an art in which knowledge of the science of human relations and skill in relationship are used to mobilize capacities in the individual, and resources in the community appropriate for better adjustment between the client and all or any part of his total environment.' The probation officer seeks to do just this in his supervisory work, *though he may attempt to do other things as well, such as discipline his client, which may put him outside the fold of caseworkers* [my italics].

Mr Eshelby goes on to discuss some of the difficulties of probation officers in 'applying social casework concepts'. The greatest difficulty he thinks is the probation officer himself.[5]

I feel fairly confident that part of the attraction of the probation service to men is the apparent opportunity to direct other people's lives. Even if I have deduced the wrong reason it remains true that a number of men officers and some women officers carry out their probation work in an authoritarian, directive way, paying little heed to such things as maintaining a non-judgmental attitude and self determination for the client, and apparently work successfully.

. . . What is emerging is that there are several

Source: Supplement to *Case Conference*, February 1964 (revised); republished in Eileen Younghusband (ed.), *New Developments in Casework*, Allen & Unwin, 1971, pp. 11–37.

types of probation depending upon the personality, attitudes and training of the probation officer. It follows that more careful matching of probation officer and client might be beneficial.

. . . At present there is no certainty that the highly trained skilled caseworker is achieving better results than the man or woman who is naturally good with people carrying out simple supportive and directive work.

There are several points that I would like to comment on here. First, the implication that the use of authority and discipline is not part of casework. This seems to me to be taking too limited a view of casework and of the kinds of relationship which may be helpful to an individual at a particular time. Surely discipline can be a valuable element in casework with certain clients, especially those who feel at the mercy of strong impulses and need help or support in controlling their behaviour, or those who have experienced insecurity and disorder in their lives and temporarily require a firm framework to enable them to function satisfactorily in society. Second, Mr Eshelby suggests that there are different types of probation work, which appear to depend on the personality, attitudes and training of the probation officer, and that in consequence consideration should be given to the matching of officer and probationer. While agreeing with his observations, I would ask whether these different types of casework should not instead depend on the needs of the client, and whether caseworkers in the probation service and elsewhere should not learn to understand better these various needs and to utilize different treatment approach with different persons. Third, the observation that there is no certainty that the highly trained worker achieves better results than the 'naturally good' worker carrying out simple supportive and directive work: this implies that in the past at least training programmes may not have emphasized sufficiently the variety of methods in casework with the result that students leaving such courses may have tended to place too much reliance on a narrow range of techniques, applying them indiscriminately until experience taught them otherwise.

These points are well brought out in a paper presented by Arthur Hunt at an Association of Psychiatric Social Workers' Refresher Course in 1960, and subsequently published in *Ventures in Professional Co-operation*. He suggests that in approximately 55 per cent of persons under a probation officer's supervision 'cultural, social and heritable' factors are prominent in causation, and he goes on to say 'I do not feel that this type of offender either needs, or could respond to, advanced therapeutic or casework techniques'. He explains that what he means by advanced techniques is:

A self conscious relationship aimed at revealing transferred residues of past experience which cause perceptual distortion, and its consequences of inappropriate action and manipulation. The use of these necessarily sophisticated techniques

has demanded . . . an appreciation of need on the part of the subject and comparative freedom from external pressures of time and conflicting obligation. Such techniques have naturally been most frequently employed in clinical settings.

Mr Hunt suggests that the bias which appears to exist in training courses is partly due to the fact that a high proportion of casework teachers have matured and developed techniques in settings appropriate to the treatment of the neuroses, as distinct from character disorders or behaviour having a strong cultural determinant, and that 'an impression is created among many students that comparatively inactive techniques are generally applicable in a setting such as probation'. He continues:[6]

I have finally been forced to the conclusion that whilst practising officers are much alive to the value of insightful and comprehensive casework in certain circumstances (usually those which are analogous to clinical situations), they have found it extraordinarily difficult to apply *advanced casework techniques* generally in the probation setting . . . All too often attempts to apply techniques considered relevant in other settings have been frustrated . . . I feel that *casework techniques*, with their underlying psychoanalytic origin, are still relevant (in the probation setting) and may be applied usefully and with demonstrable success, even though they may have to be modified until they are barely recognizable [my italics].

The emphasis here is on the relevance or otherwise, in the probation setting, of a small range of casework techniques directed towards the development of insight in the client. For conceptual convenience Mr Hunt sometimes refers to these techniques as 'advanced', while at other times he and the other authors quoted imply that this group of techniques is synonymous with, or at least representative of casework in general. This is unfortunate, but it does illustrate the tendency during recent years to think of casework in these rather limited terms. Both Mr Hunt and Mr Eshelby make it clear that in their own experience other methods of help are often more useful, and Mr Hunt has now clarified and developed his views in an interesting paper 'Enforcement in probation casework', from which two short extracts may be quoted.[7]

Personal experience of a wide range of delinquents suggests that much antisocial behaviour arises from the failure of a socialization process and that the compulsive, neurotic, affectionless or seriously unbalanced person is in the minority. Moreover, recognizable in much relatively casual delinquency is the presence of poorly sublimated aggression in which the failure of primary or social institutions of control is in evidence.

The enforced relationship and casework are not mutually exclusive. Indeed, in many respects the probation casework process is enriched by enforcement, and the explanation appears to centre on the fact that enforcement is an essential component of all early socializing processes.

Caseworkers in all settings have probably intuitively always recognized this and in practice adapted their methods to the differing needs of their clients, but it is helpful, especially for the beginning worker, to have the reasoning spelled out in print.

Casework, as I see it, is a helping activity which is made up of a very large number of constituent activities ranging from the giving of material assistance, through listening, expressing acceptance and reassurance, suggesting, advising and the setting of limits, to the making of comments that encourage the client to express or suppress his feelings, to examine his situation or to see connections between his present attitudes and behaviour and past experiences. (In a recent study of casework interviews in which I was involved at least sixty-two different activities initiated either by the worker or by the client were identifiable.[8]) These may be utilized and blended in an infinite variety of ways and the caseworker's skill would appear to lie firstly in his ability to understand the needs of his client in relation to the needs of others, and secondly in his ability to relate to his client appropriately, and to employ such methods as will most exactly meet the latter's changing needs. It is hardly necessary to say that this kind of skill is grounded in an extensive knowledge of human beings and society, and an awareness of self which enables the worker to use himself with discrimination in different situations. Since the vast majority of persons referred to social agencies are experiencing stress in some form I would guess that in practice, whatever the setting, most of the techniques employed by caseworkers are supportive in nature and to minimize the value of these by implying that they are not really 'advanced' is to present a misleading picture of casework.

Over the years various attempts have been made to analyse the casework process, to look at the numerous small activities of the caseworker during interviews and the reciprocal responses of the client, and to classify these into broad treatment methods. Until some reliable classification is arrived at, it is, of course, impossible to move on to the next stage of studying what kind of approach is successful with different clients experiencing particular kinds of problems and so to eliminate much trial and error. Before reviewing the literature, however, it may be helpful if I define the sense in which the terms 'method' and 'technique' will be used in this article. These words seem to have for many people a cold and calculating connotation, so it should be noted that neither term precludes the warm human concern that is rightly felt to be an essential part of all good social work.

Method is the more comprehensive of the two terms. The Oxford Dictionary definition is 'way of doing something, system of procedure, conscious regularity, orderliness'. I shall use it to include the use of

relationship and constituent activities or techniques in casework in a systematic way to achieve certain broad goals. For example, casework can be directed primarily towards supporting the client's ego and helping him to maintain or regain a personal equilibrium and an existing or previous pattern of social adjustment, in which case the method may be described as 'supportive'; or it can be directed towards promoting the client's self understanding with a view to effecting some change in his personality. The method might then be described as 'modifying' or as 'insight development'.

Technique is defined in the Oxford Dictionary as 'manner of artistic execution', 'the part of artistic work that is reducible to formula'. I shall use it to mean the specific response of the caseworker towards the client, such as the giving of money, expressions of interest and sympathy, suggestions, interpretive comments, etc.

In 1921, Virginia Robinson published an 'Analysis of Processes in the Records of Family Case Working Agencies.' She stated:[9]

> It is important to keep clearly in mind from the outset the distinction between those (processes) that have a significance for treatment and those that have only a temporary value—details as to the mechanical process of getting things done which have no real bearing on the development of the case.
> . . . As to the recording of the significant processes . . . there is much difference of opinion. A classification of essential processes which may be made for the convenience of this discussion is: (1) those processes which have to do with altering the material environment in order to meet the client's needs, and (2) those that have to do with the re-education of the client's point of view or habits or attitudes, or the changing of the attitudes of other people toward the client.

This is an early attempt based on observation to distinguish broad methods of casework treatment and to classify these descriptively. No attempt has been made to break down the methods into the component techniques by which re-education or the changing of attitudes is effected.

A slightly more complex analysis of treatment procedures is that described by Mary Richmond in her book *What is Social Casework?* published the following year. She says:[10]

> Before writing this page I tried the experiment of listing each act and policy of each social caseworker responsible, in the six cases cited, for the treatment described. This gave me six long items, many of which were duplicates. By combining these duplicates and trying to classify the items, I found that they fell under the two general heads of 'insights' and 'acts'. Each of these two divided once again—insights to include 'an

understanding of individuality' and 'an understanding of environment'; acts to include 'direct action upon the mind' and 'indirect action upon the mind'. Thus rephrased, my four divisions were:

A. Insight into individuality and personal characteristics.
B. Insight into the resources, dangers and influence of the social environment.
C. Direct action of mind upon mind.
D. Indirect action through the social environment.

Another early study that is of methodological as well as historical interest is that undertaken by a case committee of the Twin City Chapter of the American Association of Social Workers from 1925 to 1927. Recognizing that interviewing skills constituted an important part of casework treatment, the committee endeavoured to isolate and name the techniques used in ten interviews: two of the interviews were extracts from novels and eight were drawn from the experience of committee members. Altogether eighty-six different techniques were named. It is interesting to observe the extent to which classification appears to be influenced by belief as to what is important in the interviewing process.[11]

It was found that these techniques grouped themselves into general classifications as follows: (1) the techniques used for lessening tension in the interviewee; (2) techniques used for bringing or keeping the interviewee to the main issue; (3) techniques used for helping the interviewee to make difficult admissions; (4) techniques used for breaking defence mechanisms; (5) techniques used for influencing the judgment of the interviewee; (6) techniques used to help the interviewer gain time; (7) techniques used to help the interviewer recover from a bad start. . . . It is evident that our general classifications are really 'processes' and the committee has established, to its satisfaction at least, the conclusion . . . that a process is made up of one or more techniques.

In an account of the study, Pearl Salsberry lists the various techniques that appeared to fall into each of the above mentioned categories. The first category, for example, was made up of nine different techniques including 'simulated agreement', 'minimizing the seriousness of the interviewee's position', 'analysing a general statement into its specific parts', 'jollying', 'flattery' and 'explaining the agency'. The fourth category contained eleven techniques, described as follows: 'anticipating ultimate outcome', 'abusing for the defence', 'puncture', 'rushing', 'swaying by oratory', 'taking client off his guard', 'using acquired information', 'putting cards on the table', 'chasing into a corner', 'instilling fear' and 'negation'. A group of techniques which perhaps has a slightly more positive connotation is the fifth. It includes 'the

transition from known to unknown, reasoning from general to specific and from specific to general considerations, balancing alternatives, forestalling objections, using interviewee's phraseology, following his leads, restating the case, preparing for interviewee to state the plan, and yes-response resulting in clinching the argument.'[12] It is worth noting that silences were considered to constitute techniques in several processes!

During the decade 1929 to 1939 social workers in Britain and the United States were largely preoccupied with problems of unemployment and financial insecurity resulting from the economic depression and, in America at least, with the need to assimilate new knowledge from the field of psychiatry, and there appears to have been less interest in examining exactly what went on in casework interviews. The Milford Conference Report, however, published in 1929, identified 'three fundamental processes' of casework, and it will be observed that specific mention is made of the process of developing the client's understanding about himself, as opposed to the worker merely gaining an understanding of the client.[13]

The goals of social case treatment are both ultimate and proximate. The ultimate goal is to develop in the individual the fullest possible capacity for selfmaintenance in a social group. In attaining both immediate and ultimate goals three fundamental processes interplay at every point: (1) the use by the social caseworker of resources—educational, medical, religious, industrial—all of which have a part in the adjustment of the individual to social living; (2) assisting the client to understand his needs and posssibilities; and (3) helping him to develop the ability to work out his own social programme through the use of available resources.
. . . We could list the 'treatment services' given on the statistical cards used by social casework agencies but they would give merely the bare bones of what is involved in social case treatment. The flesh and blood is in the dynamic relationship between social caseworker and the client . . . the interplay of personalities through which the individual is assisted to desire and achieve the fullest possible development of his personality.

Other attempts to classify casework methods published during the 1930s include those by Susan Burlingham,[14] Fern Lowry[15] and L. M. Hambrecht,[16] in three papers on differential diagnosis and treatment.

An author who has done a good deal of work on this subject and whose analyses of treatment methods are more familiar in this country is Florence Hollis. One of her earliest formulations was published in 1939 in her book *Social Casework in Practice*. She divided treatment processes into 'those aiming to improve the environment in which the person lives and those attempting to increase the client's capacity for meeting whatever environment he finds himself in'.

Under the heading 'Reducing environmental pressures' she distinguished direct relief of external pressures by the worker from activity which encourages the client himself to bring about changes in his situation. Under 'Reducing the inner pressures' she identified four main ways in which the caseworker can assist the client to deal adequately with his own reality: (1) by bringing about modification of an inadequate or an over-restrictive conscience; (2) by lessening the need for repression; (3) by reducing feelings of anxiety, inadequacy, and defeat; and (4) by helping the individual to see more clearly the nature of outer reality and his own relationship to it.[17]

Subsequently Miss Hollis revised this classification. In 1949, in *Women in Marital Conflict*, she pointed out that previous treatment classifications had referred sometimes to methods and sometimes to aims and said that her own revised scheme was based on the means (i.e. the processes and techniques) of treatment rather than on its objectives. She outlined four major casework processes:[18]

Environmental Modification. . . . the steps taken by the caseworker to change the environment in the client's favour by the worker's *direct action*.

Psychological Support. . . . Encouraging the client to talk freely and to express his feelings . . .; expressing sympathetic understanding of the client's feelings and acceptance of his behaviour; . . . interest in the client, . . . desire to help; expression of . . . confidence that a way can be found to improve the situation, confidence in the client's ability to solve his difficulty, to make his own decisions; . . . direct encouragement of attitudes that will enable the client to function more realistically as well as more comfortably.

Clarification. . . . Usually accompanies psychological support . . . The dominant note . . . is understanding by the client of himself, his environment, and/or people with whom he is associated. It is directed towards increasing the ego's ability to see external realities more clearly and to understand the client's own emotions, attitudes and behaviour . . . The client must be encouraged to talk freely about the situation that is troubling him . . . Sometimes the caseworker makes direct interpretations concerning the effect of significance of the client's actions or reactions or of those of others with whom he is associated. More often the worker merely asks questions or comments on inconsistencies and inappropriate emotions. Always the effort is to help the client to think more clearly, to react more realistically, and to plan more wisely.

Insight. Insight development involves carrying understanding to a deeper level than that described in clarification . . . Current and past emotions must be relived in a therapeutic atmosphere in order that some of the affect may be discharged and in order that irrationalities

may be brought so clearly to the surface that they can be recognized, at first in the safety of the treatment situation and later in real life.

This classification was criticized by Dr Edward Bibring[19] on the grounds that the four concepts were on a different level of abstraction, but it has nevertheless been widely quoted (for example, in *The Probation Service* by Joan King,[20] *A Primer of Social Casework* by Elizabeth Nicholds,[21] and other volumes) and is obviously still being extensively used in courses of professional training. Sometimes, unfortunately, it appears to have been misquoted or quoted out of context, with the result that the inexperienced worker may gain the impression that the ultimate in skilled casework is the use of the fourth method. Florence Hollis herself specifically stated that psychological support was the most useful method with persons facing severe stress; infantile, immature individuals who are essentially in need of guidance; persons suffering from severe neuroses, severe psychosomatic difficulties and mild psychoses. She suggested that insight development could be considered with mildly neurotic persons, but only if the person desired it, could participate in it and benefit from it, and that psychological support was a valuable alternative. She further stated that full and regular psychiatric consultation was *essential* for caseworkers attempting to use insight development. It may be of interest to note that Miss Hollis looked at fifty-one cases, which seemed to have been skilfully handled and in only four of them was this method of insight development used and then along with other methods. She said: 'It is obvious . . . that the emphasis in treatment falls heavily in the area of clarification and psychological support, with environmental support also important and insight development used in only a very few instances.'[22] She also observed that in *the distressingly large number of cases in which clients terminated treatment the caseworker had not created a sufficiently supportive atmosphere*.

Several other classifications of casework treatment methods were published about this time, the one by Lucille Austin contained in her paper 'Trends in differential treatment in social casework' published in 1948 being particularly comprehensive.[23] She differentiated between two main methods in casework, 'social therapy' and 'psychotherapy', subdividing psychotherapy into 'supportive therapy', 'intermediary or experiential therapy' and 'insight therapy', and analysed each of these in terms of the goals involved and the techniques used.

These classifications indicate the extent to which social workers in the United States were making use of the concepts and methods of psychiatry and it therefore seems appropriate to refer to one of the most important of the psychiatric texts published during this period. Dr Franz Alexander in his book *Psycho-analytic Therapy* wrote in 1946:[24]

We can easily distinguish two general types of

psychotherapy—supportive and insight (uncovering) therapy. Supportive therapy is used primarily for the purpose of giving support to the patient's ego with no attempt to effect permanent ego changes; uncovering or insight therapy is used primarily for the purpose of achieving a permanent change in the ego by developing the patient's insight into his difficulties and increasing the ability of his ego to deal with them, through the emotional experiences in the transference situation. Since both types of approach are present in almost all treatments, however, this distinction is not absolute.

Thomas French, writing in the same volume, also considered that there were two main types of therapeutic approach 'which are employed in endless combination according to the requirements of each particular therapeutic problem', but he named these as 'Manipulation of the Environment' (supportive therapy is included in this category) and 'Modification of Behaviour Patterns'.[25] In 1953 and 1958 the Family Service Association of America and the Community Service Society of New York published somewhat similar analyses of casework.[26]

Meanwhile Florence Hollis in a paper presented in Boston in 1955 indicated that she had revised her earlier fourfold classification and said that she had come to the conclusion that there were really only two major forms of casework treatment—'supportive treatment' and 'development of self awareness'. Both forms of treatment had the aim of improving the individual's functioning, but supportive treatment attempted this without substantial increase in self understanding, whereas the latter aimed to increase the individual's awareness of previously hidden aspects of his feelings and behaviour. She wrote:[27] 'The most important distinction between the two forms of treatment lies in whether or not an attempt is made to bring suppressed material into consciousness, for as soon as we move in the direction of uncovering hidden material we move in the direction of arousing anxiety.'

In a more recent article Miss Hollis elaborated on this very important theme. She pointed out that development of self awareness, involving clarification and investigation of suppressed or uncomprehended material, makes great demands on the client's ego for several reasons. First because in order to encourage self examination the worker has to refrain from making reassuring comments at points where they could be made. This may mean that temporarily the client's discomfort is increased. Secondly, feelings of anger towards the worker as the source of the discomfort may be aroused in the client. Thirdly, if the client is able to think about material that has been suppressed or is consciously painful, there will inevitably be a period of increased anxiety until he has come to terms with it. Fourthly, the very business of becoming aware of and laying aside certain defences means that

he is more exposed and therefore more vulnerable to pain and discomfort.

She continued:[28]

For these reasons it is essential that when [development of self-awareness] is undertaken the worker be certain that the client has the kind of ego that can sustain itself during a period of tension without recourse to too much regression, extensive additional symptom formations, unwise acting out, or immobilization.

Furthermore, one must be sure that the techniques used in bringing suppressed ideas to the surface do not unloose more buried material than the caseworker knows how to deal with. The individual in other words must be one with a healthy capacity to both repress and suppress painful material. Otherwise both worker and client will be overwhelmed by the mental content that is unleashed when suppressed material is invited to full consciousness. This is a point particularly to be kept in mind, for it is a great temptation when people talk easily about their life experiences and feelings to think that they would be admirable candidates for this kind of help, when in actuality the very opposite may be true. Some psychotics talk very easily about things which less sick people would keep deeply buried in the unconscious.

Clarification and the pursuit of causative understanding of the self must be used sparingly. In actuality only a small proportion of our work is predominantly of this type. With many clients it should not be used at all. With many it is not needed. It should be a major tool of treatment only when the client's personality organization is relatively sound or where a circumscribed area which brings relief with a minimum of anxiety can be clarified, where the nature of the psychosocial dysfunctioning makes it appropriate, where motivation toward self-understanding can be developed, and where there are appropriate safeguards in terms of the worker's skill and the availability of psycho-analytic consultation. . . . In general the milder forms of symptom neurosis and neurotic character. When such procedures are used with other types of personality patterns it should be with caution and with particular attention to the client's anxiety and the handling of it.

Miss Hollis's latest work *Casework—A Psychosocial Therapy* deals exhaustively with these and many other aspects of casework treatment. It is the most comprehensive and ambitious book yet to have appeared on the subject and will be referred to again, when the present theoretical position is considered. In the meantime, two case illustrations may help to bring home the particular points discussed above.

In the first case a social worker tried to assist an adolescent youth towards the development of self awareness in the sincere belief that if the boy could gain insight into the connection between his barely suppressed aggressive feelings against authority and the poor relationship which he had experienced with his father, he would be better able to deal with them. All the evidence showed that, far from being 'mildly neurotic', the boy was a very immature individual with poorly developed defences against anxiety and precarious controls over his behaviour. In interview, however, the worker ignored the lad's unresponsiveness to his questioning, and in between long periods of silence probed steadily away. Every defence put up by the boy was 'seen through' and interpreted despite the latter's increasing tension. Finally, after three-quarters of an hour, the boy was dismissed with the injunction that he 'should think further about his feelings'. The worker was surprised and saddened when his client smashed the office window on the way out and careered down the street kicking at parked cars and splintering most of the milk bottles in sight.

The second case is that of Mrs T, a 31-year-old married woman who applied for help to a psychiatric out-patient clinic. At the time she was hallucinating and suffering from numerous phobias and obsessive compulsive symptoms to the extent that she was almost incapacitated. She was afraid of being alone, going out, answering the telephone, going upstairs, and was preoccupied with thoughts of death, accidents and suicide. A detailed history was obtained, which revealed that she had had an extremely disturbed background. At the intake case committee it was felt that the severity of her symptoms contra-indicated any attempt at insight therapy, and the psychiatric registrar (in his second year of post-graduate training) to whom she was assigned for treatment, was advised to use a supportive approach. From the outset, however, the psychiatrist made extensive use of uncovering and insight directed techniques. At various times he interpreted her defences, encouraged the expression of hostile feelings, and there was much discussion of sexual problems which she clearly found very disturbing. She began to be silent in interviews, then to miss appointments, and finally withdrew from treatment altogether. She stated that she felt she was not getting anywhere and felt too uncomfortable during interviews to continue.

The following year Mrs T again approached the clinic for help. She was in a state of panic and gave the impression of being a very sick woman. Once more her application was considered by the case committee and again supportive therapy was recommended. This time she was assigned to a caseworker. During the first interview she talked disjointedly and at great length, expressing extreme aggression towards her small son who she was afraid was becoming homosexual, intense fear and hatred of her mother and father, and a sense of profound unworthiness. She felt hopeless about her marriage and began to describe incidents in her very early childhood which she knew had given rise to her present fears and also recalled dreams which had upset her. The caseworker wavered between permissively listening to this outpouring of feelings, implicitly encouraging their expression by 'going along' with Mrs T's recollections of traumatic events in her early childhood, and offering active support and reassurance. During the next two or three interviews this pattern continued and gradually the caseworker, like the first therapist, was drawn into making occasional interpretive comments, with the result that Mrs T became increasingly ambivalent about continuing treatment. In reviewing the course of interviews in some detail it became clear that, following the use of exploratory and interpretive techniques, Mrs T would become resistant and disturbed, but better integrated after support had been given.

The caseworker wrote in an interim summary: About Christmas time she appeared torn between her wish to continue seeing me and to experience a corrective emotional relationship that was in many respects helpful to her, and what I now think to be her need to protect herself from my techniques. Following the holiday she 'forgot' an appointment, and it was then that I decided to use consistently supportive techniques, no matter how many opportunities she provided for discussion of her underlying problems. During the subsequent two months of supportive casework she has made good progress. Her relationship with her husband and children has improved, her appearance has altered for the better and she has shown many signs of increased ego integration. As her dependency needs have been more adequately met at home, so she has become less dependent on interviews and these have now been reduced in frequency.

The closing summary, written three months later, went as follows:

During the final three months of treatment progress has been maintained; Mrs T's pseudo-neurotic symptoms have almost entirely disappeared and she is now able to lead a fairly normal life. My techniques have continued to be primarily supportive and discussion of her problems has been indirect, for example in the context of her children's development, films she has seen and so on. As her anxiety has lessened and as her symptoms have been replaced by more healthy defence mechanisms, she has been able to move on to a constructive consideration of her basic problems, to gain some insight into the origin of these and to put her increased understanding into practice in the form of modified behaviour and attitudes towards her family. Mrs T has expressed much satisfaction in her improved condition and ability to function in the roles expected of her. She recognizes that she has not resolved all her problems, but feels realistically that she is able to manage independently for the time being.

These cases are, of course, extreme examples, but they serve to underline the point that as caseworkers we must know what we are doing. As Miss Hollis has reminded us, our methods must always be evaluated in relation to 'the nature of the problem, the client's motivation and the capacity of his ego to deal constructively with anxiety'.[29] Most of us, I think, instinctively employ supportive methods with the vast majority of persons who come for help in difficulty; nevertheless there does appear to be some tendency, particularly amongst partially trained or inexperienced workers, to regard these methods as something less than 'real casework' and to attempt to use an approach that may not be merely inappropriate, but in certain cases actually harmful. In a psychiatric setting, for instance, a patient can usually protect himself from techniques that arouse too much anxiety by failing to keep appointments. The probationer, however, is not in this happy position. If he neglects to report he commits a breach of his probation order. It is extremely important, therefore, that all caseworkers acquire skill, through training and experience, in establishing different types of relationships with different individuals and in utilizing a wide range of treatment techniques appropriate to the needs of each. As Charlotte Towle said in 1946, some clients become confused, anxious and frustrated in a neutral casework relationship and it is then advisable 'to be supportive, that is to use authority, meet dependency, impose demands and convey moral judgements in a sustaining way, so that the individual may become more self-determining or, at least, less self destructive in his behaviour.'[30]

At the present time many new social work training courses are being established in this country and it behoves those who are concerned with casework teaching to pay particular attention to the differential aspects of casework. Otto Pollak pointed out in a recent article that the principles of casework appropriate for treatment of neurotic clients have by and large been generalized in the sub-culture of the profession, so that problems arise when social workers are confronted with, for example, persons suffering from character disorder. He postulated that if most caseworkers have a neurotic type of personality, then it would be within their own experience that the treatment process is liberating rather than binding.[31] There is a good deal of evidence to support the hypothesis that workers do tend to use with their clients those methods that they may personally find or have found to be helpful. It has, for instance, often been observed that casework students and psychiatrists in training, as they gain insight into their own personalities, frequently attempt to use interpretive techniques with their patients or clients. When the response to these is unfavourable, the student may complain to his supervisor that he has not been assigned

a suitable client (patient) or that he is unable to do 'real' casework (psychotherapy). It may take a year or more before he begins to appreciate that the majority of his clients may require help of a supportive nature only and that supportive techniques can and do bring about changes in attitudes and behaviour.

In some of the group experiments that are now being undertaken in this country there is a similar need to make sure that methods that have been used successfully to develop self knowledge in caseworkers are not employed indiscriminately with groups of acting-out adolescent delinquents. Careful selection of group members and the adaptation of techniques to their needs must be undertaken if we are to avoid many mistakes in group therapy.

I should like to turn now to one of the fundamental issues facing the caseworker, namely how to help a person overcome the difficulties which are affecting his life in society. The point has been made that the skill of helping lies not only in the careful assessment of the individual and his situation, but also in the differential use of the professional relationship and associated casework techniques. No matter how experienced we are we all need to review frequently our own practice and to ask ourselves what our particular tendency is in casework. Do we adopt a rather stereotyped approach with everyone—anxious mother, delinquent youth, ambulatory schizophrenic alike—or do we vary in the relationships we establish? Are we always permissive and accepting, or (benevolently) authoritarian? Do we habitually listen passively, encourage the expression of feelings, explore our client's early backgrounds; or is our tendency to take an active part in interviews, offering advice and suggestions, and setting limits? It is so much easier to observe the characteristic approaches of our colleagues in casework than to know our own. If we think that we do tend to react similarly to different clients, is this because it is 'us', because we believe this to be the correct casework approach, or because it really seems to work best in all cases? If we vary our methods, what is our rationale? Do we respond intuitively 'playing it by ear', or have we some ideas born of our own and other peoples' experience about the kinds of methods that are successful with different kinds of individuals that enable us to meet appropriately their differing needs?

The development of casework in the United States makes fascinating reading. We are told of marked pendulum swings from overactivity and directiveness to excessive passivity and drifting, from over-intellectualized analysis of cause and effect relationships to unscientific wallowing in feelings and belittling of intellectual knowledge, from indiscriminate use of social resources to exclusive exploration of emotional factors.[32] Yet at the same time, from the literature reviewed above, we see how during the inter-war period particularly the differential methods of casework were being worked out. The techniques developed by Freud, which so influenced American casework in the 1930s, arose chiefly from his experience in the analysis of neurotic disorders—disorders which appear, in retrospect, to have been related in part to the prevailing social system. Nowadays, as Otto Pollak has pointed out, our society seems to support the development of character disorders. 'Id gratifications are prominently offered in overt and hidden form, while the waning power of generally accepted morality leaves the super-ego forces unsupported.' No longer can caseworkers rely solely on the liberating techniques that were so useful (in America) in pre-war years in helping persons to free themselves of sexual and aggressive inhibitions. We must now turn our attention to developing methods that are equally useful with individuals who have too much feeling flowing into action, too little sense of guilt, too few inhibitions —methods that lead to the development of a sense of social responsibility in the client without being a cover for counter-transference reactions;[33] in other words a more skilful, conscious use of the good parent type of relationship that has long been used by caseworkers and found to be effective.

Within recent years certain caseworkers in this country too have been working out for themselves the principles of differential treatment. Elizabeth Irvine in a paper on 'Research into problem families', published in 1954, drew attention to the extreme immaturity of many parents of such families and outlined the methods of help which seemed to have proved most effective. For example she wrote:[34]

The worker has most chance of success if he plays the part of a warm, permissive and supportive parent, thus supplying the basic experiences of the early stage of socialization, which for some reason the client seems to have missed. With great patience and tact, the client can sometimes be led through a phase corresponding to that in which the child likes to 'do it with mother' to one in which he begins to taste the satisfaction of 'doing it myself'.

Dr T. A. Ratcliffe expressed similar views in 1957,[35] and both these authors subsequently published valuable papers on the differential use of relationship which should be read in full.[36] For the purpose of this article, however, an extract from Dr Ratcliffe's later paper is given as it is especially relevant.[37]

The most important criterion of assessment [for relationship therapy] is the level of emotional and social maturity of the client . . . in terms of capacity for and experience of relationships . . . There are many clients whose early experience of relationships was so unsatisfactory that they were never wholly able to work through the initial experience of relationships within the family, the 'give and take' of such contacts, the feeling of being approved of, the capacity to internalize controls and standards, and so on. In brief they have failed to mature in this respect. They feel inadequate, and unsure of their

contacts; they still see situations narcissistically; they react badly and often impulsively to frustration and criticism. Such people need a parental relationship through which they can experience the relationship patterns they have not had; and thus a parental relationship appropriate to the 'maturity level' which the client has reached. This assessment of maturity level, and of the role needed in the relationship, is often a technically difficult task; and it may require a number of interviews to complete.

In general authors on both sides of the Atlantic have approached the subject from a developmental point of view and have laid stress on the importance of a thorough understanding of the stage of emotional maturity reached by the individual and on the use of an appropriate relationship and techniques. Reiner and Kaufman[38] give a most useful exposition of the use of a 'nurturing' relationship with immature persons suffering from character disorder, while M. L. Ferard and N. K. Hunnybun[39] describe in the main methods of casework more suited to those with neurotic disorders. Michael Power in his review of Ferard and Hunnybun's book *The Caseworker's Use of Relationships* writes:[40]

Maybe it is because this book describes so well certain kinds of casework that it becomes clearer that there are other kinds, all equally informed and guided by the same theoretical principles based upon psychoanalytic theory, but different in their techniques and application of the theory. That described in this book may be best used to help people whose ego is reasonably well developed and who have a fairly clear sense of identity, but who are beset with problems, the solution of which seems elusively beyond their grasp and who need additional insight before they are able to attain sufficient control over their own feelings and their environment. Different would be the immature people who need the experience of a relationship in which they can grow and gradually and painfully attain some degree of psychological maturity before they can be expected to carry the responsibilities of adults.

Several authors draw a distinction between those individuals who, whatever their chronological age, are still emotionally at an infantile stage of development and therefore need 'primary' emotional experiences of love, care, shelter, control and guidance, and those who have to some extent matured beyond infancy, but whose unsatisfactory experiences have given rise to conflicts, defences and inhibitions which cause problems in living, and who need corrective 'secondary' experiences.[41] (In psychoanalytic terms, the distinction is between the pre-oedipal and post-oedipal stages of development; in clinical terms it is between the psychopathic personality, character disorders, and the neuroses.) This developmental approach to the client provides a valuable guide to treatment. From our observation of his present mode of functioning, it is possible to deduce with a fair amount of accuracy the nature of his past experiences, the chief sources of anxiety, the adequacy of the defences against this and the stage of maturity that he has reached. For instance, the individual who has difficulty in establishing satisfactory relationships, who is excessively demanding, who lives solely in the present and cannot postpone immediate satisfactions for the sake of long term gains, and who has a very inaccurate perception of reality, has probably experienced insecurity in childhood and is likely to need the support of a casework relationship which provides consistent love, care, firmness, and frustration when necessary, a relationship which gradually and continuously adapts as he becomes capable of greater independence and acquires a better understanding of the outside world and capacity to satisfy his needs in socially acceptable ways. In contrast the relatively adequate, well integrated person who is able to function successfully in many areas of his life, who comes for help with some neurotic problem affecting his relationships, may come from a comparatively stable, perhaps rather inhibiting background. His need may well be for a permissive relationship. Always the caseworker's aim should be to understand the basic source of anxiety and to alleviate it in some measure through the provision of new, satisfying and maturing experiences.

The Association of Psychiatric Social Workers put it thus:[42]

> The casework relationship is not the same for every client, but should, as far as possible, be adjusted to meet the varying need of different clients. One important function of the casework relationship is to supply in some measure those experiences necessary for satisfactory emotional development, which have been lacking in the life of the individual client. Thus an inhibited and submissive client may need to be encouraged to speak his mind to the worker, and to express his feelings of criticism and dissatisfaction as a prelude to developing the ability to stand up for himself in other situations. On the other hand, a client whose pattern of behaviour is to control and exploit people until they eventually throw him over, may need to have a relationship with someone who resists all attempts to manipulate him, while remaining friendly and sympathetic. Thus the balance between firmness and permissiveness has to be finely adjusted to the needs of the client, and should not be influenced by the worker's own need, for example, to control situations himself, or to keep on the right side of everybody.

An experienced worker with advanced training recently said in the course of a case discussion, that he felt that he did not have 'sufficient ammunition to knock a hole in (the client's) wall of defences'. This and similar remarks which are made all too frequently suggests that (in this country at least) too little attention has been paid in casework courses to the constructive functions of defences and the need often to conserve and support these in casework.

Anna Freud in *The Ego and the Mechanisms of Defence* postulated that the individual develops defences against anxiety (i.e. a state of tension which it is beyond the person's capacity to master) arising from three sources—the super-ego, objective reality, and the instincts. Super-ego anxiety is the easiest to relieve. As the individual develops a relationship with a worker who is accepting and non-condemning his sense of guilt and the unconscious conflict decreases, and he becomes able to permit cautious expression of instinctual urges and feelings. Clients suffering from super-ego anxiety sometimes find their way to a probation office—their offence may have arisen from a wish for punishment, but more often they will be seen in psychiatric clinics and consulting rooms, in marriage guidance offices and in child guidance clinics. The permissive interviewing techniques which have been developed in these settings are usually most helpful to them.

Individuals suffering from 'objective anxiety' (i.e. that arising from external circumstances) are well known in most social work agencies. Problems of food, accommodation, money, work, adverse family relationships, and so on are the special province of the caseworker. Techniques, such as material help, sympathy, interest, advice, discussion, clarification, are often of great help here.

The third type of anxiety, 'instinctual anxiety', is considered by Anna Freud to be the most difficult to alleviate, particularly in an analytic situation. She writes:[43]

> The only pathological states which fail to react favourably to analysis are those based on a defence prompted by the patient's dread of the strength of his instincts. In such a case there is a danger that we may annul the defensive measures of the ego without being able immediately to come to its assistance . . . This most deadly struggle to prevent itself from being submerged by the id . . . is essentially a matter of quantitative relations. All that the ego asks for in such a conflict is to be reinforced . . . In so far as analysis can strengthen it by bringing the unconscious id-contents into consciousness, it has a therapeutic effect . . . But, in so far as the bringing of the unconscious activities of the ego into consciousness has the effect of disclosing the defensive processes and rendering them inoperative, the *results of the analysis is to weaken the ego still further and to advance the pathological process* [author's italics].

It is with persons beset by instinctual anxiety that caseworkers seem to be increasingly concerned. The suggestion that our present society in its swing away from Victorian morality has tended to ally itself with the id forces has important implications for social work. Free expression of instinctual drives in direct form is incompatible with civilization and some social workers, particularly those employed in penal settings, are entrusted among other things with the important function of helping those who have poor control over their urges to develop greater capacity to endure frustration. Techniques which relieve anxiety and strengthen precarious defences, such as consistent acceptance, limit setting, reassurance and understanding discussion within the context of a positive relationship are most likely to be of assistance here. In an article on 'Casework and agency function',[44] Clare Winnicott rightly pointed out that in probation, for example, the delinquent may be

> unconsciously looking for a human being to become a respected and controlling authority, because this is just what he had been deprived of in his family relationships . . . The probation officer can humanize the machinery of the law but he cannot side-step it without missing the whole point of the symptom and the needs of the client. If he does miss the point, the client either gives up hope or commits another offence to ensure the re-instatement of legal machinery.

J. St John quotes a probationer who complains that his probation officer had not been strict enough: 'If he'd given me a good telling off, it might have been different. I'd have pulled myself together like. Even when I'd been up for a breach he still gave me the old syrup. After that probation seemed a farce.'[45]

In casework with psychotic or near-psychotic patients the psychiatric social worker has a similar responsibility to support and strengthen that part of the patient's personality which is in touch with reality and which may be threatened by an eruption of instinctual impulses, and this means the ego, including its defensive operations. Mrs T, the patient referred to earlier, is an example of a borderline psychotic who needed much ego support. Attempts to increase her genetic understanding of her difficulties merely led to an increase in anxiety amounting to panic. Only after she had succeeded in re-establishing necessary defences was she able gradually to start working things out for herself and to begin to perceive how her present irrational fears were related to her past experiences.

Sufficient has been said to indicate that caseworkers need to apply themselves with renewed thought to 'the art of doing different things for and with different people'.[46] The point has been made that skill in casework does not lie only in the use of a small range of techniques directed towards the development of self-knowledge, although this does demand skill of a kind, but in the careful assessment of the social situation, personality structure, stage of development and sources of anxiety of each individual, and then in the sensitive, flexible, discriminating use of appropriate methods of help. Depending on the changing needs of the client at any particular time, we may be warm or detached, active or passive, directive or permissive, verbal or silent, moralistic or non-judgmental in our approach. As Florence Hollis points out in her latest book:[47]

> The treatment of any person is an individualized blend of procedures, themes, and goals. The nature of the blend is not a matter of individual worker artistry or intuition, important though these may be. On the contrary, choice and emphasis follow definite principles and rest upon most careful evaluation of the nature of the client's problem, external and internal causative factors and their modifiability, the client's motivation, and pertinent aspects of his personality. In addition, there must be comprehension of the nature, effects, and demands of the different types of casework procedures and of the criteria by which the worker can match the client's needs and capacities with the particular combination of procedures most likely to be of value in enabling him to overcome, or at least lessen, his difficulties . . . The evaluative process is an ongoing one, with the emphasis in treatment varying in harmony with the changing needs and capacities of the client.

That a careful blending of techniques is necessary in almost all cases is now fairly widely recognized in the literature.

The following short interview illustrates well the skilful, even if intuitive, use of a variety of casework techniques. It demonstrates an unselfconscious ability to communicate with and to adapt to the swiftly changing needs of a person in distress, and repays careful study.

> Sandra is a 16-year-old girl from an extremely disturbed background who spent four years at a school for maladjusted children, but who had eventually to leave because of her difficult behaviour. Turned out of home by her mother, she had problems over work and accommodation, and committed offences for which she was placed on probation. Then began a long period of shelter and hostel life with many changes of residence, Sandra making more and more demands on her probation officer.
>
> The previous day Sandra had attempted to 'phone me, but I was not available. She then visited the clinic and had a scene with the psychiatrist and refused to return. Her outburst at the clinic was mainly directed towards me.
>
> To-day she called and went as usual straight to the waiting room. I was unaware that she was there and was engaged on the 'phone. Suddenly there was a frenzied knocking on the door and a furious face looked round and demanded, 'How

much longer have I to wait?' I replied, 'I am engaged on the 'phone—would you please sit in the waiting room?' She was furious. When free, I invited her in and she said, 'May I telephone Miss L at the YWCA? It is important.' I said, 'Yes' and in an arrogant manner she went to the 'phone, but the line was engaged. She tried again and again and then threw down the telephone, using some extremely foul language. I said, 'Sandra, would you please not use this language?' For fully two minutes her jaw trembled and with difficulty she held back the tears. She then turned and said, 'You don't understand me, only Miss L does.' I replied, 'You are missing Miss L quite a bit, aren't you?' She did not reply.

The atmosphere was still very tense and she then walked over to a drawer in which I keep quite a number of personal things, including some small boxes with jewellery. (Christmas gifts from probationers.) Like a child she went through each of the boxes and played around for quarter of an hour in this way. She then got up and went to the mirror in my room, and started to pin up her hair. During this time I said nothing. She suddenly turned and said, 'So this means that when my probation is over I shall not be able to come here.' I replied, 'You know you will always have a place here. After all, haven't you been treating me as your mother over the past few months?' She answered with a smile on her face, 'My mother doesn't nag like you.' I then said, 'And what have I been nagging about?' to which she replied, 'Work and how I hate it. If only I could marry a wealthy man.' I said, 'Even a wealthy man would not want to see his wife lying in bed all day. No marriage can last in that way.'

We then went on to discuss her inability to get up in the morning and her depression, but she tired of this, or did not want to discuss it, and began to yawn. I began to put my papers away and asked her if she would like to accompany me along the street to the station. Before leaving the office she made a circle round a date on the calendar and said, 'This is my birthday.'

We walked along the street looking at a number of shops. It was a pleasant evening and she now seemed fairly happy. Suddenly and quite naturally she took my arm. At the station I purchased her ticket to the hostel and my own ticket home and said goodbye.

This article has been an attempt to summarize some of the thinking that has gone on during the past forty years about the methods of social casework and the principles which seem to be emerging concerning their differential application. (For example the principle identified by Miss Hollis that 'the more fully and deeply the worker encourages the client to know himself the more caution is needed in making certain that the client's ego is able to deal constructively with the anxiety likely to be aroused'.[48]) The value of supportive methods of help has deliberately been stressed because so much of the casework literature published in this country during the 1950–60 decade focuses on the interpretive type of work appropriate for relatively mature and well integrated individuals, and students and others seemed to be gaining the impression that this was the method *par excellence* to use with all clients. Studies such as that undertaken by Noel Timms[49] of what in fact social workers actually do in interviews are of course a most useful corrective to such impressions, but as yet few have been attempted in Britain.

It may be debated whether in the final analysis different methods and techniques have any real significance in casework. Elizabeth Irvine in 1956 emphasized the importance of the caseworker's attitude and commented on the fact that different workers obtain satisfactory results with a variety of techniques, and that any given technique could prove unsuccessful if counter-transference becomes predominantly negative.[50] Paul Halmos in a more recent article reminded us of the central place of love in various forms of psychotherapy, and questioned whether the expression of this love could be accurately described as a skill, which could be technically mastered and used deliberately.[51] I am sure that most of us would agree with both these writers that the worker's positive attitude of love and concern for the client is of far greater importance than the means by which it is expressed. But surely the mode of expression is also important. The issue is not 'Love or skill?' (to quote the title of Dr Halmos' paper) but love and skill. If casework is to be of help to the many different persons facing various problems who come to social work agencies, both these elements are essential. Love is of basic significance even when it is clumsily expressed. How much better in a professional service that it should be allied to knowledge and skill and expressed in ways most suited to the client's needs.

As caseworkers we try to communicate with a wide range of individuals in many different situations, to understand their anxieties and the manner in which these are concealed or expressed and to offer appropriate help in a form most acceptable to them. We may be required to perform some short-term material service; we may have to provide the long-term 'nurturing relationship' described by Kaufman and others[52] in which an emotionally deprived, infantile individual experiences closeness and trust, identifying with the caseworker before becoming able to function more successfully and independently—the type of casework that has been developed by Family Service Units; or perhaps with a mildly hysterical client, the need may be for a more reflective, detached approach. Such flexibility and discernment in helping does not come naturally to most of us and it is therefore important that we should be cognizant of the various methods of casework that have been identified and develop skill in using them to greatest effect.

References

1 Mary Richmond, *The Long View*, New York, Russell Sage Foundation, 1930, p. 374.
2 'The nature and definition of social casework', reprinted from *Journal of Social Casework*, Family Service Association of America, 1949, p. 3.
3 M. Brooke Willis, Foreword to *Casework in Child Care*, Jean Kastell, Routledge & Kegan Paul, 1962, p. ix.
4 *British Journal of Psychiatric Social Work*, 6(3), 1962, p. 126.
5 ibid., p. 128.
6 'The psychiatric services and the social services: II. probation', *Ventures in Professional Co-operation*, Association of Psychiatric Social Workers, 1960, pp. 82–4.
7 *British Journal of Criminology*, 4 (3), January 1964, pp. 241–51.
8 T. P. Domanski, M. M. Johns and M. A. G. Manly, 'An Investigation of a Scheme for the classification of Casework Treatment Activities', unpublished thesis, Smith College School for Social Work, Northampton, Mass., 1960.
9 *The Family*, 3(7), July 1921.
10 New York, Russell Sage Foundation, 1922, p. 101.
11 Pearl Salsberry, 'Techniques in casework', *The Family*, 9(7), July 1927, pp. 154–5.
12 ibid., p. 156.
13 *Social Case Work, Generic and Specific: an Outline. A Report of the Milford Conference*, New York, American Association of Social Workers, 1929, p. 29.
14 'Differential diagnosis as a basis for selection in a family service agency', *Diagnostic and Treatment Processes in Family Social Work*, New York, Family Welfare Association of America, 1935, p. 2.
15 'The client's needs as the basis for differential approach in treatment', *Differential Approach in Case Work Treatment*, Family Welfare Association of America, 1936, pp. 5–6.
16 'Psychiatric and social treatment: functions and correlations', *Psychiatric Quarterly*, 2, July 1937, pp. 391–423.
17 Family Welfare Association of America, 1939, pp. 294–9.
18 New York, Family Service Association of America, 1949, pp. 147–52.
19 'Condensation of the discussion', *Journal of Social Casework*, 30(6), June 1949, p. 258.
20 Butterworth, 1958, pp. 69, 75.
21 Columbia University Press, 1960, pp. 3–11.
22 Florence Hollis, *Women in Marital Conflict*, pp. 156–8.
23 *Journal of Social Casework*, 29(6), June 1948, pp. 203–11.
24 Franz Alexander and Thomas French, *Psychoanalytic Therapy*, New York, Ronald Press, 1946, p. 102.
25 ibid., pp. 132–40.
26 Family Service Association of America, *Scope and Methods of the Family Service Agency*, 1953; Community Service Society of New York, *Method and Process in Social Casework*, Family Service Association of America, 1958.

27 'Personality diagnosis in casework', *Ego Psychology and Dynamic Casework*, ed. H. Parad, Family Service Association of America, 1958, p. 86.
28 'Analysis of casework treatment methods and their relationship to personality change', *Smith College Studies in Social Work*, 32(2), February 1962, pp. 113–14.
29 ibid., p. 117.
30 'Social casework in modern society', *Social Service Review*, 20(2), June 1946, pp. 165–79.
31 'The treatment of character disorders—a dilemma in casework culture', *Social Service Review*, 35(2), June 1963, pp. 128–31.
32 Annette Garrett, 'Historical survey of the evolution of casework', *Journal of Social Casework*, 30(6), June 1949, p. 223.
33 Pollak, loc. cit., p. 127.
34 *British Journal of Psychiatric Social Work*, no. 9, May 1954, p. 27.
35 'Personality factors', *The Problem Family*, Institute for the Study and Treatment of Delinquency, 1958.
36 Elizabeth E. Irvine, 'Transference and reality in the casework relationship', *British Journal of Psychiatric Social Work*, 3(4), 1956. Republished in *Relationship in Casework*, Association of Psychiatric Social Workers, 1964, pp. 53–66; T. A. Ratcliffe, 'Relationship therapy and casework', *British Journal of Psychiatric Social Work*, 5(1), 1959.
37 'Relationship therapy . . .', p. 4.
38 B. S. Reiner and I. Kaufman, *Character Disorders in Parents of Delinquents*, Family Service Association of America, 1959.
39 Tavistock Publications, 1962.
40 'Varieties of casework' (review article), *Social Work*, 19(4), October 1962.
41 See, for example: B. E. Dockar-Drysdale, 'The outsider and the insider in a therapeutic school', *Ventures in Professional Co-operation*, Association of Psychiatric Social Workers, 1960, pp. 13–14.
42 *The Essentials of Social Casework*, 1963, p. 2.
43 *The Ego and the Mechanisms of Defence*, Hogarth Press, 1954, pp. 69–70.
44 *Case Conference*, 8(7), January 1962, pp. 181–2.
45 *Probation—The Second Chance*, Vista Books, 1961, p. 34.
46 M. Richmond, *The Long View*, loc. cit.
47 *Casework—A Psychological Therapy*, New York, Random House, 1964, p. 243.
48 'Analysis of casework treatment methods and their relationship to personality change', p. 115.
49 *Psychiatric Social Work in Great Britain (1929–1962)*, Routledge & Kegan Paul, 1964, pp. 105–8.
50 'Transference and reality in the casework relationship', p. 62.
51 Love or Skill?' *New Society*, 3, no. 77, 19 March, 1964.
52 Irving Kaufman, 'Differential methods in treating persons with character disorders', *Smith College Studies in Social Work*, 32(3), 1962.

III. 3 Once more, with feeling

Helen Harris Perlman

[. . .] Casework is the process in social work which has recently been under closest examination not only by its denigrators but also by its concerned representatives. It has had more critical scrutiny by research studies than have other social work methods. It warrants our sober attention lest more evidence accumulates suggesting that this form of help has little significance for the people to whom it is addressed.

To begin with, let us note that it is important that casework practice be placed under the microscope of research. Perhaps the lenses of that microscope are not finely ground enough and the specimen-weighing scales are not finely calibrated enough to catch the subtleties which may be of moment. But casework help has been a socially supported endeavour, costly in time, energy, and money, so it is only sensible that we begin with whatever crude instruments we possess to gauge its efficacy and outcomes. Moreover, such assays have considerable potential value to the present and future teaching and practice of casework. They may be upsetting, but they may also open doors held shut by custom and convictions.

One thing learned from these studies is that caseworkers have oversold themselves and their influence and its possible or probable outcomes. They have promised, both implicitly and explicitly, especially in the public family and child welfare services, that if enough caseworkers existed with enough time and skill, people would be taken off relief, moved out of ghettos, rehabilitated and so on. The 1962 amendments regarding public assistance services were probably based on these assumptions. What had not been faced—has it been faced today?—was that no amount of individualized help, skilled and competent though it is, can be more than individualized help. It can do no more than deal with one person or family who, at a given time and place, is suffering the effects of what

may be an endemic social problem. Lack of money, jobs, medical resources, adequate housing—these are social problems made up of complex socioeconomic-political factors. No amount of reparative or restorative work person by person, family by family, can affect poverty (though it may affect a poor person) or slum rot (though it may affect a badly housed family). Other forms of social action, not casework, are required for problems that inhere in the social fabric.

Yet so deeply does the puritan ethic of personal responsibility persist in us that professional as well as lay persons have continued, often unconsciously, to believe a person, by some combination of will, get-up-and-go, and casework, can clamber out of the disadvantageous social situation into which he was born or forced. Some people can and some do. It is also true that some by their own actions slip in to the quagmire. But the quagmire is there, and social casework is not the form of social action that can or will clear it out.

> In the past we have tended to persist indefinitely in attacking problems and in dealing with situations in which casework service was not the answer. We are coming not only to recognize the futility of persisting in situations which are beyond the scope of casework help but to realize also our social responsibility for revealing the inadequacy of social casework in these instances, in order that interest and effort may be directed toward social action. . . . Let us cease to be the great pretenders. Casework . . . cannot substitute for certain other lacks.

That was Charlotte Towle, one of casework's spokesmen, writing in the 1930s. Still, for many reasons that cannot be examined here, casework remained social work's major mode of help. When at last, in an economy of abundance, people began looking at the remaining invisible poor, there arose a cry of shock

Source: E. J. Mullen and J. R. Dumpson *et al.*, *Evaluation of Social Intervention*, Jossey-Bass, 1972, pp. 191–8.

and indignation that caseworkers had not done anything about massive, rapidly festering social problems.

We are all agreed that we have taken too long to grasp that social situations exist beyond the scope of casework help and that social casework is inadequate in these instances. Some of us still seem to blur out the difference between a social problem and the individual who suffers. There is yet another facet to this problem of our unwitting pretense. The person who suffers a social problem may want help with it; he may want to escape it, get rid of it, be provided with what he lacks, to have his deficits filled in. He may need and want someone to provide him with resources and with what he thinks he needs and to advise, guide, and counsel him, too, because as a human being he has problems common to all men. But money, employment, housing, health are first things for all of us. If social conditions are such that these primary things cannot be had or if the caseworker cannot make them available or if they do not yet exist in the community, then the victim of a general social problem feels he has been helped only negligibly. Yes, his caseworker was a nice person, he didn't mind talking with her, but what help or change was seen or pointed to or valued? When people's basic needs dominate their thoughts and their lives, a helper must be able to provide means by which deficits can be eliminated. If he does not, hope for, and experience of and assessment of change will be minimal, probably insignificant by present statistical measures.

Although technical faults may be found here and in these studies, nevertheless, it is clear that each was individually and carefully designed, according to preconceptions and hypotheses regarding the particular problem to be tackled, the maximal conditions of testing, and the expected outcomes. But the process being studied—casework—was not designed at all. There is no evidence that the caseworkers sat down and asked themselves exactly what services or provisions people with needs and deficits would want and find useful, nor did they ask what reasonable results might be anticipated. Or what, if any, special emphasis or forms of psychological influence toward change might be called for and utilized. Or, what the client's perception of service might be and, consequently, what clarifications and agreements would have to be reached. And so on. Instead, one repeatedly receives the impression that caseworkers are turned loose on clients, adjured to do casework or give casework, as if casework help were a thing to be bestowed upon a person or an immutable process, or as if casework help bore small relation to the nature of the material with which it is involved.

The nature of the material with which one works by the process called casework is an individualized socio-personal unit, one person or several, who are in some problematic transaction with a complex of social circumstances. That complex of persons with problems and those transactions determine what the focus of attention should be, what goals may be reasonably sought, and what kinds of interventions may achieve them. When a group of cases must be dealt with, some diagnosis or assessment of the particularities of the group is needed in order to design a blueprint for action. If the process is casework, each person or family is individualized within that group diagnosis. To say that a group is multiproblem or on relief or disadvantaged is not enough. One must also ask: what are the expected deficits and discrepancies between what the person wants and needs and what he has or can get, the expected disturbances or distortions of his perception, say, of the establishment representative, the social caseworker, in the light of his past experiences? And further why can't the people in this group cope unaided with their problems? Why don't they use the resources open to them? And so on.

In brief, a project that sets out to demonstrate the effectiveness of a process must assay the material and conditions with which that process is involved. Caseworkers take this requirement as an article of faith in their work with individuals, though there too it is more honored in the preachment than the practice. But examination and assessment of the probable needs, motivations, and capacities of a group of persons selected because of presumed commonalities have not occurred in these studies. Thus, the treatment offered or the forms of intervention provided have not been designed by if-then propositions.

There is a little evidence such design occurred in these studies of the effectiveness of casework; the most recently published study, the CSS-DSS Study, illustrates this lack. Those studied in this project were families going on relief for the first time. Caseworkers and researchers shared the assumption that this event would provoke a crisis in their lives. However, most of these families had lived in acutely precarious financial circumstances for some time prior to their acceptance of money; it is possible that going on relief was a small triumph, a release from anxiety and stress. If crisis were indeed the experience for most of these families, the casework design should have required immediate contact between caseworker and family at the white-hot point of felt hazard and disequilibrium. Actually the amount of intervening time was usually over a month. Crisis theory posits the impossibility of maintaining the intense feeling of need induced by crisis, and some leveling off is inevitable; thus, after a month on relief, the families' interest in casework intervention may have greatly declined.

Even if we allow for this possibility, we have no indication that what the professional caseworkers did was designed by the action theory of crisis. If it was, the study does not note it. If it was not, what was the use of the assumption that the families were in crisis? The casework services in Girls at Vocational High likewise were undesigned; they were business as usual for a group of already poorly functioning, distrustful, unmotivated girls. That was over a decade ago, but evidently, the intractable belief that casework is a package of services and techniques that can be delivered persists despite efforts to dislodge it.

It is not enough to say that casework is an individualizing process; legal and medical practices are also individualizing processes when they focus on individual cases; so are numerous other professional helping processes. We must clarify (1) the individually felt problems falling within the area of responsibility of social work as different from those which are the usual concern of other professions and (2) the conditions under which the method called casework is an appropriate social work mode and to what end casework may be utilized.

Within the purview of the whole profession of social work fall problems of person-to-person, person-to-group, group-to-group, and person/group-to-social circumstance interactions. Typically they are problems in daily social interchanges and transactions and in interpersonal relationships as experienced in their social roles. When a person (or family) finds such problems insurmountable by his own efforts or resources, he may seek or be proffered help to deal with them. Such help may make available the means by which his resource deficits are supplied or may stimulate his personal capacities for dealing with his situation effectively and satisfyingly or may do both. This help, casework, is a process focused on the person's felt need and is guided by assessments of his motivations, capacities, and resources. Its purpose is to enable a person (or family) suffering from a general social problem or a uniquely personal one to suffer less, to cope better, and, as a result, to feel able to deal with his tasks and relationships with increased confidence, steadiness, and satisfaction.

Focused on these purposes, the casework process does not even scratch a general social problem. It affects only this person or that family victimized by the social problem. True, in the course of helping an individual or family one often deals with and perhaps causes change in some large social systems which create or bear upon the individually experienced problem. Perhaps a whole school system is the cause of a single child's misery, his truancy, his failure to learn. His caseworker must attempt to deal with those persons and rulings that affect his problem. If the caseworker is successful, an environmental change has been achieved for one child. But the large system is likely to remain unmoved and intact. A caseworker may deal with the persons and forces that affect his client who is a patient in a large hospital system. This doctor, that nurse, this occupational therapist may be brought to a whole new way of dealing with his client-patient. But the caseworker cannot claim to have changed the system except in the individual instance. A by-product of the caseworker's efforts may occur if the individual case stimulates some general consideration toward change. But this occurrence is more rare than we piously hope and certainly cannot be counted on. In sum, the caseworker as a policy or program changer operates for his client; he is a case advocate. This is quite different from being a policy advocate who takes the system as his treatment target.

The basic condition for one person's use of another's help is that he both knows and feels he has a problem. He hurts, and he wants to be rid of that hurt or stress. The problem that he identifies, that he feels, and that he wants to be rid of is the crucial point of entry and connection between a client and his caseworker. Where his emotion is, there his motivation is. This point, not the social problem predefined by the caseworker or the researcher, is the starting point for giving help and taking help. It is not clear that this consideration governed the proffering of casework help in the situations under review here.

As one looks across the wide and varied range of people and problems dealt with by the process called casework the issues in education for social work interventions, even at the so-called micro-level, show themselves to be large and complex. In the effort to grapple with problems of what every caseworker should know, whether professionally educated or trained on the job, and what, in addition, only some caseworkers need to know, I put forth the following, tentatively, for consideration.

There are three main ways by which one can solve a problem or achieve some bearable relationship to it: by getting the material, tangible aids which meet present needs, such as money, a job, better housing; by having access to necessary social services so that they may be utilized in coping with the problem, such as homemaker help and child care facilities; by getting therapeutic guidance aimed toward changes of perception, affect, attitudes, and action so that the impact of the problem is decreased or the problem is dealt with more effectively than it was previously and the person's sense of mastery is increased in relation to it.

Each of these modes is contained within the problem-solving process of casework. Many cases call for all three sorts of help. Basic to each of them, to be taken account of by paraprofessionals and skilled caseworkers alike, are these elementary considerations: How the applicant-client sees his problem and what he wants to be helped to do about it should be the determinants of the caseworker's beginning actions. (Exceptions to this flat statement occur chiefly in situations where an individual's or family's 'clear and present danger' necessitates unasked-for interventions.) The need the client feels, the help he desires, the capacities and resources available to him should be the primary material for diagnostic assessment by the caseworker and the design for next steps in treatment.

Such next steps may simply be the relief of stress by the provision of necessary and symbolically vital means. Thereby a person may be freed to look ahead, to reconsider, to plan beyond the day. By the same token, all the compassionate support and reasoned guidance in the world cut little ice when one feels and is, deprived of basic needs. Unless the person is relieved of need-created stress, he tends to remain mired in frustration. Skills cannot replace goods in these instances. And although the client may be convinced of and grateful for his caseworker's goodwill and intent, he scarcely feels that any real help has been given him for the problem he finds central and omnipresent. [. . .]

III. 4 Casework and 'the diminished man'

Helen Harris Perlman

I think we are past the peak of the battle against casework. If I am not being made myopic by excesses of weariness or hope, I think we may speak of it in the past tense. It was a battle, waged with lethal accusations and crusader banners whose mottoes spoke to massive need for massive social action programs; in spots there were guerilla attacks, both unexpected and bewildering. At times some of us were bloodied and bowed too; some of us retreated from the turmoil; some of us made our way into the fray in the quest to understand why we were the enemy and what we could or should do to bring about a working coalition with those we considered our professional brothers.

I will admit that I have had my fill of being defender of the faith. It is not that I do not like a good fight about ideas or principles or purposes; I relish that. Being a defender, however, puts one into a heels-dug-into-the-ground position, and I should like to pull out and go exploring forward again. There is much yet to know, to think about and to do, even within the confines of that social work method called casework.

But first, one must take stock. The attackers of casework had—and have—a point; more than that, they have a just cause. Because of many good and bad reasons which cannot be examined here, the casework method for too many years had come to dominate social work and to be mistakenly equated with it. From nationwide governmental programs to two-person family agencies, there was an implicit belief that if only there were enough well-trained caseworkers, people in trouble could be enabled to cope with their social problems. We had banked on the great government programs of income maintenance and medical care to furnish the foundation for a living. We had lost sight of the forces and powers for human ill-being and misery that remained virulent and widespread, and in the wake of which any individual—

Source: *Social Casework*, 51 (4), April 1970, pp. 216–18.

client or caseworker—was helpless. As the spokesmen for social work, caseworkers had tacitly promised more than could be delivered by *any* one profession, whatever its nature or modes of operation. Those who attacked it, therefore, were attacking our sometimes naive and unwitting pretenses. They were calling for forms of social action based upon reforms of social policy and programs, some of which were within social work's long-marked-out (but scarcely scratched) turf, and some which called for social work alliances with popular and political as well as with other professional sources of power.

It is a long-needed movement that is sweeping through social work now. With some growing sense of their direction and some lessening of their romanticism, the 'social actionists'—whether they are community workers, social program planners and developers, consultants and stimulators to grass roots organizations, or government officials—are directing their energies now toward fighting the real enemy. That real enemy is not casework. It is social conditions that pollute social living, not only among the poor—although there the social smog is thickest—but across total communities.

Place and purpose of casework

Is there any valid place for casework in the purposes and programs of social work? To answer this question of place and purpose, we must take full cognizance of our identity. Casework is one method in social work.[1] It is not a 'thing' that can be 'given' to anyone; it is not of itself a service; and it is not an agency program. An agency whose program is to promote family welfare usually *uses* the casework method toward this end. It could commit itself to using a form of group work as its major helping mode, as indeed seems to be the case in those family agencies that are concentrating on family-group treatment. It could conceivably use community work methods, as in the organization of family groups in selected neighborhoods for parent-child socialization purposes. It could effectively use combinations of these three major methods. The casework method has this identifying characteristic: it takes as its unit of attention, as the unit to be helped, one person or one family, suffering some clear and present problem or obstacle to satisfactory or satisfying social functioning, either in carrying necessary tasks or in interpersonal relationships.

Is there then a place and purpose in social work for a helping process that, in the midst of recognized widespread social 'dis-ease,' gives attention to individual men and women and children who are in trouble and who ask for or need help?

If the answer is no, one stands on the edge-of-nihilism. If one cannot affirm the worth of the individual man one cannot affirm the worth of that man multiplied into mankind. There is no test of a social system or policy except as a measure of its effect upon individual well-being. There is no 'love of mankind' except as fraudulent rhetoric, unless there is compassion for a single human being. Casework is based upon the belief in the worth of each single person, whatever his class or creed or color, and upon the concern that when he bleeds he should be attended to. (I am simple-minded enough to say that I am not even averse to 'Band-Aids.' They are a considerable help in alleviating human hurt and in preventing further complications. They are not substitutes for major surgery nor for the complete reorganization of a hospital system. But this is not their function or their claim. Some services given by the casework method are certainly like Band-Aids. They not only make it possible for persons to carry on their necessary functioning, but they also serve as a preventive measure. Some other services given by the casework method are more closely analogous to more radical forms of medical treatment. In some instances the caseworker must use other forms of social work or other powers for attack upon the social sources of infection or wounds. But the caseworker believes that while these are being found and used, he who suffers must be aided.)

Not only do caseworkers affirm the moral question of each man's worth and right to be given the opportunity to achieve his socially approved goals, but there are some practical considerations too. A person's problems today will not wait for the wheels of justice or social reform to grind out change. Grind they must, and it is hoped that social work will accelerate them. But the man who is their victim wants help *now*, because his problems in personal and family life hurt now. And if these problems are the result of yesterday's causes, they are at the same time the causes of tomorrow's new problems.

We are not so naive as to believe that improved or even 'ideal' social opportunities and conditions (whatever those may be) result in human 'happiness' (whatever that may be). The evident fact is that improved social conditions bring with them a rising level of expectation within that intransigent, never-satisfied always striving creature called man. So, while a majority of persons might, under optimal social conditions, find themselves free to use their capacities and opportunities for self and family fulfillment, it is just possible that a substantial minority might find themselves needing or wanting more than they have, and looking to some institutionalized service conveyed in some individualized way.

It is interesting that no other profession has been censured or held culpable because of its individualized help. No one has said to the lawyer, 'Shame! You deal with your clients in antiquated courts run by often inadequate personnel and under often archaic law! Stop carrying these cases and attend instead to the necessary reformations in the legal system!' No one has said to the doctors or nurses, 'How irresponsible that you waste your time and energies in giving bedside care when there are thousands of people who need but cannot afford medical care, and when, moreover, there remain places in society that daily breed disease and malnutrition and mental sickness!' No one has said to the teachers, 'What a waste to give your attention to this child or that who is a maverick in your class, when the whole rotten school system needs overhauling!'

Perhaps the reason lies in what I proposed earlier: that in the past, individual help by the casework method was being proffered *instead* of and not *alongside* other modes of social work. I think—or hope—we are on the border now of mutual agreement: That the casework method is for helping individual people who are the victims (and sometimes the perpetrators) of social or psychological problems. But when the problems beset large sectors of the population, they must be identified, studied, and resolved or mitigated by other methods of social work and other relevant professions and groups.

Finally, I propose that casework serve—or is geared to serve—one purpose which cannot be brushed aside as trivial. Its existence stubbornly asserts the importance of individual man and of the individual, small, frail clusters of persons called families. (. . .)

Note

1 For a more detailed discussion of the author's point of view on this subject, see Helen Harris Perlman, 'Casework is dead', *Social Casework*, 48, January 1967, 22–5, and 'Can casework work?', *Social Service Review*, 42, December 1968, 435–47.

III. 5 Untrained neighbourhood workers in a social-work program

Gertrude Goldberg

Having spent its professional infancy severing ties with Lady Bountiful, social work may find itself enlisting the aid of another kind of untrained person, the neighborhood or indigenous worker. For increasingly, we note that the middle-class professional worker has difficulty both in developing rapport with lower-class clients and in offering them practical help with the everyday problems of slum life. The professional is unskilled or inexperienced in budgeting or shopping on a low income, in caring for a large family, in housekeeping under substandard conditions, and in using the public-welfare agencies as a client.

Fifteen neighborhood women were employed by a social agency as visiting homemakers whose job was primarily to teach low-income families greater competence in home management.[1] Assigned to a home for several full- or half-days a week, homemakers were to help families to improve their skills in such home-management tasks as shopping, cleaning, sewing, budgeting, taking care of their children, planning their time, and cooking.

In addition to home teaching, homemakers did a variety of other tasks, several of them indirectly educational. They offered some services traditionally done by case aides such as escorting persons to clinics and helping them to establish eligibility for public assistance or public housing (which were often efforts to teach the use of community resources). Like case aides, they also provided companionship or psychological support as part of a casework plan. Homemakers maintained a baby-sitting center where mothers could leave their youngsters while they did errands or kept appointments. Finally, they performed the mother-substitute or mother's helper type of assignment usually associated with homemaker programs when it became necessary to complement existing city-wide homemaker services.[2]

Source: A. Pearl and F. Riessman (eds), *New Careers for the Poor*, Free Press (Macmillan), New York, 1965, pp. 125–44, 148–52.

The visiting homemakers appeared to be helpful to a rather large proportion of the families served, many of whom were not likely to have been receptive to casework or counseling. During the first six months of service, homemakers were assigned to approximately forty-eight cases in which there were teaching components. Of these, only six families failed to show improvement in some area of home management or to learn how to use community resources more efficiently.[3] Among the cases regarded as failures in both respects were several in which the homemaker appeared to develop a good relationship with the client but where no noticeable changes in her pattern of behavior could be detected. In escort, mother-substitute, and companionship cases, homemakers were often very helpful although it is somewhat difficult to evaluate the results of contact.[4]

The apparent ability of the visiting homemakers to decrease the self-defeating behavior of low-income clients makes it important for us to try to understand their contribution to a social-welfare program. In this article we shall attempt to describe the fifteen women who served as visiting homemakers, their selection, training, and supervision. In addition, we shall analyze the reasons for their effectiveness, discuss the ways in which the maximum potential of neighborhood staff may be realized by a social agency, and describe the types of tasks they seem best suited to perform.

Recruitment and selection

Manner of recruiting

There were a large number of promising applicants for the position of visiting homemaker. Candidates were sought through various community agencies, by personal acquaintances of the supervisors who lived in the neighborhood, and by other applicants. Word was circulated that our agency was seeking neighborhood women for a position entitled 'visiting homemaker.' Within a month there were many more qualified applicants than openings.

Characteristics sought

In recruiting homemakers the agency sought persons whose social distance from our client group (the most deprived group in the community consisting mainly of low-income Puerto Ricans and Negroes) was considerably less than that of most members of the professional staff. At the same time, it was hoped that homemakers would have personality attributes considered important among candidates for social work and related professions. Among the women selected as visiting homemakers should be persons with skill in various areas of homemaking as well as some members of the same ethnic groups as our clients.[5]

Rejectees

A discussion of those attributes which led us to reject applicants will emphasize the kinds of persons selected from among the sixty-odd candidates. In general, we tried to avoid both those upwardly-mobile slum dwellers who tend to shun their less-striving neighbors and persons too deprived to be helpful to others.

We felt that by setting no formal educational requirements except ability to read, write, and fill out simple forms and reports we would be more likely to attract a lower-class group. However, we did turn down persons who seemed to lack a basic intelligence or who were unable to understand the service (e.g. unaware of how the position differed from domestic employment.)

We excluded persons who showed no special interest in the work and could not envision its offering more satisfaction than a factory job, for example. On the other hand, we were wary of those who emphasized the missionary aspects of the work to the exclusion of pecuniary rewards. Finally, if a candidate seemed to derive little satisfaction from managing her own home, we felt she would be unsuited to teach others.

Candidates who exhibited blatant prejudices toward minority groups, welfare recipients, or delinquents were considered unsuitable. Similarly, if they regarded themselves as utterly apart from deviant or severely deprived persons, they were excluded. For this reason, we were impressed when a candidate conceded that she could have used a homemaker at one time or that she had 'gone through some bad times.'

Selection process

Persons were seen twice, once by each supervisor, if they were at all promising. At an initial office interview we discussed the position of visiting homemaker, had them fill out a simple application, and got a general impression of their interest, availability and ability.

Applicants were asked to give three references other than former employers. We urged them to list as references community leaders such as school principals, ministers, and social workers whose opinions we might better evaluate. They usually tended to use friends' names, but we succeeded in obtaining at least one 'official' reference in most cases. However, it was probably a mistake to insist on these recommendations because we were not necessarily seeking persons with community connections. Actually, three persons who became quite satisfactory workers had no community leaders to recommend them.

We scheduled a home visit with those candidates who seemed to be good prospects. One reason for the home visit was that we hoped it would help us to assess an applicant's attitudes toward her home, homemaking, and family life. This second interview gave us a better opportunity to determine a person's proximity to the client population and to observe her in the more relaxed atmosphere of her home. In several instances, candidates who had initially seemed to be in good circumstances because they were well dressed at the interview actually lived in substandard tenements and appeared to have meager possessions.[6] More important, several of the candidates responded more spontaneously when they were interviewed at home. In the absence of trustworthy references, the home interview afforded us another chance to observe the candidate as well as an opportunity to see her in a less formal situation.

Characteristics of the homemakers

It was our goal to hire persons who, unlike many middle-class professionals, had natural rapport with the target population or the lower class. It seems important, therefore, in describing the homemakers to determine both how close they were to the clients and concomitantly how different they were from the professional staff. The fifteen persons who joined our staff apparently were able to help a large number of very deprived persons. Thus, either they were close enough to form relationships well with members of the target group, or, if they seem to be quite different from the clients, the social distance variable may be less important than we postulated. In either case, by describing the salient characteristics of the fifteen visiting homemakers, we shall be suggesting the kinds of indigenous persons who are likely to be effective neighborhood workers.

Social pathology

While we sought persons who were not so overburdened as to be unable to help others, homemakers were not by any means problem-free. To a much greater extent than professional staff who often have interpersonal problems, they revealed either at the onset, or in the course of employment, a wide gamut of social problems. At least five had close relatives, either sons or brothers, who exhibited serious social pathology such as drug addiction, desertion, delinquency, or school maladjustment.[7]

Income

The income of most homemakers was relatively low. Three of them were recipients of public assistance when they were hired. They were economically better off with their $4,000 per annum incomes as homemakers, perhaps supplemented by sporadic contributions of spouses or small Social Security benefits. One of these women commented that the salary for visiting homemakers was about as good as she could expect in view of her limited skill and education. One, and probably more, of those not receiving public assistance at the time of hiring, had an income low enough to qualify for surplus foods distributed by the department of welfare. Nine homemakers resided in low-income public housing projects. Four of those who lived in tenements were in very old buildings in problem-ridden areas. One homemaker lived in a middle-income, partially-subsidized co-operative. Only three had a family car. Most of their husbands (twelve were married) were steadily employed but in low-status occupations such as railroad laborer and elevator operator. The two most affluent women were married to a bass player in a well-known Spanish band and to a school custodian.

Attitudes toward work

It is sometimes maintained that working-class and lower-class persons regard work differently than middle-class people. For the former it is said to be 'just a job', a means of making money, or a necessary evil. Often low-status employment involves considerable physical activity, little cerebral effort, and highly routinized behavior. While the financial aspect of middle-class work is very important too, the middle-class employee usually has a more responsible job with a greater intellectual challenge than that of the lower-class worker. The middle-class person is sometimes a member of a profession which is associated with a way of life and a means of intrinsic as well as monetary satisfaction.[8] The middle-class, white-collar worker is thought to be more reliable and conscientious than the lower-class employee because his job is often more interesting and he is therefore likely to care more about it. The lower-status person is reputed to work only as hard as he has to.

Our experience with the visiting homemakers leads us to conclude either that they are not typical working- or lower-class women, or to question the assumptions regarding differential class attitudes toward work, or to conclude that this assignment evoked a conscientous response regardless of the employee's class orientation.

The homemakers responded very seriously to a demanding job. At times they seemed to resent being compelled to work so hard and complained of their fatigue. Actually, they drove themselves hard. With the exception of such vestiges of jobs with little responsibility as taking a two-week 'vacation' with one day's notice, or failing to be circumspect in

leaving messages when they called to report illnesses, they were very reliable. They were frequently more prompt than members of the professional staff and quite apologetic when they had to miss work. One voluntarily cut her vacation short to be available for shopping when a client's welfare check arrived. To miss a day's work was to fail one's personal obligation to the client rather than to be absent from a job.

Their enthusiasm and spirit were infectious. As a result, the supervisors were overburdened with work. Homemakers called us on weekends and in the evening to report 'successes' that could not possibly keep until Monday and to discuss what they termed 'emergencies.' Curiously, women who had walked close to misery all their lives treated every problem as an emergency once they were in the helping role.

Although anxiety over failure when steady work is scarce may account for some of their elan, their enthusiasm impressed even the usually impassive institutional personnel. Teachers in the neighborhood schools frequently lauded 'these dedicated women who are doing such a wonderful job,' at the same time faintly concealing their disdain for the 'cold' professional social worker. The administrator of the local welfare center declared to a group of new social investigators that 'these women are the best thing that ever happened to the neighborhood.'

The nature of this work seemed to be an important ingredient in their enthusiastic response. The job was deeply involved with the genuine needs of people, and in such a position it is hard not to take one's work seriously. One of the references we obtained from a former employer of a homemaker supports this conclusion. The respondent, who had employed the applicant as a children's nurse, described her as warm to the children but occasionally 'irresponsible' (e.g. would converse for long hours with the neighbor's cook when she was supposed to be cleaning the house). However, when the employer was ill or distressed, the candidate felt that she was needed and was especially conscientious.

The homemakers' orientation to the agency may also have contributed to their dedication. They were welcomed at a tea attended by the executive director and other administrative staff. They toured every division and were given an introduction to the various services by supervisory personnel. In the middle of the first week, one of the more noncommittal homemakers remarked, 'I took this job as if it were any other job, but now I see it's different: we really have a chance to do something for our people and our neighborhood.' Her statement indicated that a sense of self-help rather than 'pure' altruism had been generated. Another said quietly, 'We're kinda' proud to be here.' They began to feel both that the work was important and that they in turn would derive satisfaction and status from it.

Child care

The responses of most homemakers to caring for

children in our Center differed from a middle-class approach. Most of them persisted in offering custodial care (i.e. necessary physical care of the children) despite our having stressed the importance of playing with the children or supervising their activities. They felt it essential only to feed the youngsters, take them to the bathroom, and give them an affectionate hug or pat. In fact, they would have left the children in the playroom only returning to respond to a cry or to arbitrate a quarrel were it not for the constant prodding of the supervisors.

Manner of relating

The informality of the homemakers was noted by many of the more inhibited professional staff. One sucked lemons throughout a conference with the assistant director of the agency. At the staff Christmas party they distinguished themselves by 'twisting' with abandon, mostly with each other. They were disgusted with the men who stood around talking 'like faggots' instead of dancing; so they were forced to choose female partners. They were probably less self-conscious about dancing with members of the same sex than middle-class women would have been. The agency psychiatrist, who danced with one of them, asked her if he was doing all right. Undaunted by his dark vest and dangling watch fob, she replied, 'just fine, baby, but twist a little harder.' They were quite conscious of being less constrained and remarked that the professional workers needed something to drink before they could have fun whereas they required no artificial stimulant. They asked their supervisors if they were acting inappropriately but at the same time complained that many of the social workers were stiff and unfriendly.

Some of them had a saucy manner. They exchanged wisecracks with anyone visiting the Center who responded to their informality. One of them was describing Puerto-Rican foods to a group of school teachers when a rather pedantic gentleman asked, 'Is there any medical reason why you don't eat *platanos* [plantains] raw?' She retorted, 'Any medical reason why you don't eat potatoes raw?'

Some of the homemakers were annoyed with a caseworker with whom they had little rapport. A somewhat phlegmatic person, the caseworker gave vague responses like 'Well, what do you think?' or tepid affirmatives like, 'y-e-e-s.' One of the homemakers objected to her approach to a client. The homemaker described how the client, a crude, 'country' person with paranoid tendencies, was upset by the caseworker's repeating or mirroring what she said—e.g. 'You went to the department of welfare?' Instead of the desired psychotherapeutic effect of having the client look at herself or examine what she was saying, this person felt doubted, suspected. Possibly the homemaker reacted negatively because her own frame of reference or relationship, if not personality structure, was closer to the client's than to the worker's.

Social attitudes

We felt that a certain proximity to slum life would free neighborhood staff from some of the negative attitudes toward clients which is sometimes found in middle-class professionals. However, this assumption was not necessarily valid, for we found that even those persons who have themselves lived in poverty, nonetheless have many of the prevailing middle-class attitudes towards the poor (e.g. that persons are responsible for their social circumstances, that those who do not pay for a service are getting a 'favor' and have relinquished the right to make demands on the dispensers of that service). These attitudes may stem partly from negative self-images and internalization of the majority viewpoint; but they could be also the familiar reaction of persons who have bettered themselves, even if slightly, toward the group from which they have risen.

It is important to recognize that pejorative attitudes toward the deprived are not only shared by the middle classes and the more striving members of the lower-classes but by the better-functioning low-income persons as well. After all, one must shun the delinquent more when one lives on the same street or in the same housing project with him. We were, in effect, asking our indigenous staff to walk through those very doors which they had managed to slide by most of their lives. Significantly, several of our clients were considered notorious by homemakers who knew their reputations.

Real vs. assumed attitudes

Some of the homemakers' attitudes toward the poor seemed middle-class. Yet, one had to distinguish between what they really thought or said among themselves, and what they believe others want to hear and, in effect, demand of them. In some layer of their personalities, unlike persons who have not experienced economic and social deprivation, they both felt and knew that social opportunities are important and middle-class norms and values do not necessarily apply to their way of life.

Early in her employment, we gave a homemaker some material on teenage behavior prepared by one of the large insurance companies. She accepted the interpretation without qualification, and when we questioned her, the only argument she supplied in its behalf was that it was 'just what the teachers say.' On another occasion she was upset by a school principal's extreme concern over a pornographic note written by her eleven-year-old daughter. When we helped her to separate her opinions from the judgment of the principal, she conceded that such notes are quite common and certainly not worthy of an emergency call to a parent.

The disparity between this middle-class compliance and genuine attitudes was illustrated during a training session when one of the Negro women rudely denied that color affected one's opportunities. 'If you do not get a job, it's your own fault,' she maintained. Later we learned that she was one of the staff who most keenly felt and expressed the sting of inequality. Once she plaintively asked a supervisor if she thought the time would come when people would judge her as a person instead of as a Negro. Such a blatant denial of her opinions as she initially attempted suggests that she was not accustomed to express her feelings candidly in a mixed group, particularly in the presence of a middle-class person who was also her supervisor.

Social class

In much of this discussion we have referred to 'the homemakers' as if they were a homogeneous group and have also implied that this group was lower-status, probably somewhere between lower-class and working-class.[9] They were neither the 'down and out', although some have been at one time or another, nor the stable working class with skills, homes, and cars. They were, however, obviously different from middle-class professional personnel and from the clerical staff, as well. One simply could not visit the homemaking Center without tasting their salt; one could enjoy the flavor or prefer something more bland. They, in turn, felt different and thought they had a distinct contribution to make. In the ensuing section, we shall try to analyze that contribution and to account for their success.

The homemaking relationship and role

The capacity of homemakers to develop rapport with their clients is evident from a cursory reading of cases, even some where failure is noted. Above all, one is impressed by the unusual feeling of warmth between worker and client. The relationship resembled that of friends rather than of worker and client. Like friends, they were usually on a first-name basis. Significantly, some homemakers felt snubbed when they were not treated cordially by a client, e.g. offered coffee or a snack. We sometimes felt such reactions were inappropriate to the helping role partly because we failed to recognize the friendliness implicit in such responses. Clients spoke of going to a party or other social events with homemakers, and they would come to the Center to chat or visit when there was no pressing problem or official business. It is not surprising that clients revealed themselves quickly to homemakers and that a homemaker could obtain in a few visits what would have taken her supervisor quite a number of interviews. Other indications of the warm relationships are the mother who asked a homemaker to be the godmother of her child or the young woman who wanted her homemaker to be the matron of honor at her wedding.

Although the homemakers were usually better off or better able to manage than most of their clients, there was a lack of *felt* social distance. There was, of course, less actual disparity in life circumstances between indigenous staff and clients than between clients and professional workers. The position of neighborhood worker in relation to clients was illustrated when a homemaker introduced a client to some friends whom they met while shopping. This client was flattered and thanked her. Although the worker and her friends had some 'status,' they were within the pale of the client's set, visible enough to respect and aspire toward. Similarly, a homemaker, in speaking of one very poor housekeeper, remarked, 'I wouldn't see her socially.' Although the worker was being snobbish, the thought of social contact with the client occurred to her whereas it probably would not have entered the mind of the professional worker.

The difference between our ability to form relationships and that of the homemakers was apparent when supervisors introduced a neighborhood worker to a family. We sometimes felt like inhibiting influences. When we left, they could speak their own language or vernacular. We were eager for the homemaker to return to the office, for she and the client would often have conversed freely and fully. They had something to talk about instead of problems—the neighborhood, a mutual friend, a place on the island if they were both Puerto Ricans, or other common experiences.

One indication of the lack of condescension is the reciprocity between client and worker. For example, one family gave a homemaker some surplus butter they did not intend to use. Although her income was too high to get surplus foods, they felt she could use the butter and wanted to thank her for her help. When a homemaker lost a family member, two clients who had heard the news in the neighborhood, went to the funeral parlor or paid a condolence call at her home. Another family surprised a worker by bringing gifts to her on Mothers' Day. A housewife stopped by the Center to tell a homemaker about some bargains because the worker had given her so many good tips previously. The homemakers were not perceived as belonging to the 'giving class.' And, in turn, clients did not see themselves as the 'receiving class.' Homemakers were neighbors, perhaps a little better off, but, nonetheless, persons with whom one reciprocated and exchanged.

It would be inaccurate to stress the warm feeling between homemakers and their clients without also pointing out that homemakers in some respects were less accepting than trained middle-class staff. As noted in our section on their social attitudes, they sometimes looked down on deprived people and they were contemptuous of persons who managed less well than they in what seemed to be comparable circumstances. A few homemakers were particularly offended by slovenly housekeepers. Those who had budgeted thriftily when they were penurious or had adjusted to a husband's desertion had difficulty understanding persons who handled their troubles with less pluck. They tended to be less disciplined in their responses to clients than professional workers. For example, they would fail to recognize that to berate a deprived client for inappropriate behavior was often to compound her deprivation. Similarly, they would show favoritism to one child in a family, scold a deviant youngster by saying, 'If you were my child . . .,' or become offended when a client was not 'grateful' enough.

Ironically, these 'mistakes' and rather punitive attitudes impaired relationships between workers and clients less than might be expected. For example, a homemaker with genuine contempt for a wretched housekeeper nonetheless helped her to improve her housekeeping. Rather than reacting negatively to the worker's judgmental attitude, the family responded warmly to her. It is possible that the professional worker may also harbor prejudices towards clients but tends to express them in subtler ways that are nonetheless apparent to low-income clients. Then, too, the discipline of the professional worker may seem colder or more rejecting to the client than the homemaker's direct, candid reaction even when it is harsh. Social-class and professional barriers may be more inhibiting in the helping role than personality factors. Another reason for this seeming paradox may be the one we shall discuss below, namely the difference in the type of helping roles performed by professional and indigenous workers.

Although homemakers were in some respects less accepting than professional workers, they were more tolerant in another. They did not perceive people as problems, or at least, they disagreed with professionals about what constitutes a problem. They could understand why a client refused to discuss interpersonal problems when her welfare check had not arrived. Such behavior would not be considered 'resistance.' Somehow Mrs Smith was less forbidding to the homemaker than to the caseworker. To the homemaker she was well-meaning, easily misunderstood, temperamental—'She falls out with everyone but me.' To the caseworker she was, 'paranoid, rejecting and abusive to her children.'

The homemakers reacted to physical 'emergencies' and were quite annoyed when caseworkers did not treat these conditions rapidly. On the other hand, they thought professionals made too much over 'little things.' 'That child didn't try to commit suicide; he ran up on the roof to hide.' More important, deviance did not suggest hopelessness or that people were beyond help. And indeed, homemakers sometimes may have brought about changes in persons who seemed too self-destructive to be aided. One young woman seemed determined to be killed by her common-law husband who had already stabbed her several times. With a homemaker's support, she managed to take him to court, decorate her apartment, and to obtain badly-needed medical care for herself and her children. Recently we learned that she had gained enough skill in using community resources to escort a neighbor to the clinic. It is not as though homemakers could not diagnose psychological causation, e.g. that a child did not 'want' to hear, but they were less prone to assume it and, they were not trained to emphasize psychological problems.

Type of helping role

It is perhaps misleading to speak to homemakers as untrained, for it suggests that they were unskilled. Yet, as we have suggested, they had considerable ability to cope with their environment and therefore much to offer a client who was less resourceful than they. They knew how to live on a low income, to stretch leftovers, to use surplus foods (including powdered skim milk and canned meat which must have the preservative removed before it is edible), to buy inexpensive material and sew an attractive garment with it, to recognize a bargain. They had taken care of a large family and planned their schedules well enough to have some time for themselves. They were both skilled and experienced in caring for young children. They knew what detergents would best clean an icebox or a stove and which made sense on a low income. They knew their neighborhood, what stores were good, and where bargains could be found. They also had learned how to deal with the local merchants. In fact, they insisted on accompanying a supervisor to the food stores because they feared she would be cheated. They were familiar with the neighborhood clinics, the welfare center, the child health stations, and the schools, and they could show a client how to fend with these institutions—not like a professional who relies partly on the agency's power and partly on his polish, but the way a lower-class person does it for himself.

A homemaker's know-how makes it possible to get by on a little, to negotiate life in a slum. She exploits every opportunity—the barber school for free haircuts, the thrift shop, the remnant heap, free recreation, public clinics, surplus foods (if she qualifies or if her neighbors do and don't use their supply). She is not under any illusion that it is easy to get ahead. But she creates some regularity and routine, some security, and some freshness amidst the uncertainty, the squalor and chaos that surround her.[10]

The position of visiting homemaker permitted the neighborhood worker to impart her skill and know-how to clients. The following are some clients' descriptions of the homemaking service:

The homemaker didn't talk about how to shop or bargain or sew. She showed me how, helped out, lent a hand, went along when I might have been afraid to go alone. When we went to the project office to ask them to fix the broken window, nobody hit her when she spoke up for me. She didn't do all the talking for me. I said enough to have the courage to do it alone next time. If we'd just talked about how to ask them to make a repair it wouldn't have helped.

When she came, we got things done together— she ironed while I cleaned, or sewed while I cooked. When we budgeted and shopped I found it was possible to have a full icebox even when you live on welfare. I also began to believe that a cleaner house and a better way of running the house would really make a difference to the kids and me.

It was awful nice to have her around. She was someone to talk to. I don't have much of a chance to get out and see grown folks. It seemed like the only people I knew were the kids. The time went fast when she worked along with me. I hardly knew we were working. Meantime she got me into the swing of things; she kept talking about having a routine or a schedule. Sometimes she made it a little easier for me to do things. Like she stayed with some of the kids while I took the others to clinic or came along to help watch a few during the long wait. Sometimes when I had to go somewhere she would come early to help me feed the kids and get them dressed. Once she even made dinner when I came back from welfare feeling too tired to do anything.

The important component in this admittedly idealized description of the service is not so much the homemaker's personality or her ability to form a relationship with the client but what she could do for and teach the client. If, for example, a child were sick, and they went to clinic, the homemaker served as interpreter, guide, and supportive companion. When this type of active and immediate service was offered, the client did not have to ask what might be called relationship questions. The service itself demonstrated the worker's concern.

The role of the visiting homemaker led to a friendly, peer relationship. If a worker shops, sews, or cleans with a client, she is perceived differently from someone who offers help from behind a desk. Homemakers performed the same kinds of physical and domestic tasks as the clients, who did not have to wonder, as did one client about the author, 'Do *you* cook, Mrs Goldberg?' In addition, a worker who spent considerable time (a half or whole day, several days a week) in a client's home was likely to develop an informal relationship with her. Under those circumstances, they may have got on each other's nerves, but the homemaker would not seem distant or aloof.

The issue of dependency

A homemaking service in which the worker actually did some of the client's work might be expected to conjure up severe feelings of dependency that would limit effective use of help. It was our observation, however, that while some clients did rely too heavily on a homemaker, hostile feelings engendered by excessive dependency usually did not keep them from being helped by the service nor did such feelings, if they were in fact present, need to be handled in any depth through casework intervention. Frequently the client became more restive as she became more efficient, and we felt this was an appropriate response and that the service should be gradually reduced, if

not terminated quickly. Sometimes a client would resent demands made on her by a homemaker (e.g. if she had to work much harder than usual in order to move to a new apartment) and would discharge her. If we were convinced that the client could use additional help and that she would be unable to accomplish an important task without us, we attempted to prevail upon her to keep the homemaker until it had been completed.

Some clients either became overly dependent on the homemaker or tried to use her as a maid. In the former case, we slowly tapered the service; in the latter, we carefully instructed the worker to do household chores only when the client did, and if the client could not respond to this setting of limits by working along with the homemaker, we probably could not help her and would have to withdraw completely. In this approach, we were using a time-honored method of social work: doing *with*, not *for* the client.

The nature of an indigenous staff is another factor which may mitigate problems of dependency in a service for low-income clients. We have noted that there seemed to be less condescension between homemaker and client than between professional worker and client and that there was, instead, reciprocity and friendship. The relatively small social distance between homemaker and client may have made it easier for the client to accept help. The homemakers seemed like older, better-established women who traditionally help neighbors who are less capable or experienced. They also conveyed to clients that they had themselves faced similar problems. What they were doing for clients was for the neighborhood as well as for the particular individuals being helped. Their assistance to clients therefore benefited them. Homemakers may have communicated a sense of their self-help to clients who in turn did not need to feel so grateful. [. . .]

Tasks suited to an indigenous homemaking staff

Teaching the newcomer, the young housewife, or the inadequate homemaker how to manage and to exploit community resources was the most significant task done by homemakers. Here they were imparting the methods they had themselves acquired in coping with slum life. Homemakers did group teaching or community education as well as individual assignments. That is, they could offer sessions to groups of clients on such homemaking subjects as budgeting, shopping, cooking with surplus food, and sewing.[11] Unlike a class taught by a professional home economist, these were informal activities. There was no basic orientation or scientific approach to cooking or meal planning. Lower-class clients are likely to be more responsive to an informal approach because they can identify more readily with the leader and because the presentation will not be academic.

Education of professional personnel was another important task of an indigenous staff. A neighborhood worker can help to bridge the gap between middle-class staff and the lower-class community. For example, homemakers introduced school teachers in the neighborhood to Puerto-Rican cuisine by cooking them a meal and talking to them informally about the various *productos tropicales*. The workers' enthusiasm and pride was intended to help teachers gain more respect for the Puerto-Rican culture. Homemakers also explained to professionals how it feels to be a newcomer, to try to talk to a teacher when you do not speak well, to live in public housing, or to receive public assistance. In addition to developing the professional's understanding of the culture of poverty and of various ethnic groups and underprivileged minorities, the indigenous worker can help the professional know how he is perceived and how certain of his methods and techniques are viewed by lower-class clients.

There is a specific community-organization task which homemakers can perform. If community resources such as a public clinic are under-used because of poor transportation, then failure to obtain medical services is not simply a matter of self-defeating patterns of behavior. In such a situation, indigenous workers could involve residents in a campaign to secure adequate transportation. Similarly, shopping and budgeting may be difficult because neighborhood stores have over-priced items as do many shops in slum areas. Also, members of certain ethnic groups have to spend time traveling out of the neighborhood to purchase special products. Homemakers could organize a boycott, visit a merchant, or publicize exploitative practices in the newspaper in order to alter those conditions which inhibit sound home management.[12]

The mother-substitute homemaker service performed by our homemakers is not new to social work but can be offered more effectively as a neighborhood program. There are several reasons why a neighborhood-based homemaker service is preferable. Because of its proximity to clients, workers can be assigned more rapidly. A smaller, neighborhood program is also likely to involve less red tape. Further the service can be shaped to the particular problems and needs of the neighborhood. Finally, the homemakers are thoroughly familiar with the homemaking resources if they are assigned on a neighborhood- rather than city-wide basis.

Child-care out of the home or a group baby-sitting service is appropriately staffed by neighborhood workers. The homemakers were ill-suited to develop a formal program or to cater to what might be called nonessential needs of children. They were, however, perfectly able to give adequate physical care while parents did errands or kept appointments. They might also be used to help organize cooperative baby-sitting groups among low-income residents, staffing them initially to encourage participation and to demonstrate the usefulness of such a facility but eventually turning the task over to participating parents.

Conclusions

An indigenous staff can be an invaluable part of a social agency's efforts to help low-income clients, providing the agency appreciates and knows how to realize their potentiality. Untrained neighborhood workers are sometimes viewed as poor substitutes for professionals, hired because of a shortage of funds or trained staff. Consequently, the goal of supervision, training, and administration may be to make them as 'professional' as possible. The aim is sometimes to teach them without learning from them. (Of course, they must be oriented to agency and social-work goals as well as freed, if possible, of social attitudes and actions which are clearly hostile and damaging to clients.) Because we would sometimes prefer to hire professionals if given the choice, we tend to seek upwardly mobile slum dwellers or middle-class persons who lack social-work education. We find such persons, who usually serve as case aides, easier to get along with than lower-class persons because they are more likely to share our values. Unfortunately these middle-class and middle-class oriented workers also share our difficulties in developing rapport with clients. They have neither the know-how of the lower-class worker nor the skill of the trained worker.

To a certain extent a lack of respect for the work of lower-class neighborhood staff stems from a clinical approach to the problems of the poor. We have acknowledged that our neighborhood workers were indeed unskilled when it came to psychosocial diagnosis and to psychotherapy. They were neither caseworkers nor case-aides. However, if we regard social deprivations as critical barriers for many lower-class clients, then providing them with skills for coping with difficult management problems (as well as expanding social opportunities) is an important goal of social-work practice. In this type of social treatment, an indigenous staff can make a substantial contribution. Even where there are severe psychological problems, bread-and-butter difficulties often need to be alleviated before the client can concentrate on inner or intra-psychic help. In several of our cases the homemakers' help with environmental problems was an important prelude or concomitant of psychological treatment by the casework staff.

A truly professional service is one in which diagnosis is based on social as well as psychological problems or in which the role of the total environment is recognized. Based on this comprehensive understanding, help is then offered by the staff best qualified to assist the 'client-in-situation.' In seeking the most suitable staff, it is important to acknowledge the limitations of trained workers, who, as we have emphasized, cannot be expected to know how to manage a low-income household or to cope with slum life. It is, however, possible to find neighborhood workers who have this competence and who can thus make it possible to offer a professional service.

Notes

1 The homemaker service and a number of the observations and conclusions of this article owe a great deal to the imagination and skill of my colleague, Dorothy Yates. In preparing the text, I am also indebted to Florence Galkin and Phyllis Melnick for their careful reading and thoughtful suggestions.

2 Homemakers were part of the casework department of a social agency. Some families with whom they worked were receiving help from a caseworker either in that agency or another. In these instances, the supervisors of the homemaking program, both social caseworkers, participated in case planning with the referring worker but rarely saw the family except in emergencies or to introduce, interpret, or terminate service. Where the homemaking need was primary or the only one a family was willing to deal with and they were consequently not receiving casework help, homemaking supervisors handled the necessary caseworker as well as case planning and supervision of homemakers. Usually the casework role entailed referral to and intervention with social agencies, particularly the department of welfare. Homemakers sometimes reported progress informally to caseworkers or spoke to them regarding day-to-day problems that arose in a household. Case planning and evaluation of the client's use of the service, were, however, done by homemaking supervisors and caseworkers, with the homemakers participating in preliminary discussions and occasionally, in the joint conferences.

3 These figures do not pertain to changes in interpersonal relationships, nor is there any claim that a family was 'cured'. Rather, each of the families with whom we had some success learned to cope better with some aspect of home management.

4 To measure the effectiveness of the homemaker service a much more specific evaluation covering a longer period is, of course, necessary. The impressionistic evidence given above is all that is currently available and is cited only as a general indication of the value of neighborhood workers.

5 While the project described above had predetermined entrance requirements, it is the thesis of the principal authors that prejudgment of qualifications for aides prior to training may preclude both those most in need as well as those most able.

6 It has been observed that today's poor are misleadingly well-clad. However, they are well-dressed but nonetheless ill-housed and ill-fed. See Michael Harrington, *The Other America: Poverty in the United States*, New York, Macmillan, 1962, pp. 4–7.

7 Because of the social problems of neighborhood staff, it was necessary to spend considerable supervisory time offering casework help (mainly referral) to those who requested it. We referred a daughter to a vocational guidance service, obtained casework service for a brother, discussed a marital upheaval, saw a homemaker's mother who was concerned about a delinquent son, etc. In addition to the obvious justification of this use of time, that of extending help to persons who asked for professional assistance, we felt it an important supervisory role. The homemakers would never have believed we cared about people and, in turn, would not have respected our judgment if they felt we could only respond to client's problems.

8 In a study of a group of workingmen, the authors report that the only group which deviated from the overall pattern of about 80 per cent of the workers wanting to remain working if they inherited enough money to retire, is the unskilled group. Only slightly over 50 per cent of them would want to continue working. The authors also observe that middle-class people see work as a chance to accomplish something or to make a contribution. Working-class people view it as synonymous with activity; the alternative to working would be to lie around. Nancy Morse and R. S. Weiss, 'The function and meaning of work and the job', *American Sociological Review*, 20, March 1955, pp. 191–205.

On the other hand, some commentators have emphasized that there is little work in contemporary society that is creative and satisfying, regardless of one's social class. See, for example, Paul Goodman, 'Youth in the organized society', *Commentary*, 26 February 1960, pp. 95–107 and C. Wright Mills, 'Work milieu and the social structure', *People at Work: a Symposium*, San Francisco, Mental Health Society of Northern California, 1954, pp. 20–36.

9 This discussion has omitted ethnic differences among the homemakers. (There were six American Negroes, six white Puerto Ricans, an American of Cuban descent, a second-generation Italian-American, and a first-generation German-American.) While significant differences in behavior and attitudes between the two major groups, especially, could be noted, the social-class variable seems most pertinent to a consideration of assistance to low-income clients. One observes, furthermore, that professional workers who are Negro or Puerto-Rican experience many of the difficulties and disadvantages of other middle-class workers in developing relationships with lower-class Negro or Puerto-Rican clients.

10 The homemaker service was part of a social-welfare agency that was attempting to broaden social opportunities. At the same time it was helping clients to forego self-defeating patterns of behavior so that they might use new opportunities and efficiently exploit those which existed. The homemaker service was not based on a static concept of opportunities, and there was very clear recognition that it is much more difficult to manage under adverse social conditions than with an adequate income and modern home conveniences. There is, however, abundant evidence that some lower-class persons, largely because of the effects of social barriers, do not make maximal use of the advantages that are available. Far from lulling persons to accept their lot, a program of this sort helps them to assert their rights and to have the confidence and competence to work for their social betterment. The homemakers, themselves, were examples of lower-income persons who made the most of their opportunities but were hardly contented with their situations. Some of them were active in efforts to improve social conditions in the neighborhood, and few would allow themselves to be exploited.

11 Within a year's time the only class offered on an ongoing basis was a sewing class. There were a few scattered cooking sessions, too. We had little doubt, however, that classes in other areas of homemaking are feasible and could have been developed had time permitted.

12 Other social problems, notably substandard housing and restrictive policies of the housing authority and department of welfare bear directly on home management.

However, social action in these major areas is too extensive for a homemaking staff to mount without dissipating their function in regard to self-defeating behavior. Such activities also fall out of their range of competence. Homemaking staff should certainly lend appropriate support to community action to improve these conditions.

III. 6 Improving the effectiveness of volunteer work

Roger Hadley, Adrian Webb and Christine Farrell

Ways of organising a volunteer programme: three models

As far as one can tell from the statements of the founding members, Task Force was conceived as a means of providing an extensive service. This is certainly the way in which it has developed. The chief attraction of an extensive model is quite simply the scale of operations it makes possible: large numbers of people can be helped by mobilising very substantial numbers of volunteers, with the assistance of a small full-time staff. In the Task Force version the ratios of volunteers and old people to full-time staff are very high. It is true that the staff are not systematically trained to detect or handle complex emotional or relational problems, but it could be argued that such skills would not be greatly used in an organisation designed to provide a widely, but thinly, spread service. Although some individual members of staff undoubtedly do devote much thought to the matching of old people with volunteers, volunteers must necessarily draw largely upon their own abilities and experience or find support among their own friends and relatives. The weakness of this approach is the uneven and sometimes poor quality of service achieved.

An alternative way of organising volunteers would be to develop an intensive approach which concentrated upon the issue of quality. A far smaller number of volunteers and old people would be involved and the volunteer-staff ratio would be more favourable. High quality work would be pursued by improving the selection, training and allocation of volunteers, the assessment of needs, and the monitoring of relationships. This would clearly accord with the complex and demanding needs presented by many of the old people we interviewed.

A third, composite model, could combine elements from both these approaches. The accent would then be on a selective and flexible response to clients' needs; in some cases an extensive and in others an intensive, service would be provided. The full-time staff would have the key tasks of deciding when each approach was applicable and providing, or organising, the supportive services needed in the intensive area of the work.

Since there is a choice about how a volunteer organisation operates we will make proposals for changes in Task Force using each of these models in turn. It must be emphasised that there can be more than one version of each model and our examples are therefore intended to be illustrative rather than definitive, but we hope they will provide some basis for judging the merits of different ways of organising volunteers.

We have been critical of the effectiveness of the extensive model adopted by Task Force. It could be argued that our contention, that success is largely fortuitous, could also apply to professional social work agencies. But where volunteers as young as thirteen or fourteen are involved there are good reasons for being particularly careful how they are used. Both these volunteers and the old people they are supposed to be helping could suffer greatly if things go wrong. This immediately leads to a second criticism. Even if one accepts that successful relationships can largely be left alone, there is every good reason for trying to reduce the extent of failure. We will therefore begin by looking at an intensive model which would seem to minimise these problems, and also have other advantages.

The intensive model

In our version of this approach we will assume that it has been decided to restrict the service offered to social visiting. We will also assume that the organisation has chosen to concentrate its resources on the old people who are most in need, and to work with only those

Source: *Across the Generations*, Allen & Unwin, 1975, pp. 173–85 (adapted).

volunteers it believes to be capable of achieving successful relationships [. . .] We would therefore make two kinds of recommendations: those affecting organisational procedures and those concerning staffing and management.

Organisational procedures

1. *The identification of the most needy.* Although most of the old people accepted by Task Force appear to be amongst the most needy in the population, in terms of social isolation and loneliness, the organisation had no means of identifying the relative levels of need among those it had accepted. If the number of clients was to be restricted, a standardised means of measuring need on a systematic basis would be required. The method used to establish need in our study of the longitudinal survey might prove suitable for this purpose. It has the merit of using a mixture of 'objective' data about isolation and old people's own estimations of their loneliness.[1] Once criteria were established, each centre would have to decide in the light of its own resources at what cut-off point referrals would have to be turned down.

2. *Assessing the kind of help needed.* The staff would be required to identify as far as possible, in interviews with the old people, the kind of social contact needed and therefore the type of volunteer most likely to succeed in establishing a successful relationship. We do not suggest that such information could always be acquired before the allocation of the volunteer, but we know from our study of the partially successful and unsuccessful relationships in the longitudinal survey that in many cases old people had clearly developed interests and preferences which were ignored in allocating volunteers.

3. *Selecting volunteers.* The organisation would no longer accept virtually all offers of help. Volunteers would be carefully screened, including in each case a personal interview. Any who exhibited obviously disqualifying characteristics such as low motivation or severe personality problems would be counselled out. Volunteers who had already acquired relevant experience before coming to Task Force could be allocated to old people straight away. Other volunteers might be asked to graduate to social visiting through a three-stage preparation. First, they would attend seminars on relevant topics such as the problems of the old and the nature of the volunteer–client relationship. Second, they would be offered experience of helping elderly people in the context of a group, for example on a decorating project or in an old persons' club. Finally, they would be reinterviewed to determine whether they were ready to undertake social visiting.[2]

4. *Allocating volunteers.* The hit or miss methods of the present would be abandoned and allocation would only be made when the basis for successful relationship appeared to exist. This would mean that in many cases volunteers, and possibly the old people too,

would have to wait some time before they were allocated. Proposed allocations would be discussed with both parties before they were made.

5. *Introducing the volunteer and old person to each other.* A full-time staff member would be required to introduce the two parties to each other and to help the relationship get off to as good a start as possible.

6. *Support during the relationship.* Task Force staff gave little or no support to volunteers in the relationships we observed. We believe that reversing this situation could play an important part in improving the quality of the work done. For example, each staff member could be responsible for providing help and advice to a quota of volunteers. Regular meetings could be held with volunteers, either individually or in a group, at which the progress of relationships could be discussed and any problems raised. The staff member would also visit the old people to check on the relationships from their points of view and to see if any additional help could be offered. Group meetings with volunteers might also have an additional function. Assuming a fairly stable membership, they could become important normative reference groups for the volunteers concerned and a source of reward over and above the intrinsic satisfactions of the work itself.

Where evidence accumulated that a relationship was not working out to the satisfaction of the parties involved, in spite of counselling, it would be the responsibility of the staff to examine the possibility of reallocating the volunteer and client. Given the knowledge that would have been acquired of both during the relationship, there should be a better chance of arranging a successful allocation at the second attempt.

7. *Termination.* If the support procedures outlined above were systematically applied, staff would be alerted well in advance if a relationship was likely to end through the withdrawal of one or other party. It would then be the responsibility of the staff to help both the old person and volunteer cope with the end of the relationship, and to find another volunteer if the old person wished it. If the staff member had done his job well during the earlier phases of the relationship he would have discussed termination with both parties long before it happened and they would be well prepared for it.

These are all quite obvious points; the fact that they have to be made underlines the degree to which the extensive model adopted by Task Force has neglected the organisational prerequisites of high quality work. If the decision was made to adopt a more intensive approach, could these changes in procedure be superimposed on the existing organisation?

Staffing and management

It is one thing to prescribe organisational procedures but quite a different thing to create the setting in which they can be successfully carried through. In our view the application of the intensive model would presuppose considerable changes in the type of staff employed and different management methods from those which characterised Task Force at the time of our study. The staff would differ both in skills and orientation. Intensive work with old people and volunteers of the kind we have described calls for the ability to diagnose needs and potentials and the capacity to help others build effective relationships. These are the types of skills which the good social worker is supposed to have and it may be that an organisation designed on the intensive model would do well if it could recruit its field-staff from this profession. Nevertheless, skills alone are not sufficient, for the orientation or commitment of the staff is also a vital issue. When we studied Task Force most of the staff appeared to give higher priority to social education and community action than to direct involvement with old people. It is likely that the model could be made to work only if the staff had a preference for intensive work.

One of the major problems posed by this approach is precisely that of recruiting such staff in sufficient numbers. People of this kind are much in demand by statutory and voluntary social services where they have better pay and career structures than a volunteer agency is likely to be able to offer. A number of strategies might be developed to make employment in a voluntary organisation more attractive. An arrangement could possibly be reached whereby the 'career' organisations would unequivocally recognise employment with an organisation like Task Force as relevant experience for their staff. [. . .] Second, the volunteer organisation might seek to recruit people with the potential to become skilled staff, but who as yet had little relevant training or experience. [. . .] Third, the organisation might try to improve career prospects within its own structure. This could be done through the formalisation of the hierarchy that already exists, but it could also be accomplished through the creation of posts for specialists in particular fields. [. . .]

Assuming that sufficient staff of the calibre needed to operate the intensive model could be recruited or trained by Task Force, the organisation would still have to devise methods for defining and maintaining a high standard of work. It seems unlikely that the grant-aiding bodies will create the pressure for the organisation to raise its standards; the main impetus to achieve high quality work would therefore have to come from inside the volunteer agency. New structures would be needed to enable a consensus to be reached on aims, and reporting and evaluation procedures would have to be established to check on progress. These might restrain the actions of the individual staff member more than does the existing system; this is one possible cost of working in an organisation that has a clearly stated purpose which is systematically pursued.

Table 1 Clients helped and estimated success rates in a typical Task Force centre: present model and intensive model

	Present model	Intensive model
1. Staff members	4	4
2. Supposed active list of old people	800	200
3. Actual active list of old people	560	200
Tasks undertaken		
4. Regular and occasional jobs	140	—
5. Regular visiting	380	200
Success of visiting		
6. Successful relationships	85	160
7. Partially successful relationships	135	40
8. Unsuccessful relationships	160	—

Outcome

It is difficult to forecast with any confidence the effect of making the kinds of changes we have proposed. So many other factors are likely to change at the same time as those deliberately manipulated. Nevertheless, [. . . if] we assume a success rate of four in every five relationships under the intensive model, the overall success rates of the existing system and the intensive model might work out as shown in Table 1.

It will be seen that the intensive method might be expected to create about twice as many successful relationships as the present system and few, if any, outright failures of the kind which were so numerous in the centres we studied.[3] Further, the termination of those relationships which were established might be expected to be of a much higher standard and the gaps between one volunteer going and another being found could be eliminated. Although the cost per old person nominally helped would rise by at least four times what we are suggesting that the cost for each successful relationship could fall below the present figure. It must be remembered that while the staff-client ratio would be nearly comparable with that in many branches of professional social work, the frequency and duration of contact received by each old person would be much higher than that received by most social work clients. It is not simply an intensive model of volunteer organisation: it is a means of providing quite an intensive domiciliary service. The full-time staff might also be involved in some work of an extensive kind (organising decorating work on much the same lines as at present) and in activities which relate to social education and community action.

The main drawback to the intensive model, it would seem, is that while it is likely to ensure that a high standard of work is achieved with the minority of old people accepted for help, it leaves the majority without support of any kind. We would argue, however, that it is better that the position should be presented clearly rather than concealed, as it has been with the present model, behind an impressive array of statistics. The cost of providing a decent service to *all* old people in need of help can then be seen and the inadequacy of the present service can be plainly demonstrated.

The extensive model

The extensive approach adopted by Task Force has a number of serious defects as we have shown. Nevertheless, it has its strengths, and variations of it could be devised. We will look at those features of the present Task Force approach that might be worth preserving and then outline possible developments which, assuming the existing staff complement, offer the hope of reducing failure to a minimum.

The great advantage of the extensive model is the number of people which it brings into contact with each other. We have implied that it would be better for the old people not to have contact with volunteers at all than to experience an unsuccessful relationship. But it must be said that some old people might see things differently. Given their isolation even a mediocre or poor relationship could be important as a recognition that they had not been forgotten by the world. In other words, the weight attached to the question of quality is a matter of judgement. When one turns to the volunteers the problem is even more difficult. Involving large numbers of young people in a community-based activity could certainly raise their consciousness of social problems and foster an alertness to the power of the community as a caring agent which could remain with them into adulthood. We certainly have evidence that many of the volunteers became more aware of the problems of old age as a result of their work, but we cannot predict how this experience will affect their attitudes and behaviour later in life. And on the negative side there is always the possibility that some volunteers may be badly disillusioned by a traumatic experience with a difficult or very lonely, demoralised old person. The lack of support for volunteers is bound to be worrying in this context for some of them may be left with profound feelings of failure, inadequacy and guilt.

Even though the extensive model may have a strong, positive value from the point of view of volunteers, one is still left with the difficult task of weighing this argument against the gains and losses for old people. But the appeal of the extensive model remains. It means giving a lot of people a potentially educative or supportive relationship, and it clearly works in some, perhaps many, instances. Can one simply modify it a little in order to reduce the extent of failure?

One possibility would be for the organisation to restrict its activities entirely to work which required little supervision. For example, it might be decided only to accept referrals for jobs and to pass on other referrals to other organisations. In this case the staff could concentrate their efforts on the selection or screening of volunteers and on maintaining a simple checking procedure to see that work was done. No time would have to be spent in support of either old people or volunteers. If a volunteer lapsed for any reason he could simply be replaced and, since the organisation would only be concerned with the completion of jobs and not the formation of friendly relationships, termination problems would not be encountered. This model depends upon the organisation's capacity to recruit large numbers of young volunteers wanting to provide effective practical help for the large numbers of old people who need it. We do not know if they would be forthcoming but if they were staff would not need to be highly skilled to operate the simple procedures involved: willingness to stick to the routine and a commitment to helping the old would be the main requirements.

Another possibility would be to concentrate resources on selection procedures. [. . .] Very young volunteers, for example, might be automatically excluded. Similarly, categories of volunteers likely to include many with low motivation might be dropped, such as those for whom community service is simply an alternative to other school subjects. The old people, too, might be more carefully screened and both the most difficult cases and the least needy could be excluded. Given the effective application of these procedures the number of unsuccessful relationships should be substantially reduced without the need to increase the input of staff advice and support.

A major difficulty posed by both the intensive and extensive approaches is that the work involved would probably seem much less stimulating to the full-time staff and the appeal of the organisation to the volunteer could also be considerably reduced. These disadvantages would not be likely to apply in the third scheme, the composite model.

The composite model

There are several ways in which features of the extensive and intensive models could be incorporated in the same organisation. To achieve a high standard of performance in an organisation mobilising relatively *large* numbers of volunteers would require a substantial input of staff time. But need all the staff be full-time, paid personnel? If volunteers could be used in some staff functions as well as in the 'coal-face' activities, the low staff-volunteer ratio of the extensive model could be retained while pursuing high quality intensive work. It may not be appropriate to use the more experienced young volunteers to select and allocate other volunteers, but there seems to be no obvious reason why they should not be employed in training and advising their less experienced colleagues. If they were to carry a small 'case load' they could keep in sufficient contact to ensure that all was well and give advance warning of problems to the full-time staff. Full-time, trained staff members would still be required to cope with volunteer selection and allocation, with difficult crises in relationships, and with termination. But a high quality service could be offered to a larger number of old people than in the intensive model.

An alternative would involve the flexible use of volunteers and would therefore concentrate attention on allocation rather than support. The first composite approach, outlined above, assumes that the weakest volunteers will be excluded and that the rest will be used intensively. This second version would involve using all volunteers in a non-intensive way at first, allocating them to jobs or group tasks. A much smaller group would then be selected for intensive work through a process of elimination. The extensive phase would test motivation, act as a period of training and socialisation, and make it possible to identify and select the most dependable volunteers for long-term visiting. The advantages of using a large number of volunteers would be combined with those of providing a visiting service with a low failure rate. Specialisation by staff members in extensive or intensive work would probably be necessary, with the possibility of making a rudimentary staff 'career' from the former to the latter.

If it proved possible to combine these two approaches in a single organisational structure, the model would contain both the intensive and extensive use of volunteers, a degree of staff specialisation, and a volunteer 'career' pattern (from extensive work, to intensive work, to staff support work), while retaining an overall staff-volunteer ratio that would be considerably higher than in the intensive model. The organisation would be based on the flexible use of its volunteers and would demand more skill of at least some of the staff than it does now. The advantage would be that without abandoning any category of volunteer, or existing untrained staff members, the organisation would provide a larger number of old people with a high-quality visiting service, as well as many more with jobs and decorating. More particularly, there would be little chance of the inexperienced volunteer or staff member becoming solely responsible for the help given to isolated old people within a few days of entering the Task Force world.

Recommendations

The models which we have presented here should have applicability far beyond the particular case of Task Force, and in this broader context it would be inappropriate to recommend one as preferable to any of the others. Each has its merits and could be relevant in some situations. The choice of approach must largely depend upon the type and supply of volunteers, the clientele, the nature of the problem they present, as well as the careful costing of alternatives, and an assessment of the probability that appropriate staff could be recruited to run the organisation in the manner required. In the case of Task Force, however, it is more relevant to make specific recommendations.

In spite of our criticisms, this study has made it abundantly clear that Task Force has made an important contribution through its present extensive mode of operation. Nevertheless, our evidence suggests it should seek to adopt an intensive or composite approach in the next stage of its development. The potential of the organisation for achieving high-quality work is very considerable, especially with older volunteers. Given the extent of unmet need for visiting amongst isolated and lonely old people the expansion of this work and the reduction of failure should, in our view, receive first priority. Whether an intensive or composite model should be chosen must depend on the circumstances of the organisation including the attitudes of the funding bodies, and the interests of existing staff. It may be that different centres could experiment with different versions of one approach or the other. But whichever structure is chosen we believe that the emphasis on quality should be paramount.

One problem inherent in our recommendations is that they imply an increased degree of central control over activities throughout the organisation. Each centre's control over its volunteers would have to be matched by a centralised monitoring system, operated by the headquarters staff, designed to establish and maintain good quality staff work. This emphasis on control is likely to pose a major dilemma for the organisation. One of the attractive features of Task Force as it is run today is its freedom from the worst defects of a highly centralised bureaucracy. Its staff exhibit an enthusiasm and commitment for their work which is sustained by the fact that the individual centres can see themselves as virtually autonomous in many of their activities. A normative orientation predominates; staff actions are guided more by loyalty and identification with Task Force as an ideal than by bureaucratic rules. If this is to be changed much else could also change and in unpredictable ways: the type of staff: their material rewards and conditions of service; and their willingness to innovate.

Would our suggested pursuit of high quality work necessarily give rise to these other changes? We would argue that they need not, providing the problems were recognised and allowed for in the process of reshaping the organisation. Apart from the youthfulness and orientation of the staff, which would make any apparent increase in centralisation such an explosive issue, there are several other features which make for a relatively decentralised and informal organisation. Each of the centres is small, with no more than four full-time staff, each operates in a distinctive sociogeographical context in which the problems vary quite considerably, and the headquarters staff is also small in number. Consequently, each centre tends to be a group of peers rather than a firmly hierarchical organisation, and the centres can only be guided in general terms by the rules and procedures formulated by the director. In short, Task Force staff have to be convinced of the value of high quality work; it cannot be imposed on them and to try to do so would be a fundamental mistake.

The most important point, however, is that the existing 'clearing house' function has in practice given only limited independence and job satisfaction to staff. It is a rather mechanical administrative process. While our recommendations do imply a greater responsibility at headquarters for the quality of work done, and therefore for generalising guidelines about good practice throughout the centres, they also offer the prospect of greater discretionary activity and more interesting work for centre staff. At present many staff turn to the social education and community action as ways of finding the job satisfaction missing in the volunteer work with old people. This has resulted in a *de facto* reduction of the importance of what is officially still the first goal of the organisation. However, the co-existence of these activities does not seem to us to be a problem for they are to a large extent mutually supportive. The real need is to increase the inherent interest of organising volunteer work. Moving away from the idea of acting merely as a 'clearing house' and taking on responsibility for the quality of work done could do precisely this even though it will involve putting greater emphasis on the control functions of each part of the organisation. A fuller involvement of volunteers in Task Force work, as was suggested in discussing the composite model, could help prevent increased control leading to rigidity. An organisation like this depends upon commitment and must therefore exhibit a regard for individuals' expectations, interests, ideas and beliefs, as well as use their abilities. Control over the quality of work and the preservation of areas of autonomy and job satisfaction need not be mutually exclusive. They depend upon a managerial approach based on consensus and the toleration of diversity within agreed limits, rather than one that seeks to achieve uniformity through the imposition of bureaucratic procedures. The 'agreed limits' must in part be set by the staff themselves, although funding bodies must obviously have a voice in their determination and the clients' interests should also be consciously incorporated in discussions about the organisation's goals and procedures. This last point is one we would want to emphasise, for in all our time studying Task Force we never felt the client's viewpoint was adequately presented as such—a defect which we feel is reflected in the fact that we have had to argue the case for aiming systematically at a high quality of service.

Given a managerial context such as we have outlined, a higher quality of work could be achieved through the promotion, rather than the restriction, of those features of Task Force which have made it attractive to committed young people: its informality and its reputation for giving individual staff the scope to develop their own talents in the service of the old people and volunteers.

Summary

[. . .] A substantial increase of resources in any one volunteer organisation, or the volunteer sector as a whole, would change the policy context and make possible a wider variety of developments than we have discussed. Similarly, we have noted that volunteer organisations do not necessarily have to confine themselves to the provision of a direct service to individuals; such activities as community development and political action are also important. But the recommendations made in this chapter arise from and remain within the limits set by our empirical research.

Notes

1 An interesting discussion of the relevance of self-rated needs (particularly in relation to health cases) is to be found in Malcolm Johnson's recent article, 'Self-perception of need amongst the elderly', *Sociological Review*, 20(4), November 1972.
2 A rather similar screening process has been used in the selection of volunteers for the Blackfriars family counselling scheme.
3 There is no inherent reason why help with jobs should not be provided in an intensive model, but we have restricted our example to visiting to simplify the model.

III. 7 A systems approach to social work intervention: its uses for work with individuals and families

Anne Vickery

Introduction

The merits of the general systems approach to social work have been amply expounded in a number of recent papers in American journals and collected readings. A few relate solely to casework,[1] but more typically they relate to social work practice as a whole and argue that the approach is conducive to building a unified theory of practice.[2] At a 1968 workshop held by the US Council of Social Work Education several papers were presented and later published under the title 'The General Systems Approach: contributions toward an holistic conception of social work'.[3] In the introduction, the editor, Gordon Hearn, writes:

> This volume may be regarded as a benchmark in the continuing inquiry concerning the real nature of social work. It supports the hope that we may eventually develop a substantially inclusive, internally consistent, and organized conception of social work practice and its approach to the human scene. It indicates, in particular, the contribution that the general systems approach may be expected to make this much-needed overall conception.

In 1973 two important publications presented overall conceptions of social work practice, one by Allen Pincus and Anne Minahan,[4] the other by Howard Goldstein.[5] Both draw on general systems theory; Pincus and Minahan implicitly, and Goldstein explicitly.

At the outset it should be stated that, in our view, general systems theory applied to social work is not an alternative theory to the many upon which social workers need to draw. Rather, we perceive it to be a theory that can help social workers to organize and integrate a multitude of perspectives and methodological approaches that may be used in attempts to achieve change of various kinds. As far as social work is concerned a general systems model serves to map

Source: *British Journal of Social Work*, 4 (4), 1974, pp. 389–404.

out the variables in professional practice in such a way as to highlight the connections among variables within personality systems and within social systems. A model, as distinct from a theory, does not say which variables in a given situation are the strongest determinants of behaviour. Its purpose is to describe the various parts or factors that are relevant to a phenomenon and how these parts appear to be related to one another. A model based on systems theory tends to encourage social workers to take into account a far wider range of variables than they otherwise might, and to see personal well-being not in terms of a static equilibrium, but in terms of openness to exchange with the environment.

It would be impossible to do justice to all the arguments that have been put forward in favour of a general systems approach both by behavioural scientists and social work educators. The aim of this paper is to use a general systems model for the following purposes:

(1) To pinpoint where the focus of social work most appropriately lies.
(2) To examine choices of social work goals, targets of intervention and client systems.
(3) To identify points of intervention within the defined system.
(4) To examine the implications of a general systems approach for the role of the social worker with individuals and families.

The focus of social work

It might seem paradoxical that in recent years it is the caseworker, the person relating face-to-face with individuals and families, who has been seen as a force for conformity and who has been so frequently criticized for acting more in the interests of society than in the interests of clients. In contrast, community workers, who relate more with collectivities than with individuals, have been welcomed for their wholehearted alliance with the interests of those whom they serve. They are seen as a force for liberation of individuals from an oppressive system. Thus, those who are most concerned with methods by which to liberate the individual are seen as 'oppressive', while those who concentrate on fostering communal-collective action are viewed as liberating. Of course, as soon as the notion of 'an oppressive system' is introduced, the reason for this apparent paradox is clear. Caseworkers have perhaps too exclusively confined themselves to psychological and psychoanalytic theory as their knowledge-base, and to a belief in the efficacy of the relationship between two people as a means of recovering 'the wholeness of being human';[6] whereas community workers, drawing more exclusively on sociology and political science as their knowledge base, believe that individuals can be wholly human only within the context of a benign environment and a just social order. Changing the social system of those who are oppressed by the collective efforts of the oppressed themselves is, for the community worker, not only a means of attaining social justice, but also of promoting individual human dignity and happiness.

Recent efforts to correct a view of social work that perhaps over-emphasized individual emotional development and underplayed environmental factors, have not entirely released us from the tension that exists between these perspectives. Here we refer to the strain that is invariably experienced by a social worker who may have to choose between serving a caseload of individuals and families in great need or devoting his energies and attention to the structural problems of how the community allocates its resources and organizes its service delivery. Development of new theoretical perspectives based on systems theory have helped the professional who works with individuals and families to take a broader view of his or her role and to see that with some of the perspectives of the community worker the behaviour of individuals can be better understood and a more appropriate range of methods of intervention can be used. We shall develop this point later.

The general systems approach does not support the dichotomization of the individual and his environment; it does not allow the supposition that a complete shift of effort from the psychological to the sociological aspects of human life will yield better results in all cases. William E. Gordon[7] points out that the focus of social work has concentrated at times on the side of the human person as interpreted by psychological theory, and at other times on the side of the environment as interpreted by sociological and economic theory. But in his view the mainstream of social work practice has become neither applied psychology nor applied sociology. Rather, he says, 'the central social work focus is placed at the interface between, or the meeting place of, person and environment . . . The phenomenon of concern at this interface is the *transaction* between person and environment.' Harriet Bartlett[8] adopts the same view of the essential nature of social work practice. Social work

practice, Bartlett says has to do with people's social functioning, their capacity to cope with the demands of their environment; it is, therefore, about an 'interactional field' in which transactions occur between environmental demands on the one hand and people's coping capacities on the other. If the feed-back to the individual from the environment is positive his coping capacity is likely to be enhanced and his subsequent behaviour likely to elicit still more positive responses from the environment; if the feedback from the environment is consistently negative, the individual's ability to cope may often be diminished and his subsequent behaviour likely to elicit still more negative responses. She writes: 'In such ways the social environment fails to meet the needs of large segments of the population, and places demands upon them that are far beyond the limits of their coping capacity.'[9]

The general systems approach focuses the attention of social workers to the point where it belongs, the transactions that occur between individuals and their environments and the potential of the transactions for enhancing or diminishing the capacity of individuals to gain satisfaction from life and to promote the satisfaction of others.

Choice of goals, targets of intervention and client systems

'Goals' refer to the aims or objectives that client and worker are hoping to achieve. The 'target of intervention' is the person, group or organization that the worker decides to act upon in order to further the attainment of the goal. This means that the interventional target in work aimed at bringing about change in an individual client may be the client himself, in which case social work is *direct*; or, the interventional target may be members of his family, his school, or part of the 'helping system' e.g. a department of health and social security or staff in a residential home, in which case social work is *indirect*. Although the casework literature has tended until recently to concentrate mainly on the interaction between worker and client, it is evident that in most agencies a great deal of work is indirect.

Although individuals and families might be the beneficiaries of social work, interventional targets are appropriately located in a variety of systems.

$$
\begin{array}{l}
\textit{Personality} \\
\textit{system}
\end{array}
\text{---individual} \left\{ \begin{array}{l} \text{intra-personal} \\ \text{psycho-biological} \end{array} \right.
$$

Social system—dyad
family
group (non-
familial) interpersonal
organization
community socio-cultural
society

It is important to emphasize the distinction between personality and social systems. A personality system refers to the relationship among parts of an organism;

this involves complex physiological as well as psycho-logical physico-chemical energy inter-changes. But the relationships among parts of a social system are primarily psychic involving complex communicative processes of information exchange. Walter Buckley[10] makes this distinction as follows:

> society's 'individuals' are *not* discrete. What is discrete to the human observer's limited sensory apparatus is simply the physical organism. The behaving individual—the psychological person—is essentially an organisation that is developed and maintained only in and through a continually on-going symbolic inter-change with other persons. . . . It is these psychosocially developed and supported webs of communicative interrelations of varying degrees of permanence that give society some degree of wholeness, or make it an 'entity' in its own right, to be studied by techniques and perspectives different from those used in studying the entity called 'the individual'.

Buckley's comment is salient to the issues that we are considering. Since different theoretical frameworks are appropriate to different kinds of systems, social workers must be clear about which of the systems they are responding to, in which of the systems they are intervening, and what the effects of change in one system might have upon the others.[11] For example, a source of strain to a family social system might be a difference of values between father and son, resulting in conflict and threat to the family's cohesiveness. The father may try to resolve the conflict by forcing the son to abandon his beliefs. The father may succeed, but in restoring cohesiveness to the family social system the strain may be transferred to the son's personality system. The social worker's intervention might be in response to the needs and feelings of either the father or the son; he might respond to each in turn. This would be intervention at the personality system level. He might respond to the social system, asking father and son to identify and discuss the range of agreements and disagreements between them. The nature of the problem and the aims of the social worker should influence the choice. The aim might be to change the father's attitude or to prevent the son from getting into trouble or to help the son to leave the family and help the family survive its partial dis-integration. Bringing about change in either father or son might be worked at individually with each other or in joint interviews together. Enabling the son to leave the family may depend upon individual work to help him strengthen ties with social systems outside his family. Helping the family survive its partial dis-integration might require family therapy, the strength-ening of family ties with other social systems, or individual help for one or more of its members. The choice should depend on a judgement as to which type of intervention is likely to bring about the desired change most rapidly.

Assuming that all behaviour has meaning only within the context in which it arises, this kind of analysis of the inter-action between systems helps the social worker to clarify the meaning of the phenomena he observes and to be sensitive to the requirements of the system in which he is intervening. It does not, however, help him to decide which values or whose interests he should pursue. In the above example, who might be considered to be the client? The son or the whole family? The son within the family? The son independently of the family? The definition of the client-system and the aim of social work intervention are mutually dependent. In part, the aims, methodo-logy and clientele of a social worker are predetermined by his agency's definition of its mission; in part, the client system, methodology and aims are determined by the aims of social work; and, in part, the selection of aims, targets and methods of intervention are determined by the client. As well as illustrating the distinction between personality and social systems, the above example also shows that in some cases it is difficult to distinguish between a client system and an interventional target. If the son alone is the client and the social worker's aim is to change the father's attitude by intervening in the father's personality system, the father becomes the interventional target in indirect work on behalf of the son.

It may be useful to extend this kind of analysis to a situation involving a social system of a larger scale than the family unit. An example is a client, Mrs X, married with four children, two of whom are under five. She is being seen monthly at a psychiatric out-patient clinic and treated for depression. Her husband is an unskilled worker who manages to stay in work despite the fairly high unemployment rate in the area. The family income, however, can only cover bare necessities. The family has never had a holiday and has no affiliations with outside organizations or groups. There is no extended family within visiting distance. This family is not unlike many other families in the neighbourhood. Other families are even worse off financially, housing is in poor repair and lacks basic amenities like a bath and an inside lavatory. There is a lack of play space in the area, poor facilities for leisure activities, poor shops, no community groups. Interaction among residents is minimal. Mrs X is referred to the social worker by the psychiatrist because Mrs X has told the psychiatrist she cannot manage the children. One child recently started refusing to go to school. The two children under five are irritable, disobedient and destructive but easier to manage when Mr X is at home. Mr X is reliable and conscientious and doing his best to be kind and sup-portive to his wife. Recently, however, their relation-ship has deteriorated. Quarrels occur much more frequently and are more bitter. Assuming the social worker wishes to improve the total social functioning of this family, and sees the children's disturbed be-haviour as the product of a disturbance in the parents what choices are open in terms of interventional targets? The following is a list of the immediately obvious systems:

Personality system

Individual

Mrs X
Mr X
Children

Social systems

Interpersonal

Dyads. Mr and Mrs X
Dyads and triads of various family members
Family Unit as a whole

Family Unit's interchanges with total social network

e.g. School
Home Help Service
Day-Care Services for Children
Housing Department

Community

e.g. Residents in the neighbourhood ⎫ Any one of
Planning Department ⎪ these might
Housing Department ⎪ be an inter-
Education Department ⎬ ventional
Social Services Department ⎪ target or a
Voluntary Organizations ⎪ combination
⎪ of them in
⎪ interaction
⎪ with each
⎭ other.

It is probable that the social worker would intervene in those systems where intervention was most likely to bring about the quickest change for the family. For example, a sympathetic home help who would both rescue the house from squalor and also befriend and encourage Mrs X might be the most effective way of halting the downward spiralling of the family under the weight of accumulated problems. At the same time, questions have to be asked about Mrs X's depression. The psychiatrist reports that Mrs X has been receiving treatment for six months and had no previous history. She is now lethargic, irritable, sleeping badly, disinterested in the family. Prior to the illness she was hard-working, inclined to worry about the family's well-being and a good manager on their low income. She has always been shy with strangers but was well-liked by the few friends she had made in childhood. She is now living in a different part of the country from where she was brought up.

If Mrs X were living in a bright, cheerful neighbourhood among people who were outgoing and friendly, the social worker might take the view that Mrs X's depression stemmed from intra- and inter-personal conflicts and inadequacies. However, the lack of rewarding experiences to be derived from interaction with people outside the family means that the family X is deprived of sufficient positive transactions with their environment for the maintenance of psychosocial health.[12] Without excluding the possibility that intra- and inter-personal factors need attention, it would seem reasonable to ask questions about the extent to which depression is endemic in the neighbourhood, to what extent other families suffer from the community's lack of social cohesiveness, inadequate housing, poor social facilities and employment opportunities. The evidence may point to the need for intervention in the community social system. From the point of view of effecting change in the family X, the community may be thought of as an interventional target for indirect work on their behalf. However, from the perspective of a community worker, the community can be viewed as a client system in its own right. Keeping for the moment to the family worker's perspective, it is easy to see how social group work with Mrs X and other similarly placed mothers might be the method of choice and that it might be more effective if based on a 'social goals' rather than on a 'remedial' model.[13] Becoming a member of a residents' association or a play group scheme might do more to relieve Mrs X's depression than several hours of social work interviewing or even of home-help time. Both the psychological benefits of social interaction and the benefits accruing from the achievement of goals, such as improved play and leisure facilities, would make a contribution to this family's well-being. This does not imply that domiciliary services and a relationship with a social worker might not be an essential bridge in helping Mrs X to transfer from her role of 'patient' to that of active group member. But if social workers are to be sensitive to the need for improved transactions between individuals and the social network outside the family, at least two requirements have to be met. The first relates to the availability of knowledge about *the community* and the second to the knowledge about *the means of effecting change within the community*.

Arguing first for the need for easy access to knowledge about the community one has to extrapolate from the learning theory approach to social casework.[14] In order to understand behaviour it is not enough to have knowledge about its roots in past experience. Knowledge about factors in the present that are contributing to, maintaining or exacerbating the behaviour is certainly equally important. For example, the social worker working with a withdrawn child will always ask whether there are emotional problems that prevent the child from reaching out for and using the things in its environment that will meet its needs, or whether those things are simply not there for the child to reach out for and use. The same questions have to be asked about a family in trouble. But answers to such questions must be based on an adequate knowledge of a community's strengths and weaknesses, and the availability of essential resources.

The second requirement is that the worker should have some knowledge about the means available in the social structure of the community to affect social interaction and the definition of common goals and policies. The means for effective change are frequently deficient. That is, social workers may well be aware of the need to intervene in the community system but agencies may be too overburdened by responding to individual and family problems on a short-term basis to be able to divert the necessary resources required for community action. Nevertheless, it becomes clear that just as residential care and field work services have to run concurrently if either are to be viable, so must social work with individuals and families and social work with groups and communities operate in conjunction with one another.

Having put the case for multiple and mutually interdependent approaches it is necessary to develop the point made earlier about the tension involved in

basis. Thus, choices of client system and interventional targets are not simply methodological questions. To choose to work solely with individuals and families is to run the risk of ignoring factors of social injustice and the need for positive discrimination in the allocation of resources; conversely, to choose to work with communities is to run the risk of ignoring or underestimating the interests of those individuals whose needs will not be met through collective action.[15]

The general systems practice model[16]

We have examined some of the uses that a general systems model has in clarifying the technical and value issues involved in choice of client system and targets of intervention. It is important also to consider the ways in which a general systems model facilitates the examination of crucial points in the transactions between client-system and environmental system. Once

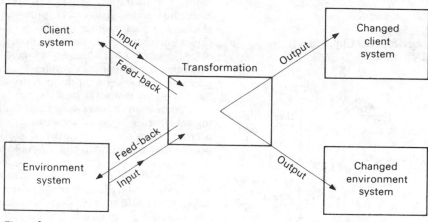

Figure 2

choosing whether to work with individuals or with communities. Greater knowledge about the community enables workers to uncover the ways in which the nature of the community contributes to individual problems. In addition, it helps in identifying many other factors that do not easily lend themselves, as in the case of the family X, as leverage points or targets of intervention in harmoniously furthering the goals of effective work with individuals. Here we include such factors as substantial quantities of unmet need, structural social inequalities, unequal distribution of resources and the failure of public services to reach the people most in need. Attention to these factors tend, for the reasons outlined above, to divert attention and resources away from the detailed and painstaking work of meeting the needs of specific individuals who one way or another come to the agency's notice. Even if they have knowledge about these factors, agencies with limited resources are forced to make choices between work aimed at alleviating present individual suffering, or intervention aimed at longer-term results benefiting the community on a broader

the client system is defined there are four points in the inter-system between it and its environment to which attention must be given, namely, 'output', 'input', 'transformation' and 'feed-back'.

Output

This is perhaps the key point of control for both client and worker. At an early stage in the development of a social worker's relationship with a client, discussion is focused on the question of what it is that the client wishes to achieve, what the worker sees as desirable for him to achieve and possible discrepancies in their objectives. Without open discussion, the objectives of the social work process are not clarified and controlled by either party and the client cannot exercise effective choice. For example, one of the client's outputs might be a poor performance at work resulting in long periods of unemployment between jobs. The social worker may think that the output of the total social work process should be a more adequate work performance, and a reduction in unemployment. The client, on the other hand, may not be concerned about his own outputs, but he may wish the output of the social work process to be clearance of his debts by financial help from the agency. J. E. Mayer and Noel Timms[17] provide many examples of how the social worker's failure to discuss with the client discrepancies between their respective 'output' objectives negatively affects the outcomes of the casework.

Input

Part of the output of one system contributes to the input to the other. Outputs of the client system may be based on inputs from the environment system. The input of the environment system has to be considered from three points of view, namely, what is actually available in the community, what inputs have been lacking in the client's past experience, and how the client selects from the inputs that are currently available. The earlier example of the X family described the deleterious effects of a lack of life-enhancing inputs from the environment. The approach to casework outlined by Elizabeth McBroom[18] identifies lack of educational inputs as being the key problem in families with multiple problems in poor districts. She suggests that the teaching of social skills may be the most important input for the social worker to make.

Transformation or processing

These terms refer to the manner in which the client-system uses inputs from the environment. In situations of conflict the primary task that is likely to absorb the energies of the client is directed elsewhere than at appropriate life tasks. William Jordan, for example, has illustrated this in his description of the ways by which clients manage to influence a social worker against his better judgement to collude with the client's fantasies.[19] Psychoanalytic transference is a particularly important conceptualization of one type of transformation of inputs.

Feed-back

This is a concept borrowed from cybernetics. When the output of the client system does not satisfactorily 'match' the demands of the environment, feed-back may help the client system to correct itself and thus encourage more appropriate behaviour. If, however, the client-system is insensitive to feed-back it will have the reverse effect, reinforcing the negative self-damaging aspects of the inappropriate behaviour. The same is true of the environment system and its interaction with the client system. The most effective point of intervention may sometimes be in the feed-back of the environment system, helping it to understand how its outputs may be reinforcing the behaviour in the client system that it most abhors. An example would be helping adults to avoid punitive responses to certain adolescent behaviour. Equally important is the need to teach clients how their own behaviour elicits the responses in others that they find uncongenial. This is well exemplified in marital work or family therapy. A concentration of attention on the point of feed-back is perhaps characteristic of a systems approach.

It may be helpful to illustrate the use that can be made of these four points in the inter-system of client and environment by a single case example. Let us suppose the client is a forty-year old bachelor, Mr A., living alone in the suburban terrace house where he was born. His parents have been dead for ten years. He is referred by the local authority housing department to the social services department. In order to make way for a large housing scheme his house is due for demolition. Mr A is refusing to co-operate with plans for his re-housing in council property. He will not open the door to housing department officials and has for some time exchanged acrimonious correspondence with the department. The worker offering help to Mr A discovers that he has worked for twenty years as a messenger and that he has very little verbal communication with anyone. He was an only child and his elderly parents used him as an almost constant companion. They discouraged him from forming outside relationships even while at school. His house is in ill-repair and very dusty inside. Mr A is thin, and he looks tired and undernourished. He is sleeping badly and complains of being miserable and anxious because of threats from the housing department and also because of seemingly sinister things done to him by neighbours' children playing outside his house.

Mr A might be most concerned about the output of the housing department. That is, their pressure on him to co-operate with their redevelopment plans. But also he will be suffering from his own output of anxiety and depression. The output about which the worker might be most concerned could be Mr A's refusal to consider rehousing. If so, the initial stages of the social work process would be devoted to the development of mutual understanding and agreement as to the focus of work and its desired objective.

Adequate *inputs* are lacking on both sides mainly because in the past Mr A has been deprived of adequate socialization into an adult role. Having been held back from further education and from experiences such as joining a mixed social club or pursuing hobbies involving other people, Mr A in the present is unable to make use of available recreational facilities that would encourage emotional maturation and maintain mental health. He has become socially isolated. As with Mrs X, the worker would need to play the role of the good father, gently but firmly encouraging Mr A to try out new experiences which would bring vital inputs to him, as well as allow him to make inputs to the environment. Other possible inputs for Mr A are medical attention and domestic help.

Mr A's *transformation* of inputs is unhelpful because he transforms innocuous everyday occurrences such as children playing in the street into sinister happenings which frighten him and drain his energy.

The worker must understand the nature of the transformation in order to avoid becoming part of a similar process. In some cases it might be appropriate to try to alter the transformation either by interpretation or by behavioural modification, but in this case it might be wiser to aim to bring about change through more remote inputs such as the ones already mentioned, medical treatment, social experiences, domestic help.

As far as *feed-back* is concerned, Mr A and the housing department are in a vicious circle spiralling downwards. The more aggressive Mr A's letters become the more threatening become the replies from the housing department, and the more aggressive becomes the next letter from Mr A. The worker might well decide for the sake of Mr A and others like him to seek intervention in the housing department's style of communication as well as to intervene with the particular officer dealing with Mr A.

This outline of a practice model exemplified by the case of Mr A does not say anything new to social workers but it does help to present a unified view of the social work process and to identify what are likely to be the most effective and essential points of entry into the client and environment inter-system and the most appropriate inputs for the social worker to make. The model can be applied to social work with families, groups and communities as well as to individuals. Clearly, though, the complexity increases as the social system grows in size and heterogeneity.

Implications of a general systems approach for the role of the social worker with individuals and families

As we have indicated, much of the work of social workers who are concerned with individuals and families is indirect, such as arranging for services that repair gaps in people's material and social environment, advocating on behalf of clients both within and outside one's own agency, simulating volunteer groups to meet gaps in the service to individuals and families, working with the 'caring system' itself, such as in work with foster parents, neighbours and residential staff. All these activities seem to be entirely appropriate for the social worker. Nevertheless, they are activities with may not always have been seen as part of the core of casework, and for this reason may have been devalued. However, if the definition of casework is, broadly, to be concerned with social work focused on helping the individual rather than narrowly directed to intervention in the individual's personality system and inter-personal relations, it is clear that the caseworker has to play a very wide variety of roles and enter into a wide variety of activities. At the same time, the caseworker has to be knowledgeable about the contributions that other kinds of workers can make; and having defined certain social work goals, he must be able to judge whether they can be best achieved through the caseworkers's activity or whether they need a worker practising different methods and skills. The case of the X family is an example in which casework and community work would both be needed. In the case of Mr A, casework alone might be effective but at a later point success might depend on there being a suitable club with a sufficiently skilled club leader to help Mr A to integrate as a member. Casework with a delinquent adolescent who belongs to a delinquent peer group might never be effective in changing his delinquent behaviour unless it includes work with the peer group as a whole. Social workers must not only be skilled in judging what methods to apply within the range of their own competence, they must be able to judge the circumstances under which these methods are either insufficient or irrelevant to the objectives they wish to achieve. This is particularly true in circumstances where resources are inadequate.

The recent Home Office study of after-care units for discharged prisoners shows that despite the wish of the social workers to provide long-term help through a casework relationship, the service they actually provided was overwhelmingly concerned with material needs.[20] Paradoxically, the material resources of the units were relatively insignificant. 'The inadequacy of the Service at coping with their short-term needs may well have influenced the clients' views on its ability to cope with their long-term rehabilitation.' The inter-relations between urgency of clients' immediate material needs, lack of pre-release visiting, lack of information on clients, the bargaining nature of client-worker interactions, lack of material and treatment resources are some of the variables that appeared to be directly related to inadequate diagnosis, difficulty in establishing a professional relationship, parcelling out of clients to different agencies and lack of an overall casework plan. This kind of system of interacting variables could certainly be seen to account for failures in social work in many social work agencies.

It becomes apparent therefore that social workers of all kinds have to be concerned with the total network of social provision, and should contribute to policy formulation. This is not easy. Harry Specht[21] argues that the call for social workers to 'get into the political arena' however temporarily inspiring is likely to leave many feeling inadequate. But he goes on to point out that policy formulation is a process entailing many different tasks and roles, and that all professionals can learn to contribute to the process in whatever is the most appropriate way for them. He sets out a model of the process which specifies the professional tasks and roles that are relevant at various stages. It suggests that the social work practitioner with individuals and families has tasks to perform at the stages of identification of the problem, implementation of new policies and their evaluation; and that the community organizer has tasks at the stages of bringing the problem to the attention of the public, developing policy goals and building public support. The manner in which Specht classifies social work roles and specific tasks, based as it is on the American experience in 1967, may not precisely fit our own current situation. Nevertheless, the point that all social workers, no matter what positions they occupy or what methods they are using, can and should play a part in policy formulation holds good. Besides contributing to changes in policy within one's own agency there is the need to help other agencies to come together to work out policies that ensure helpful transactions between providers and consumers of services. In other words there is a need to be aware of and to work with the social service system as a whole. It may be that within the whole, one of the most important contributions that social workers with individuals and families can make is to act as mediators, helping the consumers and the social service system to communicate directly with each other in a manner that helps consumers to make better use of the system, and helps the system to make better adaptations to the consumers.

Conclusion.

In this paper we have attempted to use the general systems approach to sketch the outlines of social work intervention. We have intentionally stressed how this approach can be used by the worker with individuals and families. This is not to devalue the contribution of other kinds of workers. On the contrary, we have argued that the social problems experienced by individuals and families are seldom susceptible to treatment at the individual and the family level alone, and that caseworkers, group workers, residential workers and community workers must see themselves as part of a service team intervening in the social system as a whole; as much dependent on other kinds of workers such as teachers, doctors, lawyers, planners and managers as they are upon each other.

References

1 Mary Paul Janchill, 1969, 'Systems concepts in casework, theory and practice', *Social Casework*, February; Ann Hartman, 1970, 'To think about the unthinkable', *Social Casework*, October.
2 Gordon Hearn, 1958, *Theory Building in Social Work*, University of Toronto Press.
3 Gordon Hearn (ed.), 1968, *The General Systems Approach: Contributions Toward an Holistic Conception of Social Work*, New York, Council on Social Work Education.
4 1973, *Social Work Practice: Model and Method*, F. E. Peacock.
5 1973, *Social Work Practice: a Unitary Approach*, University of South Carolina Press.
6 R. D. Laing, 1967, *The Politics of Experience*, Penguin Books, p. 45.
7 1968, 'Basic constructs for an integrative and generative conception of social work', in *The General Systems Approach*, ed. Gordon Hearn.
8 Harriet E. Bartlett, 1970, *The Common Base of Social Work Practice*, New York, National Association of Social Workers.
9 ibid., p. 106.
10 1967, *Sociology and Modern Systems Theory*, Prentice-Hall, p. 44.
11 Harris Chaiklin, 1969, 'Social system, personality system and practice theory', in *Social Work Practice*,

New York National Conference of Social Welfare, Columbia University Press.
12 Gordon, op. cit.
13 Beulah Rothman and Catherine Papell, 1966, 'Social groupwork models, *Journal of Education for Social Work*, no. 2, autumn.
14 Derek Jehu *et al.*, *Behaviour Modification in Social Casework*, Wiley.
15 Dorothy Runnicles, 1971, 'The relation of community work to casework', unpublished paper prepared for NISW Workshop.
16 The following draws largely on the framework presented by Donald Lathrope in 'The general systems approach in social work practice', *The General Systems Approach*, ed. Gordon Hearn, 1968.
17 1970, *The Client Speaks*, Routledge & Kegan Paul.
18 1970, 'Socialization and social casework', *Theories of Social Casework*, ed. Roberts and Nee, University of Chicago Press.
19 William Jordan, 1970, *Client-Worker Transactions*, Routledge & Kegan Paul.
20 Home Office Research Studies, 1971, *Exploration in After-Care*, HMSO.
21 1967, 'Social policy formulation: the role of the social caseworker', in *Social Work Practice*, National Conference on Social Welfare, Columbia University Press.

III. 8 The tasks and functions of residential institutions

E. J. Miller and G. V. Gwynne

Characteristics of the intake

[Here] we examine certain essential features of residential institutions catering for the physically handicapped and chronic sick and begin to analyse their consequences.

At one level the function of such an institution can be defined quite straightforwardly: it imports cripples and looks after them. But if we are to understand and try to tackle the problems of operating these institutions, it is necessary to be a good deal more precise about what it is that is being imported and the nature of the task that the institution is being called upon to carry out.

[. . .] every institution has to contend with social attitudes towards disability. These not only impinge on the institution from outside, but are imported into it, by managements, by staff, and by the inmates themselves. [. . .] Infirmity has psychological—even psychopathological—consequences which are often insidious and even irreversible. If I have a visible handicap, your behaviour towards me will be different in gross or subtle ways from your behaviour towards able-bodied associates; accordingly, my response to you is different from theirs to you; your image of me as different is confirmed; my image of myself is affected by your image of me; thus I am in reality different. The problem of being set apart in this way is one with which every cripple has somehow to cope.

Although inmates of residential institutions are often more physically (and perhaps psychologically) handicapped than those who remain in the community, this is by no means necessarily so. The more critical difference is that they have been rejected. They have for the most part been rejected as individuals, in that their families are no longer willing or able to look after them. More importantly, by crossing the boundary into the institution, whether voluntarily or not,

they fall into a rejected category of non-contributors to and non-participants in society, and indeed are virtually non-members of society.

Individual rejection

Individual experiences of rejection are often blatant. The case of Mrs Atkins is an example:

Mrs Atkins who is now in her middle fifties, has Parkinson's disease. Her speech is difficult to understand. Two operations have made it possible for her to walk—an awkward, shuffling gait. She easily loses her balance, falls over and bruises herself, and because of this she cannot go out alone. She is able to dress, wash and bath herself, but it is a painfully slow business: to get dressed takes her about an hour. Her disease began shortly after the birth of her daughter. The first thirteen years of her marriage were spent with her in-laws. Because of her own frail health her mother-in-law brought up the child. By the time Mrs Atkins and her husband were able to afford a home of their own, she was already too incapacitated to manage the housework. She recalled that her husband stayed up until 4 a.m. cleaning the house on their first Christmas in the new home and that he then had to leave at 6 a.m. to go on shift duty. 'He was good to me then.' Subsequently the husband brought another woman into the house; Mrs Atkins was relegated to the spare bedroom. He was violent with her on several occasions and once, when she could no longer cope adequately on her own, left her for three months. Three years ago she saw an article in a local paper describing the institution where she now lives and she herself applied for admission. She later divorced her husband. She showed neither bitterness nor recrimination towards him and could

Source: *A Life Apart*, Tavistock Publications, 1972, pp. 72–90.

see the strain that was imposed on him by twenty-five years of marriage during which his partner became progressively less able to cope and to provide a normal home life. Plainly, however, his cruelty to her during the last few years was calculated, consciously or not, to drive her away and rid him of an intolerable burden. The daughter is now married with three children of her own and lives only a few miles from the institution. Despite the proximity she apparently visits her mother only about once a year. 'She can't really come with three children.'

[There is a] high rate of divorce or legal separation among inmates. For many of those still classified as married, the status was largely nominal. An exception was Mrs Brown, whose husband moved house to be close to the institution in which she lived: he was able to visit her daily and take her home for a few hours at weekends. Much more often, visits by spouses tend to become increasingly infrequent and perfunctory.[1]

Like Mrs Atkins, many inmates disguise their feeling of rejection and try to cover up: 'He's good to me really but he's busy at weekends.' But such feelings can be painful. The inmate who commented to the interviewer: 'Matron says we're only here because our relatives won't put up with us', was perhaps asking to be reassured that her statement was not really true.

Of the inmates who are or have been married, women out-number men – partly because the caring role is socially defined as a feminine role and this makes it more appropriate for a wife to look after a disabled husband than vice versa. This is reinforced by the structure of financial aid. The disabled husband normally has some kind of pension which makes it at least possible, if difficult, for the wife to devote her time to looking after him without having to take up other employment. No corresponding financial help is available if it is the wife who is disabled. Unless, therefore, the husband's financial resources are substantial, he cannot arrange for someone to look after his wife at home. It is then difficult to find any alternative to an institution.

The married inmates are, of course, for the most part those who have been disabled only later in life. Those who have been crippled at birth or in childhood are much less likely ever to get married. They have usually experienced a lifetime of successive rejections.

As a child of seven Mr Collins had a disease which caused a great deal of pain, hampered his growth, and led to a weakened heart. He stopped going to school and his life from then on was confined to a series of hospitals, where he received little tuition. He claims that he taught himself to read. His deprivation was intensified by a permanent rift between his parents. His mother, he felt, wanted nothing to do with him; his father could not cope alone; so he stayed in hospital until he was moved to the home where we met him. His father had continued to visit him until

his death some years previously; his mother never contacted him.

In other cases, lengthy periods of hospitalization have been accompanied by strongly supportive parental relationships.

Miss Davis, for example, who has Still's disease, is one of a family of five children. She spent most of the first nine years of her life in a leading orthopaedic hospital, which she entered at eighteen months. Diagnoses in the early days were uncertain. Towards the end of the stay in hospital there was a suggestion that her legs should be amputated below the knee since it was thought that she would never be able to walk, but her mother would not agree to the operation and she was discharged. Her memory of the years in hospital is vague. At ten she went to school for the first time. This was a primary school for normal children. At first the school had refused to take her on the ground that the responsibility for a crippled child was too great; but her mother was determined that she should go to an ordinary school rather than to a special school and successfully appealed to her Member of Parliament. Miss Davies feels that it was due to her mother's determination that she learnt to walk. Despite her prolonged stay in the orthopaedic hospital she had been unable to walk when she left. The local GP's advice was to keep her moving as much as possible and her mother insisted that she practised walking daily around the garden. If she fell, she had to pick herself up. Now, at the age of thirty, she has had to come into an institution because she is also going blind. In view of this second disability she thinks it particularly fortunate that her mother did not agree to the amputation.

It is important to recognize that although in retrospect Miss Davies's mother can be seen rationally to have been supportive and helpful, the child's subjective experience was nevertheless one of rejection by her mother. Whatever the compelling reasons, the mother did not look after her, but sent her away. This deprivation of the child's normal experience of reliable mothering is common among those who are hospitalized in infancy or early childhood.

Social rejection

So far we have been considering manifestations of personal rejection, which, to a greater or lesser degree, has been experienced by almost every inmate coming into an institution of this kind. This will obviously have psychological effects on them as individuals and thus on the relationship they make with the institution. The second type of rejection we mentioned was social rejection – the rejection of inmates as non-contributors to and non-participants in society. While this will also be experienced by inmates individually in various ways and will often be bound up with personal rejection, we are more concerned here with its impact on inmates as a category and thus on the relation between all institutions of this type and the society that has exported them.

The cripple who has not been put into an institution clings on, albeit often precariously, to some kind of status within the wider society. Least socially handicapped is the cripple who is not only in work but is also a breadwinner. The roles conferred by his job and by his position in the family override his status as a cripple: he thus approximates to a 'normal' member of society.

Jobs, however, are more difficult to find for cripples than for the able-bodied and, once obtained, more difficult to hold.[2] However irrelevant it may be to the individual's work capacity, the disability almost always obtrudes into the relationship between employer and employee. Cripples frequently report peremptory dismissals without explanation. Whether they are in reality victimized is, of course, impossible to ascertain; nevertheless, the feeling of victimization is real and inevitably colours the relationship with the next prospective employer. The cripple is suspicious and distrustful of the employer's motives; aware of this, the employer is himself on guard; and the outcome is all too predictable.

One should perhaps be surprised that more cripples do not give up the struggle and seek some kind of sanctuary. Giving up the struggle, however, also means giving up the social status that goes with the job. Although to most of us this may not seem a social status that confers a great many privileges, the lack of it certainly carries with it major deprivations.

Rehabilitation was defined for us by the head of one rehabilitation unit in terms of acquiring the status of a tax-payer. This reflects the value that our society assigns to work. Society both applies pressure on every child to assume this status and invests substantial resources in educational and therapeutic institutions whose task is to prepare people for this status or to restore them to it. In some cases these resources seem not to have been deployed as effectively as they might have been.

Mr Edwards, now fifty-three, is an example. He contracted polio as an infant. He has no movement below the waist and his right arm and hand are completely useless. He can just manage to store a cigarette between two fingers on his right hand, but cannot move the hand. His left arm, too, has very little movement but his left hand is extremely good. This is his principal asset. He was kept at home for a few years as a child but spent most of his life in hospitals or institutions. His parents died when he was in his late teens and although he has a number of brothers and sisters they don't want to know him. He had been at a hospital fairly near his home in Kent until the war broke out, when he was evacuated to

Lancashire. He stayed in a hospital there throughout the war. (This distance from home made it almost inevitable that he would be cut off from family and relatives.) Shortly after the war he was transferred to yet another hospital in the south. From there he was sent for a twelve-week period to a rehabilitation centre, the object being to assess his capacity for work. Because of his chequered history of hospitalization he had received only two years of schooling; such proficiency as he had in reading and writing was largely self-taught. To assess his capacity he was given a number of tests which he passed fairly well. He was told that he was fit to hold down a job. He was also told, however, that it was up to him to get a job to hold down. That was out of the question, so he returned to hospital. Somewhat later a welfare worker suggested that he should go in for book-keeping. Various half-promises were made but nothing came of it. Subsequently a surgeon suggested that he should have his useless right hand amputated and replaced by an artificial hand which would enable him to do a little more. Again, nothing came of this. Finally, he got himself transferred from hospital to the residential institution where he now lives. This is a place that offers him a much more benign environment and also relative security of tenure. After he had been there for two years the notion of his taking up book-keeping was raised again and it was suggested that he be transferred to another establishment which specializes in retraining the physically handicapped. How far these previous episodes had come to nothing because of his own reluctance is impossible to tell. He himself says that he was not enthusiastic about having his hand amputated but he was willing. By the time this final proposal to take up book-keeping was made, however, he certainly felt that he had had enough. He understood that if he failed the proposed training course there was no guarantee that he would be able to come back to the institution he was in, and if he passed, there was similarly no guarantee about where he might be transferred. He therefore elected to stay where he was.

However one may apportion responsibility for the outcome between Mr Edwards and his rehabilitators, the fact is that rehabilitation, though evidently regarded by both as the desirable objective, remained a chimera. In this respect, his case is not atypical of the reported experience of a great many in these institutions. Their lives before they were institutionalized have been a succession of hopes raised and hopes dashed. By external criteria they have failed.

The sense of failure seems particularly strong in those who as children have been to special residential schools for physically handicapped and have received along with their education and training the impression that when they grow up they will be able to find employment and take their place in society. Others, as children, have no doubt been buoyed up through a series of difficult and painful operations by the hope, explicit or implied, that the next operation would bring recovery or at least an improvement in functioning; and, too often, it has not done so. Work, and the status that goes with it, is highly important as an aspiration.

The cripple who cannot work and is supported by parents or by a spouse feels deprived and the deprivation extends to other members of the family. From time to time the plight of these families is publicized in the press: for example the husband who is trying to hold down a full-time job and also look after his incurably ill wife. But what is important is that the deprivation is shared; and the dependent cripple (even a Mrs Atkins) still retains a vicarious social status as a member of a family which has a place in society. The husband just referred to asked through the columns of the newspaper whether he should give up his job so as to devote his full attention to his wife. Readers earnestly advised him not to, on the very real grounds that by doing so he would be further attenuating his wife's vicarious link with the social world outside.

For inmates in a residential institution even this vicarious link has been severed.

Consequences for the primary task

This examination of some characteristics of the 'human throughput' enables us to define more rigorously the task of these residential institutions and to see in what respects they differ from other residential institutions that superficially seem comparable.

Physical handicap by itself is not the discriminating factor; nor is the experience of personal rejection. More critical is the fact that when people cross the boundary into such an institution they are displaying that they have failed to occupy or retain any role which, according to the norms of society, confers social status on the individual. Even in this respect, however, the crippled inmate is comparable with the convict committed to prison or the patient committed to a psychiatric hospital. What is significantly different is that the prison and, nowadays, the psychiatric hospital sooner or later discharge almost all their inmates and have grounds for hoping that some will be reformed or cured and take up socially valued roles in the outside world. By contrast the boundary of the kind of institution we are discussing is, by and large, a point of no return. It is exceptional indeed for an inmate to be restored to some semblance of a normal role in the wider society. Usually he will remain in the institution, or in another of the same category, until he dies.

To lack any actual or potential role that confers a positive social status in the wider society is tantamount to being socially dead. To be admitted to one of these institutions is to enter a kind of limbo in which one has been written off as a member of society but is not yet physically dead.

In these terms, the task that society assigns – behaviourally though never verbally – to these institutions is to cater for the socially dead during the interval between social death and physical death.

Compensatory values

A few inmates recognize this implicit definition of the task of the institution. It is a receptacle for those who are beyond salvage – 'the scraphead of human rejects' (Brown, 1966, p. 140). In January 1968, when the 'Back Britain' movement was sweeping the country, a macabre joke was going about in one institution: 'Let's back Britain', it was suggested, 'by all committing suicide. We could save the country £30,000 a year.'

If one is in a situation of hopeless adversity, cynicism is one form of defence. No doubt some of the inmates who refer to themselves as being on 'the scrapheap of human rejects' are half hoping to be contradicted – and they usually are. An able-bodied commentator who makes a remark to this effect is liable to arouse angry protest. Indeed, although there may be some inmates who, however reluctantly, see the reality of the situation they are in, the majority of inmates and almost all staff and members of the wider society find the notion of the social death sentence altogether too painful to contemplate.

Both the widespread use of the specialized 'limbo' institutions and the attitudes towards them are the result of three features of contemporary society. First, medical advances designed to prolong life have often succeeded merely in postponing death; second, the diminished size of the family unit has reduced its viability in holding its sick or ageing members; and third, the declining force of the values and rituals of Christianity has left society without any adequate cultural mechanisms for coping with death.

The last point is particularly important. As Geoffrey Gorer (1965) and others have pointed out, death in contemporary society has come to be looked upon as obscene. In contrast to, for example, the Indian joint family, where the growing child experiences the cycle of birth and death as being almost as natural as the cycle of the seasons and the crops, in our own society many adults have yet to see their first corpse. The idea of death – the death of others and, more particularly, the death of oneself – is shut away. We lack socially sanctioned devices to express our grief and share our work of mourning. To die or to be bereaved is to commit a social gaffe and, as with social gaffes of other kinds, the recommended procedure is: 'Least said, soonest mended.'

The cripple, of course – especially the victim of an incurable and progressive disease – is an ugly reminder of mortality. It is perhaps for this reason that we are particularly prone in contemporary society to put these rejects out of sight in special institutions of their own. By the same token, the reality of what is being done must also be denied.

Since it is too painful to acknowledge explicitly what society is implicitly asking these institutions to do, two sets of values are commonly brought into use as defence mechanisms. These may be labelled the humanitarian or medical value that prolongation of life is a good thing and the liberal or anti-medical value that the handicapped inmates of these institutions are 'really normal'.

The humanitarian defence

Although the social death sentence has been passed, the pressure of humanitarian values is to keep the interval between social and physical death as long as possible. The medical profession is one of the carriers of these values on behalf of society. Doctors and nurses are committed to preserving and prolonging life without asking for what purpose. Not long ago there was a public outcry in Britain when it was disclosed that a hospital consultant had issued written instructions that resuscitation procedures were not to be applied in cases of heart failure if the victims were over the age of seventy. If doctors exercise any discretion of this kind, they are expected to do so quietly and discreetly. When the demand for life-saving apparatus, such as kidney machines, outstrips supply we give the medical profession no guidance as to whose lives to save and whose to sacrifice. This is a painful reality that we prefer not to discuss and by and large the medical profession colludes with the rest of society in this respect.

In a hospital ward set aside for the 'young chronic sick' we saw a young man who had suffered brain damage through oxygen starvation during a heart operation. His body was largely paralysed, he had no speech, and he showed no signs of awareness of what was going on around him. He frequently screamed and occasionally tried to attack the nurses. When we asked the specialist whether he didn't think that both the patient and his family might be better off if he were dead, the specialist was indignant. It was his job, he said, to preserve life 'and we must never forget that in another ten years there may be a cure for this'. Later he acknowledged the conflict he felt when faced with such cases.

While humanitarian values apply pressure to postpone physical death for as long as possible there is reluctance to acknowledge the unhappiness and lack of fulfilment of many of the lives that are so prolonged. Society wants to believe that the inmates are happy and contented and demands that they behave as if they were happy and contented. We heard of one institution where the chairman of the Management Committee would stride in breezily every morning and say: 'Oh what a happy place this is! It always gives

me such pleasure to come here.' As one inmate commented: 'How can we tell her what we really feel like?' For the inmate to show discontent is to show ingratitude and this is an affront to humanitarian values.

The liberal defence

In this respect, superficially at least, the liberal value is at variance with the humanitarian. The abnormality of the inmates is denied: it is claimed that they are 'really normal'. It is the liberal conviction that the institutionalized cripple ought to be accepted by the rest of society and it is implied that if he develops the capacities remaining to him he will in fact be accepted. Hopes of physical and, more particularly, social rehabilitation are thus encouraged.

However, any inmate who takes too literally the liberal protestations that he is really normal, and who behaves accordingly by trying to cross back to the other side of the boundary, quickly discovers his mistake. The encouragement given to an aspiring foot- or mouth-painter tends to be in inverse proportion to the income that his paintings produce: if his income as an inmate approaches income levels in the world outside he becomes an awkward anomaly in the system.

Earlier we described the case of Mr Edwards, who refused to risk the uncertainties of giving up his place in an institution for the doubtful fruits of a course in book-keeping. He nevertheless did not stagnate. Exploiting the dexterity of his good left hand, he began to manufacture costume jewellery and took samples of this to a department store where one of the buyers said that they would sell as much as he could provide. He could not work very fast but over a period of about eighteen months began to build a modest business, clearing a total of some £40 after his materials had been paid for. At the end of this period he received a visit from a Customs and Excise official who said that he understood that he had been selling jewellery. Mr Edwards was required to show the official his receipts and it was pointed out to him that under the purchase-tax regulations he was obliged to pay 50 per cent of his takings to Customs and Excise. They agreed to waive any tax due on the work he had done already but told him not to undertake any more unless he was prepared to pay the purchase tax. Mr Edwards concluded that if he put his prices up to a level that would still give him some profit margin, he would price himself out of the market. He therefore gave up making costume jewellery. Nowadays he is still active in the workshop of his institution and satisfies his entrepreneurial drives by being the institution's tobacco and cigarette merchant. He buys these at wholesale prices and gives 50 per cent of his profits to the institution's welfare fund.

Like others receiving social security benefits, a handicapped person has his allowance cut if his earnings exceed £2.05 per week. Similarly, the inmate whose upkeep in an institution is paid for by a local authority ceases to be eligible for support if he is gainfully employed – even though there may be an unbridgeable gap between what he earns and what he would need to support himself. This is reminiscent of trade union protests against prison inmates being allowed to earn money from real work in contrast to the make-work of sewing mail-bags. The inmate must not compete with normals. Society is curiously intolerant of the half and half, of the uncategorizable.

Staff who profess liberal values frequently proceed to infantilize inmates by claiming, for example, that their home is 'one big happy family'. The analogy is clear: they identify the inmates with children and themselves with parents. Their assertion that they believe inmates are 'really normal' is all too often belied by some disparaging remark: for instance, 'I think it's good for them to have boyfriends but of course [with a laugh] their little affairs don't last very long.'

Two models of residential care

Associated with these two values, the humanitarian and the liberal, we have identified two models of residential care which we call here the Warehousing Model and the Horticultural Model. These define the primary task of a residential institution in rather different ways.

The warehousing model

In the warehousing model, the primary task becomes: to prolong physical life. It represents an attempt to translate the model of the hospital into the setting of the residential institution. The intake into the system is a patient defined in terms of physical malfunctioning. The conversion process entails the provision of medical and nursing care. This provision is facilitated if the inmate, as the object of these ministrations, accepts his dependent role in the system. Acceptance of temporary dependency is functional in the hospital setting as a means to an end: the output, it is hoped, is a person restored to his normal roles in the world outside. Doctors and nurses derive satisfaction from their contribution to this process. Institutions for incurables, however, can provide neither the hope for the patients nor the conventional satisfaction for staff. In the hospital, the patient who dies, however inevitable his death may be, is the failure of a process directed towards cure; in the institution, there are no cures: the only outputs are dead patients. Medical and nursing skills are thus redirected from the familiar task of curing to the task of postponing death.

We discuss in a later chapter the problems for both parties of providing and receiving intimate physical services. Both the anxieties of the ordinary hospital situation and the defences used to cope with them are magnified in the long-stay institution. One common defence that may be mentioned here is the depersonalization of patients into 'cases'.

When one of us visited a special ward set aside for young chronic sick within a larger hospital, the consultant in charge, despite our protestations that our interest and qualifications were non-medical, proudly showed off each patient in turn, describing his condition, treatment, and prognosis. In one case – a woman crippled with arthritis, compelled to lie permanently on her back – the consultant had a screen put round the bed, raised the woman's nightdress to her thighs and, with something of the pride of a philatelist displaying a rare stamp, drew detailed attention to her deformed and twisted legs. In this ward the performance of the primary task that the warehousing model implies could hardly have been surpassed. One cannot but be reminded, however, of the efforts made in prison to prevent the convicted murderer from dying in any other way than through judicial execution.

To the extent that effective performance of the warehousing task requires the inmate to remain dependent and depersonalized, any attempts by the inmate to assert himself, or to display individual needs other than those arising from his specific disability, are in the warehousing model constraints on task performance. They are therefore to be discouraged. The 'good' inmate is one who accepts the staff's diagnosis of his needs and the treatment they prescribe and administer.

The horticultural model

In the horticultural model, by contrast, it is needs for physical care that are the constraints. The intake into the system is conceived as a deprived individual with unsatisfied drives and unfulfilled capacities. The primary task is to develop these capacities. Thus the conversion process is concerned with providing encouragement for the individual development of inmates in the direction of greater independence – in complete contrast to the dependency orientation inherent in the warehousing model. The role of staff that follows from this horticultural ideology is thus not to treat the disability but to provide opportunities for the growth of abilities.

The horticultural model is a relatively recent development. The warehousing model represents the conventional approach to residential care and is still to be found in relatively pure form, especially in some medically based institutions that are as yet only slightly tempered by what we describe here as liberal values. The horticultural model, on the other hand, is less likely to be found in a pure form – it is an aspiration rather than a reality – and in some institutions the two models coexist somewhat uncomfortably together.

The models as social defence mechanisms

[. . .] Here [. . .] we wish to draw attention to the use of these models as defence mechanisms.

In order to look at them in this way it is necessary to try to break out of the straitjacket of one's own value system. We ourselves, when we embarked upon this study, were very much caught up with the liberal values of the horticultural model. We were captured by the plight of intelligent cripples in particular who were forced to lead stunted lives in institutions that did not provide opportunities for their development. We were antipathetic to the warehousing ideology. There seemed to be no point in prolonging physical existence for its own sake and we would argue that individuals should be given a greater opportunity to determine their own lives and to take risks, even if this might mean shortening their life-span – though it was comforting to believe that, despite the risks, the fuller and richer life that the horticultural model offered might actually postpone death rather than hasten it.

It is not difficult to recognize the inadequacies of a warehousing system in which inmates are treated as helpless bodies to be processed – to be got out of bed, washed, dressed, fed, put on the lavatory, entertained, and kept busy. If emotional and psychological needs are denied or discounted, the most expert and devoted care of the body can destroy the person. The system all too readily projects into the patients its own image of their helplessness, which then pervades their whole life.

It is less easy to see that the horticultural mode is also inadequate. The philosophy that people are more than their disabilities and the emphasis on development of individual capacities seem unexceptional. Yet paradoxically this approach may deprive at least some individuals of their real needs. The pressure to maintain or increase independence may be inappropriate and even distressing to someone with multiple sclerosis or muscular dystrophy who, as his disease progresses, faces a gradual or stepwise decline. Acceptance of dependency may fit the needs of some much better than the struggle against it. Thus the declining multiple sclerotic may feel just as deprived in the horticultural climate as the lively youngster with polio in a warehousing culture that is geared to brain damaged 'vegetables'.

Few inmates, therefore, fit either model entirely. The same individual may feel somewhat more comfortable with one model in the earlier stages of his institutionalization and with the other model later. We argue that the models cannot be adequate because the tasks they represent are not real tasks. They are essentially social defence mechanisms set up to cope with the intolerable anxieties that are associated with the task that society implicitly defines for these institutions. Like other social defence mechanisms, they are obviously, in part, functional. They support individual defences both of the inmates and of the people who look after them. They also support the

defences of members of the wider society who are, however occasionally, reminded of the existence of these institutions. As with other defence mechanisms, however, they have a dysfunctional component as well.

What both models neglect and deny is that, if we are correct in our interpretation that by the very fact of committing people to institutions of this type, society is defining them as, in effect, socially dead, then the essential task to be carried out is to help the inmates to make their transition from social death to physical death. Denial of the meaning of this boundary between the institution and the wider society, between the 'dead' and the living, can lead [. . .] to splitting within the institution between staff and residents or between one group of staff and another, and also to processes of canonization and scapegoating.

What is most intolerable about the real task as we define it here is that it might imply the the individual himself could have a choice about when to die. Paradoxically this is still regarded as an affront to society, even though society has effectively washed its hands of the inmates as significant social beings. Pressed to its logical conclusion, the real task would imply that the inmate on entering such an institution could be given a capsule that would bring about instantaneous and painless death whenever he chose to take it. Such logic, of course, transgresses too many deep-seated cultural values: even to suggest such a possibility would be regarded as outrageous.

Yet so long as the unthinkableness of this alternative persists and is in effect repressed and denied by the substitute tasks derived from the humanitarian and liberal values, it may also become impossible to contemplate more appropriate approaches to the processes of residential care in institutions of this kind. Perhaps we are too guilty about the social death sentence (that behaviourally we have passed and verbally deny) and we fear that if they are given the opportunity of electing when to die the inmates will affront us by swallowing the capsule forthwith. It may be salutary to recall the well-known story of the judge who passed sentence of death on a prisoner but showed clemency by allowing him to choose the manner of his death. The prisoner's retort was immediate: 'I'd like to die of old age, sir.' The corollary of recognizing that the social death sentence has already been passed and that the individual may be left with the choice of when and how to die is the recognition of the individual's right to determine how he would like to spend the intervening period. This includes the right to choose dependency, or to take advantage of developmental opportunities. It then becomes the task of the institution first to help the individual to make his decision and second to provide him with the facilities to implement it.

This definition of the task challenges the warehousing assumption and defence that inmates have only physical needs. It also challenges the horticultural assumption and defence that they are 'really normal'. It demands recognition that, while on the one hand inmates have in common the experience of having been extruded from the wider society and of no longer being able to aspire to its norms of achievement, they are at the same time widely diverse individuals with diverse and changing needs. It implies that it is the task of the institution, without either destroying the inmate's individuality or denying his dependence, to provide a setting in which he can find his own best way of relating to the external world and to himself. [. . .]

Notes

1 Other studies have confirmed the strong inverse correlation between length of stay in an institution and frequency of visits (e.g. Wing, 1962).

2 Townsend (1967) asserts that some employers abuse the Disabled Persons (Employment) Act 'by persuading some lightly handicapped persons . . . to register as disabled . . .' Others, he maintains, pay low wages.

References

Brown, H., 1966, 'Some anomalies of social welfare', in Hunt (1966), pp. 133–41.

Gorer, G., 1965, *Death, Grief and Mourning in Contemporary Britain*, Cresset Press.

Hunt, P. (ed.), 1966, *Stigma: the Experience of Disability*, Geoffrey Chapman.

Townsend, P., 1967, 'The disabled in society', lecture read at the Royal College of Surgeons.

Wing, J. K., 1962, 'Institutionalism in mental hospitals', *British Journal of Social and Clinical Psychology*, 1, p. 38.

III. 9 I give them money

Geoffrey Parkinson

While I was visiting Pentonville prison, Ronald White, aged twenty-four, with twelve court appearances behind him, called at the probation office and asked to see me. I have known him for a number of years and watched him grope his way from gas meter thefts to the impressive delinquent heights of robbery with violence. He was now a voluntary after-care case and my aim was to maintain some sort of coarse, casual contact until perhaps age and an overdose of prison made him more benign.

On being told I was away Ronald asked to see somebody else, which meant the duty officer. That day the duty officer was an experienced worker, specially trained in psycho-analytically orientated casework and familiar with Ronald White and his history. What went on between them is not clear but my colleague left me a brief note giving his impression of the interview:

> Ronald White called at the office today. I remembered him because he was under my supervision once in Hampshire. The interview started by his asking for financial help but it soon became apparent that he had more fundamental worries; his marriage has just recently broken down after only six months and I felt he had quite deep feelings about this. I am sure he would welcome seeing you again and you may be able to help him work through his difficulties in this area.

A week later I saw Ronald. 'What's all this about your marriage?' I asked. 'Oh that ain't nothing much. I didn't want to marry her anyway,' he answered casually. 'When you saw my colleague he felt you were pretty fed up.' 'Yeah well, it was like this, I was a bit short of money and I thought you might loan me a dollar or two. When they told me you were out I saw Mr T. I was once under his supervision. I told him

what I wanted and he started to ask me some questions about myself and when I told him about my marriage he got very interested and wanted to know all about it. I really didn't want to go into it but he seemed pretty keen. He is a nice bloke and after all the interest he was taking. I didn't feel I could end our talk by saying, "I have not come here about my marriage, I want some money," because it might have seemed ungrateful for all the trouble he was taking with my problems. So anyway, I decided I would have to get the money from somewhere else and I thanked him and pushed off.'

There is nothing very momentous about these two interviews. I told Ronald that I felt he could cope with his marriage breakdown, that he would be a bloody fool if he allowed it to lead him into more crime, and I then gave him ten shillings, a letter to the Ministry of Social Security, and asked him to keep in contact. I think it is highly likely that he will, while I give him cash and boost his fragile ego.

This little incident is too fragmentary for any deep analysis but it illustrates two methods of approach towards clients that arise quite frequently in the probation service and in other casework agencies. My colleague, in classical style, got past the 'presenting problem' to a fundamental area of Ronald's life—his broken marriage. Ronald at an earlier interview had assessed me as 'a hard sod, good for a soft touch'. I am, as one of my colleagues aptly described it, a shallow caseworker.

In the late 1950s and early 1960s deep casework appeared to offer almost magical possibilities for the treatment of clients. Crude assumptions about human motivation were being swept away in our social services. When I had entered the probation service in 1954, reports to courts were little better than police antecedents with a dash of Patience Strong sentimentality. They were mostly based on the 'pull yourself together lad' theory of life. Many advanced voluntary social work agencies looked unhappily at the work of the probation officer. The good Family Welfare

Source: *New Society*, 5 February 1970, pp. 220–1.

Association supervisor of those days could almost be induced into a fit if one said one had given a client money without an analysis in depth of his personality and problems. There was a biblical zeal about the contempt for money shown by those early case-workers of the New School. Old charity organisations like the Family Welfare Association were particularly vigorous in the pursuit of the pure air of casework, since their histories were usually stained with chronic almsgiving. They had decided money solved nothing, it was merely the symptom of the disease. What was needed was an understanding of the fundamental problems. Giving money made the client dependent on the social worker; giving insights into the cause of his moneyless state, on the other hand, gave the client independence. The tradition nostalgically lingers on. Good casework is associated with insight, limited casework with giving money.

I gave Ronald money. I give most of my clients money. I give it because it is the one thing they all accept joyfully; it makes them feel valuable; it breaks down, if only for a moment, their sense of isolation. It makes them believe that I may solve their problems, it buys their co-operation and their friendship which invariably they would not sell for any other price. It shows my concern in the only way they understand. I give money with all the difficulties and dangers of dependence it can produce because I feel I have precious little choice within the context of the situations my clients offer me. There is one further reason: 'conning' money out of the probation officer is perhaps a continuation of the client's delinquent activities, but performed within an accepting environment; it is one of the first steps away from actual stealing and as such is to be welcomed.

My clients cannot accept insight; even if they understood what I was trying to get at, the experience would be too claustrophobic for them. They have no 'reasonable ego', they are emotionally frozen, non-verbal and unmotivated towards change, except perhaps when afraid of the punishments the court may impose on them. Helping my clients with cash is like giving a frozen man brandy before asking him to recount the adventures that caused his condition. The sum does not have to be large. I hand out perhaps £2 a week. But the fund available to the Inner London Probation Service, from which I draw this money, can be vital in opening up relations with a client.

On all this there would, I think, be relatively little disagreement nowadays, just some mild regrets and the hope expressed that gradually the client would be able to use the casework situation more constructively. At one time, however, it was the subject of great and terrible casework war, with all the theorists cursing cash.

The theorists in social work have been a great worry to practising caseworkers. Whilst initially helping, they thereafter probably delayed many agencies in delineating their function, except perhaps by means of protest. For its part, probation had a love affair with psychoanalysis. Many of the noted social work theorists of recent times have plagiarised their insights from the works of Freud and Melanie Klein and hoped that we would match our methods with their ideas. Carmelite casework, its nods and grunts and germ-free insights, was offered to clients in mouldy little offices all over England. We weren't too worried if the clients didn't like it. The theorists had explained that quite easily as 'resistance'. What mattered was the technique, radiating from its centre, that Vatican of casework, the Tavistock Clinic. It took us years to realise that 'the truth' did not always set our clients free.

The probation service is crammed full of dedicated officers who have an accumulation of complex, though partial and half-digested, psychoanalytic theories and insights into human behaviour. Well-meaningly they blunder their way through their caseloads, hoping it all makes some sort of sense. Some may even abandon native intelligence to will-o'-the-wisp theorisings about unconscious motivation. It may even make sense when read in their records and receive high commendation from supervising officers who share the same culture of half-formed theorisings. Yet the central question is, 'What does it mean to the client?' There are a large number of Ronald Whites on our caseload, not so eloquent but probably more shrewd. Time and time again the situation repeats itself. The caseworker, desperately looking for a client who will talk about problems, finds one who is willing to meet the demand. Then off goes the client, followed in hot pursuit by the caseworker, feathers fly in hours of deepening insight until at last the probation officer returns to his case conference exhausted but happy and the client returns unaffected to his crimes. Caseworkers are continually bewildered by the continuing delinquencies of their best clients!

Visiting a prisoner at Springhill some years ago I noticed that he had once been on probation. I asked him how he got on. 'Fine,' he said, 'it was very helpful. We used to talk all about my problems, I was going through a difficult time with my wife.' I said it couldn't have been all that helpful since he had ended up doing more bird. 'No, no,' he replied without showing any signs of regret, 'it was valuable, but you see my probation officer never told me that if I ever got into trouble again I would end up in a place like this.' His remark may have been naive, but its message for treatment is profound.

Marriage problems, for example, may excite and interest a caseworker, but if the client is before him for criminal activity the focus ought to be on the effect a broken marriage may have on the possibilities of further delinquent breakdowns rather than on the marriage as such. There can be no assumption that the client will make the necessary links between matrimonial disharmony and criminality, if links there are. He must be told and told again.

In so far as they have a theoretical knowledge about life, our clients resort to old saws and maxims of the 'it takes two to make a quarrel' variety. These sayings are the client's intellectual contribution to the casework situation and are patronisingly, though not necessarily unsympathetically, assessed by the worker. What the worker may not realise is that invariably he is offering the same sort of patterned stereotyped material back to the client, only it is middle class, more 'psychological' and better presented. The client has learnt a fragmented philosophy which hasn't much bearing on his behaviour. The social worker has a psychology more sophisticated but often almost as rigid, which has little to do with the client's real life, or indeed the social worker's real life, in many cases.

In the future we may have to face in our society not the ignorant inflexibility of much social welfare, but a new insightful inflexibility that comes from knowing 'the truth.' Local welfare authorities, members of the clergy, marriage guidance councillors and a variety of social work agencies, are already frequently offering, with rigid hygienic zeal, something of the medicine that has been so ardently advocated in the name of insight, progress and reform.

I recently experienced this situation in small detail when I took one of my children to a local authority pre-school playgroup, highly commended for its new knowledge about children and play techniques. The staff seemed to know all about my child before they knew my child, and almost parrot-like repeated the truths of child development we social workers know so well. Not surprisingly they took rather less interest in the child than in their theories and their self-preoccupation and general casualness towards the children under their care was slightly distracting, though of course it was explained away by a 'psychological' theory: 'This is the child's world. We won't interfere unless we have to.' This playgroup was probably in many respects a great deal better than the old disciplinary groups, but it revealed the special diseases of its conception.

An ex-colleague of mine, back from the United States, said social workers are more and more leaving their clients to their secretaries to deal with and devoting themselves to case conferences about clients. The joke, I think, is serious. The flight from the client is probably on the increase; the gap between casework theory and practice is not as great now as it once was, but it is still leaving students ill-prepared for what they have to meet in the field and encourages some to withdraw to the shelter of administration, social work training or research.

This situation has revealed itself most clearly in the super-ego, middle-class preoccupations of many social inquiry reports and casework records, and a curious idealisation of clients' problems and attitudes. With amazing speed, feelings of guilt are discovered in clients and trifling gestures are interpreted as the hallmarks of subtle reparation: 'His father was once a criminal; now he feels a bad side in himself and is ashamed,' one recent report said of a young man who was clearly going through a mild attack of remand-home remorse.

Middle-class assumptions are legion. Descriptions of home surroundings frequently convey more about the social worker's emotional background than about that of his client. This is particularly true in assessments of the delinquent's mother. Officers are always discovering that she is 'over-protective' and 'over-anxious' and while these descriptions may be justified at the time of the court appearance, the way the mother has dealt with her anxieties in her day-to-day life by behaviour may be far more damaging to her children: her arid emotional life and self preoccupation, her extended absences to enjoy the social life of the pub or the launderette, her obsession with bingo or, more frequent than is generally believed, her promiscuous sexuality.

The idealisation of clients' motives is seen in assumptions about their preoccupation with relationships, most characteristically illustrated by my colleague's contact with Ronald White. This particular client's anxiety about his wrecked marriage was a luxury that only the caseworker could really afford. Ronald's narcissism put forward his real priorities. He could stand a broken marriage, but not half an hour without cigarettes. The Family Welfare Association was, I felt at one time, the most pathetic example of the tug of war that can exist between the client's narcissistic preoccupations and the worker's relationship preoccupations. Clients tried to talk about the gas bill, workers tried to talk about the client's mother. Perceptive clients got the gas bill paid by talking about mother.

A great danger in the field of social work is the rigidity of established concepts among those who see themselves as belonging to the casework elite. In their ranks there are many with that curious instinct which allows life to be seen only through a filter of words and concepts. It is understandable that many social scientists and social workers, having gained new knowledge at great personal sacrifice, will not relinquish or amend it willingly. Flexibility seems a thin return for deserting impressive theoretical superstructures, particularly as it leaves a great gulf of uncertainty which feels, even though is not, unprofessional.

Social workers perhaps more than any other professional workers should have means to correct their faults. Extended research into the clients' experiences of social work would be a good starting point.

III. 10 Social work as the privatized solution of public ills

Geoffrey Pearson

It is the purpose of this paper to explore the possibility that there exists a fundamental tension between the motivation which brings a person into social work as an occupation and certain aspects of our culture, and that this opposition finds some reflection in the relationship between social work's system of values and features of everyday life in urban-industrial society. The social worker is usually taken to be a neutral semi-professional; it is my intention to champion a competing definition of social work by a presentation of the social worker as *essentially* a political deviant. In order to get this argument under way it becomes immediately necessary to clear the ground, for as he is commonly conceived the social worker is regarded as something less than political, and quite beyond the possibilities of deviance. Indeed, stereotypically, the social worker is conforming to a fault—grey, jolly perhaps, but uninteresting.* There is some support for this in Coxon's recent work on occupational attributes.[1]

Images of profession

The attempt here is to approach an important aspect of social work—namely, occupational choice—from outside the limits of this stereotype, or, as Becker, borrowing a term from Freidson, expresses it, with a lack of 'sentimentality'.[2] Becker makes the distinction between 'conventional sentimentality' which acts to place outside the arena of study those cherished myths and beliefs—for example, of the 'highly principled' absence of self-interest in our higher professions, or the impartiality of the police—which are fairly typically unquestioned, and sometimes unquestionable, conventional assumptions, and 'unconventional sentimentality'. Unconventional sentimentality also constitutes a refusal to challenge assumptions, but of a different kind: an example of unconventional senti-

Source: *British Journal of Social Work*, 3 (2), 1973, pp. 209–10, 215, 219–27.

mentality would be the refusal to question the belief that physicians are essentially self-interested, career-oriented, and money-grabbing rather than patient-oriented, or that coppers are necessarily bent. 'Whatever form sentimentality takes', writes Becker, 'its distinguishing mark is a refusal to consider distasteful possibilities.'[3] What one finds distasteful, however, will vary with custom, and whether a social worker would regard as insult or self-affirmation the imagery of the sensibly shod, stereotypical social worker will depend on that actor's purposes and preferences.

'Sentimentality' in attitudes towards occupations reflects what one group or another would like the occupation to be. We can recognize in different sentimentalities what Strauss has called 'segments' of professions which are the diverse and heterogeneous orientations—some well organized, others relatively less so—within a profession which underly the often well-managed public face of a homogeneous, unified professional identity.[4] Sentimentalities reflect factional interests as to what a profession is about: what its proper activities are; how its membership should be trained, recruited, etc.

One interest group largely ignored in considerations of struggles within professional groups is that of the 'raw' recruit. Indeed, in so far as a 'proper' function of a professional organization is to socialize him into professional understandings and routines, and to rob the initiate of his 'lay' conceptions of professional activity, recruits are persons without social weight. Here, the attempt is to cut through that web of interests by replacing it with another: namely, that of the people who choose social work as a career. In terms of *their* plans and projects, therefore, we will ask what are their attitudes to social work, and what kind of an occupation do they think they are entering; what are recruits looking for, and what does this tell us about social work, about the world in which recruits live, and about the relationship between social work and that world. [. . .]

The 'professional solution'

That which the student hopes to avoid, and the problem which he confronts in his attitude, is well recognized in the literature of the social sciences. He is, for example, refusing to be the 'cheerful robot' which is how Mills describes man in mass society where there is 'rationality without reason'.[5] A more graphic picture of the normal man is drawn by Becker when, writing of the way in which man had once been so ridiculously proud to believe that he stood at the centre of the universe, he had now lost everything of which he could be proud as it was replaced by 'hiring lines, time-clocked work, efficiency and dedication to profit'. He goes on:[6]

> The critical intelligence of all but perhaps a privileged minority of scholars was gradually shaped by this new dedication, so that by and large proud *Homo Sapiens* has today (in Western society) become the finicky peruser of brand names, the covetor and consumer of gadgets and junk.

[. . .]

Who are they fighting for?

The social worker has identified for himself a major life problem—how to work out effective means of relating to self and others in mass society—and has provided for himself through his choice of occupation some sort of solution whereby he might more easily experience himself as a human being in his public life as well as in his private life. Social work as a career becomes for some a limited solution to the problem of mass society. But, unwilling or unable to extend the diagnosis of his ills and their prescribed remedy to his clients, and searching in his professional life for the differences between himself and clients rather than the shared features of their lives, the social worker's solution remains privatized. Indeed, to the extent that his solution remains the privatized pursuit of a privileged minority, it must be an open question as to whether or not we have the right to claim that action as 'political' action.

I want to argue that social work has a very poorly managed public face; 'poor' in the sense that no clear *imagery* is made available to the public as to what kind of occupation it is, or what its core practices are. Therefore, recruits have no ready-made vocabulary of motivation thrust upon them. Theoretically, there is scope for a high degree of individual improvisation in the articulation of motivation in social work; certainly under such circumstances motivational accounts can be expected to tell much more about the entrant than the occupation itself. Given these conditions, it is the high degree of consistency of the motivational accounts from recruits which suggests that attention be directed firmly to the comprehension of social worker motivation as an attempt to act on *a common universe of problems*. These are not best understood as 'personal' expressions of problems, hang-ups and inadequacies; here are potentially successful and 'decent' citizens commenting on the futility of their lives *as* successful and decent citizens, and grasping at social work as a potentially liberating enterprise. The consonance of their articulated motives with many of the issues in the current moral–political debate within social work should further direct us to understand that social work's internal disputes are not simply 'internal-professional' matters. In that all members of society can lay moral claims as rightful judges of welfare programmes,[7] social work is not the kind of occupation which can simply dismiss recruit opinions as 'under-socialized' or 'amateurish', and the recruitment of personnel holding to beliefs such as those outlined is a potentially crucial instrument of professional change.

Thus, organizationally, social work is grounded in what can best be briefly signified as 'managerialism': the philosophy that our social ills demand routine, technical mastery rather than a sweeping confrontation couched in 'political' or 'ideological' terms. Motivationally, however, we find the expression of a politics which takes as its calculus a libidinal self-maximization. It is not a politics of managerialism—instrumental, systematic, grounded in consensus—but of the enragé: expressive, utopian, uncaring for the restrictions of the mundane. It is a politics which, if developed, could only undermine the structures of self-denial and the work ethic which it confronts, but which social welfare *organizationally* is thought to uphold. There is more than a hint of 'postscarcity' politics about the social work recruit's motivation, and there is thus a direct tension between the *organizational* and *motivational* components of social work. Which is not to say that such thoroughly deviant politics is unambiguous; it is not to say that the social worker's commitment to these values is entirely single-purposed.

Here our explorations can add some substance to speculation in Gouldner's *Coming Crisis of Western Sociology*. Gouldner writes about the rise of what he chooses to call 'Psychedelic Culture'—as opposed to 'Utilitarian Culture'—and he suggests that there is a new style of deviant today. He characterizes them—'the cool cats, the beats, the swingers, the hippies, the acid heads, the drop-outs, and the "New Left" itself'[8]—as one symptom of a resistance to utilitarian values, but also as a deviant class who are not on their backs with their palms upturned, and eyes lowered, waiting for the dole, but are fighting for their rights, rejecting labels and stigma, and turning these labels and stigma back onto the authorities: black is beautiful; gay is good; off our backs. Gouldner[9] speculates on the relationship between the 'new deviance' and the traditional strategies of the welfare state. A crucial shift in their relationship, which Gouldner understands, is that the deviant life-style is no longer restricted to the ghetto, or the lumpen poor, but is embraced by some sections of the young and potentially professional middle class, even if for many

'Psychedelic Culture is just a last fling before they surrender and become the conforming cadres of a utilitarian culture'[10] Gouldner asks how the welfare state will adapt to these developments, for:[11]

> The welfare apparatus that will be used against the middle-class deserters of utilitarian culture will be staffed by their class kindred, who may have already caught or who are vulnerable to the very malaise they will be asked to stamp out. They may, in parts of themselves, be drawn to the subversion of our utilitarian social order.

Gouldner's speculative conclusion is that whatever their private adaptations, welfare personnel will 'shop' their kin, continuing to define the various forms of resistance to utilitarian culture as 'sickness', requiring 'humane, and expert treatment by competent authorities—psychiatrists, social workers, counsellors, etcetera'.[12] The style and ideology of recruits to welfare elites, I would want to argue, has wider implications for the welfare state than simply the management of middle-class deviants, and this is to add nothing to what is already implicit in Gouldner's account. An inability to do more than substantiate the general drift of Gouldner's argument, without being able to confirm or refute his conclusion, is a limitation of this paper and, in other areas our account is also inadequate. There is, for example, an historical dimension to social worker motivation. If here I have framed the motivational accounts of recruits in the vocabulary of the 'New Left' of the late 1960s, it must be allowed that there was a not too distant past when people were attracted to psychoanalysis because *it* seemed to offer a liberation from a morality which restricted both personal and sexual expression.

Similarly, the fate of the recruit's perspective during his term of apprenticeship is here left open. In an unpublished paper, Deacon and Bartley suggested that professional social work education 'cools out' political criticism, transforming considerations of social structural problems into an impotent psychological form.[13] Invariably, professionalization is regarded as a conservatizing force, putting out the student's fires. What hard data evidence there is, however, does not support this conclusion. Epstein, admittedly employing a measure of 'radicalism' quite different from anything in the present account, has demonstrated how under certain conditions professionalism has an 'intensification effect': those who are 'radical' become more radical, while those who are 'conservative' consolidate their conservatism.[14] Epstein's work also suggests that it is not the training situation itself, but rather the transition to employment which is likely, if anything is, to 'de-radicalize' social workers.

A final and crucial, limitation is the absence of any consideration here of theoretical tendencies which mirror the political and personal ambitions of social work recruits. Elsewhere,[15] I have written of what I call 'misfit sociology': a broad mixture of social psychology, the sociology of deviance, anti-psychiatry,

'labelling theory', and the life-style and radicalized client organizations of the 'new deviance'. With a widely dispersed theoretical and empirical base which has meant that a rich variety of uses have been made of it, misfit sociology is bound together by a method of study often taken as 'phenomenological' which allows authenticity to the deviant's actions, a sympathy with the underdog, and a theoretical de-reification which is explosive when set alongside routine welfare professionalism.[16] To give a single example: the misfit paradigm demonstrates conclusively, in the work flowing from the seminal contributions of Becker, Matza, Erikson, and others,[17] how the 'reality' of the deviant's 'pathology' is *negotiated* by client and professional. Moral crusades, the attachment of deviance-amplifying labels, moral entrepreneurship, the invention and transmission of stigma to clients—even what Young calls, 'the translation of public fantasy into reality'—are all part of the professional's activity.[18] A de-reified world where the client's deviance no longer stands *out there*, thinglike and independent of professional activity, is thoroughly subversive of the professional's claim to both technical and moral authority. What Becker calls the 'credibility of hierarchy' whereby 'in any system of ranked groups, participants take it as given that members of the highest group have the right to define *the way things really are*'[19] is also dismembered within the tradition of misfit sociology.

Any rigorous discussion of the issues at hand would require a detailed appreciation of the misfit paradigm which has served as a powerful legitimator of activism in the field of welfare, and has a contribution to make to the growing edge of social work which struggles within its self-imposed definitions of professionalism to give birth to a new and vital conception of 'profession'. Social work stands at the point where it seems that many wish to do more than hold the hand of the distressed client, and would galvanize that limp hand into a clenched fist. But, bound by his conception of the neutral, non-judgmental professional, the social worker dithers: 'What right has he to action when the robot is, after all, cheerful?'

It is here that the argument is customarily left to fend for itself. To do that, however, is to act in bad faith since the argument to this point allows only for the development of the social worker's identity one-sidedly—placing emphasis on his managerial, technocratic professionalism, and ignoring that aspect developed here which depicts the social worker as an enragé with more of an eye for the main moral chance than is customarily allowed. The social work professionalism which stutters past these arguments has many peculiarities. It has a false sense of the need for professional consensus when social work is not, and probably never could be, a consensus profession, its very guts being in the operation of moral choice. Estranged from its moral roots, it has an over-technical sense of itself, although at the same time a lurking moral spirit within social work is always threatening by its own movements to overturn this technocratic professionalism.[20] In the profession's accounts of its members' responsibilities and obligations, its reification of the social order threatens to rob the social worker even of his rights as citizen. Likewise, in professional accounts the 'goodness' of social work is always surprisingly and solidly unambiguous, despite much soul-searching about 'effectiveness', meeting 'real' need, and the limits of the 'client-worker contract'. But even if it does sometimes appear to have bogged down into a routine professionalism, social work is always recognizable as something more than a lexicon of techniques or a system of offices. One core element in any account must be its moral programme; the idea of setting out to help others and to do it in such a way as not to do violence to their human agency. Another, the one explored here, is the *living* commitment of its membership, expressing a 'politics' which, while it has been very recently crudely categorized as a form of marxism,[21] is a much more complex blend of political traditions. While some social workers—students and practitioners alike —may employ the rhetoric of Marx, there is no indication of any serious attempt to understand matters of social welfare and deviance in terms of a marxist theory of political economy.[22] Rather, the politics of the social work recruit mixes together humanism, pluralism, Christianity, the Fabian tradition of social reform, and snatches of Marx in a sort of political 'soup'; his ambitions fly between a revolutionary utopia and a careful case-by-case appraisal of distress. Fundamentally, he wants desperately to 'do good'.[23]

> his object is comparatively modest. He protests not against the fact that peasants are poor and oppressed. He seeks to establish or to re-establish justice or 'the old ways', that is to say, fair dealing in a society of oppression. He rights wrongs. He does not seek to establish a society of freedom and equality. The stories that are told about him record modest triumphs: a widow's farm saved, a local tyrant killed, an imprisoned man set free, an unjust death avenged. At most —and the case is rare enough—he may . . . order bailiffs to give bread to their labourers, to permit the poor to glean, or he may . . . cancel taxes.

In these words Hobsbawm describes not an earlier form of social work, but the social bandits of peasant society. He goes on:[24]

> The traditional 'noble robber' represents an extremely primitive form of social protest, perhaps the most primitive there is. He is an individual who refuses to bend his back, that is all . . . They cannot abolish oppression. But they do prove that justice is possible, that poor men need not be humble, helpless and meek . . .

The similarity between this and aspects of the social work enterprise which emerge from our discussion is too remarkable to go unnoticed, and there is a temptation to crash the gears of history, geography and culture, and transpose directly from the rural peasantry to highly developed urban-industrial complexes the notion of a primitive political rebellion hidden within social work asserting itself against the forces of unfreedom. What can be said less contentiously is that the moral implications of the rise of the welfare elites are ambiguous. It is greeted by some, such as Halmos who talks of a 'moral reformation of leadership'[25] with optimism; others are more cautious, or even straightforwardly pessimistic.[26] However we choose to characterize the welfare professions—as a new reformation, dispensers of 'happy pills', or as the 'brain police'[27]—the growth of their power is a significant *societal* shift. *Individually*, the decision to enter the welfare professions is also ambiguous. For some it represents an accommodative and privatized solution to estrangement; for others, especially I suspect among the young, it is an attempted active resolution of some central cultural problems concerning work, identity, leisure, meaning and value. It represents a tradition which refuses to lie down, asserting the dignity of man against oppressive social forces; and in this sense social work recruits sometimes appear within the arena of professional education as the sole representatives of dignity and outrage, thus carrying on a rear-guard defence of elements of even social work's own traditions against its technocratic-professionalism.

There is, nevertheless, in our estimation, a shortage of consciousness in the recruit that his action signifies anything beyond an escape from the world, and the professional socialization process only seems to encourage a splitting of his ambitions so that the recruit's idealism comes to confront him as something alien, a symptom of his 'immaturity'. Thus, except in the psychodynamically distilled accounts of 'working through one's own problems', the idea of making the social worker's choice of occupation accountable *as human enterprise* is scandalously ignored. Mayer and Timms are wrong when they assert in their recent and fashionable work, *The Client Speaks*,[28] that it is the client who is neglected in the social work literature; rather, it is the social worker himself, the actor who attempts to negotiate unguided the menacing no man's land of social work's politics. If one does not understand the social worker in his 'natural' environment, and what constitutes success and failure in his life, how can one hope to judge 'success' or 'failure' in clients, or their expectations of 'success' and 'failure'. Framed as these issues must necessarily be in the designs and projects of the social work actor and his ideology, they can be studied apart from the social worker's life and the world he inhabits only by refusing the possibility that social work action is itself problematic, and by accepting a narrow and over-professionalized view of social work as 'what is done in the agencies' and 'what it appears to be'. The decision by early social workers—in the days long before the 'end of ideology'—to work among the poor and the 'depraved', to whatever effect, was born out of a complex of moral and political impulses: moral outrage, political ambition, a fear of 'the mob', and a fear even sometimes of politics itself, to name only a few. If social work is to return from the problems of juggling something defined as 'need' against something defined as 'help', where in each instance the properties of those definitional acts remain assumed, it must regain a hold on its moral-political roots. For those who accept this challenge, which will certainly involve more than a re-learning of catechisms, the commitment will involve the consolidation of what can only be described as the deviant enterprise of the social worker.

Note and references

* A simply impressionistic view of the presentation in the mass media of the social worker suggests that the stereotype does also contain 'interesting' possibilities that he (or, more commonly, she) might have 'quirks' in the sense of hidden longings, or not altogether 'pleasant' motivations. It is a mistake to assume that stereotypes must be monolithic and self-consistent: social workers are pretty as often as they are plain, and not infrequently manneristic. Media imagery, it seems, present an important but neglected aspect of occupational identity.

1 A. P. M. Coxon, 1971, 'Occupational attributes: constructs and structure', *Sociology*, 5(3), pp. 335–54.

2 H. S. Becker, 1964, *The Other Side*, New York, Free Press, pp. 4–6; and see E. Freidson, 1961, *Patients' Views of Medical Practice*, New York, Russell Sage Foundation, p. 20.

3 ibid., p. 5.

4 A. L. Strauss and R. Bucher, 1961, 'Professions in process', *Amer. J. Sociol.*, 66, January, pp. 325–34.

5 C. W. Mills, 1959, *The Sociological Imagination*, Oxford University Press, pp. 170–6.

6 E. Becker, 1968, *The Structure of Evil*, New York, Braziller, p. 38.

7 See K. Davis, 1936, 'The application of science to personal relations: a critique of the family clinic idea', *Amer. Sociol. Rev.*, 1(2), pp. 236–47.

8 A. W. Gouldner, 1971, *The Coming Crisis of Western Sociology*, Heinemann, p. 78.

9 See L. Taylor and I. Taylor, 1972, 'Changes in the motivational construction of deviance', *Catalyst*, no. 6, Fall, pp. 76–99; I. L. Horowitz and M. Liebowitz, 1968, 'Social deviance and political marginality: toward a redefinition of the relation between sociology and politics', *Social Problems*, 15(3), pp. 280–96; and P. Walton, 'The case of the Weathermen: social reaction and radical commitment', in I. Taylor and L. Taylor (eds), 1973, *Politics and Deviance*, Penguin.

10 Gouldner, op. cit., p. 79.

11 ibid., pp. 80–1.

12 ibid., p. 81.

13 B. Deacon and M. Bartley, 1971, 'Becoming a social worker: a study of an experimental student social work placement', unpublished paper.

14 I. Epstein, 1970, 'Professionalization, professionalism, and social-worker radicalism', *J. Health and Soc. Behav.*, 11(1), pp. 67–77.

15 G. Pearson, 1972, 'Misfit sociology: a study in scholarship and action', Eleventh National Deviancy Conference, University of York, 19 September 1972; and 'Misfit sociology and the politics of socialization', in I. Taylor, P. Walton and J. Young (eds), 1975, *Critical Criminology*, Routledge & Kegan Paul.

16 For accounts of 'reification', see P. L. Berger and T. Luckmann, 1967, *The Social Construction of Reality*, Allen Lane, p. 106; K. Marx, 1961, *Capital*, vol. 1, Moscow, Foreign Publishing House, p. 72; J. Horton, 1971, 'The fetishism of sociology', in J. D. Colfax and J. L. Roach (eds), *Radical Sociology*, New York, Basic Books, pp. 171–93.

17 For example, H. S. Becker, 1962, *Outsiders*, New York, Free Press; D. Matza, 1964, *Delinquency and Drift*, New York, Wiley; K. T. Erikson, 1966, *Wayward Puritans*, New York, Wiley.

18 See T. Duster, 1970, *The Legislation of Morality: Law, Drugs and Moral Judgement*, New York, Free Press; Becker, op. cit., pp. 121–63; R. A. Scott, 1971, 'The construction of conceptions of stigma by professional experts', in J. D. Douglas (ed.), *Deviance and Respectability*, New York, Basic Books, pp. 255–90; J. Young, 1971, 'The role of the police as amplifiers of deviancy, negotiators of reality and translators of fantasy', in S. Cohen (ed.), 1971, *Images of Deviance*, Penguin, pp. 27–61; T. J. Scheff, 1968, 'Negotiating reality: notes on power in the assessment of responsibility', *Social Problems*, 16(1), pp. 3–17.

19 1967, 'Whose side are we on?', *Social Problems*, 14(3), pp. 239–47.

20 See recently, N. W. Timms, 1971, '. . . and Renoir and Matisse and . . .', an inaugural Lecture, University of Bradford.

21 B. Munday, 1972, 'What is happening to social work students', *Social Work Today*, 3(6), pp. 3–6.

22 Compare I. Taylor, 1972, 'The criminal question in contemporary social theory', *Human Context*, 4(3), pp. 633–40; P. Q. Hirst, 1972, 'Marx and Engels on law, crime and morality', *Economy and Society*, 1(1), pp. 28–56; and I. Taylor and P. Watson, 1972, 'Radical deviancy theory: a reply to Paul Hirst', *Economy and Society*, 1(2), pp. 229–33.

23 E. J. Hobsbawm, 1972, *Bandits*, Penguin, p. 55.

24 ibid., p. 56.

25 P. Halmos, 1970, *The Personal Service Society*, Constable.

26 See Gouldner, op. cit.; H. Marcuse, 1964, *One-Dimensional Man*, Routledge & Kegan Paul; M. North, 1972, *The Secular Priests*, Allen & Unwin.

27 K. Keniston, 1968, 'How community mental health stamped out the urban riots (1968–1978)', *Trans-action*, July–August, pp. 21–9.

28 1970, Routledge & Kegan Paul.

Part IV Social work evaluated

The main purpose of this Part is to illustrate the central role ongoing research plays in social work practice and social policy. Social work is a relatively new profession and, indeed, its professional status is still in question. Is the service offered adequate? Are clients' opinions and self-evaluation being properly considered in casework practice? Do social workers have adequate training and supervision to fulfil their role successfully? Do residential institutions truly care for inmates or does institutionalisation add to their problems? Does a concentration on individual problems lead to a corresponding neglect of the wider causes of social problems? All these are highly debatable areas both for social workers and policy-makers. As is the case of any new project, research is vital to guide future practice and to evaluate the success or applicability of the project in the first place. Hence the nature of the research at this stage is highly evaluative and policy directed. Success and positive results are much sought after to assure both government and public that the social services are 'helping' and are not a waste of valuable material resources.

One note of warning though should accompany any attempt to translate research project results directly into future social policy action. While the goal is always to gain an objective assessment of the situation all social scientific research is dogged by an inevitable influx of subjective opinion which determines the choice of research material, the methodology used, the questions asked, and thus the types of 'solutions' and 'answers' offered.

For this Part we have chosen research projects which cover a wide range of social work interests including the client's perspective, the receptionist's role, social work teams, school social work, residential care and community development. They in turn enable us to look more closely at *specific* developments within the present-day social services, and view how the issues surrounding social work (Part III) are translated into everyday practice.

A. S. Hall provides us with a case study of the reception facilities provided by a local authority Children's Department. As the receptionist is frequently the first point of contact between prospective client and social service organisation, he assigns great importance to the role a receptionist (who is unqualified in social work practice) may play in making the initial evaluation of a client's case, and thus in the type of help (if any) which is made available. Contrary to earlier research, Hall concludes that such administrative roles are not ones of passivity and neutrality, but can be effective bridges or barriers between client and professional.

Another relatively unexplored field is the attempt to obtain the clients' own view of the services being offered. McKay *et al.* have studied the clients' subjective perceptions of the services offered by the Southampton Social Services Department. They are justifiably eager to point out that they make no attempt to evaluate the service, and that all such consumer research is highly speculative. Nevertheless such attempts to assess the views of those 'on the other side of the fence' would seem vital if social workers are to offer the best possible help available.

Evaluation of social work intervention has probably come under most scrutiny. Again assessment can be expected to differ given the lack of a precise definition of a social worker's tasks and the wider issue of whether social workers should be offering a less personal or a more political type of help. Hey and Rowbottom direct their interest to how social workers themselves perceive their own role, and how they function within a social services organisation. They conclude that social work is more efficient when it is directed towards fulfilling specific tasks. Evaluation of social work becomes the concern of managers and supervisors; the caseworker's actions being accountable to them. In this way Hey and Rowbottom are chiefly concerned with efficiency and day-to-day organisation, and as a result can turn away from the more theoretical and broader evaluation of the role social work plays in society.

Tony Marshall and Gordon Rose's contribution similarly advocates the increased deployment of social workers in schools, given their effect on reducing the delinquent tendencies of some pupils. Again such research is illustrative of attempts to work within present constraints; the concern is for effectiveness and evaluation from the institution's point of view, rather than the client's.

The relative merits of task-oriented work or client-oriented work is similarly raised by Tizard *et al.* in a comparative study of the care offered to subnormal children in traditional hospitals and children's homes. In terms of 'educating' the children, they conclude that the hierarchical, highly centralised and task-oriented hospitals did much to retard a child's development, rather than enabling him to profit from 'special education'.

The focus of attention towards a more structural analysis of social problems is provided by a paper offered by the Community Development Project Information Unit. Correspondingly concern is directed more towards areas of high social deprivation than towards cases of individual maladjustment. The national CDP, set up in 1969, here offer an alternative analysis of social problem causation and thus differing strategies of problem solution. The issues raised are concerned with problems of employment, income maintenance, housing, community education and neighbourhood participation, which are to be resolved by some structural change, rather than by piecemeal work on specific tasks. The types of research methods used also notably differ from those of the research projects previously described. Here the method is action-research, whereby the community development officers themselves gather research data while working in and with the community. Action and 'objective' research thus become blurred in that the data collected may play a strong part in supporting a change in social policy.

The diversity of research project orientation, the methods used and the policy directives offered by these illustrations in themselves serve well once again to indicate the issue-oriented nature of social work practice. It would seem important to remember that many diverse policies and actions are being advocated, and that a consensus of opinion is hard to find.

Consequently we may expect that the evaluation of social work and community work is likely to continue, not only as a speculative, but also as a highly controversial, activity.

IV. 1 Client reception in a social service agency*

Anthony S. Hall

Introduction

A number of functions performed within any organization are generally accepted as essential to its efficient operation but are rarely considered to exert any *direct* impact upon its primary tasks or objectives. The typist and the clerk, for example, are usually recognized as being extremely important within the bureaucratic framework but because their function is assumed to be a passive one[1] their influence on the organization is seldom closely examined. The reception of clients to social service agencies is one such task which because of its assumed passivity has largely been bypassed in the literature of social administration.[2] In view of the situation of Reception as the clients' first point of contact with the social service organization it was decided to examine the validity of this assumption.

What follows is based on a case-study of the reception facilities provided by a single local authority Children's Department. [. . .] The intention was to analyse the effects of the arrangement of reception facilities and the activities of receptionists upon the provision of child care services by the social work staff. The performance of the 'reception function', far from being a passive administrative expedient, was found to have a profound influence upon the way the agency operates, the services it provides and to whom they are provided. In the Children's Department studied few of the component parts of this function fall within the 'officially approved version'[3] of the receptionists' role—the majority are not even recognized. [. . .]

The duties of the receptionist

In his study of interpersonal relations in a State Employment Agency, P. M. Blau analyses 'the modification of rules that occurs as they are interpreted and applied in a particular situation'.[4] [. . .]

Source: *Public Administration*, 49, spring 1971, pp. 25, 26, 27, 28, 29, 30, 31, 32, 33, 34, 35–40, 41, 42.

Such an analysis of the operation of the Reception Office in the Children's Department was the original intention of the present writer. It soon became apparent during the course of the study,[5] however, that the situation was far less formally structured than that encountered by Blau. No official statement of the duties and functions of the receptionist, or the role of reception, is recognized within the department. At best there is a fairly widespread agreement among senior administrators of what the functions of receptionists are, or at any rate, ought to be. It was possible to use this consensus as a yardstick when examining what the reception staff actually do. [. . .]

The *formal duties* of receptionists in the Children's Department are far less well defined than those of the interviewers in the Blau study. No official statement of procedures and principles exists in any easily identifiable form. [. . .]

In view of the absence of any precise outline of their duties and function it is perhaps not surprising that none of the staff received any instruction or training for their work. Principles and procedures are simply passed on by existing staff to any new recruit by word of mouth. This practice was extended to the new supervisor when she was appointed.

In such an unstructured situation it was difficult to discover any formal procedures governing the reception of clients. The lack of any clearly communicated statement of function from an administrative or supervisory source results in the work of receptionists being based almost entirely on an informal code of practice.

What then are the bases of reception activities? As has already been noted, the only 'official' attempt to define the receptionists' role [in an O and M Report] was seen by only one of the present staff. However, many of the practices employed were attributed by all the staff to this document. It could be argued that *notions of what the Report contained* provides a formal basis of the receptionists' perceived role. The almost total reliance upon word of mouth in interpreting the contents of the Report has produced some gross distortions of the original outline, but the staff maintained that they were working essentially within this framework.

A second basis of procedure could be termed *quasi-formal verbal instructions* given to receptionists by the staff of the departments with which they have contact as to how they should deal with their clients. The child care staff, for example, frequently provide instructions about the treatment of their own clients or those of a particular sector. Interpersonal and intersectoral variations in practice are considerable, but over time the reception staff become aware of such variations and attempt to abide by them. Quasi-formal instructions (discussed in greater detail below) form an important part of the framework of procedures.

The picture would be incomplete without reference to the least tangible of the bases of procedure. Each of the receptionists made it very clear in discussion that they believed their *own judgment* to be of paramount importance when deciding what to do in particular situations. One summed this up very adequately and concisely when asked about the existence of formal rules: 'No one has ever told us what to do. You just pick it up as you go along. Let's face it . . . reception is just common-sense really . . .'

Given the lack of any readily available statement of formal duties and functions, and the wide range of sources of quasi-formal instructions to receptionists, it was not possible directly to examine the modification of formal rules by informal procedures as did Blau. In a very negative sense, however, there does exist a 'manifest' or 'officially approved version' of the receptionists' role. It was possible in discussions with both senior administrators and child care officers to discern a fairly standard explanation of the duties of the receptionist; an explanation which, for the most part, was endorsed by the receptionists themselves. In view of the non-intervention of administrative staff one must assume that this widely accepted description of duties and procedures represents the formal framework of practice. It is possible, therefore, to outline this statement of what is believed to be the reception function and to use this as a basis for analysing the observed reality.

The 'manifest functions' of the reception staff can be outlined very simply. The primary task is to receive visitors, to ascertain which department they require (Health or Children's) and to bring them into contact with the correct official. If a visitor has obviously called at the wrong building the receptionist is expected to redirect him.

A small proportion of visitors to the Health Department are dealt with by the receptionists themselves. This involves stamping and signing vaccination certificates and such like documents. For the rest—the vast majority of callers—the procedure is to ascertain the nature of the inquiry and to contact the relevant official in one or other department. Clients of the Health Department, if the officer is available, are directed to the correct room on the eighth, ninth, or tenth floor of the building.

The procedure for clients of the Children's Department varies according to whether or not they are already known to the agency. It they are known, the relevant sector is contacted by telephone and informed that 'Mrs X is here to see Mr CCO'. The client is asked to wait in the office until the child care officer collects her to go to one of the nearby interviewing rooms. If the CCO is not at the office or is, for any reason, 'not available' the client is given the option of waiting, calling back, or of seeing the sector duty officer if the situation is urgent. Many clients are asked to come back later on a specific day, or a choice of days is given when the CCO will be at the office. There is no appointments system as such in operation.

Where a client has had no previous contact with the department, the receptionist records basic information about the client (name, address, number and ages of children) on a 'Record of Inquiry' form. A telephone call is made to the 'Records Office' to see if 'anything is known' about the client, and only then is a call put through to the sector responsible for the area in which the client is at present resident. 'Unknown' clients are seen by the duty officer of that sector.

Modifications of the officially approved reception function

The observed reality of the functions performed by the reception staff differs from the officially approved version of their role in response to three main factors:[6]
(1) The *inappropriateness* of the officially approved version.
(2) The response of reception staff to *quasi-formal instructions*.
(3) The use of *discretion*.

The repercussions and unintended consequences of these variations from, and extensions of, the 'official' role ascribed to receptionists have a profound influence upon the operation of the agency.

The 'inappropriateness' of the officially approved reception function

The term 'inappropriate' can be applied to the official version of the reception function in two respects. The first of these relates to a general misunderstanding of the conditions faced by the reception staff which has caused the official versions to be based, in part at least, on false premises. The second involves the *inevitable* unintended consequences of placing certain duties upon the receptionists—consequences which were considered undesirable by all the departmental staff interviewed. Each aspect will be discussed in turn.

In the Children's Department 'Reception' has for the most part operated outside the arena of debate about the activities of the agency. Visitors are received; child care officers are told that clients are waiting to see them, and clients are interviewed. As the reception function appears to be operating smoothly very little attention has been paid to the work of the reception staff since the office was established at the end of 1967. As a result the writer found a very low level of awareness among both child care officers and administrative staff of the conditions and bombardment levels faced by the receptionists and their methods of work. The same lack of understanding could be said to underlie the official version of the reception function. The validity of the assumptions on which this version is based, and the operation of the staff within this framework have never been called into question. The first area of deviation from the 'official version', therefore, is due to certain false premises on which that version is based.

One important misconception [. . .] is that a sizeable majority (usually stated to be between 65 and 75 per cent of the total) of all clients calling at the office want the Health Department; only about one-third to a quarter are thought to be clients of the Children's Department. [. . .]

The receptionists, on the other hand, are well aware of the preponderance of Children's Department clients, and as a result are orientated towards the work of that department. They see themselves primarily as 'working for Children's' and have modified the official version of their role accordingly. They perform the duty, as prescribed, of stamping vaccination cards and the like—a Health Department function—but other Health clients are dealt with very abruptly. The 'official version' requires receptionists to ask all clients to wait in Reception while the relevant official is contacted. For Health Department visitors this procedure is rarely, if ever, followed. They are immediately asked to inquire at one or other of the offices on the eighth and ninth floors. It is left to the inquiries clerks in these offices to ascertain whether or not the relevant health official is available.

One result of the receptionists' perception of their role, therefore, is that they 'underplay' their responsibilities to the Health Department, and exaggerate and extend their involvement in the work of the Children's Department. This development is functional for the reception staff in that it helps to clarify their somewhat ambiguous position in the Health Department and elevates their self-perceived status through the process of specialization. The potential dysfunctional aspects for the Health Department and its clients are obvious.

[There are also] a number of other basic assumptions which are widely held within the department about the bombardment faced by reception staff, which do not appear to coincide with the reality. The first concerns the level of bombardment; the second the proportions of 'known' and 'unknown' clients calling at reception. [. . .]

The second way in which the 'officially approved version' of the reception function could be deemed to be 'inappropriate' is through the inevitable and unintended consequences of placing certain duties upon the reception staff. This again is in part due to the lack of understanding of the reception situation.

The official version of the receptionist's duties requires the receptionist *to ascertain the requirements of visiting clients*. As has been recorded on a number of occasions, details of the allocation of functions between local authority departments are not widely known among clients and potential clients of the personal social services. Social work staff from a variety of agencies—both central and local—are not generally differentiated but are referred to as 'the man from the Council' or 'the lady from the Welfare'.[7] By the same token, clients approaching the Reception Office for the first time often do not know which department has the responsibility of dealing with their particular problem. The receptionist's task, therefore, is not simply that of asking the client which department they want and putting them in touch with the relevant officer. It is one of listening to the clients' account of their problem and on this basis deciding which is the responsible agency.[8] For this reason the 'ascertainment function' involves the reception staff in conducting the *initial interview*. Receptionists take on this task even when a client names the department they wish to contact as they know from experience that many clients are wrongly informed (or have made incorrect assumptions) about departmental responsibilities.

The 'quasi-official support' given to this practice (discussed in the next section) has led to its development and extension over time to cover both clients who have had no previous contact with the agency and 'known' clients. In the case of 'unknown' clients in particular receptionists may be involved in deciding not only which department they require but also for which service they ought to apply. For example, when a client informs the receptionist that she wishes to have her children received into care, this is, on the basis of the information given, the responsibility of a child care officer. The receptionist may, however, extend her function to ask why, and on the basis of the reply suggest that what is really needed is a day nursery placement. Such a client, if 'persuaded', will then be referred to the Health Department with his or her 'service request' *already formulated*. In this type of case—a number of which were observed during the study period—the receptionist is going far beyond the prescribed role, but in a logical development of that role. At the same time the receptionist is providing a 'service' which would rank among those normally attributed to the social work staff.

This extension of the 'ascertainment' responsibility is not confined to new clients. It is extended further to some current case clients, especially when the relevant child care officer is not available. In the absence of a client's own CCO it is accepted practice that he or she should be given the option of calling back later when the officer is more likely to be available or of seeing the duty officer. The option, more often than not, is couched in the terms, 'Is it urgent or can it wait?' The response is usually a detailed account of the problem which the receptionist then assesses as urgent or non-urgent. In this situation the receipt of the immediate assistance of a social worker is dependent upon the judgment of the reception staff.

The conditions under which reception interviews are conducted are far from ideal. Clients are expected to relate the nature of their request to the receptionist on duty in a room which is often crowded with other waiting clients. The opportunities for privacy in such a situation are necessarily limited, especially when the staff fail to see this as a problem. (At the risk of becoming anecdotal it is worth relating one instance of a receptionist calling across a crowded room to a client, 'When did your wife leave you, Mr—?') This lack of confidentiality can be seen to produce anxiety and distress in a sizeable proportion of the clients interviewed.

The discussion so far has been concerned with variations from the formally approved version of the reception function which result from the 'inappropriateness' of that prescribed function. Most of the observed variations must be ascribed to the failure accurately to define the role of Reception which, in its turn, is the result of incomplete knowledge of reception conditions. Such modifications are the almost inevitable consequences of the prescribed functions themselves rather than of informal modifications introduced by the reception staff themselves in response to their own needs and wishes.

The response of receptionists to quasi-formal instructions

It has already been suggested that in the absence of any clear hierarchy of responsibility for reception, the staff respond to the quasi-formal instructions of child care officers and other personnel with whom they are in immediate contact. These instructions tend to result in extensions of the formally approved reception function, and the reception staff accept their validity and act upon them in the absence of any official directive to the contrary. At the same time, as a result, the receptionists are drawn increasingly into the work of the deptarment with which they are primarily involved. Such instructions have a two-fold effect in extending the receptionists' role. In the first place, they have the *indirect effect* of providing quasi-official approval for procedures and activities which have developed in response to other factors; secondly, they are *directly* responsible for the institution of new procedures which extend the formal reception function.

The indirect or 'supportive' element can be illustrated with respect to the receptionists' role as initial interviewer. The Chief Welfare Officer, for example, instructed the reception staff to telephone his department with a detailed account of the problem of any potential client of his department before referring them on. In asking receptionists to perform this task

the officer was not only giving his approval to, but extending, their initial interviewing function. Child care officers provide similar, if less authoritative, incentives for this development by asking the receptionist on duty to supply further details about a particular client before conducting their own interview.

The unofficial interviewing function of reception staff is further supported by child care staff by the latter's reaction to certain clients being referred to them for interview. There is no official procedure for assessing the performance of receptionists, but the reaction of child care officers to their work provides an indication for the reception staff of their perceived 'efficiency'. The occasional remark from a CCO is interpreted as a mild rebuke and has an effect on their subsequent activities. For example, during the study one CCO informed the duty receptionist that 'Mrs—who I saw just now didn't want to see me . . . she only wanted a day nursery so I sent her up to Health'. The implication in this kind of remark is that the staff of reception are not adequately performing their screening function, and such comments inevitably influence future practice. In response to these kinds of pressures reception staff exaggerate their interviewing responsibilities even beyond those necessitated by the official and quasi-official instructions on which they operate.

Quasi-formal instructions from child care staff also have a *direct* influence on the reception function, placing additional tasks upon the receptionist and further defining their framework of operation. It is the general practice of individual child care officers and sectors to instruct reception staff not to disturb them during certain times when clients call at the office. These may take the form of 'standing instructions' or 'temporary measures' introduced during a particular 'crisis' period. The object of this practice is to enable child care staff to take an undisturbed lunch-hour or to attend a weekly sector meeting without fear of constant interruption. There is considerable variation in the practice of different sectors. Some will 'close down' for an hour at each lunch-time; others make it a general principle to keep at least one officer available at all times to answer 'duty calls'. Several request no interruptions at all during meetings; others accept 'necessary interruptions' with varying degrees of 'good grace'.

A major consequence of these individual sector requirements is that the reception staff are made responsible for the regulation of bombardment on different sectors during certain specified periods and, where sector practice dictates, for adjudicating on what constitute 'necessary' interruptions. For the most part they are left with the task of resolving the problems of inaccessibility as and when this situation occurs.

The receptionist's response to this additional task of regulating bombardment varies according to the receptionist involved and the attitude of the client.

The simplest outlet which is employed in the majority of cases—at least initially—is to explain to the client that the officer he or she wishes to see is not available until a particular time and to give the option of waiting or of calling back later. For some clients who have 'to get back to work in an hour' or have another appointment elsewhere, this option is not sufficient. Difficulties of this type are resolved by the reception staff as the circumstances dictate.

The receptionist may 'confide' in the client, sympathize with the problem and imply criticism of the CCO for not being available. (This kind of reaction is particularly likely when the client has been given an appointment which the officer has failed to keep.) Clients may be asked to wait on the pretext that their officers 'will be down in a moment'. On occasions clients themselves are criticized for not keeping a previous appointment and are told to call back. Each response, 'designed' to relieve a possible conflict situation between receptionist and client, clearly shifts the responsibility for the client not being seen on to someone other than the receptionist herself—usually a child care officer; occasionally the client. This kind of response to the daily problems of administering the reception function is discussed more fully in the next section.

Modifications of the manifest reception function introduced by the use of discretion

In analysing this area of variation it is useful to consider the relationship between the reception staff and each of the groups with which they are primarily in contact—clients and social workers. Considerable space in the literature on social work is devoted to the client-worker relationship. In the agency setting, however, the receptionist acts as an intermediary between these two groups and in certain circumstances exercises a profound influence on the nature of this relationship. There is an inevitable degree of overlap but as far as is possible the importance of the reception function for each group is considered in turn.

The reception function *for clients* is not limited to that outlined in the official version of the receptionists' role but involves the provision of a range of more positive services. Possibly the most important of these (in terms of the number of clients involved) is the ability and willingness of receptionists to act as *advocates* on their behalf in contacts with the social work staff. The 'official version' places the responsibility on receptionists to inform child care officers that clients are waiting to see them. When a client is not seen quickly, however, the receptionist will frequently make further telephone calls (often stressing urgency) to ensure that the client is eventually seen and as quickly as possible. Subsequent calls may be made directly, as a simple reminder, or indirectly on the pretext of forgetfulness.

The extent to which a receptionist is prepared to perform this function is dependent on a variety of factors. In large measure it is related to her own assessment of the needs of a particular client, or upon the opinion that he or she is being treated inappropriately or 'unfairly' by a child care officer. It may depend simply on more personal considerations such as her 'likes' and 'dislikes' of certain individuals. One receptionist, for example, objecting to the length of time a particular client had been kept waiting by a duty officer remarked: 'I like him. The hours he's sat out there without once getting "stroppy". They [the child care staff] really are terrible. I'll stick up for him. I'll keep ringing them up until they do something.'

While the advocacy function can be an important asset for visiting clients, the reverse process can also be identified. Clients can be 'suppressed' in a variety of ways. [. . .] The receptionist conducts an initial interview identifying the reason for the visit. The subsequent telephone call to the CCO concerned may be used to exaggerate the urgency of the problem to attempt to ensure that the client is seen. By the same token, the conversation between receptionist and CCO may *understate* the problem and result in delay before the client is seen. The outcome is the same when the advocacy function is withdrawn from certain clients to whom the receptionist 'objects'. Both processes—advocacy and suppression—were clearly illustrated in the response of one receptionist to the question 'Do you treat clients differently for any reason?':

'No. It doesn't make any difference to me . . . Well . . . there are those who you feel particularly sorry for, who you think are getting a rough deal. Very often it depends on how hard you push the CCO or the duty officer as to what gets done. On the other hand, you don't put yourself out for someone, who annoys you. Like that woman just now . . . She'd only been in here five minutes before she asked how long she'd have to wait. I don't like that'.[9]

A second important 'reception service' is the provision of *advice and guidance*. Reception staff are constantly faced with the problem of dealing with clients when no child care officer is available to see them. The lack of any specific appointments system, coupled with other factors such as the high mobility of officers in the course of their work, result in a large number of 'wasted visits' by clients to the office.[10] [There is a] range of negative responses employed by reception staff in this situation to deflect the expression of client-dissatisfaction with the agency from themselves on to the social worker or even the client. Far more frequently the reaction is a positive one: an attempt to provide a service for the client in the absence of the help of a social worker. This may simply involve the receptionist undertaking the task of attempting to ensure that the officer sees the client at the earliest possible opportunity. It may involve advising the client of other agencies which might be able to offer assistance, or even providing advice and guidance on the problem facing the client. This advisory role is a further logical extension of the initial interviewing function. Where a client has explained 'her' problems to the receptionist and a CCO is unable to see her, the natural reaction of the receptionist is to advise as best she can in the absence of more professional assistance.

The role of the receptionists brings them constantly into contact with the *social workers* in the agency. For the most part, it must be stated, the relationship between these two groups is cordial, each recognizing the valuable role played by the other—if misunderstanding the true nature of that role. In certain circumstances, however, the objectives of the child care officer and the receptionist may be said to be in conflict.

The primary task of the reception staff is to ensure contact between officer and client. Achievement of this goal may be possible with a single telephone call to the officer; it may involve persistent calls before the client is eventually seen. For the social worker, interviewing clients who call at the office is only a small part of their day-to-day work. In a situation where an officer is already deeply involved with several cases, and a constant 'barrage' of paper-work, interviewing a client in Reception may be considered more of an 'inconvenience' than a primary duty. This reaction is particularly acute amongst sector duty officers who are concerned not only with their own cases, but with seeing the clients of absent colleagues as well as dealing with new cases as they arise. Under the circumstances a visiting client may receive rather less attention than the reception staff think they deserve.

For the receptionist, the visiting client is the sole responsibility and, therefore, the major priority; for the child care officer in the sector priorities may be somewhat different. The possibility of conflict and abuse of procedures in such a situation is considerable, not least because of the lack of understanding by both parties of the problems faced by the other.

The child care officer, faced with other problems on a duty day, may tend to place the greater part of the responsibility for clients visiting the department upon the reception staff. This is perceived by the latter group as an attempt by the child care officer to abdicate 'his' responsibility for the visiting client. All the receptionists admitted considerable problems in this connection in their relationships with CCOs. [. . .]

[. . .] Criticisms directed at the field staff can be seen to fulfil two criteria. Firstly, in the opinion of the receptionist the client is being treated 'unfairly' or inappropriately; secondly, the officers' action (or inaction) places the responsibility for dealing with the client upon the reception staff. The receptionist may exercise some influence over the CCO by acting on the client's behalf, but only within the limits of manipulating a relationship in which she is subordinate. This limit is revealed in cases where the CCO decides to place the onus of responsibility upon the receptionist. This may involve the provision of a service which the reception staff consider to be the duty of a CCO; it may place them in a potential conflict situation which they then have to resolve.

For at least some child care officers, the existence of Reception permits the delegation of certain responsibilities which they themselves (for a variety of reasons) feel unable to fulfil. Perhaps paradoxically this practice also has functional aspects for reception staff, despite their declared criticisms. This informal extension of their discretionary powers helps to increase their own job satisfaction whilst at the same time making it easier to deal with difficult situations as and when they arise.[11] In the process the reception function takes on further facets which are seldom officially recognized. [. . .]

Conclusion

Despite its description as 'social administration' few students of the discipline have made any systematic attempt to study the processes involved in the administration of the social services. [. . .] This should not be the case. It is not only possible but, I would suggest, essential to study the workings of social service agencies *as organizations* in an attempt to understand the administrative processes involved and the problems which inevitably arise. [. . .]

Notes

* The ideas contained in this article have since been developed and are now published by the author in *The Point of Entry*, Allen & Unwin, 1974.
1 The concept of 'passive function' refers to activities which may or may not be essential to the workings of a bureaucracy but which, in either case, exert *no direct influence* upon the performance of the agency's primary tasks or objectives – in this case the provision of child care services. An 'active function', on the other hand, implies a *direct* involvement with primary tasks or goals.
2 The few contributions to the study of reception activities are contained within: Adrian Sinfield, *Which Way for Social Work*, Fabian Pamphlet 1969. I. Duetscher, 'The gatekeeper in public housing', in *Among the People: Encounters with the Urban Poor*, 1968.

3 Administrative concepts may be given four different meanings: *manifest* (officially approved version), *assumed* (interpretation offered by individuals concerned), *extant* (the reality) and *requisite* (recommended version). Wilfred Brown, *Exploration in Management*, 1960. Quoted and refined by D. V. Donnison, *Social Policy and Administration*, 1965.
4 P. M. Blau, *The Dynamics of Bureaucracy: a Study of Interpersonal Relations in Two Agencies*, 2nd ed., 1963, p. 21.
5 The writer was in the Children's Department for over a year prior to the specific study of reception practices Observations of reception procedures were made throughout February and March 1970.
6 This classification suggests a degree of mutual exclusiveness and clarity which is far from apparent in practice.

7 For example: Hilary Land, *Large Families in London*, 1970, p. 107.

8 See A. Leissner, *Family Advice Services*, 1967, p. 10.

9 Note the nature of the reason given for withholding the advocacy function.

10 During the two-week period for which records were collected, one in four calls at Reception by clients of the Children's Department did not result in an interview with a child care officer. In addition, almost as many clients were seen by a duty officer as were seen by their own CCO.

11 P. M. Blau (op. cit., p. 87), notes a similar reaction among receptionists in the Employment Agency. 'The exercise of discretion enabled receptionists to derive satisfaction from helping people. It also made dealing with aggressive clients less difficult, since it provided receptionists, who could refuse such a client special consideration, with sanctions to discourage aggressive behaviour and to release their emotional reaction when it occurred. The clerk who exercised least discretion found conflicts with clients so irritating that he alone preferred other duties to those at the reception office.'

IV. 2 Consumers and a social services department

Ann Mckay, E. Matilda Goldberg and David J. Fruin

Introduction

The reorganisation of the social services has taken place with little attempt to obtain the consumer's point of view. In 1968 the Seebohm report referred to consumer participation and placed considerable emphasis on the 'accessibility' and 'acceptability' of the proposed social services departments. Yet the Seebohm committee reported that it was 'regrettably, unable to sound consumer reaction to the services in any systematic way'. Even the recent literature on social work research in this country reveals that clients are rarely asked for their opinions of the service although the importance of the consumer's views is becoming increasingly recognised. Mayer and Timms[1] carried out an exploratory study with a small group of clients from the Family Welfare Association, but as far as we know the present study is the first systematic attempt to obtain the views of a random sample of a social service department's clients.

This study of consumers' attitudes was one part of a programme of action studies that the Research Unit of the National Institute for Social Work is undertaking with Southampton Social Services Department. At the same time, we carried out a study to document the views and attitudes of social workers in Southampton.[2] The findings from both studies are to provide baseline data for ongoing action research in one of Southampton's area offices.

Our main aims in the consumer study were to discover how clients had initially come into contact with the service and what expectations they had of it. We also tried to find out what they thought of the services and how much they knew about them. In this article we will concentrate on the clients' expectations and views of the service and how they correspond with those of the social workers on which we reported [recently].[3]

Source: *Social Work Today*, 4 (16), 15 November 1973, pp. 486–91.

At the outset we would like to stress that the present study is essentially an investigation of the consumers' subjective perceptions of the services and not an attempt to evaluate the service. We have no means of knowing whether the clients' reports reflect what actually happened, as no independent observations were made and the social workers' views as reflected in the social worker study were global impressions.

How the study was carried out

Our first problem was to define who was the client. We excluded clients in residential accommodation since we feel they need a different approach and we hope to carry out a separate study in residential establishments. We also excluded consumers living outside Southampton and those whose address was incomplete, in order to minimise unprofitable fieldwork. Cases referred by the police where only one enquiry visit had been carried out were also omitted.

It seemed reasonable to interview those who had used the services of the department, though this person was not necessarily the 'main' client. We excluded children under 16 but saw their parents where they had been in contact with a social worker from the social services department. In cases of severe mental handicap we interviewed the caretaking person, and where the name of a whole family appeared on the case file we interviewed the member who was available, providing he or she had contact with a social worker from the department. In short, our criterion was that the person interviewed should be a consumer and not necessarily the person whose name appeared on the case file.

Although we aimed at a representative sample certain biases crept in due to some of our exclusions, and in consequence the sample interviewed may be somewhat unrepresentative. Some children's cases were excluded because their parents were not traceable or had no contact with a social worker, and a number of children were in foster homes and community homes outside Southampton. We do not know in what direction these omissions have biased the sample, except that it is fairly certain that many of these children were long-term cases. On the other hand, cases whose contact with the department was only a short one may be under-represented since they never become 'cases' on case files. Despite these possible distortions it is noteworthy that the social character-istics of the sample are in many respect similar to those of other client populations studied in Buckingham-shire,[4] Bradford,[5] and Camden.[6]

We carried out a series of exploratory interviews and gradually developed the questionnaire which we piloted in other local authorities. Finally, after several modifications we developed a structured interview which lasted for approximately one hour. A team of eight trained interviewers, none of whom were social workers, carried out the fieldwork in May 1972. Southampton's Director of Social Services wrote to 537 consumers inviting them to participate in the study and giving them at least a week in which they had the chance to refuse. Sixty-four consumers (15 per cent) felt they were able to refuse to participate. Almost two-thirds of these refusals were elderly or disabled clients, many of whom replied that their ill-health, deafness or old age prevented them from participating. Seventy-two could no longer be traced at the address given on the case file. This is partly an indication of the high mobility of many of those who contact the department, and from an administrative viewpoint reflects the difficulties of maintaining up-to-date files.

Who are the consumers?

The final sample interviewed consisted of 305 con-sumers of the social work services provided by South-ampton Social Services Department. Their demographic characteristics differed in several respects from those of the general population in Southampton, but as we have mentioned were similar to other client popu-lations. Three-quarters of the respondents were women in contrast to Southampton's population where the ratio of men to women is almost equal. As Table 1 shows, the greatest deficiency of men occurred in the 20–44 age group. The greater availability of women for interview in the economically active age groups may partly account for this. However, al-though demographically speaking women outnumber men in the over-sixty age groups, the problems of retirement, chronic illness and disability in the pre- and post-retirement age groups bring men more within the scope of doctors and social workers as studies of general practice have shown.[7]

The large proportion of elderly clients was another striking feature of the sample: more than a third were over sixty years of age, compared with a quarter in Southampton. The difference between the consumers and the general population is even more marked among the over seventy-fives. The consumers also differed

from the Southampton population in their marital status—almost one-third being widowed, separated or divorced compared with only 12 per cent in South-ampton as a whole. The client groups in Buckingham-shire, Bradford and Camden showed similar distribu-tions. This did not reflect solely the large number of

Table 1 Age and sex ratios of social work consumers and Southampton population

Age group	Consumers		Southampton population[a]	
	Sex ratio Male : female	% of total sample	Sex ratio Male : female	% of total sample
20–44	16 : 84	42	51 : 49	47
45–59	23 : 77	22	49 : 51	27
60–74	35 : 65	20	45 : 55	20
75 and over	36 : 64	16	33 : 67	6
Total	25 : 75	100	49 : 51	100

[a] Census 1971

elderly in the sample as in each age group there were considerably more widowed, separated and divorced among the consumers. Proportionately more con-sumers lived in large households and in overcrowded conditions (using the definition of more than 1.5 persons per room). All these factors indicate that the social services are reaching some of the groups in greatest need of the services such as the very old, broken and large families.

There were more semi- and unskilled workers in the client sample, as has been found in other studies of clients in welfare settings. In contrast, in Camden where a social worker functioned in the setting of a general practice, the social class distribution of the social work clients was similar to that of the borough.[8]

The housing situation also presented some inter-esting differences. Proportionately fewer consumers owned their own homes than did the general popula-tion in Southampton. Twice as many lived in local authority rented accommodation, and possibly because of this exclusive possession of all three amenities was high (fixed bath or shower, running hot water and WC). As considerably fewer consumers than the general Southampton population lived in unfurnished privately rented accommodation where disadvantaged groups are often found, we may have missed them in the sample or alternatively they were not social work clients. On the other hand, slightly more consumers lived in privately rented furnished accommodation.

Finally, the types of problems which brought the consumers into contact with the department were as follows: about half were elderly and disabled; two-fifths were child care and family relationship problems; and less than 10 per cent were cases of mental disorder. These proportions are very close to those quoted by the social workers when describing their caseloads for the social worker study.

Referral route

We were interested in tracing the path of the consumers to the department and who the referral agents in the community were. In over half of the cases, contact had been initiated by the department and in the majority of these cases a third party, most frequently a health service, had been involved. No other agency was responsible for the initial referral of more than a small proportion of consumers. Of those (111) who contacted the department on their own initiative, less than half went at the suggestion of a third party—most frequently a friend or relative.

Expectations and help received

What did the clients initially expect from the social services department? This proved a difficult question to answer. Expectations are affected by one's experience and this also applied to the consumers whose expectations seemed coloured by their experiences and their images and perceptions of their own social workers. Other research has suggested that expectations from social work agencies are hazier, in contrast to the more definite expectations from better-known services given by doctors, lawyers etc.[9] We did not really find evidence to support these ideas. Less than a third of the consumers said they did not know what to expect or that they did not expect any help. However, we did find some link between lack of expectations and lack of knowledge about the department. Only a third of those who expected help had not heard of the department, compared with two-thirds of those with no expectations. Any kind of prior knowledge seemed, to be the important factor rather than what they had heard about the quality of the department. This seems to suggest that if the department were better known, people would be clearer about what to expect from it, something which was also mentioned by the social workers. Several of the social workers considered that clients came with unrealistic expectations and that more public education would lead to a clearer and more realistic idea of the services offered. Lack of expectations was also related to being contacted by the department; just over 10 per cent of clients who went to the department on their own initiative said they did not know what to expect, compared with almost half of those contacted by the department. Age also made a considerable difference to whether consumers had expectations or not. Over half of those who did not know what to expect were aged over sixty.

When comparing the consumers' expectations with the social workers' perceptions of what they thought the clients wanted from them, considerable differences emerge. Whereas the majority of Southampton social workers thought clients expected most of all to be able to discuss personal problems and to receive advice, sympathy and information, less than 10 per cent of the consumers said they expected help of this kind, confirmation to some extent of Mayer and Timms' findings.[10] Consumers mostly expected practical help

such as aids, services, clothing and bedding. Their expectations coincided with what they actually received, practical help being among the most frequently mentioned types of help received (Table 2). One might suggest that because practical help is more tangible it is more easily remembered than advice and sympathy.

Table 2   Type of help received

	No.	%[a]
Miscellaneous action	110	36
Aids	96	31
Material: clothes, bedding etc.	76	25
Advice	72	24
Community facilities	61	20
Services	59	19
Arrangements/support: children	48	16
Listening/talking	40	13
Finance	35	11
Housing	31	10
Adoption	15	5
No help	29	10

[a] Respondents could specify more than one type of help received.

A further discrepancy appeared between the clients' perceptions and those of the social workers. Almost 15 per cent of the consumers said they expected help with housing difficulties and just over 10 per cent said they wanted financial help, whereas the social workers on the whole thought clients did not expect help of this kind. Although both housing and financial difficulties often coincide with other social problems one can still ask why people go to the social services department rather than the housing department or the Department of Health and Social Security. Perhaps it is as one client said: 'We didn't know—we just went on the off-chance, we hoped they would talk the council into giving us something on the ground floor.'

One can speculate whether these clients find their way to the social services department through misconceptions about its function, or whether they are hoping that the social workers will use advocacy on their behalf. Both these points were also mentioned by the social workers.

The emphasis on practical help did not mean that consumers did not appreciate help in the form of listening and sympathy. Just over one-third of consumers mentioned that the help they had received had resulted in some relief of emotional stress, they had become less anxious or depressed, more confident or stable.

'It improved me as I was getting to the stage with Pat where it was getting me down. It helps a lot when I'm worried about her.'

'I was immature, she'd [the social worker] told me what to do but I didn't always listen.'

'I feel much brighter now there is someone trying to do something for me.'

Some 10 per cent of this group said that ventilating their feelings by talking provided an emotional outlet; having someone to talk to or someone who would listen, was helpful to their emotional well-being.

'I can talk to her and tell her anything I like—it helps a lot to talk to her.'

'It was at least someone to talk to and gave me hope, yes it improved things.'

Consumers' perceptions of the qualities needed to be a good social worker also reflected their appreciation of the non-material aspects of help. Respondents laid the greatest stress on personality characteristics such as understanding and sympathy, a pleasing personality and social skills such as the ability to put one at one's ease.

Ninety per cent of consumers said they had received some help and the few who did not were mainly under sixty years of age. Practical help in the form of aids, services, outings, holidays was most frequently mentioned by the elderly. Few consumers over the age of sixty said they had received what might be termed 'casework help'. In contrast, advice, information and 'casework help' were mainly mentioned by those under sixty. This suggests that the predominantly practical needs of the over sixties are more easily recognised than their needs for other forms of help. Because the elderly need so much practical help their care is often entrusted to the social workers with the least skill and experience, such as welfare assistants. Though the older people may well have more practical needs because of their increasing physical frailty, this does not preclude them from having other emotional and social needs.

Satisfaction

Satisfaction is clearly one of the crucial elements of interest in consumer research. Two-thirds of the sample said they were satisfied and less than one-fifth expressed dissatisfaction. On the whole consumers liked their social workers. Over 80 per cent found their social worker understanding, sympathetic and easy to talk to. Nearly all thought they were good listeners, and many made appreciative comments about their personalities and the help they received. Whether our summary question: 'On the whole would you say you felt satisfied or dissatisfied?' was bound to elicit a stereotyped response is difficult to say. Kogan *et al.*[11] found that clients who were judged to show no improvement were just as likely to place a high valuation on the help they received, on their worker, and on the agency, as were clients who were judged to show great improvement. Also, even though we tried to make it clear that our interviewers were not connected with the social services department, there may well have been confusion between them and the social workers which could have influenced the consumers' replies. We, therefore, tried to relate satisfaction to other factors.

Satisfaction was clearly related to the amount of help received. Those who said they had received no help were the least satisfied and the proportion of satisfied consumers increased with the amount of help they had received, until practically all those who said they had received five or more types of help were satisfied.

Age, too, was related to satisfaction. The elderly appeared to be slightly more satisfied, particularly those over the age of seventy-five. This may well be linked to their lack of expectations which we have already discussed and perhaps also to a feeling of dependency on the goodwill of the services. It is, however, reassuring that the elderly seem on the whole satisfied because the social workers' answers indicated that they were more interested in work with younger age groups.

We thought that frequency of contact with the social worker would be related to feelings of satisfaction but this was not a straightforward issue. On the whole consumers were satisfied with the frequency of visiting. Those who saw their social worker most frequently were most satisfied and fewer of those who saw their social worker every three months were satisfied. However, it was very puzzling to find that out of nine clients who saw their social worker less than every three months, eight said they were satisfied. A close inspection of those eight cases revealed that all but two considered that their 'problem' or reasons for contact with the department were solved, and they were receiving infrequent visits as a routine measure to keep an eye on them. The remaining two were foster mothers who received statutory six monthly visits. One might also expect consumers who said they were not going to continue seeing their social worker to be less satisfied. However, there were no differences between them and consumers who said they intended to continue contact. This finding is consistent with other research which has found that clients who do not return to the service are not necessarily dissatisfied, rather the contrary, they may well have got what they wanted.[12]

It is reasonable to postulate that those consumers whose expectations had been fulfilled would be satisfied. More of those whose expectations were fulfilled were satisfied (80 per cent) than were those with unfulfilled expectations (50 per cent). Also, not surprisingly, most of those who had no expectations but received help were also satisfied. It is, however, surprising that half of those who had some expectations but felt they had received no help were also satisfied. One can speculate that this could be related to the haziness of their expectations. If one has definite expectations or views one has something against which to measure what one receives.

One way of tapping dissatisfaction was to ask the consumers whether they thought that their social workers could have done more for them. About two-thirds of the consumers were satisfied but one-third thought their social worker could have done more for them. This was related to whether they had received help. Far more of those who felt they had received help said there was nothing more that the social worker could have done, and they were on the whole satisfied clients. The most frequently mentioned type of additional help wanted was practical such as clothes, furniture and bedding. The question of advocacy was again raised. Fifteen per cent of consumers made comments such as 'Push the telephone installation' or 'Put pressure on the housing authorities and get us out of this house.' A plea for more help in the form of more regular or frequent visits, or on the other hand for social workers to be more accessible was made by just over 10 per cent of the consumers. Some of these were from the very lonely, particularly the elderly on their own, highlighting the need for more informal social work help such as would be provided by volunteers.

The consumers' feelings of satisfaction were also bound up with attitudes towards their social workers. Although we tried to differentiate between the consumers' attitudes towards the department, the services received and their individual worker, it proved difficult to achieve. Consumers who expressed negative attitudes towards their social workers were more likely to be dissatisfied; three times as many of the consumers (30 per cent compared with 10 per cent) who reported receiving no help thought that their social worker lacked understanding or sympathy. However, help received made little difference to whether they were easy to talk to or good listeners. On reflection this apparent contradiction makes sense: if one does not receive appropriate help one is likely to perceive lack of understanding and sympathy but one can still acknowledge that the person concerned was a good listener and easy to talk to.

Only a few social workers mentioned in their questionnaire the personal relationship between worker and client as something the majority of clients appreciated, yet nearly all clients appreciated the visits and liked their social workers. In reply to our question 'What differences would it make if your social worker stopped visiting?' about one-fifth of consumers gave replies which indicated that they would miss their personal relationship with their social worker.

'I would be very sorry, during the year I have come to look upon her as an acquaintance not a child care officer. I like to see her as a person not what her job stands for.'

Most of the social workers thought that clients valued a feeling of security from the support that was available from a beneficent department. This view was in part correct: nearly a third of consumers mentioned that the help they had received had given them a feeling of security—someone in the background on whom they could rely.

'It gives you a sense of security, with someone to turn to.'

'It made me feel that I've really got someone behind me. The more I become disabled the more help I'll want.'

A similar number mentioned that it was not so much the individual relationship that they would miss if their social worker stopped visiting but the services or the material benefit.

'If he stopped visiting it wouldn't make any difference because I'd visit him if I need him.'

When we looked more closely at the fifty-four consumers who had expressed dissatisfaction, two typical situations could be discerned. A quarter of these consumers had children in care and their resentment about their child being away seemed to be directed against their social worker.

'They are just wrecking the boy's life. We want him home and in a good school, he needs his brothers and sisters. A good social worker could help us to get him home.'

'I have heard of a scheme where if the child had got into trouble he could report every Saturday and do some work. I thought this would do the trick. If they had gone to court and had this it would have been much better. The school was rather drastic.'

The second largest group of dissatisfied consumers (twelve) were elderly or physically handicapped. As on the whole the elderly and physically handicapped are a satisfied group, it seemed worthwhile to look at the twelve dissatisfied cases closely. Most of them mentioned the need for more regular or frequent visits.

'Much more constant visiting. I need to talk, we've had problems, we don't know who to see.'

'Since the young lady took over she never comes to talk privately.'

These cases highlight once again the needs of the elderly and physically handicapped for help other than practical.

Accessibility

The Seebohm report stressed the importance of the accessibility of the social services. We therefore examined quite closely some of the factors involved, such as how easy it was to find the office, ease of access by telephone and the kind of reception experienced. At the time of the survey the social services were still located in centralised offices. Just under half of the consumers said they had never visited the office. Those who had visited did so infrequently—a quarter had not been for more than a year, the majority had not visited in the three months before the interview, and only one-fifth had called during the preceding month. Three-quarters of the clients who had been to the office said they had difficulty in finding the building on their first visit. The consumers displayed a general lack of knowledge about how to contact a social worker. Although social workers carry cards, eighty-three of the consumers did not know where the office was and even fewer (just over 10 per cent) knew how to contact a social worker in the evening or at the weekend. Increased publicity and information of the services may remove misconceptions in some people's minds, and increase their awareness of services available.

A number of consumers were not clear as to whether they were in contact with the department and their perceptions did not always coincide with recorded information. Ten per cent of the consumers who thought they were in contact with a social worker were, in fact, sampled as 'closed' cases. In contrast two-thirds of those who thought they were 'closed' were, in fact, 'active' cases. From the department's viewpoint, about half of the 'closed' cases thought they were still in touch with a social worker and one-fifth of the 'active' cases considered they were no longer in contact. This raises questions about the clarity of procedures and whether there should be a policy of social workers letting clients know when they intend to cease contact.

Access by telephone was considered to be inadequate by both social workers and those clients who had ever used this means of contact (about half). However, an interesting discrepancy arose between the clients' and the social workers' views of the office and the reception met there. The workers thought that the clients' main complaints would be about administrative delays, and the problems of contacting their social workers. The clients on the other hand made few overt complaints about the services. Those who had visited the office were critical of amenities rather than of the personnel. They did not have to wait long and they said they usually made contact with a social worker easily.

Consumers reported that they were most commonly seen at home. A similar pattern of home visiting was found among social work clients in Buckinghamshire over ten years ago[13] and in the more recent workload studies carried out in Northern Ireland and England and Wales.[14] Barely 10 per cent of the Southampton consumers said they were seen regularly at the office. Their preferences for home as opposed to office visiting reflected what actually happened: this may be a further illustration of their adapting to the services they received. However, this may also be linked with the very small proportions of clients who contacted the department on their own initiative. As area offices are established and become known to consumers, it would be interesting to see what the effect will be of encouraging clients to come to the office rather than be visited at home. One wonders whether given the opportunity of visiting a pleasant, conveniently situated office, a number of clients might not prefer this to a home visit. An office interview could then provide an outing or 'a change' particularly for the elderly living alone, giving them an opportunity of meeting others.

Finally, we thought it was important to explore consumers' views on having a say in the running of the services. The Seebohm report emphasises the importance of the maximum participation of individuals and groups in the planning, organisation and provision of the social services. A quarter of the consumers said they would like to have some say in running the service. Very few of the elderly, particularly those over seventy-five, felt they wanted to participate. We felt it would be interesting to follow up those who did respond positively and we are exploring the possibilities of doing this.

Conclusions

This study is based upon the consumers' views and perceptions only and does not purport to show what actually happened or attempt to evaluate the quality of the service. It is an attempt to bring the consumers' point of view to the notice of those who provide the services and to provide a baseline for any changes that may be introduced to the service.

The study highlights some of the difficulties involved in carrying out consumer research. One may question how realistic it is to expect people to be able to say what they wanted or anticipated from a service whose scope is indeterminate and ever-changing. One must also bear in mind that one's perceptions are affected by one's experiences. However, even bearing in mind the limitations of the study, some useful issues and points for action become apparent.

The importance of access and publicity on the part of the social services departments, though well-known, emerged. The establishment of area offices (now complete) may lead to more people contacting the department rather than the other way round. Increased publicity and information would increase the potential client's awareness of the services available. The consumer's general lack of knowledge about how to contact a social worker and even whether they were still in contact, illustrates the need for more information and clarity about procedures for clients.

The pleas of some of the consumers for more regular or frequent visits highlights the scope for using volunteers and other informal social work help, particularly for the lonely, elderly and disabled clients.

The discrepancies found between worker and client perceptions also prove interesting. It is encouraging that at a time when reorganisation was affecting staff morale, the clients expressed positive views about the services they were and had been receiving. Some of the discrepancies about expectations may be reduced by the development of more clearly defined aims which are explicitly understood and agreed upon by both client and worker. [. . .]

References

1 J. E. Mayer and Noel Timms, 1970, *The Client Speaks*, Routledge & Kegan Paul.
2 June E. Neill *et al.*, 'Reactions to integration', 1973, *Social Work Today*, 4(15).
3 ibid.
4 Margot Jefferys, 1965, *An Anatomy of Social Welfare Services*, Michael Joseph.

5 Jean P. Nursten, John Pottinger and Maureen Anderson, 1972, *Social Workers and their Clients*, Research Publications Services Ltd.

6 E. Matilda Goldberg and June E. Neill, 1972, *Social Work in General Practice*, Allen & Unwin.

7 M. Shepherd *et al.*, 1966, *Psychiatric Illness in General Practice*, Oxford University Press.

8 Goldberg and Neill, op. cit.

9 Charles D. Bolton and E. Kammeyer, 1968, 'The decision to use a family agency', *Family Co-ordinator*, 17.

10 Mayer and Timms, op. cit.

11 Leonard S. Kogan *et al.*, 1953, *A Follow-up Study of the Results of Social Casework*, New York, Family Service Association of America.

12 Mayer and Timms, op. cit.; William J. Reid and Ann W. Shyne, 1969, *Brief and Extended Casework*, Columbia University Press.

13 Jefferys, op. cit.

14 Vida Carver and J. L. Edwards, 1972, *Social Workers and their Workloads*, National Institute for Social Work Training; Rea Walker, E. Matilda Goldberg and David J. Fruin, 1972, *Social Workers and their Workloads in Northern Ireland Welfare Departments*, National Institute for Social Work Training.

IV. 3 Task and supervision in area social work

Anthea Hey and Ralph Rowbottom

[. . .] In this paper we shall discuss firstly a particular task-centred definition of work and describe how some social workers (engaged for the most part in casework) have seen their work in terms of this definition. Secondly we shall report certain generalized findings about how the management and supervision of this work is currently organized and the views of some social workers about this. Thirdly we shall argue (contentiously if necessary) for the advantages of clear definition of social work tasks and a clear structure for the management of this work in which what we shall call 'managerial' and what we shall call 'supervisory' roles are properly differentiated. [. . .]

The research project and conference programme

The method used in our research includes a series of unstructured interviews with staff in the area of work which has been chosen for analysis by a steering committee. Those interviewed have all volunteered to collaborate. In the interviews we explore with the worker such things as: the nature of his work, his duties, the discretion he has in following through his work, his authority in relation to others in carrying out his work, and theirs in relation to him. We offer various conceptual tools to clarify the situation. (As time goes on the concepts are naturally modified and extended in the light of experience.) At the end of this mutual exploration the material is committed to paper and checked with the individual concerned, who is able to correct and delete if he wishes until he is satisfied that the report reflects his view of his situation.

The material at this stage is neither more nor less than a statement of the assumption of an individual about his work and situation as an employee. However, as the perceptions of a number of individuals in an area of work are drawn together the picture becomes

Source: *British Journal of Social Work*, 1 (4), winter 1971, pp. 435, 436, 437, 438, 439, 440, 441, 442, 443, 444, 445, 447–8, 450–2.

more and more complete; that is, of what the organization is really doing and how it does it. Further clarification is usefully obtained as individuals give permission for their perceptions to be shared with each other and then the points are identified where change of a specified kind might be appropriately instituted. The exploration is a continuous process, as apart from changes that arise from project work, people's work and relationships are always changing in some degree or other in the normal course of events. [. . .]

Problems in defining the nature of social work

One of the first things apparent from the research is that whilst apparently sharing certain general views about what they are doing or hoping to do to assist their clients, social workers seem to find it peculiarly difficult to be precise in their articulations and, in particular, to identify for others the processes by which they expect to promote change. We are, of course, not the first, nor will we be the last to remark on this. Much of professional literature is concerned with attempting to describe the processes involved. [. . .]

Our aim is not, however, to produce another theory of social work, but merely to report some descriptions of the work that social workers see themselves as doing and of the organizational framework within which the work is done, and various apparent implications for supervision and training. [. . .]

Duties, discretion and tasks in social work

We will now proceed to outline some of the basic concepts we have used and give examples of the kind of descriptions that result from exploring with social workers the work they actually do in these terms.

For a start, we take the basic model of the nature of work in organizations developed by Jaques (1967), which in a highly compressed form may be summarized as follows.

Work has a physical dimension and a psychological dimension. The psychological dimension may be described as the exercise of discretion. In an organizational role discretion is exercised towards some prescribed ends implicit in the duties prescribed for the role, or explicitly in specifically assigned tasks, and within certain limits, for example, of policy and resources, explicitly or implicitly prescribed. Thus a relevant definition of work in an organizational setting becomes: the exercise of discretion towards prescribed ends within prescribed limits.

Within this context the duties or functions in any role are the generalized expectations of the ends to which the role occupant must work. They describe the general character of the role; what it has been set up to do. In responding to these expectations the occupant may initiate particular tasks at his own discretion, or alternatively, he may be set tasks by specific assignment. It is not possible in a sense to perform duties themselves—duties have to be broken into pieces of work with specific intended results which the worker expects himself, or is expected by others, to attain within some explicit or implicit time-scale. That is, he is expected to produce results, and he has not got for ever to do so.

[. . .] It is only when duties have been broken down into tasks [. . .] that work becomes evident and concrete. A task can be defined in general as a specific piece of work with an end-point, which requires a comprehensible programme of activity in order to attain it, and which has in it implicitly, if not explicitly, a timescale.

In responding to this idea of task, a number of social workers with whom we have worked suggested that in the nature of social work, with its complex emotional interactions between workers and clients, the purpose of intervention is to meet and work with these interactions on an *ad hoc* basis, as it were situationally, visit to visit, interview to interview, and that the notion of task can hardly apply. Case planning in this context is thought to be a matter of determining objectives—hoped-for results which do not necessarily have an implicit or explicit time-scale attached. These objectives serve rather to condition the responses that workers might be expected to make to situations as they arise, rather than as specific tasks, i.e. specific end-points which require programmes of active intervention to achieve [. . .]

All work, however, we must reassert, is in fact carried out in task-form, whether wittingly or unwittingly. Those workers believing in situational responses only, are seeing in fact short tasks; whilst those working through on a programme of intervention see longer ones. Is there perhaps some relationship between the inability to perceive longer tasks and the felt lack of a special area of competence and an exclusive body of social work knowledge (Wilensky and Lebeaux, 1965) either in the individual social worker, or in the profession as a whole? [. . .]

Obviously all social workers have a lot of short tasks which are easy to identify; for example:

to phone another agency (matter of days)
to make referral (one day)
to produce a social history report for court
(a matter of up to four weeks).

Many of these are fairly repetitive. In other cases a number of tasks may be being pursued simultaneously. For example, in a large family with multiple problems, where both parents were deaf and without speech, the worker saw the general duty of supporting the family as giving rise to the following tasks at various times, some concurrently with others:

to provide an escort (matter of hours)
to act as an interpreter, for example at court
(matter of hours)
to obtain a grant for school uniform (one month)
to obtain reconnection of electricity supply
(two months)
to get two-year-old boy placed in a nursery
school (six months)
to supplement parental role, in providing sex
education (six months)
to help mother to be able to undertake part-
time employment (nine months)

Most social workers who have been able to describe their work in task-terms beyond the one visit situation-response type of task mentioned previously, have been able to identify some tasks in the time range three to six months (some of these occur in the example given immediately above). A smaller number of longer tasks in the six to twelve months range have also been identified, and a smaller number still in the range of one to two years. [. . .]

Advantages of clarity in task definition

There are a number of ways in which greater clarity of definition of social work tasks might arguably be of advantage. Firstly, identification of tasks of social workers in the way we have suggested might itself contribute to improved services to clients. Unless you know what you are trying to do how can you begin to know whether you have done or are doing anything? In the new local authority social work situation, as social workers acquire duties in respect of a wider range of clientele the advantages of specificity are very obvious. It can no longer be assumed that workers will know intuitively what can be done, or how to do it. For those committed to the generic view of social work, the identification of specific tasks may help to demonstrate the similarities in the work and show that the work is not essentially different because of the client's age or health. And if this is so, the recognition should help to build up confidence in workers as they find their present skills can be used more widely.

A second possible advantage of explicit task definition is in relation to social work training. Social work trainers of course have for long been teaching the relevance fo treatment planning based on thorough study and diagnosis—students on placement are assiduously guided by their supervisors, too, in this way of working. But how many students, hatched into workers overnight on completion of their courses, find the supervisory arrangements very different, and their discretion in how they structure their work with clients extended to a seemingly limitless degree? The selection of cases for students to give them sufficient range of experience within the time available is always difficult, though perhaps longer placements in agencies, arising in response to the reorganization of departments, may provide scope for students to work on longer tasks with time-scales which are more explicit (i.e. continuing the assumption that there are many longer tasks available to be undertaken if clients are to get the help they need). Using the idea of tasks, tutors (who are usually experienced and skilled social workers themselves) may perhaps consider, in conjunction with students' supervisors, a more specific programming of student experiences, and at the same time it may be possible to achieve greater clarification of the tasks of the supervisors themselves.

Thirdly, the explicit definition of task may provide a means both of adjusting work to the particular level of capability of the individual social workers, and of helping that capability to become more fully realized. In discussing tasks to be carried out, the individual social worker can see clearly what is being expected of him or her, can comment on the feasibility of the expectations, and can participate in the exact formulation of the task. At the end of the day, the existence of a specific task to which the social worker has committed himself or herself makes an objective standard against which the worker's actual performance can be judged (taking due account of unexpected difficulties encountered en route). This can help to move the assessment interview out of the morass of psychological comment and on to the firm ground of discussion of effective or ineffective methods of work. [. . .]

The role of supervisors

[. . .] One of the assumptions voiced time and again is that only the social worker in direct contact with the client can know what needs to be done, and that whilst the supervisor's deeper experience can often be drawn on for support, the individual social worker alone remains accountable for his work with his client. It is inferred from this view that the supervisor should have no right to instruct the social worker as to how to work, though it is recognized that the supervisor sometimes may have the right to refuse resources within his discretion, and to insist on compliance with statutory or departmental requirements, e.g. frequency of visiting or mode of recording. This basic doubt as to whether anybody has the ultimate right to prescribe to the social worker appears to be compounded by the feeling that supervisors should provide consultation whose aim is to stimulate the social worker's professional development. Prescription of work is felt to be directly at odds with the training method preferred by most supervisors.

Further confusion in the supervisory role often arises where certain action or expenditure is not within the authority of the supervisors, so that recommendations made by the social worker and supported by a supervisor pass for decision to a more senior officer. (This senior officer is then of course implicitly reviewing the work not only of the social worker but of the supervisor who has supported the recommendation.) If the senior officer then deals directly with the social worker bypassing the supervisor, as is often the case in practice, this adds again to the doubt of supervisors as to their accountability and authority.

However, when the question of the autonomy of the individual social worker is really analysed, it has generally been our experience in discussions that the existence of accountability as an undoubted fact of the situation is recognized, and that it follows that authority to prescribe work, to assess, to sanction, and in an extreme case to transfer or dismiss a social worker, is seen as necessarily resting somewhere in the department. If so, what is at issue is not whether social workers should have complete freedom or whether their work should be completely prescribed at every point, but how much discretion social workers should have, how they should be helped to exercise this discretion, and at what points their actions need to be sanctioned, vetoed or prescribed by others (presumably of greater capability). [. . .]

Managerial and supervisory roles

[. . .] It has been argued so far:

(a) that there is some case for the more explicit definition of specific tasks in social work
(b) that some review of the quality of social work actually performed is unavoidable and that review mechanisms of various kinds are already to hand; and
(c) that authority to prescribe work to assess performance, and (if needs be) to apply sanctions must therefore, in all logic, be placed somewhere in the departments, and presumably not just at director-level.

In examining in this project the various ways in which authority and accountability may be, and is in practice, distributed amongst the higher-level roles in existing departments, we have found it necessary to distinguish two kinds of role—the *managerial* and the *supervisory*. (It appears that these two roles have not commonly been distinguished in thinking about the management of social work.)

The managerial role is one which carries the fullest degree of accountability for the work of others and requisitely therefore (it may be argued) needs a degree of authority as follows:

(a) to approve or veto the appointment of subordinates, because unless he can secure the people he thinks are suitable to carry through the work the manager cannot be held to account for the discharge of that work;

(b) to be able to prescribe the work of his subordinates, in order to be able to ensure that work actually done is in line with his perceptions of the work needing to be done;

(c) to be able to assess the performance of subordinates, in order to make the best use of their capacities and to guide their careers in their best interests;

(d) to be able to initiate the transfer of a subordinate from his teams, given that the manager has done everything possible to enable the subordinate to be effective and still finds the quality of his work unacceptable.

Where managerial accountability is unclear and diffused it is not only that the work done may be ill-controlled. From the point of view of the individual worker there is a lack of one definite person who is accountable not only for dealing with his work, but also with his problems; for attending to his individual career-progression; for listening with particular care to his own ideas on how the policy of the department might be shaped or reshaped.

It has been pointed out by Jaques (Brown and Jaques, 1965) that the effective operation of a managerial relationship implies some optimum distance of what he calls 'capacity' (the generalized ability to cope with executive or managerial work at various levels) between the superior and the subordinate. Too much difference, and the subordinate finds the boss unapproachable—a figure of some awe in terms of professional and administrative standing. Too little distance (and our research suggests subjectively that this is far more likely to be the case in social work departments) and the so-called superior is a figure whose assessments of one's own performance cannot really be taken too seriously—not so much a 'boss' more a 'senior colleague' (or if the circumstances suggest that his assessments are in danger of being taken seriously, this becomes a matter of considerable anxiety). By extension, there is presumably an optimum number of managerial levels for the running of a particular department of given size. However, if a manager has either a large number of subordinates or smaller numbers employed on complex duties, he may need assistance in managing them, and in this situation supervisory roles may well become established. The supervisory role has more limited authority:

(a) to assist in inducting new workers into their duties;
(b) to allocate and prescribe work within the manager's policy;
(c) to help and advise on a day to day basis;
(d) to carry out routine checks in work.
[. . .]

Possible implications for organization of area teams

With these factors in mind a number of general alternatives for the organization of a typical fieldwork team of, say ten to twenty social workers, may be considered.

One possibility is to assume that every difference in grade should be accompanied by a full managerial relationship. Assuming senior grades, basic grades and welfare assistant (or similar) grades, this would result in a structure with three managerial tiers, and no supervisory relationships, as shown in Fig. 3A. Evidence of the kind quoted above, however, throws very great doubt on the reality of this proposal.

To go to the other extreme, all members of the area team, at whatever stage of development, might be

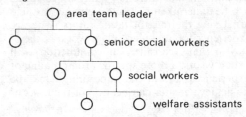

A Full managerial relationships between successive grades

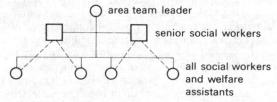

B Full managerial relationships only with area team leader

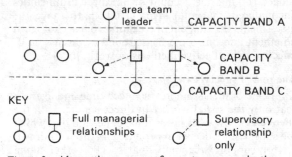

C A possible requisite alternative

Figure 3   Alternative pattern of area team organization

considered direct subordinates of the area team leader, with senior social workers playing a supervisory role (Fig. 3B). This feels a more likely possibility but for some evidence from our project-work that, for example, so-called 'supervisors' usually see themselves as fully accountable for the work of trainees or students allocated to them. Might this not apply to the more junior social workers?

Maybe in order to see this problem clearly it is necessary to step out of the framework of existing grades for the moment and attempt to see the variety of workers in any area not in terms of particular skills (psychiatric work, work with the blind, etc.) but, for the purposes of this exercise, in terms of a spectrum of capacity-levels. Perhaps the workers could be classified in three broad bands—A, B and C as shown in Fig. 3C —where the differences of capacity between the adjacent bands are just such as to promote an easy managerial relationship. Thus all workers in Band B would look upon the worker in Band A (the area team leader) as a 'natural' manager. On the other hand, the workers with Band C would naturally 'look' for managers in the band above, in Band B that is.

In terms of supervisory relationships, some of the higher capacity workers in Band B might well be given supervisory duties in relation to some of the workers at the bottom of Band B; but to the extent that these supervisors, or other workers at the top of Band B themselves needed case-supervision or support, they would probably look for it directly to the area team leader.

Returning to existing grades, one might *speculate* that most senior social workers were in the top of Band B, whether or not they carried supervisory roles, without ignoring the possibility that some basic-grade workers were extantly in the same position (and whether or not the latter should therefore properly carry a senior-grade is another matter). Most basic grade workers would no doubt fall in the lower half of Band B; but some, newly-qualified, unqualified, or less capable, might extantly again, be judged as coming within Band C. Band C might usually contain trainees, students and welfare assistants, who would thus just be 'supervised' but extantly 'managed' by senior workers at the top of Band B.

Needless to say, as workers developed, their position in these bands would change, and of course it would very much be the job of those with managerial responsibilities to be alive to these developments, and do their best to restructure the situation accordingly.

References

Brown, W. and Jaques, E., 1965, *Glacier Project Papers*, Heinemann, chapter 7 and 8.

Jaques, E., 1967, Equitable Payment (rev. ed.), Penguin Books.

Wilensky, H. L. and Lebeaux, C. N., 1965, *Industrial Society and Social Welfare*, New York, Free Press, N.Y.

Conclusion

Drawing on some evidence from field-research work and conference discussion over the last two years with social workers of various grades, it has been suggested:

(1) that there are obvious advantages to be gained from a more explicit definition of the tasks to be carried out in fieldwork from the point of controlling and balancing the services to clients, and of aiding the training and individual development of social-workers;

(2) that social workers (in local authorities at least) find themselves for the present at least in hierarchical organizations in which accountability is a fact; and hence review, prescription, assessment and sanction are necessary consequences;

(3) that the management of their work can be effected through at least two different types of role, here called the 'managerial' and the 'supervisory', and that various important alternative patterns of area-team organization become apparent when this distinction is recognized. (Important in the sense that quite different modes of behaviour become appropriate when the distinction is made.)

In a sense, the general trend of many of these arguments is to suggest that local authority social service departments call for stronger and better-defined systems of management than exist at the moment. To counter the inevitable reaction one must stress that better management does not necessarily mean more restrictive or more authoritarian management. Some individuals may indeed need more authoritative direction than they are getting at the moment, but others may need less. The supposition is that there is an *optimum* level of freedom for each worker, given his particular stage of development, and that defining his work accordingly will enhance rather than reduce the scope for truly creative work to be done.

IV. 4 An experimental evaluation of school social work

Tony F. Mashall and Gordon Rose

[. . .] The present paper is a summary of the results of the Central Lancashire Family and Community Project (1965–73). Financial resources limited the project to five workers operating in co-educational schools varying from 500 to 1,000 pupils: two comprehensives and three secondary moderns. One was a Catholic school; the remainder were non-denominational. One school had later to be excluded from the research because the managers withdrew permission for psychological testing, an outcome that emphasised the importance of creating good relations from the outset of a large-scale community-based project of this kind, and also the difficulty of maintaining them throughout. Despite this setback, a complex research design was maintained for almost eight years, due largely to the emphasis placed on close liaison with the local authorities concerned.

The professional backgrounds of the workers, and hence their styles of work, were varied: two fully-trained social workers (a family case-worker and a probation officer), a nurse with a social work diploma and psychiatric hospital experience, a person with residential child care and youth work qualifications, and a teacher who had completed a one-year school counselling course; three of these were trained teachers and another was qualified to teach by holding a university degree. The nature of the work was not therefore narrowly defined: it embraced any kind of work which operated through personal relationships to help children and their families to solve or adjust to personal and social problems. The defining characteristic of the work was its *setting*. Each worker was based in a single school as a staff member, able to undertake a small teaching load in addition to their primary counselling or social work functions (the worker who was not qualified to teach was able to contribute to remedial lessons). From their school base they were expected to provide a home-school link and to engage in family social work where necessary.

Methodological considerations

So that the process being evaluated could remain natural, without an obvious experimental component, workers and schools were allowed complete freedom to pursue their own ends. Necessary research activities were unintrusive, amounting to an annual spell of testing with no obvious link with the social worker. Although it was monitored carefully, selection of cases was left to the worker and his school: teacher referrals always predominated, but as the social worker became known, parents and the children themselves brought their problems along. The social workers also discovered some cases for themselves, through teaching and other activities with pupils. Further referrals also came from other agencies, such as education welfare and police juvenile liaison.

One of the project's aims was to reduce delinquency, but this was considered inadequate as a sole aim for two reasons: firstly, reliance on official data, such as police records, could introduce an unknown bias which would invalidate the evaluation process (Short and Nye, 1958; Gold, 1966; Hood and Sparks, 1970, chapters 1–2; Steer, 1973); and secondly, we expected that delinquency was sometimes but one sign among others of an underlying maladjustment problem, which might be the more appropriate problem to investigate. The scope of the project was accordingly widened to encompass all that is implied by the concept of maladjustment.

This broadening of the project produced thorny problems of definition. What is good or bad adjustment depends upon whose point of view is taken – the teacher's, the parent's, that of the police, the social worker's or that of the child himself. Teachers tend to be preoccupied with classroom disruptive behaviours rather than with withdrawal symptoms (see Wickman,

Source: *British Journal of Guidance and Counselling,* 3 (1), January 1975, pp. 3–14.

1928; Stouffer and Owens, 1955), while parents and social workers are likely to have a contrary or at least a different bias (see Mitchell and Shepherd, 1966; Rutter *et al.*, 1970). Moreover, the academic literature contains a wealth of definitions of adjustment (see Rose and Marshall, 1975, chapter 2), and evidence of distinguishable forms of maladjustment with different antecedents and different consequences (e.g. Hewitt and Jenkins, 1946).

Questionnaires answered by the children themselves were used as the basis for our analysis, providing us with a number of measures of different aspects of a child's behaviour, environment, attitudes and personality. Three successive year-cohorts answered a questionnaire relating to home, school, peer group and self-concept, as well as completing a standardised personality inventory (Cattell and Beloff, 1962), in both their second and their fourth years at school. Data on attainment and attendance were also recorded. To simplify the fifty-four principal variables obtained, they were subjected to oblique factor analysis. At the simplest level, two factors (only slightly inter-correlated) were obtained, which were interpreted as representing two basically different types of adjustment problem:

(a) *Social adjustment* – referring to the child's relationship with, or adjustment to, other people and society in general (including home and school relationships and general attitudes to social norms).

(b) *Personal adjustment* – referring to the child's relationship to himself or his internal adjustment (e.g. anxiety, self-esteem).

It was clear that therapeutic change would need to be evaluated separately in terms of each of these dimensions: a unitary conception of adjustment would not be appropriate.

As a check against the children's self-report data, behavioural reports were obtained from teachers and parents (on the basis of symptom check-lists), from police records, and from a psychiatrist (on the basis of interviews with a random sample of children—see Leslie, 1971). Henceforward, the term '*behaviour*' will be used to refer to these observations by other people, and the term '*adjustment*' to refer to the self-report data.

There was an association between the behavioural observations and the self-report data, particularly the social adjustment components, which confirmed the relevance of the self-report data to what is seen as maladjustment by others. The correlations were not, however, high enough to predict a child's behaviour *at any given time* from test scores alone—a finding which concurred with that of other studies (e.g. Simon, 1971; West and Farrington, 1973). Poor test scores apparently represented a predisposition to misbehave, but did not necessarily represent persistent misbehaviour or even misbehaviour at all from some children. Moreover, when considering change over a period of time, the relative independence of *behaviour* and *adjustment* was even more evident: each

tended to show separate 'careers', later adjustment being relatively more influenced by earlier adjustment, and later behaviour by earlier behaviour.

There are good reasons why a less than perfect correlation between adjustment and behaviour might be anticipated. One is that the self-report data were time-specific, describing the state in which a child appeared at that moment (including temporary aberrations of mood or atypical crises), while the behavioural observations (based on knowledge of the child over a considerable period of time) allowed an assessment of his usual or average state of adjustment. In addition, though, any disposition which a child may have had to behave in a particular way, as revealed in the adjustment score, might have been 're-pressed' in the face of social pressures, in which case the adjustment problems would have remained concealed. *Adjustment* therefore varied with changes in situational or environmental problems and in the child's ability to cope with them, while *behaviour* was more subject to social conformity pressures. The results in fact show that, without social work intervention, there was much more improvement in behaviour than in underlying adjustment. But the social pressures which resulted in greater outward conformity—represented most extremely by taking a child to court—also had a *negative* effect on adjustment scores.

It was accordingly necessary to differentiate carefully between the two basic kinds of adjustment, and between them and their behavioural manifestations. The existence of multiple effects, however, made it necessary to analyse any interactions between them. It emerged, for example, that changes in personal and social adjustment among non-cases were *inversely* correlated: i.e. in normal circumstances an improvement in the child's predisposition to conform (social adjustment) was likely to be accompanied by increased anxiety (lower personal adjustment), while, vice versa, an improvement in personal adjustment tended to lead to poorer social adjustment. The children treated by the school social worker did not however manifest this association, so that it appeared that social casework or counselling could effect improvement in one dimension without adversely affecting the other.

Furthermore, changes in behaviour and adjustment over time, in both treated and untreated cases, were correlated, in this case positively. Thus if a child's adjustment was deteriorating it would be more difficult to improve his behaviour, and vice versa. The social workers, it was found, were more likely to receive deteriorating children as referrals, and this had to be allowed for in the evaluation.

A further methodological problem related to the environment within which the research took place. It is common in evaluative exercises of this sort to set up a simple experimental paradigm designed to test the bare hypothesis that the treatment in question effects greater improvement in its recipients than would otherwise be expected. In so doing, extraneous influences and circumstances are either eliminated or

ignored, while no attempt is made to look for consequences for anyone other than the clients. If however
the research is to have practically useful results it is
important that an effort is made to evaluate these
contingent variables as well: adoption of the new
treatment methods as part of general policy would not
occur in a vacuum, but in an ongoing social situation
which cannot usually be controlled just to facilitate
the treatment process. Thus the introduction of a social
worker into a school is more than a new method of
helping or reforming maladjusted children. It has,
or might have, effects on the whole school (children
who are not clients, teachers, school organisation and
structure) and on others outside (the families of the
children, other social services). Just as important are
the effects that all these in turn might have on the new
treatment process: for instance, the way the school
might alter or limit the social workers' aims and
methods. Thus although the main research was geared
to analysing change in individual children, an attempt
was also made to look at such variables, independent of
the treatment process, which might modify its effects.

We also carried out some testing in other schools in
the locality, and in two of them a full test–retest procedure was carried out on a complete year-cohort,
just as was done in the experimental schools. These
were not strictly 'controls': although collectively they
had an initial delinquency rate equivalent to that of
the combined experimental schools, their initial
maladjustment rates were different. But they made it
possible to match individual pupils from the control
schools with treated ones in the experimental schools,
which—when added to untreated matches from within
the experimental schools themselves—increased the
number of individual controls to a feasible level.

Even so, serious problems arose with respect to
matching. Even if cases with certain 'social adjustments'
scores, say, were matched with non-cases with similar
scores, certain difficulties remained:

(a) If selection of children as cases was very good,
there would be no non-cases with such bad scores.
The opportunity to inflate the sample of 'untreated'
children by using members of the 'control schools' was
helpful here.

(b) The fact that the cases were referred must mean
that there was something different about them—
worse behaviour, deteriorating more, worse underlying problems, etc.—so that the cases might have had
a worse prognosis despite comparable scores on one
test measure.

(c) Test-errors were likely to be non-random: i.e.
cases were more likely to have initial scores which
were falsely high (at the well-adjusted end), and non-
cases ones which were falsely low (because the fact of
referral confirms the low scores among the cases and
the higher ones among the non-cases). Due to the
improbability of test-errors being repeated in the retest,
this would mean that cases were likely to appear to
move as a whole towards *lower* average social adjustment, and non-cases to higher.

(d) Children identified as 'problems' might thereby
be 'labelled' by others as such and treated differently
from non-cases by teachers and other children, so
that they would be unable to overcome the effects of
their bad reputation. In fact, most of the referrals that
did occur were of children who were already widely
recognised as problems and were thus unlikely to be
labelled as a result of the referral. In any case, if
referral to a social worker involves such effects, and
these are disadvantageous, they should be evaluated
along with the treatment as inevitable components of
it.

The only overall solution was to control for as
many aspects of the child and his situation as possible.
Adequate matching was achieved on the basis of
prediction scores employing prior test-scores, prior
indicators or misbehaviour, and contemporary measures of situational problems. By using such a wide
range of information, good prediction could be obtained—for example, fourth-year social adjustment
scores showed a product-moment correlation of 0.68
with the predicted scores. Cases and non-cases (from
experimental and control schools) could then be
matched according to predicted outcomes, so that
differences in actual outcomes could be ascribed to
treatment differences. Full details of the analysis are
contained in Rose and Marshall (1975).

Effects on treated children

Since the research took place in a natural community
setting, some of the children in our sample received
forms of treatment different from, or additional to,
that provided by the social workers—police juvenile
liaison work, court appearances, and probation, for
example. This clearly had to be taken into account in
the evaluation. Controlling for these other treatments,
the results of the work of the school social workers
were shown to be clearly positive: both behaviour and
social adjustment scores improved by comparison with
untreated controls. Some equally interesting results,
however, emerged when the effects of different forms
of treatment were analysed. The results for the different
forms were always ranked in the same order as their
position on what might be called a 'controlling'/
'supportive' continuum: from court appearance (with
a sentence other than probation), through probation
and juvenile liaison, to school social work. The more
controlling the treatment, the more likely it was that
the misbehaviour would be repressed in the immediate
future; social adjustment scores, however, deteriorated
with more controlling treatments, auguring badly for
the more distant future when, perhaps, new crises
would have to be faced. On the other hand, the more
supportive the treatment, the more social adjustment
scores improved, while—as we have already seen—
behaviour also improved by comparison with untreated controls (though not as much as in response to
the controlling treatments). These differences were
highly significant statistically.

Such were the outcomes by the child's final school year, still a relatively short-run period. For longer-term evaluation there were available only police records of cautions and court appearances up to the age of 17–18. Comparing the boys in the experimental and control schools, where similar delinquency rates had obtained in the first year (12 and 14 per cent respectively), a substantial relative improvement in delinquency rates was evident in the experimental schools: by the fourth year there were only three-quarters as many delinquents as in the control schools, and by the age of 17–18 (amongst former pupils) only two-thirds as many. These figures may indeed under-estimate the extent of improvement, since on the basis of their better test scores the control school boys would have had not an equal prognosis but a better one. There was some evidence therefore that the effects of school social work were long lasting, pro-ducing an improvement in underlying adjustment which provided a good foundation for future be-haviour.

But although the experimental results showed positive changes in delinquency, general misbehaviour, school attendance and social adjustment scores, there were no differences between cases and non-cases in terms of changes in personal adjustment scores. Per-haps more personal aspects such as anxiety level are less readily changed, or perhaps social work is not an appropriate way of changing them. Another possible explanation is suggested by an analysis which indi-cated that the meaning which could be attached to personal adjustment scores depended on the child's level of social adjustment at the same period. For children with below-average social adjustment, the lower the personal adjustment the poorer the prognosis for future behaviour; for children with above-average social adjustment, however, a certain degree of anxiety appeared normal, and a high personal adjustment score was associated with a relatively *poorer* be-havioural prognosis. One might hypothesise that a high personal adjustment score here is indicative of repression of problems, since many of the children identified solely by the psychiatrist as mentally ill were in the latter category—especially among the girls. At all events, we should obviously not be looking for any unilinear change on the personal adjustment dimension as a result of school social work.

The success of school social work appeared to be spread evenly across different types of problem, but a relationship did emerge between the level of a child's prognosis (prediction score) and the optimum amount of supportive work necessary to produce benefit. The more severe the case, the more intensive the work needed to produce positive results. This was hardly surprising, but less obvious was the corollary that the less severe the case, the less intensive the work associ-ated with a successful outcome. In short, too much work applied to minor problems usually resulted in deterioration rather than improvement, a result sup-ported by similar effects found in some cases of multiple treatments. In fact, the workers were usually accurate in their assessment of the amount of work needed, although outside pressures might at times lead to over-concentration on a minor case. But this finding also has implications for cases where different workers may be working simultaneously with the same child, which might result in over-saturation: such overlap, of course, was one of the problems that the Seebohm Committee sought to overcome. It also suggests the need for a school social worker or counsellor to liaise closely with other social workers whose caseloads may overlap. Alternative explanations for the finding may, however, be possible: the 'over-saturated' children may for example have had different kinds of problems, which were not identified and which re-quired different forms of treatment.

In addition to *type* and *severity* of problem, another important variable is that of the *timing* of treatment intervention. The stage in the child's 'career' at which he is identified and referred carries important implica-tions for the likely success of treatment. Traditional social services usually begin late, after marked symp-toms of maladjustment have appeared. By this stage the consolidation of a deviant self-concept and habituation to a particular line of personal development (e.g. the 'hardened' delinquent) may make treatment effects difficult to achieve without prolonged effort. School-based social work has the important advantage of finding early signs of trouble and thus contacting cases at a much earlier stage in the development of a deviant life-style. This suggests that primary-school social work might bring even more impressive economic and therapeutic returns.

Other effects

As was mentioned earlier, the well-being of treated children was not the only therapeutically beneficial outcome hoped for from the project. It was also hoped that there might be effects on families, on untreated children, and on schools and teachers.

On *home relationships* no overall significant effect was visible, which was hardly surprising in view of the very small proportion of cases in which social work with families was undertaken. In those families where there had been some social work contact, however, substantial improvements were evident on scores of 'parent-child relationships' obtained from the question-naire.

Measurable effects on *untreated children* were not really anticipated. But close inspection of delinquency rates in the experimental schools showed that al-though the greatest improvements were among treated cases, there was a small but positive effect among un-treated pupils. The reasons are worthy of investiga-tion. It might be that the presence of the social worker had influenced the ways in which some teachers related to pupils and dealt with misbehaviour.

This latter interpretation would seem to be sup-ported by the effects that were observed on the *teachers* themselves. These effects appeared to differ according to the teachers' attitudes to, and relationships with, children. Initially, the more child-centred teachers had feared that their opportunities to relate helpfully to children might be diminished by the introduction of an 'expert', but in the end they felt they were able to contribute even more effectively than before in their pastoral care functions through their co-operation with the school social worker. The less child-centred teachers—who exercised more control in the classroom, were more formal in their relations with pupils, and sharply distinguished teaching from social work—were inclined to be less favourable to the project both before and after experiencing it, though they became less antagonistic as time went by, Paradoxically, the latter group of teachers were often a fruitful source of referrals, perhaps in an attempt to use the social worker as an aid in asserting control over difficult children.

The school's influence on the social worker's role

At the start of the project, it was intended that the workers should perform a solely counselling, supportive role, in contrast to the controlling methods that are more customary responses to deviance. It was anticipated that they would delve beneath the surface of symptomatic behavioural disturbance to the underlying problems so as to untangle and interpret them in the course of a long-term relationship with the child and his family. These were also the original aims of the workers, to which they were inclined by training and personal conviction. But the school is a fairly inflexible organisation whose objectives differ from those of social workers, and the introduction of such a novel role makes great adaptive demands on *both* sides. While the school seeks to incorporate this new kind of person both ideologically and structurally, the worker is also forced to make some concessions to the unfamiliar milieu in which he finds himself.

The schools had two expectations of the new staff, both of which were legitimate and reasonable from their point-of-view and both of which were antipathetic to the social workers' aims. One was expecting the rapid reform of misbehaving pupils; the other was expecting that the social worker would be closely identified with the staff and become involved in the school organisation. The first of these expectations brought great pressure for a tough approach to disruptive children. Because the workers needed to win acceptance and build up their positions within the schools, they succumbed to some degree, *wanting* to 'improve' behaviour in order to be seen to be effective by teachers many of whom were sceptical of the value of school social work with delinquents. Using the descriptions of their work in the social workers' own case-records, we found that these pressures had resulted in the use of more 'controlling' methods in a few cases: changes in these cases were more likely to be in behaviour than in adjustment, although the latter

was still improved to some extent. As for the second expectation, this led to workers becoming substantially involved not only in teaching but also in such school activities as house activities and clubs. While such involvements helped to serve some social work purposes, they brought a marked reduction in the time available for casework, and certainly curtailed its more time-consuming aspects such as family visiting.

The kind of case the workers received was also affected by the teachers' bias toward recognising the socially-alienated disruptive children who 'acted out' their problems rather than the quiet, withdrawn and highly conformist child who internalised them. We cannot of course be sure that they would have been successful with the latter type of child, and when they did come across more psychiatrically abnormal children they tended to refer them to child guidance clinics rather than attempt to tackle such problems themselves. Even so, the identification of problems needing specialist attention and making the appropriate referral could be a valuable function of the school social worker—assuming the specialist services have the capacity to take on such an increased caseload. Any widespread adoption of school social workers should, therefore, be matched by increases in the resources of other agencies that seek to help children or their families.

Though for convenience this account of the influence of the school has considered common features, in practice one is conscious of their differences. The composition of the teaching staff, the Head's style of organisation, his efficiency, and the power structure of the school all make a great difference to the way in which the worker is accepted and the kind of role he is able to fashion (see Rose and Marshall, 1975, chapter 8). Such matters will decide both whether a social worker can function effectively and also what kind and range of help is appropriate.

Conclusions

This research has established that school social work can reduce the incidence of maladjustment and deviant behaviour to a degree sufficient to warrant the wider deployment of social workers in schools. Moreover, such side-effects as we could measure were positive, if slight. Certain limitations to the effectiveness of such work were imposed by the nature of the school setting, but on balance it certainly appears that the school is extremely promising as a setting for the development of social work with children and young people.

Unfortunately, however, the interdepartmental co-operation which is necessary for dealing with the child with problems and his family is seriously handicapped by the administrative structure. Education and social work are developing separately and not by any means in the same direction, and few social service departments have either taken over some part of the social work role in school or even made adequate arrangements for establishing relationships with the schools in their areas. We would strongly recommend that the various ministries concerned should jointly institute a survey of the needs of individual schools and the ways in which these could best be met. In this survey, consideration should be given to the needs both of the school social worker for adequate supporting services

from other departments, and also of the outside agencies themselves for a social base within the school—such as social centres housing counsellors and other kinds of workers, including youth and community workers.

References

Cattell, R. B. and Beloff, H., 1962, *Handbook for the High School Personality Questionnaire*, Illinois, Institute for Personality and Ability Testing.

Gold, M., 1966, 'Undetected delinquent behaviour', *Journal of Research in Crime and Delinquency*, 3, pp. 27–46.

Hewitt, L. E. and Jenkins, R. L., 1946, *Fundamental Patterns of Maladjustment: the Dynamics of their Origin*, Illinois, Green.

Hood, R. and Sparks, R., 1970, *Key Issues in Criminology*, Weidenfeld & Nicolson.

Leslie, S. A., 1971, 'The Prevalence of Psychiatric Disorder in the Young Adolescents of an Industrial Town', MD thesis, University of Liverpool.

Mitchell, S. and Shepherd, M., 1966, 'A comparative study of children's behaviour at home and at school', *British Journal of Educational Psychology*, 36, pp. 248–54.

Rose, G. and Marshall, T. F., 1975, *Counselling and School Social Work: an Experimental Study*, London, Wiley.

Rutter, M., Tizard, J. and Whitmore, K., 1970, *Education, Health and Behaviour*, Longmans.

Short, J. F., Jr. and Nye, F. I., 1958, 'Extent of unrecorded juvenile delinquency: tentative conclusions', *Journal of Criminal Law, Criminology and Political Science*, 49, p. 296.

Simon, F. H., 1971, *Prediction Methods in Criminology*, Home Office Research Studies 7, HMSO.

Steer, D., 1973, 'The elusive conviction', *British Journal of Criminology*, 13(4), pp. 373–83.

Stouffer, G. A. and Owens, J., 1955, 'Behaviour problems of children as identified by today's teachers and compared with those reported by E. K. Wickman', *Journal of Educational Research*, 48, pp. 321–31.

West, D. J. and Farrington, D. P., 1973, *Who Becomes Delinquent?*, Heinemann.

Wickman, E. K., 1928, *Children's Behavior and Teacher's Attitudes*, New York, Commonwealth Fund.

IV. 5 The care and treatment of subnormal children in residential institutions

Jack Tizard et al.

Those whom we in this country call the severely subnormal, and who are referred to as trainable and custodial children in the United States, and as imbeciles and idiots in the continent of Europe, provide a test case for the concept of educability. Because their handicaps are so severe they have been denied educational services in most countries, on the grounds that they cannot benefit from them. In some countries, such as England and the Soviet Union in which they do get education—or 'training'—this is organized under a different Ministry from the one which is responsible for the education of ordinary children, and the actual teaching is carried out by people who are not qualified teachers.

A number of studies have shown that even severely handicapped children *do* profit from special education (it would be incredible if they did not). We know, alas, that when we compare the abilities and attainments of severely retarded children who live in their own homes with those of similar children resident in hospitals or institutions for the retarded, the hospital children are seen to be more backward than their peers who live at home (Lye, 1959, 1960; Tizard, 1964). The question arises, therefore, as to what it is in the hospital environment which retards their development. This question formed the starting point for the work to be described.

The need for residential places

About the need for residential provision for many of the severely retarded there can be no doubt whatsoever. Figure 4 gives data obtained from a survey carried out in London in 1960 (Goodman and Tizard, 1962; Tizard 1964).

It shows how the proportions in institutions in each age-group of severely retarded persons known to the authorities rises with each decade of life.

Source: 'What is Special Education?' First International Conference of the Association for Special Education, 25–28 July 1966, pp. 164–76.

These are London data, and in other areas the proportions will of course vary; but a similar *trend* is almost certain to be found. Since more severely handicapped and dependent persons are now surviving till

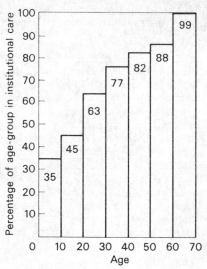

Figure 4 Percentage of London retardates in institutional care (IQ < 50)

adult life, it seems inevitable that in the future the numbers of residential places required for them will increase. The problem of how best to provide these is a growing one.

The present investigation

During the last three years we have been studying some sociological aspects of institutional care for children. A detailed survey has been made of a large mental subnormality hospital, with several hundred beds for children, and of long-stay paediatric wards in a hospital for children who are physically but for the most part not mentally handicapped. The patterns of management found in these two institutions have been compared with those found in two large Children's Homes for deprived ('dependent' in American terminology) children.

Table 1 Percentage of children in each age group (years)

	birth–2	2–5	5–11	11–15	15+	Total (%)
Subnormality wards	1	10	54	35	—	100
Paediatric wards	13	21	30	19	17	100
Children's Homes (average)	—	12	46	36	6	100

To check some of our findings and conclusions we have also carried out studies of two other, smaller institutions for mentally subnormal children.

This paper first describes the findings obtained in our study of the two large hospitals and two large Children's Homes, and then gives an account of our survey of children in the other two, smaller, mental subnormality units. Then we discuss some of the sociological factors which appear to be responsible for the differences in patterns of management which we have found.

First, then, the four large institutions. They were all of comparable size, each having between 300 and 400 beds for children. All four establishments were divided into cottages or wards, consisting of detached or semi-detached units set in the grounds of the institutions. In one of the two Children's Homes and in both of the hospitals there were on the average between sixteen and twenty children in each unit; the other Children's Home had just over ten children on average in each cottage. In the two Children's Homes and in the mental subnormality hospital the age-distribution was very similar.

About half the child population was between five and eleven years of age, and there were few children less than two years of age. In the long-stay paediatric wards of the other hospital one child in eight (13 per cent) was less than two years of age and one child in six (17 per cent) was more than fifteen years of age. The babies were in a special ward, as were the adolescents; and in the remaining long-stay paediatric wards the distribution of children by age resembled that in the other three institutions.

In other ways also the four institutions were very similar. In all of them, boys outnumbered girls; and in all four institutions the majority of children had been in residence for years rather than months. The constituent units—wards or cottages—nearly all had children of both sexes; and except for the two special wards in the paediatric hospital, they nearly all had both boys and girls of widely differing ages. Thus in size, lay-out, sex and age distribution, the length of

stay of the children, the constituent units in all four establishments were fairly similar.

Where they differed widely, of course, was in regard to the children's handicaps. In the subnormality hospital all children were severely retarded: 40 per cent of them had IQs of less than 20 points; 30 per cent had IQs between 20 and 30; fewer than 20 per cent had IQs between 30 and 40; and only 10 per cent had IQs of more than 40 points. In the paediatric wards a quarter of the children were rated as subnormal, but no intelligence test scores were available for them. The children in the two Children's Homes were for the most part within the normal range of intelligence.

The children in both *hospitals* also included many more who were handicapped in other ways. Nearly half of the children in the mental subnormality hospital, and as many as 70 per cent in the long-stay paediatric wards, were classed as non-ambulant. A large proportion in both hospitals were incontinent, many of them doubly incontinent. About half required help with feeding. Very few could dress themselves without help.

Most children in the paediatric wards had normal speech or at least could make themselves understood through speech. In the subnormality wards, however, lack of speech was a major problem. No fewer than 76 per cent of the children had no speech at all for practical purposes; 11 per cent had single words only, and a mere 13 per cent could talk even in simple sentences.

In the Children's Homes few children suffered from these disabilities—though many children in the Homes had of course other problems—educational, physical, emotional and social—to be coped with by the staff.

The nursing problem both in the subnormality hospital and in the paediatric hospital was a formidable one, and that part of the nurses' day which was not devoted to the general management of the ward was taken up with the feeding, washing, dressing and changing of severely handicapped children. However, in the subnormality hospital about a third of the children attended a hospital training centre, and in the paediatric wards all children except the subnormal ones had bedside or ward teaching by qualified teachers. For the children classed as mentally subnormal who were in the paediatric wards, no formal educational provision was made, though many of them might have benefited from it.

In the Children's Homes, all children went to school during the day—to a nursery school, infants' school or junior school situated in the grounds, in the case of the younger children, or to one of twenty or more ordinary secondary schools outside the establishment which were attended by all children over the age of eleven.

The children's day in the hospitals and homes

Let us now consider the manner in which children were brought up in each of these four establishments.

A convenient way of doing this is by looking at some aspects of a typical day in each.

A day begins with waking, and getting dressed. In the subnormality hospital dressing the children was in some, but not all, wards a responsibility of a night nurse; the children had to be toileted and dressed, and made ready for breakfast when the day staff came on duty at 7.30 a.m. The night nurse therefore had the task of coping with up to twenty handicapped children, and the job had to be finished by 7.30. The nurse would, moreover, often be dealing with children whom she did not know—thus in one typical ward, for example, forty-two different night nurses were on duty in the course of a single year. The nurse would therefore go from bed to bed waking each child in turn and taking him to the toilet or sitting him on a pot in the ward. The children were then washed, and either dressed and sat on their beds or left in their beds in their nightclothes.

All this of course takes time; and in two of the sixteen wards we studied, the process started at 4 a.m. In another nine wards it began at 5, and in the remaining five wards it started at 6.

In three-quarters of the paediatric wards, nurses began getting the children up at 6, while the remainder started at 7. Curiously enough, in two paediatric wards which had a high proportion of subnormal children as patients, the process of dressing the subnormal children started at 4, whereas the other children were not wakened till between 6 and 7.

What did the children do after being dressed? To answer this question, enquiries were made about a random sample of *ambulant* children in each of the two hospitals. In about two wards in every five, in both hospitals, the children merely remained in or on their beds after being dressed. On other wards, however, though they still stayed in the dormitory, they had toys or books to get on with. There was only one ward in the subnormality hospital where the children moved out of the dormitory into the day room before the day staff came on duty.

Getting-up times in both hospitals were the same at weekends as during the week—indeed except for schooling during the week, ward routine remained much the same throughout the year.

In the Children's Homes, the children could for the most part dress themselves, and no night nurses were employed. In different cottages they were wakened between 6.45 and 7.30. On Saturdays and Sundays, however, things were very different, and getting up was anything from a quarter of an hour to two hours later than during the week. The children, and the staff, would have a 'lie in'.

In the hospitals and in the Children's Homes, the children went to bed at very different times. In one ward of the subnormality hospital, bedtime for the youngest children started about 4 in the afternoon, and in nearly half the wards it had started by 5. In the remaining wards, however, if didn't start till 6 in the evening, and in two wards it was as late as 7. The older, active schoolchildren started to go to bed about 7 in most wards, though not till 8 in three wards, and as early as 6 in another.

In the paediatric wards, the pattern was rather similar to that of the subnormality hospital, except in the adolescent ward. In the two Children's Homes, bedtimes were much later than those in the hospitals, and the timetable was much more flexible.

Now let us look at meal times. In both hospitals meals were prepared in central kitchens and taken in hot containers to the wards, where they were served by nursing staff. This meant that the children did not see the main meals prepared, though there were ward kitchens in which snacks and hot drinks were made. The staff did not eat with the children, so that the patients, while they were in hospital, never sat down to a table with an adult, or indeed actually saw an adult eat at all.

In the Children's Homes, food was ordered from a shop in the establishment and meals were prepared and cooked by the housemothers in charge of the cottages. The staff ate with the children, serving from the table as is done in an ordinary family.

In both hospitals there was a marked lack of contact between children on different wards, except when they were at school; visiting another ward for a meal hardly occurred at all. One consequence of this was that when a child was removed from one ward to another, which happened not infrequently, he might never again see either the staff or the children in his old ward. In the Children's Homes, on the other hand, it was common for visitors to be invited into meals, not only for birthday parties and on special occasions, but also at other times when children brought friends home or visited.

Let us now look at toileting—clearly a major problem in a hospital in which four-fifths of the children were incontinent, or where, as in the paediatric wards, though one-third of the children could recognize their own needs to go to the WC, more than 90 per cent were dependent on staff at the toilet because of their physical handicaps. How was this organised?

In all wards except one in the mental subnormality hospital, there was a regular session before and after each meal at which all children were toileted. Most wards, however, had more sessions than this, and although not all children attended all sessions in all of the wards, there were some wards in which all children were taken to the toilet irrespective of need. In both hospitals, half of the wards had five or more regular sessions during the day, and as each took upwards of half an hour, a large proportion of the day might be spent simply attending to the toileting of the children. In wards where feeding was also a problem, meals and toileting might leave little time for anything else. In nearly half the wards of the subnormality hospital, all children would be taken into the lavatory at the same time, and all would wait there till the last child had finished, when they would all return to the day-room.

A similar pattern was seen in the organization of bath times. In the mental subnormality hospital, bathing took place in the evenings before the children went to bed—at a time, incidentally, when there were usually fewest staff on duty. Because of the lack of staff to attend to the children in the dormitory and day-rooms, the children were often kept in the bathroom for the whole period of bathing. Since the bathing followed on from one of the toilet sessions in these wards, they would have been in the bathroom from the time at which the toileting had begun. In half of the mental subnormality wards children were all kept in the bathroom waiting for their turn to be bathed, and the same pattern occurred in a quarter of the paediatric wards. Similarly, in a quarter of the wards in each hospital, all children remained in the bathroom till all bathing was finished before being returned to the dormitory.

In the Children's Homes these problems of toileting and bathing did not arise in this extreme form. About a third of the children required supervision or assistance in bathing, but this was always done individually, and in only one of the fifty-eight separate cottages investigated was the system adopted of having one nurse bath the child and hand him over to another for drying and dressing. This practice was found in more than half the wards of the subnormality hospital and in nearly half of those in the paediatric one.

There are many other ways in which the lives of the children in the two kinds of establishments differed. All children in the Children's Homes had their own clothing. Clothing for the younger children was bought by house-mothers from the local shop, whereas the older children had a clothing allowance of their own. Virtually all of them had their own toys, and most their own books; and there were in addition communal toys which were very much in evidence in the cottages. The children lived lives which were free and unregimented; they used the gardens as they wished; they mostly had the run of the house; few places were out of bounds. The houses were full of their possessions, including paintings and handwork brought from school and displayed in the living rooms or in their bedrooms. Treatment was individual and personal, adapted to the child's age and maturity.

In the mental subnormality hospital only coats, slippers, shoes, toothbrushes and combs were supplied individually to children. Few children had their own shirts and blouses, trousers, underwear or dressing-gowns. Only a third had their own cardigans or pullovers. In the paediatric wards things were better, but only just over half of the children had their own jumpers or cardigans, and only one child in four had his own shirt or dress, whether supplied by the hospital or by his parents. No child in the subnormality hospital had free access to the courtyard, and in the paediatric hospital fewer than half of the ambulant children, and none of the mentally subnormal ambulant children, had free access to it. Indeed, one of the remarkable things about both hospitals, to a visitor, was how few of the children were to be seen outside even in fine weather. Once they were outside they usually had no free access to the wards, in spite of the fact that the only toilets were inside the building.

It has already been mentioned that the children in hospital got up remarkably early, and that, not surprisingly, many of them went to bed when the sun was still high in the sky. They didn't, however, sleep undisturbed. In most of the wards the children were potted at intervals throughout the night. It was common for all of them to be lifted three times; in some wards it was as often as five, and in some it was only twice. It was not uncommon for all children in the ward to be potted, and not just those who wet their beds. After all, the night nurse didn't know the children, since she spent on average just over a week in any particular ward.

In the Children's Homes little if any potting was done at night, though the bedwetters might be lifted once before the staff retired for the night. It is generally believed that waking children in the night to pot them is a waste of time. Can it be that the practice is continued in the hospitals largely to give the night nurse something to do?

So much, then, for aspects of the children's day. The contrast between two patterns of care is a striking one, as this brief account of them shows. It would, however, be a mistake to conclude that the staff in the hospitals ill-treated their patients. Limited and regimented their lives might be—but the handicaps of the children, and the work-load, appeared to give the staff little alternative but to act as they did. The description of the children's day in a long-stay ward of a hospital is therefore not intended as a criticism of the nursing staff, but rather to illustrate that children in such hospitals lead drab and uninteresting lives compared with those led, not only by children in their own homes, but also by those in other large Children's Homes.

Children's Homes for the mentally retarded

It is sometimes argued that the nature of the children's handicaps in long-stay hospitals is such that a tight and rigid, though kindly, regimen must inevitably be followed. This, however, is not the case. We know from other studies (e.g. Tizard, 1964) that mentally subnormal children can be brought up very differently; and there are, both in this and other countries, special schools for spastics and other *physically* handicapped children which are run on lines very similar to those followed in the Children's Homes we investigated. To see how such places cope with the formidable problems of nursing and caring for severely handicapped children we have made a special study of two other residential establishments for subnormal children. These were not run as hospitals at all, but rather as Children's Homes.

One of these places was a residential hostel for retarded children, organized by a local authority. It had sixteen children in residence, and it was staffed by house-mothers. The pattern of management resembled very closely indeed that followed in the two Children's Homes, in that the children had individual attention, their own clothes and possessions, and a large amount of personal liberty. Their speech, and personal and social behaviour, contrasted markedly with those of children in the subnormality hospital who were judged to be of comparable ability.

The second establishment we studied was a voluntary home in which there were two units, one for trainable and one mainly for idiot children. The trainable children of school age constituted a group with disabilities similar in range and severity to those found in one or two of the wards in the subnormality hospital—wards in which most of the children were ambulant, and had IQs of over about 20 points. The other unit contained idiot children (with IQs of less than 20 points) and children with multiple and very severe physical and mental handicaps. The children in this unit were, as far as we could determine, comparable with those in the most difficult wards in the subnormality hospital. This latter unit was the same size (twenty beds) as the wards in the subnormality hospital. Yet in even this unit the children received a great deal of personal attention; they had their own clothing; there was a nursery which provided schooling; the children appeared much more lively and responsive than the idiot children in the subnormality wards of the hospital.

A child management scale

We have not yet carried out intensive psychological studies over a period of time to see how children in

of the garden, dormitory or courtyard by children who are ambulant, meal-time and bathing practices, leisure-time activities, personal clothing, toys and books, and the extent to which ambulant children have free access to various parts of the unit. It is a crude scale, with a range of scores from zero to 36, a high score being one characteristic of a ward or house in which rigid rules are in force, where there is block treatment of the inmates, where individuals have few opportunities to express their individuality, and where there is a large social distance between children and staff. Figure 5 shows the pattern of scores obtained on this scale in the two children's hospitals and in the Children's Homes.

The scores obtained by all wards in the subnormality hospital are very high—they range from 22 to 32. The paediatric wards also have high scores, ranging from 16 to 23, so that they overlap somewhat the scores obtained by the subnormality wards. There is, however, no overlap whatsoever between the scores obtained by any ward in either hospital and those obtained by any cottage in the Children's Homes. The two large Children's Homes for deprived children had scores which ranged from zero to 7.

The local authority home for retarded children (who are similar in age and attainments to children in some of the wards of the subnormality hospital) had a score of only 6. And the two units which made up part of a voluntary home, and which also contained children similar to those in our subnormality hospital, scored 11 and 15 points respectively. The unit which scored 15 points is that which contained the idiot children. It has already been mentioned that this unit was com-

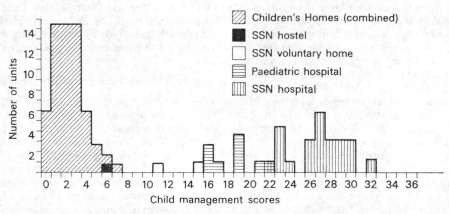

Figure 5 Distribution of child management scores

these units progress; we have, however, attempted to quantify our observations of child management practices in the various establishments we have surveyed. A scale of child management practices, consisting of eighteen items, all of which can be objectively rated and scored, has been devised, and applied to all wards and cottages in each of the institutions (King and Raynes, 1968). The scale deals with such matters as variations in bedtime and getting-up time, the use

parable with the most difficult wards in the subnormality hospital. Yet it comes out very differently in our ratings.

How are these results achieved? Let us look at some features of staff organization to see.

Sociological aspects of child care

First the point must be made that the differences between the hospitals and the Children's Homes are not due to the fact that in the one group staff are trained, whereas in the other group they are not. Nurses have a three-year training, and although about one third of the nursing staff in both hospitals were untrained, nursing assistants or 'aides' all senior positions were filled by trained and experienced staff. By contrast only about one-quarter of housemothers and very few assistants indeed in the Children's Homes had had even the formal one-year child-care training organized by the Children's Department of the Home Office: one-quarter to one-third had had no formal training whatsoever—not even a short refresher course or a period of in-service training. Training itself clearly does not provide the answer.

There were also differences in the number of child care staff available to look after the children. In the mental subnormality hospital there were six or seven nursing staff on day duty for each ward of twenty children. In the special care unit there were also seven day staff, but in addition there were several part-time staff whose combined hours of work added up to the equivalent of between two and three full-time staff. In the local authority hostel for subnormal children (which had only sixteen children, most of whom went home for weekends) the staff ratio was only one to every four children, and in the Children's Homes it was one to five or one to six.

Considering only the subnormality units it is evident that the special care unit for very severely handicapped children in the voluntary home was considerably better staffed than more comparable wards in the subnormality hospital. But the local authority hostel was not better staffed than were those wards in the subnormality hospital with children with a similar range of disabilities. When we examined the way in which staff were deployed—both during times when these various units had their full staff complement, and during 'emergency' conditions of staff shortages—we became convinced that difference in the numbers of staff available could not in themselves account for the marked differences in child care practices which had been described. A more significant factor appeared to be the striking differences in the ways in which the various establishments were organized—and our interest has been to document and classify these in order to try to understand some of the factors which influence the ways in which institutions serving children actually function. Underlying this attempt is the belief that the differences in functioning are largely a product of the social structure of establishments rather than the characteristics of their staff.

The delegation of authority

One striking difference between the Children's Homes and the hospitals lay in the amount of authority and responsibility delegated to the child care staff in individual units in the two kinds of establishment.

Broadly speaking, the housemothers in the Children's Homes (and also in the two small subnormality units we studied which resembled them in patterns of child management) had almost sole responsibility for the management and upbringing of the children in their care: for their food and clothing, for deciding what they should and should not do, the secondary school they should go to, where and when they should take them for holidays, when meals and bedtime should be, how the children should be punished and rewarded. It was they who decided within wide limits how the cottage should be furnished, what the crockery should be, what food should be ordered as well as how and when it should be cooked, and who should wash up afterwards. They had, in other words, much the same range of authority and responsibility as an ordinary parent: and like ordinary parents they had a housekeeping allowance which by and large they spent as *they* thought best. The very small administrative and supervisory staff at the centre had of course the power to overrule decisions at cottage level: but in practice this seldom happened, and the superintendent and his deputies acted largely as consultants and advisers. They only visited cottages perhaps once or twice a fortnight, but they could be turned to for advice or help as required, and they were readily accessible to *all* grades of staff. Apart from this they concerned themselves largely with external matters and with broad policy affecting the whole establishment.

By way of contrast, the major decisions affecting many of the matters already mentioned—food, clothing, holidays, schooling, toys, furniture and crockery, and so on—were settled largely off the ward, in hospitals. Ward staff might indeed not be consulted at all about them, or only rarely. The area of responsibility of the ward staff was less, their duties were more tightly circumscribed, the detailed supervision of their work was much, much greater. And with every additional specialist and department the power and responsibility of the nurses at ward level was diminished.

In short, many of the areas of decision-making, which in the Children's Homes were largely the responsibility of the housemothers and which were therefore settled at cottage level, were centrally initiated in the hospitals.

It was remarkable also that the delegation of authority from the centre to the housemother staff at cottage level had its counterpart in the manner in which decisions were arrived at, and tasks actually apportioned, among the child-care staff working in the cottages themselves. Perhaps because authority was so widely diffused in the Children's Homes, and because so much responsibility was given to the housemother staff, they themselves shared more of this responsibility with their assistants. There was very much more informal consultation and communication among staff of various grades in the Children's Homes than in the hospitals. This was shown by their responses to questions asked in interview, and it could be readily confirmed by direct observation of how things were actually organized in cottages as opposed to wards. This speed and ease of communication were facilitated by the fact that the Children's Homes were much less hierarchical and much more informal in their organization than were the hospitals.

There was an additional factor which undoubtedly contributed to the informal democracy of cottage organization, namely that in the Children's Homes staff remained in the same units over long periods of time, whereas in the Hospitals there was constant movement of junior staff from one ward to another. In the hospitals we studied both student nurses and nursing assistants spent on the average less than two months in any particular ward; in the Children's Homes on the other hand it was very *rare* indeed to find even junior staff moved from one cottage to another.

What, one may ask, is the reason for these differences? Why should staff remain always in the same unit in the Children's Homes, and why should they be required to move so frequently in the hospitals?

The answer is in part at least to be found in the different perception of staff roles and staff training in the two types of institution. In child-care practice, staff changes are avoided wherever possible because it is considered highly undesirable for children to have to keep meeting, and trying to make relations with, new staff every few weeks or months. The 'experience' which an assistant in a Children's Home acquires is therefore an experience in child care; and to gain this she has to be involved in the day-to-day upbringing of a small group of children, whom she comes to know intimately, over a lengthy period of time, and for whom she is in a real sense responsible. The title of her post accurately describes her role—it is assistant housemother; and if she stays in the service for long enough the promotion she will get is to a position of housemother—the person who acts as a substitute mother to the children under her care.

A student nurse in hospital is moved from one ward to another also 'to gain experience'—but the experience she gains is in the recognition and treatment of diseases, the carrying out of orders, and the performance of what are accurately called *duties*. These duties are highly predictable and standardized from one ward to another so that the nurse can fit in easily to the pattern of routine in any ward in the hospital.

Because of the nurse's preoccupation with duties, which have to be completed stage by stage and in an order which is determined by the demands of ward routine rather than the individual needs of the children, it is very easy for the childish and human needs of the patients to be given a lower priority than other matters: the elucidation of the causes of their condition, the 'treatment' of their disabilities, the arrangement of the duty rota, the cleanliness of the ward, the adequate keeping of records and what not. The role of a nurse is a very different one from that of a housemother, and the differences reflect profound differences in what one can call the ideology of the two types of institution. There is time for only a few remarks about this now.

Ideology

By the ideology of an institution we mean the system of beliefs and values which govern its practice, the ends it aims to serve. The ideology of the child-care service was in England authoritatively stated by the Curtis Committee, twenty years ago. It is to protect children, to keep them with their families whenever possible, to return them to the care of their own families as soon as possible. While they are in residential care the object of the service is to give them an environment which as closely as possible resembles that of an ordinary home, with ordinary standards of affection, companionship, security, good physical care, adequate education.

No comparable statement was made by the British Royal Commission on Mental Illness and Mental Deficiency and there is still in practice a good deal of confusion about the goals of care and treatment for the subnormal, both in this and other countries. The function of the institution at present is neither to cure subnormal children—since their handicaps are nearly all brought about by damage which is irreversible—nor is it to return them to their families, since in practice this only rarely occurs. The goals of clinical medicine are too narrow; but they have not been adequately supplemented by others. The data presented earlier, on the characteristics of the six institutions we have studied, illustrate contrasting ideologies in action. They also take us a little way towards the answer to the question which is a theme of this Conference: What is special about special education? If you see your role primarily as that of treating patients you will develop one type of institution in which to do it. If you see it as your role to bring up and educate handicapped children you will regard rather different issues as important. The differences between the children's hospitals and the Children's Homes for the subnormal reflect differences in outlook which on the one hand is narrowly medical, and which on the other is broadly educational, in orientation. These differences in ideology influence every aspect of institutional life, though there has been time to touch on only a few of them here.

Summary

A study has been made of six long-stay institutions for children. Two of these were hospitals run on traditional lines and staffed by nurses. The other four were run as Children's Homes, though in two of them the children were as handicapped as the children in the mental subnormality hospital we studied. The two hospitals resembled each other very closely even though they had different kinds of patients. All four Children's Homes also conformed to a common pattern, though two of them had ordinary, normal children as inmates and two had severely retarded children. When we assessed the six establishments on an eighteen-item scale of child management practices there was no overlap in score between the most liberal ward in either hospital and the most restrictive cottage in any of the four Children's Homes. It is postulated that the reasons for the contrasting patterns of up-bringing as between the two types of institution are to be found in characteristics of their social structure: the hospitals are hierarchical, overdepartmentalized and too highly centralized. They are task-oriented rather than child-oriented. A narrowly medical ideology leads staff to see themselves primarily in the role of treating patients. But in practice these two hospitals were custodial institutions—though they need not have been.

References

Curtis, M. (Chairman), 1946, *Report of the Care of Children Committee*, Cmnd 6922, HMSO.

Goodman, N. and Tizard, J., 1962, 'Prevalence of imbecility and idiocy among children', *Brit. Med. J.*, i, 216–19.

King, R. D. and Raynes, N. V., 1968, 'An operational measure of inmate management in residential institutions', *Soc. Sci. and Med.*, 2(1), 41–53.

Lyle, J. G., 1959, 'The effect of an institution environment upon the verbal development of institutional children (I)', *J. Ment. Defic. Res.*, 3, 122–8.

Lyle, J. G., 1960, 'The effect of an institution environment upon the verbal development of institutional children (II)', *J. Ment. Defic. Res.*, 4, 1–13, 14–23.

Royal Commission on the Law Relating to Mental Illness and Mental Deficiency, 1957, *Report*, Cmnd 169, HMSO.

Tizard, J., 1964, *Community Services for the Mentally Handicapped*, Oxford University Press.

IV. 6 National CDP Inter-project Report (extract)

CDP Information Unit

Action and research strategies

Confronted with [the] wider canvas of population movements, employment and housing changes, local teams have increasingly questioned and moved away from the original 'social pathology' assumptions of the experiment. They have begun to develop perspectives which better account for the unequal distribution of both private and public goods and services, and provide explanations for the powerlessness of CDP populations to influence these distributions.

But in addition they have to locate their own action and research programme in this developing framework. Inter-project debate and discussion have increased awareness of this wider context, and the strategies of several later projects particularly have been influenced by this approach. But in practice on the ground there is great diversity. Programmes and strategies attempted by each team reflect different assumptions and different opportunities for action in each area; and they reflect too the different ideas of how social change is achieved. To understand these differences, it is helpful to set out, systematically, possible strategies open to local teams, beginning by distinguishing three main models of social change. This is a first attempt at such a scheme, and the categories may have to be revised as a result of further analysis and debate.

(i) *Consensus* models of social change are based on the assumption that social problems are 'malfunctions' which can be cured by adjustments and re-arrangements within the existing operating systems. The problems are defined mainly in terms of failures of co-ordination and communication, and the focus of change is thus on management and administration and the non-participant. The central tactic is debate.

(ii) *Pluralist* models of social change are based on the assumption that social problems arise from 'imbalances' in the democratic and bureaucratic systems.

The problems are defined mainly in terms of failures of participation and representation of certain interests in the political process, and the focus of change is thus on politicians, policy-makers and the disenfranchised. The central tactic is bargaining and negotiation.

(iii) *Structural conflict* models of social change are based on the assumption that social problems arise from a fundamental conflict of interests between groups or classes in society. The problems are defined mainly in terms of inequalities in the distribution of power and the focus of change is thus on the centres of organised power (both private and public). The main tactic is organisation and raising of levels of consciousness.

These are over-simple definitions, but they imply important differences of emphasis. Given the possibility of developing change at three main levels—national local and grassroots—it is possible to distinguish nine different, though overlapping, strategies (Figure 6). In using this diagram it is important to point out that in practice individual CDP strategies will not necessarily fall neatly into one category. The figure is intended as a guide to sort out broad difference—not a strait-jacket. In most projects there is a mixture of approaches, and some degree of ambiguity and even contradiction in the strategies being attempted. This is partly because few team members bring a completely clear or consistent set of theoretical assumptions to the experiment; and partly because the problems being tackled are complex and contradictory themselves. In practice too, a project's strategy on any one issue may vary over time, especially if one approach is tried and found unsuccessful.

In the following paragraphs we briefly outline the main features of each of these strategies.

(1) *Social planning* aims to bring about changes in policy by planning as comprehensively as possible taking into account the physical, social and economic aspects of total situations. Problems are defined primarily as technical, rather than political, and conflicts

Source: *National CDP Inter-project Report*, February 1974, pp. 23–38.

of interest are seen as reconcilable if they are treated within a more total system. Commitment to the comprehensive social plan is sought first from senior professionals and the role of the politician is seen as one of ratification for a rational solution to an agreed problem.

(2) *Organisational development and service-delivery* aim to bring about changes in organisational practices, by managerial and administrative re-arrangements. Re-groupings between various parts are made to achieve better communications, both between themselves and with the outside environment. Better communication is assumed to lead to closer co-ordination, and hence a more efficient and relevant service. The overall goals of the organisation are not questioned, so much as the means of achieving those goals. Organisational consultants are often employed to propose, or legitimise, such re-arrangements.

of at least two of the pilot phase projects (Coventry and Southwark) has led to a questioning of the relevance of those assumptions and strategies at least to problems like redevelopment. Attempts to improve co-ordination of the clearance operation and increase communication with residents by reasoned well-argued debate with officials, has proved futile in both areas. A number of projects are still basing much of their work (community education programmes, development of services for young people, support for community groups) on this set of assumptions. Pilot phase experience suggests that these approaches may be able to achieve some greater flexibility in the face to face delivery of services, but that they are much less effective where there needs to be basic changes of policy.

(4) and (5) *National and local lobbying*. Strategies (4) and (5) assume a state of competition and bargain-

Basic assumptions / Level	Consensus	Pluralism	Structural conflict
National	1 Social planning	4 National lobby	7 National pressure
Local	2 Organisational and service development	5 Local lobby	8 Local pressure
Grass-roots	3 'Traditional' community development	6 Community organisation	9 Community action

Figure 6   Models of social change and posssible strategies on three levels of operations

(3) *'Traditional' community development* aims to bring about changes in the functioning of individuals, groups, and 'communities' by facilitating their integration into more coherent wholes. The 'community' is assumed to be homogeneous in its needs and where conflicts of interest are found, these are reconcilable through better communication and inter-group relations. The process of community development is often seen as more important than any product, that is development of community relationships is seen as an end in itself, rather than primarily as a means of solving common external problems. Nevertheless, new more comprehensive structures, like neighbourhood councils, are sought as a means of representing the neighbourhood more effectively in relation to external decision-makers.

Each of these three strategies assumes a basic consensus of purpose between CDP, the client-population and the relevant agencies. The solutions are to be sought through better co-ordination and communication. The original CDP design was based on a simple combination of strategies (2) and (3). The experience

ing between different interest-groups within a plural system. They seek changes, therefore, not first in the technical or bureaucratic systems but in the political arena. The arenas for bargaining over policies and the allocation of resources are assumed to be those of the formal governmental process, so strategies are pitched at politicians, councillors, parties and pressure groups. Support is lobbied on the basis of reasoned evidence, and the expressed needs of constituents.

(6) *Community organisation* is probably the closest description of much of the neighbourhood work going on currently in local projects. The powerlessness of residents to control their own life situations, or to influence the decisions which affect their areas, is seen to be related partly to their lack of information, access to relevant expertise and advocacy, and poor organisation. Information centres, neighbourhood newspapers, legal and welfare rights campaigns, financial and technical support for residents associations all aim to equip the residents of CDP areas with a greater capacity to bargain for the protection of their interests. The provision of 'hard' information and 'hard' skills

seems to have helped resident groups to gain some points of leverage to claim their rights under existing legislation and policy (supplementary benefits, GIAs) and to expose instances of poor quality service from local agencies. However, much of this has been limited to very here-and-now issues, and has been in reaction to agency programmes, rather than any real claiming of initiative for change. The question is how far alliances can be formed between these different action groups, and momentum kept up to sustain the necessary long term processes of improvement and change.

(7), (8) and (9) *National pressure, local pressure and community action.* These assume a longer term historical analysis, and aim to relate selectively to the local community, forging links between its more active members and groups, and organised sections of the working class. The intention is to sharpen local consciousness of the underlying problems, and relate action and pressure to the activities of the wider labour movement. The question that remains is whether a clear enough awareness of the underlying issues can be developed to stimulate a powerful movement for change from a local base.

CDP is an Action-Research programme, and research assumptions and strategies must also be looked at briefly. Research was originally seen as a data gathering resource; researchers would both act as 'consultants' on action programmes, and evaluate their success or failure. Research teams were based in universities and polytechnics to increase the chances of objective evaluation. This arrangement, particularly in some of the pilot projects, was marked by friction and tension between the two teams, underlining the fact that in action-research the two processes are rarely so distinct that they can be carried on independently by two separate groups. Even monitoring and evaluation require close co-ordination and co-operation. Increasingly, action and research have moved closer together as a co-operative team in most project areas, resulting in some cases in shared accommodation and shared administrative structure. There is a progressive blurring of the role of action and research, particularly where analysis is called for. Here research can play an action role in that the data it collects may powerfully support a change in policy. With this development the main contributions of research are seen as the following:

(i) *Information.* CDP needs to gather information about conditions within an area and local attitudes towards these conditions. Where appropriate, such findings can contribute directly to the various action strategies described above.

(ii) *Experiment/demonstration.* Some aspects of CDP, particularly in the field of service delivery, may be tied to an experimental design which will allow for careful assessment and possible replication elsewhere.

(iii) *Processes.* There is a need to describe accurately and to attempt to assess the various issues and strategies that CDP undertakes and to examine the effects of action in different context. It is important to have on record what procedures are used and how effective CDP programmes prove in influencing the way policies develop. In this way, both the achievements and obstacles to progress can be mapped in.

(iv) *Basic research.* Research can explore existing explanations of phenomena which might lead to a recasting of the ways in which problems are identified and resolved.

The differences in basic assumptions among the projects are gradually helping to develop a more critical assessment of different strategies, but with a general move towards analyses that emphasise structural explanations of the problems of CDP areas. The staggered start of the projects means that some are less able than others to test these perspectives in their work. The earlier projects have much of their work grounded in earlier perspectives and governed by the original narrower definitions of the experiment. However, their experience will be important in showing whether different approaches can produce change, and if so what kinds of problems they can solve.

Issues

Each project has selected a set of issues for its programme of action and research; the choice is determined by the context of the project area, and the analysis of the area's problems made by the project team. Generally in each project, programmes form an inter-related attempt to tackle the problems of an area, rather than a collection of independent activities which happen to be administratively combined. In this section, where we set out some of these issue areas on an inter-project basis, the danger is that by divorcing one piece of action from another on the same project, the overall shape of the project's programme will be lost. It is also difficult to convey the generally close daily contact between project and local residents. [. . .]

The pilot phase of the experiment was characterised by local diversity, and little comparative work. With the full complement of projects there has been an increase in inter-project discussion, and this has encouraged the identification of critical issues in common. In general, projects do not follow a 'comprehensive' or 'total' strategy—what in practice might easily become a 'little bit of everything', but are searching for the key issues. In this section we examine some of these and highlight different approaches.

Employment has become an issue of central importance, not merely because of the deteriorating economic conditions of many areas, but because it is clearly a key variable, with repercussions across the board. Thus, several projects' findings have underlined the difficulties which unemployed or low paid people have in obtaining adequate housing, even in the public sector where they tend to be concentrated in hard-to-let and stigmatised 'problem' estates. In Glyncorrwg, the project is examining the linkage between economic and social problems.

Four of the projects are developing analyses of the wider dimensions of the employment problem. Glamorgan and Cleator Moor are focusing their attention on governmental policy (regional policy; the 'growth point' principle), whereas Newham and Newcastle are focusing on the private sector, particularly the effects of changes in a firm's investment upon the workforce and population of small areas. In the first case, the main emphasis is on a 'social planning' approach; the process has included data collection, a report by an economic consultant, and the development of a set of proposals for a more sensitive and flexible regional employment policy. These have been used to open up debate with the relevant government departments (DTI and Welsh Office). The Welsh project is also involved in a working party with the local council examining employment problems in the area and in similar valley communities of South Wales. The Glyncorrwg team is documenting the relative success and failure of their general approach, and it will be important to compare their rather pessimistic experience so far with the alternative approach of Newham and Newcastle. In these projects, data will be gathered on the investment patterns and operations of local firms. The differential effects of these trends will be analysed and discussed with local workplace contacts (Trades Council, shop-stewards committees). The aim is to provide discussion and organisation to look at the industrial issues of the neighbourhood as a whole and plan necessary action.

Seven of the projects have programmes to develop new job opportunities or to improve accessibility to existing employment. Cleator Moor is examining tourism as a generator of employment, while Newcastle is exploring the potential of the local authority in creating jobs. These two projects also hope to promote small businesses and co-operatives. Glyncorrwg has set up action programmes aimed at creating local jobs, and to increase the chance of workers getting to jobs elsewhere it is subsidising transport schemes.

A further group of projects (overlapping with those already mentioned) is focusing on support services for the unemployed. Cleator Moor and Paisley are planning to survey the special needs and problems of the unemployed themselves, and Glamorgan has studies in progress of recent redundancies in both the private and the public sector, and their impact on individuals and the community. They are also working on the development of more relevant retraining programmes for those out of work. Coventry and Liverpool have concentrated on the support services for the young person making the transition from school life to work life. Coventry has commissioned a consultant's report which has recommended major changes in the role and structure of the youth employment service, as well as changes in practice in schools and in industry. The report has now been lodged with the central youth employment executive, and a test-bed for implementing the recommendations is being sought. Liverpool is involved in several schemes for this age-group and a

research project is following the progress of a group of school leavers with regular surveys of their job records and experience.

These various measures are valuable in their own right, and may point the way to wider improvements in practice, but they can only have at best a marginal impact on the long term structural problem of employment [. . .] These demand a major piece of social accountancy. However, CDP can provide analysis and data on employment conditions of small disadvantaged areas—a condition which is often masked by their incorporation for statistical purposes in larger units; these figures alone should be a powerful argument for changes in policy.

Income and income maintenance. This issue is closely related to that of employment. Project areas generally have higher than average unemployment for their region and higher than average dependence upon state incomes and welfare benefits. In Ferguslie Park some 22 per cent of men were unemployed on the 1971 census figures (compared to 8 per cent for the Paisley Burgh) and in the Newcastle project area the figure was 13 per cent at this time. Here, three-quarters of the unemployed were labourers and more than half of these had been unemployed for over a year; two-thirds of labourers aged fifty-five and over had been unemployed for more than two years. More than 80 per cent of these unemployed men were receiving supplementary benefit and for more than 70 per cent this was their only source of income.

In Coventry, the differential operations of social security have been approached via survey and research. This has revealed very limited knowledge of rights and an extensive range of unmet need, both among pensioners and other claimants. These findings have been presented to the appropriate departments (DHSS, Cabinet Office) and support gained from MPs, the national pressure groups (CPAG, Age Concern), and from local Trades Union organisation. But the question remains whether this type of approach which has been extensively tried by the poverty lobby for some years can achieve the necessary shifts in policy or practice. The Batley project is attempting to get change at the local level with a concerted programme to disseminate information on welfare rights and stimulate maximum take-up. Part of their strategy has been to place an 'expert' within a key agency. As the appointment of 'welfare rights officers' to social service departments is gaining momentum, it will be important for CDP to examine this approach carefully and compare its effectiveness with other strategies which aim not only to disseminate information, but to place hard knowledge and advocacy more directly in the hands of claimants themselves. Almost all projects are attempting this by setting up information centres and involving local residents closely in casework. This is proving to be effective as a crisis service, getting a better deal from social security for individuals in need, but it is not so effective in developing a collective response to the problem. Newcastle is attempting this by informal adult education; Coventry by opening up discussion with shop stewards and the Trades Council; Batley by working through a Claimants and Unemployed Workers Union and other community organisations. Such an approach may be the most effective way of raising awareness of the main issues, and creating the greatest leverage for change.

This raises the question of what is CDP's particular contribution in a field where there are already other well organised pressures at the various levels. Experience suggests that it may be in relating income maintenance and welfare rights to other inter-connected issues, for example legal rights (through community lawyers in Liverpool, Coventry and Newham), housing and planning rights (through a public health inspector in Southwark, planners in Coventry and (shortly) in Newcastle and Birmingham).

Rates are another issue with immediate relevance to income levels, and the recent revaluation, shifting the burden of this tax away from industry and commerce on to the domestic ratepayer, has highlighted the problem. Among domestic ratepayers the burden has also shifted disproportionately on to council house tenants, and in some areas on to the occupants of lower valued property. This has hit many residents of the CDP areas hard. In Birmingham for example, the increased rate contribution from the CDP area easily outstrips the extra amount of money CDP brings in. The two responses are action and analysis. In Birmingham, the strategy has been to employ a worker to prepare collective appeals with residents, and in Coventry information on differential rate levels has been fed out to resident groups and to the local Federation of Council Tenants, and to local councillors where it was linked to another related issue—that of Fair Rents set by the Rent Scrutiny Board.

Housing is perhaps the most complex issue faced by CDP teams. Yet housing and environmental problems are most likely to stir resident groups to collective action, and are obviously central to the future of CDP areas. CDP activities here can be divided into action and analysis on the broader policy issues, and the neighbourhood strategy adopted by action teams. The housing dynamics of the CDP areas [were] outlined [earlier]; several projects have set up research to examine these processes in more detail, particularly the working of new housing legislation and other national influences on their areas. Birmingham is tracing housing movement in the fluid situation of a rapidly changing multi-racial area now under the shadow of a renewal programme, and is looking closely at the micro-level of movements within single streets. The Newham project is charting how the different forms of investment in housing affect people's chance of being housed. They aim to explore ways in which the potential advantages of municipal housing can be more adequately related to the interests of working class people. The Coventry project is commissioning a research study of the wider interests which appear to have influenced the allocation of land, and investment in renewal in

the city since the war. They also aim to explore this theme in terms of a social history of decision-making in which the residents of the older housing areas have been important actors. One of the main audiences for this research is seen to be local residents who have organised around housing issues. At the neighbourhood level the common method of operation is to organise and support resident groups which form around housing issues, though there may be quite different aims behind these apparently similar exercises. In some cases problems can be tackled at the local level because they centre on small areas—a group of streets with similar physical problems. For example, Tynemouth and Batley have encouraged resident initiatives over modernisation programmes on council estates. Similarly Glyncorrwg are exploring the possibilities of linking local job creation with grants for house improvements.

In other areas problems are more long term and intractable. Most projects service groups concerned with redevelopment. But there are two different approaches. Projects may take up a housing issue, and encourage resident group development as a way of solving that particular problem; or they may see the process of involving people in collective action over housing problems as a means of promoting a wider understanding of the political system, and a catalyst for their engagement in more basic political activity. The experience of the pilot projects with redevelopment schemes underlines some of the reasons for this shift in objectives.

The pilot projects began by dealing with redevelopment problems primarily in terms of management and administration. Concerted attempts were made by Southwark and Coventry to press for a more total approach, more coherent control and more sensitive co-ordination of the whole operation—a better flow of information about rights and about the timetable of clearance; more efficient boarding-up of empty property to stop the chain of dereliction; more participation and choice in the whole question of the future of the area; more forward planning of general improvement areas, and the declaration of whole districts to guarantee their security and arrest blight. Their cases were argued on the basis of both local evidence and comparable experience from other authorities. The central Home Office team added their weight and dialogue was established with senior officials in local, regional and central government.

This approach followed the original Home Office model of change through dialogue—better communication leading to better co-ordination. However, neither team found these approaches effective in bringing about even relatively simple and inexpensive changes of practice. This experience underlined the crucial political interests at stake in urban renewal; it was not merely a question of technical adjustment. Later projects are involved in more sophisticated and long term attempts to tackle renewal problems from a similar standpoint. Birmingham, for example, proposes to set up an environmental team in the period before the renewal programme begins to operate, to work with local authority departments and yet be in a position to respond to residents' priorities. And Oldham is encouraging the formation of representative resident associations to process problems of renewal. These experiments should show whether intervention at an earlier stage in the renewal process and backed by hard technical skills will prove to be more effective in relating renewal policy and practice closely to local needs.

Following this pilot phase experience several projects have placed much greater emphasis on the second aim of using housing issues to develop wider awareness. Several projects (Newham, Batley, Southwark, Coventry, Tynemouth, Glyncorrwg and Cleator Moor) are servicing groups of residents on local redevelopment issues with technical expertise from planners and public health inspectors acting as consultants to the local group. Although this intervention is on a very narrow front (involving small groups of streets at a time) experience suggests that through this combination of advocacy and community organisation, residents can bargain more powerfully for investment in their area, and in the process they can develop a much clearer awareness of the wider factors governing and constraining their housing opportunities. Newcastle is undertaking research on housing careers in the private and public sectors, which is intended to provide a general analysis and to inform and raise levels of consciousness about these issues among local residents.

Besides the redevelopment issue, several projects are experimenting with ways of stabilising local housing conditions and increasing security in the short-term, as well as 'alternative' housing opportunities. Birmingham is involved with problems of industrial intrusion into residential areas, and the problem of short-leases particularly local operation of the various leasehold reform acts, both of which contribute to the immediate insecurity of the area. Coventry has appointed a consultant to study the feasibility and to set up a pilot resident-controlled housing co-operative. The idea of co-operative tenant control is an important alternative to traditional housing relationships. However, experiment in this field is restricted by the fact that such associations are bound by the same national constraints as traditional housing, thus clearly limiting the control which tenants can effectively exercise. Again this raises a basic question for pilot projects when they wish to experiment with new ideas which lie outside the scope of existing legislation.

Education. In the first pilot projects education was a major field of expenditure. Education was seen as an important link in the distribution of opportunities, and one open to change. Emphasis on education fitted with the early assumptions of the CDP experiment, and several of the earlier projects took up ideas developed in the Educational Priority Areas programme, but others have avoided involvement in conventional education completely, or have experimented with education away from a school base. The central question is whether and in what form educational change can promote wider changes, and the ensuing debate has called into question several of the assumptions underlying the initial importance given to education.

Educational activities in CDP fall into three main types:

(a) *Conventional education development*: improving and extending existing facilities, introduction of new equipment, development of pre-school provision, more teaching resources. The assumption is that the system could be effective but needs more resources to work.

(b) '*Community education*': particularly developing home-school links, the need for a curriculum relevant to inner-city areas, and the idea of the 'community school'. The aim is to change relationships between school and community and develop 'constructive discontent' which will encourage a critical stance among children towards their environment. The assumption is that this can best be done by working through schools.

(c) *Emphasis on work outside schools*, on informal adult education, dealing with real life situations—problems of work, unemployment or rents with groups not already involved in the educational process. The aim is to stimulate knowledge and awareness, and encourage pressure for change among those directly affected. The assumption is that this can best be done outside schools or other formal institutions.

Liverpool, Coventry, Southwark, Glamorgan and Batley all have work of the first two categories under way. In Southwark, besides work in the school system with the provision of a Home/School Officer, the needs of the pre-five age group are being thoroughly examined. This involves the development of child-minder training and pre-school visiting services using both statutory and voluntary resources. Student teachers also participate in these schemes, providing important experience of the conditions under which they are likely to work when qualified. Similarly in Glamorgan there is work with homes through a Parents' Forum, playgroups and playschemes, and the setting up of a community resources centre. These developments will add to the experience gained in the earlier EPA programme, though it will be important to collect more evidence on the wider and long term effects of 'community education'. At this stage EPA approaches seem to have had some success in 'loosening up' professional thinking and practice at the level of the local school, and in opening up the possibility of greater interaction on a day-to-day basis between pupils, teachers, parents and the local neighbourhood. The repercussions for central policy or the allocation of educational resources are more difficult to discern, though in Coventry the Community Education programme has contributed to a movement of political and professional pressure which has led to a policy of positive educational discrimination towards disadvantaged areas and some shifts in resources. But in general though many children in CDP areas are experiencing more exciting and open teaching, they are still taught in old buildings, with inadequate equipment and without supplies even of basic books; and the very conditions that increase the disadvantage of the area, contribute to teacher turnover and absenteeism, a problem highlighted by the recent report from Newham's Comprehensive Headteachers.

Other projects are developing work outside the school context, an area less well explored by the EPA projects. Newham plans to work with groups of parents approaching the idea of what is 'community education' from this angle. But it is work in adult education, informal sessions with resident groups and organisations which develop around concrete local issues, where CDP can make a distinctive contribution. The programmes developed in Liverpool have influenced the approaches to adult education adopted by other projects.

Cutting across these major issue areas, several projects are closely involved with a range of services for particular groups in their local population.

(a) *The elderly*. Coventry, Cleator Moor and Southwark are all involved with research into the needs of the elderly, though their emphases differ. Coventry is more concerned with the loss of status among the elderly and the possible reinforcement of this by existing welfare services which seem to set in motion a self-fulfilling prophecy of decline. The research aims to form a basis for proposals for radical changes in the structure of services for the elderly, with an emphasis on enhancing rather than undermining their status. Cleator Moor, focusing on felt need and inadequacies of provision, is also attempting to explore ways of involving the elderly in developing plans to meet their needs. Southwark's approach contains both elements—examining the effectiveness of traditional services, and initiating new services where there is a clear need, for example an employment bureau for over-sixties, a visiting service using local residents, and supporting self-help initiatives.

(b) *Young people*. Many of the projects, as part of their neighbourhood work or education programmes, have become involved in supporting the development of services for young people—whether this is nursery and pre-school provision, adventure playgrounds, or summer play programmes. Cleator Moor and Southwark, however, are committed more substantially to developing a comprehensive and more relevant pattern of provision for young people. Both have appointed a play organiser to study the needs, set up pilot projects and recommend modification of existing services with an emphasis on the use of locally recruited workers and locally based management and control structures.

(c) *Race relations*. Birmingham and Batley are both conducting research into the needs of their immigrant (mainly Asian) populations. Both are concerned not only with the special ethnic aspects but with the fairness and adequacy of existing policies. Birmingham has taken up questions on the administration of the 'Pakistan Act' which affects many of the project residents, particularly the processing of applications and the problems of access to information. As part of its adult education programme Coventry has established a network of language groups for Asian men and women. These meet in homes, religious temples, schools and in one case on the factory floor, and aim to equip the immigrant with basic skills in communication.

Interwoven with these major single issues of employment, income-maintenance, housing and education and particular groups serviced by the project are a set of organisational arrangements and developments, ways of increasing the co-ordination of local services by promoting neighbourhood work, of increasing local participation and control, and of making local authority structures more responsive to the needs of CDP areas. Many of these developments overlap, and there are, as usual, quite distinct approaches being tried out by different projects.

Neighbourhood work, information and advice. CDP is a neighbourhood based experiment and all projects have rooted their work in this way. A very similar range of activities characterises the projects:

(i) shop front information centres, either shared with the project offices or as independent resident-controlled centres;

(ii) work with community groups offering information, advice, technical expertise (e.g. legal, welfare and housing rights), grants and hardware (duplicating facilities, video TV equipment);

(iii) project news-sheets disseminating information and data, or community newspapers run by local residents with support from CDP.

Despite these common activities, there are underlying differences. A major distinction is the degree of selectivity over the issues taken up. One extreme would be to respond to any issue brought forward, and the other to define in advance the problems to be handled. Projects are spread out between these extremes, most trying to balance and relate their own views on key issues to resident priorities. These distinctions are apparent in the range to be found in information centres: for example a generalist information service (and Community Resource Centre) at Cleator Moor, consciously trading in the whole range of issues from school bus fares and dangerous parking to vacant housing and welfare benefits; the semi-specialist services (Coventry's emphasis on legal and welfare rights); the selective service, like Newham, which consciously restricts its focus to those individuals and groups who are potentially going to work for change. Similarly the resident groups which form round these centres, and the supporting community newspapers or newsletters, reflect these differences of approach. In several projects the move has been to strengthen information centres with the 'hard' skills of lawyers or planners, or through these centres attach such skills to resident groups. The assumption here is that resident-controlled Information Centres backed by these skills may be a more potent instrument in crisis situations, like eviction, than similar workers inside the local authority or schemes to co-ordinate local services. This strengthening of information and advice centres thus provides an alternative strategy to the currently popular development of multi-service centres or schemes for integrating local authority services.

Service delivery. A major concern of the original CDP objectives was to promote greater integration of services at the local level. Though this has become less central an objective in several projects, in others it remains a major element. Liverpool has developed an extensive Community Services Centre which brings together several local authority services into a common building, and seeks to integrate their activities and policies for the area. The scheme is linked to a resident-run information centre, and related to other changes in the local authority. Paisley is developing a similar centre.

Both these developments in multi-service centres, and information and advice centres in fields as diverse as housing, consumer affairs, career guidance and employment bureaux, are increasingly being turned to as solutions to the problems of disadvantaged areas. Within CDP there is a chance to assess the workings of these two approaches both individually, and in a comparative way, where they appear to play overlapping roles.

Neighbourhood democracy. With its heavy investment in neighbourhood work, stimulating and sustaining resident organisations, it is inevitable that CDP should be drawn into experiment and debate over schemes such as neighbourhood councils. Several projects are moving ahead to formalise the federation of resident groups that have grown up around the project, into embryo community councils. Others like Coventry have found that umbrella organisations of this kind are more likely to succeed as providers of general services (secretarial, banking, administration of grants, to community groups, salaries to staff) than

as a representative forum or as a campaigning body on behalf of the neighbourhood. Again CDP should be in a position to compare these different approaches.

Local authority. Change at the local level, neighbourhood work, participation and local control have to be seen in relation to the role of the local authority. CDP projects are in a position, if they choose, to work at both the local community and the local authority level. But over and above the way particular services operate, is the role of the local authority in distributing goods and services within the area, the way it resolves policy and conflicts of interests and how it is geared to variations in local need. Coventry, Liverpool and Paisley are all involved in research on decision-making at the local level. Liverpool is examining the framework of managerial processes within local authorities and in particular the trend towards more centralised and 'rationalised' planning, the corporate management structure and its responsiveness to pressures for participation. Paisley is exploring where power and influence lie in local political decision making in Paisley. Coventry is investigating the wider structure of interests which have influenced the allocation of resources (particularly land and housing) locally.

A further major issue which a number of projects have been exploring concerns the finance which is available to local authorities tackling disadvantage. Local authorities with CDP areas are increasingly constrained by the problems of decreasing resources with which to provide services where there is growing demand. The Rate Support Grant formula currently[1] is such as to penalise:

(i) areas in decline with a high proportion of industrial and commercial property

(ii) areas higher than average family sizes

(iii) areas with relatively high proportions of children

(iv) areas trying to attract new industrial and commercial development, as any increase in rate income resulting from new development is matched by a £ for £ reduction in the 'resources' element.

Note

[1] From April 1974 a new Rate Support Grant formula comes into operation. This new formula deals with some of the points made here. See White Paper, Cmnd 5532 —'The Rate Support Grant 1974–75'.

Part V Welfare under attack

The development of social welfare has not been without its critics. Particularly in the last twenty years, since the 'rediscovery' of poverty in the early 1960s, increasingly radical attacks have been launched on social welfare legislation and its consequences. There has been a concern to 'demask' social policy, and to make explicit and challenge the assumptions on which it is based. Such critical analysis has been developed not only by social theorists and researchers, but by the 'clients' themselves. The past decade for example has witnessed the emergence of broad-based movements amongst gays, claimants, prisoners and mental patients. Allied to this has been the formation of radical groups of social workers, lawyers and probation officers.

In this Part we look at 'welfare under attack'. Robert Holman attempts to demonstrate how the social policy programmes of the two major political parties use a similar model of poverty, and are premissed upon the same sort of assumptions about the society we live in. While not denying that certain differences do occur between the Conservative and Labour Parties, his comparison of the speeches and writings of Sir Keith Joseph, a former Tory Secretary of State for Social Services, and Roy Jenkins, former Labour Home Secretary, underlines the fundamental convergence of their analyses, and the consequent similarity in policy proposals. Holman goes on to develop a number of 'proposals for change' based on an alternative theory of poverty. He concludes that the growth of community groups has provided a political voice for many of those 'written off as the casualties of society'.

The attempts to organize and mobilize two sections of these 'casualties' are discussed by Hilary Rose and Paul Harrison. Most fundamentally, perhaps, they describe the attempts by claimants in the first instance, and by mental patients in the second, to redefine the terms in which they are considered a social problem. Rose's paper discusses the origins and emergence of

the claimants' unions in the context of the 'working out of the Welfare State, and the changing consciousness of its inadequacies during the 1960s'. In contrast to the Child Poverty Action Group, the claimants' unions were set up to work *with* rather than *on behalf of* the poor. The unions emphasize that the 'help' of politically committed individuals was often provided at the expense of claimants increasing the control they have over their own lives. Rose charts the expansion of the initial idea, from the original group in Birmingham in 1968, to some ninety unions in 1973. She argues that the core of the strength of the movement 'lies in the way that the unions have shown how it is possible to create a collective organization in opposition not merely to the "meagre hand-outs" of the Welfare State, but to its increasingly intense individuation.' Most importantly, the movement has struggled to overcome the isolation and dependency of the claimant.

The article by Paul Harrison is similarly concerned to show how mental patients have come together to try to protect themselves from the consequences of the allegedly liberal Mental Health Act, 1959. In examining the practical outcome of the Act, he records that, although they have declined proportionately, the absolute number of compulsory admissions to mental hospitals has continued to rise. Partly in response to this, and to the new techniques of control (particularly drugs and electric-shock treatment), the Mental Patients' Union was originally formed in 1972 during the patients' demonstration against government proposals to close down the Paddington Day Hospital in London. Attacking psychiatry as one of the means used to ensure that frustration and anger are internalized, the MPU drew up a charter of demands, including a demand for the abolition of compulsory hospitalization. In 1974 there were fourteen unions scattered around the country, with about 1,000 members. A decision was then taken to decentralize the union, allowing each group full autonomy. Harrison moves on to discuss the 'reform' groups, for example Mind, which are involved around the mental illness issue.

Pat Carlen's article is rather different. Her concern is to depict the social meanings of magistrates' justice, using a critique of 'games theory' to analyse the courtroom. While acknowledging the important contributions which games theorists have made to an understanding of how the courts operate, she emphasizes that for one player at least—the defendant—'the law game is no game at all', and in recognition of his status, she labels him 'the Dummy Player'. She examines the various strategies which different professionals use to maintain and extend their credibility, and comments on their performances in court. She shows how the rules of the game are made, interpreted and broken, and by whom, drawing out the distinctions between those which are formal and those which are informal: 'the mark of the *competent* professional in court is that he should know the informal rules both explicit and implicit.'

The final contribution to the Reader traces the origins and development of imprisonment, and attempts to predict future trends of penal policy. Arguing that 'the prison is the ultimate depository of changes that happen elsewhere', Stan Cohen shows how we have only recently begun to situate imprisonment in its proper historical context. Using the work of Foucault and Rothman, the article explores how features of today's prison system are to be found in the earliest conceptions of incarceration. The article concludes that the most important movement is from the concentrated surveillance of the asylum to the dispersal of social control beyond the walls of the institutions: 'overtly or covertly, more of our lives will be under central surveillance and control.'

V. 1 Poverty: concensus and alternatives

Robert Holman

The purpose of this article is to examine the published views of two leading politicians who can claim to speak for their parties. From their discussion of poverty and social deprivation (and the terms will be used inter-changeably) an attempt will be made to demonstrate that their policies or proposals rest on similar assumptions about society and a similar model of poverty. Their consensus of approach will mean that no alternative policies are being seriously mooted within the party political system. Their assumptions will be examined critically and the suggestion made that an approach deriving from an alternative model is required to counter poverty.

Sir Keith Joseph has been a notable Secretary of State for Social Services. His keenness to 'see for himself', his grasp of detail and his humanity have been impressive. He has given much thought to poverty and in June 1972 he put his ideas together in a speech to the Pre-school Playgroups Association. Obviously, the minister placed some importance on his now well-known 'social deprivation' address, for he caused it to be circulated widely.

The speech contains a graphic description of features associated with poverty, low income, poor educational attainment, inadequate housing, depression and despair. This prompts the minister to ask why social deprivation can persist in a period of relative prosperity. The answer, he suggests, can be found in the concept of a cycle of deprivation 'by which problems reproduce themselves from generation to generation'.

Sir Keith then outlines a theory of 'the phenomenon of transmitted deprivation' in which the carriers of poverty are the families themselves. He accepts that the early years are the most vital ones in shaping the

social and emotional development of children. They are the years in which the way they will function as adults is established. Certain inadequate parents do not provide the love, firmness, guidance and stimulus which most normal children receive. Being poorly socialized, their children do not acquire the motivation, skills and capacities necessary to avail themselves of educational and job opportunities. In turn, they will grow up only to transmit the same behaviour patterns to their offspring who, therefore, will also remain in poverty. A cycle is in existence which condemns any joiners to poverty as the following quotations will show:

> Do we not know only too certainly that among the children of this generation there are some doomed to an uphill struggle against the disadvantages of a deprived family background?

> Do we not know that many of them will not be able to overcome the disadvantages and will become in turn the parents of deprived families?

> large numbers of children [are] doomed to lives stunted physically, emotionally and intellectually because of their early years.

> Parents who were themselves deprived in one or more ways in childhood become in turn the parents of another generation of deprived children.

So serious, antisocial and unresponsive are the behaviour patterns of these families that they actually militate against the steps taken by the social services and prevent efforts to help the new generation of children.

> I must revert, finally, to problems of family background, which lies behind so many of our other ills—mainly because of their effects on children here and now, but also because they

Source: *British Journal of Social Work*, 3 (4), 1973, pp. 431–45 (reprinted in Butterworth and Holman (eds), *Social Welfare in Modern Britain*, Fontana, 1975, pp. 403–19).

prejudice everything we are trying to do for children in the next generation.

As an example of 'transmitting' families, Sir Keith instances 'problem' families who not only pass on deprivation but because of their breeding habits, do so to a very large number of children.

The cycle of deprivation theory is not new. Indeed, Sir Keith's exposition is similar to that published by Jamieson Hurry over 50 years ago. It is new to find a minister embracing a theory so fully and being prepared to shape public action accordingly. For beyond the basic social security system, which acts as a minimum level safety net, he is calling for forms of social intervention which will change the behaviour pattern of poor persons. In particular, he believes the cycle of deprivation can best be broken into by improving and supplementing the families' child rearing practices which shape the later behaviour of their children. Thus the minister advocates measures which reach children in their most formative years— playgroups, compensatory education and 'preparation for parenthood' schemes—and measures which have a direct influence on the immediate behaviour of adults, for instance, therapeutic relationships with an increasing number of social workers. He hopes that by the shaping and changing of their behaviour, families will learn how to function adequately in society. Further, the numbers joining the cycle can be reduced by teaching families to use one of the minister's favourite projects—family planning schemes for the poor.

The concept of the cycle transmitted deprivation is related to certain assumptions about society. At the risk of over-simplification, certain of these assumptions, upon which Sir Keith appears to base his poverty policies, can be identified. On the whole, the economic and social machinery of society is regarded as working well, providing a tolerable standard of living for most people. Unfortunately a minority of certain families are the grit in the machine, being unable to use it themselves and causing trouble for other people. The deprivation of this minority is due mainly to their inadequate child-rearing practices which fail to instil in their children the skill and will to perform like the rest of the population. If these family habits and practices can be improved, however, the minority will be enabled to achieve better education and jobs and so move out of poverty. The other sections of society wish to abolish poverty and will willingly provide the necessary resources and be prepared to incorporate the poor into their ranks.

Roy Jenkins, Home Secretary, and former Chancellor of the Exchequer and Deputy Leader of the Labour Party, is a political heavyweight who commands much support in his party. His wide-ranging interests, in particular his views on poverty, are presented in his latest publication, *What Matters Now*. Here Jenkins eloquently, even passionately, describes the many faces of poverty, stressing that it involves not just a lack of money but also deprivation in terms of health, education, housing and employment. Moreover, he makes it clear that these factors are multiple and interrelated, with one deprivation leading to another.

Housing standards affect attitudes and the ability of children to learn. It is difficult to perform effectively outside if the home circumstances are those of over-crowding or damp.

Further, he perceives that poverty characterizes certain localities as well as individuals, and he details the vast differences in resources and standards of living between regions, especially between the south-east and the rest of Britain. He strongly states his belief that such discrepancies are socially unjust and should be rectified.

In *What Matters Now*, Roy Jenkins devotes more space to describing poverty and suggesting solutions than to making explicit the reasons for its existence. However, from the whole of the book it is possible to discern the conceptions of society and poverty on which are based his policy proposals. First, he views society mainly within an economic framework. It is a market and being an uncontrolled market it 'strengthens rich regions at the expense of poor regions, successful firms at the expense of small men, the well-organized at the expense of the badly organized'. Those unfortunate enough to live in depressed regions are likely to be poor, for 'poverty is a matter of employment prospects'. Second, his economic orientation does not mean that he under-estimates the role of family socialization experiences in perpetuating poverty. He refers to the 'cycle of deprivation' less often than Sir Keith Joseph, but clearly accepts that deprivation is transmitted when parents are unable to pass on the skills which give access to higher education and well-paid jobs. Third, he believes that basically the different sections of society will act together to remove poverty. Acknowledging that strong groups 'load the dice in favour of their members' he yet believes that a call to idealism can persuade them to favour policies to combat deprivation. He regrets class politics and confrontations and puts his faith in the 'generosity of all men and women of goodwill, irrespective of their economic interests or class positions'.

The solutions proposed by Jenkins, following his analysis, require an improvement of the social services within the context of a better economic climate. He uses the term 'social services' broadly (as it is held in this article) to cover those services with a social work orientation (usually called the personal social services) those which operate on a selectivist basis to provide financial support to people in need, and those of universal application such as the National Health Service and educational services. Jenkins advocates an expansion of the personal social services in order to provide individualized guidance; higher social security benefits, a new child endowment payment and tax reforms to aid those with low incomes; increased retraining schemes to equip the unemployed and low wage earners with better earning skills; an extension of the priority area approach to include the National Health Service as well as education; and an enlarged urban programme to stimulate voluntary and local authority projects. These and other improvements, he believes, would 'break the cycle by which the children of the poor become poor themselves'. However, the advances in the social services, he warns, would be dependent upon a revitalized economy and decreasing unemployment. His faith in solutions through a combination of more social services and an expanding economy is revealed in his conclusion:

> Poverty can be eliminated only if we improve the standards of our social services . . . [only] if we make it a goal of our general economic policies.

Consensus of approach

At first sight Jenkins's analysis may appear to differ from Sir Keith's. He gives more prominence to economic factors, concedes that different social groups may have differing interests, and desires a greater degree of social equality. But these differences may serve to hide the fundamental similarities in analysis and the consequent similarity in policy proposals. Both politicians accept that poverty is an unfortunate occurrence, with no specific function to perform in society, with the result that they focus on the inadequacies or inabilities of poor families rather than on the structures of a society which tolerates or even requires poverty. Not surprisingly, Sir Keith and Jenkins conclude that poverty can be overcome simply by directing social services towards deprived families or by creating an economic climate through which the families can reach higher benefits. The families are not quite blamed for their plight but their lack of skills or abilities are seen as the cause. Thus the families—not the rest of society—are expected to change. Moreover, both politicians accept that the social services are effective instruments through which the changes can be wrought, so that if the services are expanded poverty will be correspondingly decreased. Further, both implicitly assume that 'experts' can devise solutions which will be both effective and acceptable to the major political parties. The emphasis is on policies made from above, transmitted downwards via social and economic services, with the expectation that those in poverty will respond and change.

The basic homogeneity of the two approaches— which reflects that of the two major political parties— is further revealed in three omissions or defects in both analyses. First, neither concedes or even discusses the point that to concentrate services on changing the deprived will be of limited value if the causes of deprivation rest mainly in the social structures of society rather than in the personalities of the poor or in their immediate environment. The emphasis on better socializing experiences for children will avail little if schools are required to maintain present hierarchies by ensuring that some children fail. The counselling or training of parents into different forms of behaviour will have little outcome if the public and private housing market is such that some people must be 'selected' for, or 'rationed' into, private slums or local authority sub-standard property. Increased job training will mean little in a situation where institutionalized occupational prejudice operates against the poor. In other words, why change people if the opportunity structures of society remain unchanged? Indeed, if poverty inheres in factors outside the control of the poor their reaction in terms of despising school, lacking motivation to work, and refusal to conform to middle-class behavioural standards, may be regarded as a rational adaptation to intolerable circumstances rather than as the direct result of inadequate childhood socialization experiences.

The questioning in the above paragraph of the politicians' assumptions about the causes of poverty should not be interpreted as an argument against the expansion of the social services. But the social services may not be the only weapon needed to attack poverty. The second omission made by both politicians is that their assessment fails to lead to proposals that require changes in those who are not poor. An effective attack on poverty needs not just a break into the familial cycle of deprivation but radical changes in the opportunity structure, in the methods of allocating resources and in the power structure of society at large. Neither makes much reference to it. Sir Keith gives no indication that a reduction in poverty may be dependent upon a reduction in wealth and privilege. Jenkins discusses economic factors and makes nodding mention of the unequal distribution of economic power, but his proposals concentrate on traditional social services for the poor. Both politicians apparently assume that poverty can be tackled by more of the present social services operating within the existing pattern of society.

Third, in their eagerness to make a case for the expansion of the social services in their present form, they give little if any attention to their negative effects. They mention that the services may be ineffective in reaching certain clients, but they do not appreciate how the same services may actually reinforce and perpetuate poverty. For instance, they do not discuss how services can act as social regulators containing the discontents of the poor within social agencies, and so preventing the build-up of pressure for reform. Nothing is said of the conveyance of official judgements of inadequacy or fecklessness which clients may eventually accept and to which they then conform.

Another model of poverty

It is not claimed that certain differences do not occur between the two major political parties. The parliamentary scene does witness forceful arguments over superannuation plans, immigration bills, means tests and so on. However, this paper has aimed at demonstrating that two leading spokesmen for these parties hold a similar understanding of poverty and hence propose similar kinds of solutions within an agreed framework. Obviously, the criticisms made of them spring from an alternative analysis of society in general and poverty in particular. This analysis will be briefly outlined but first of all a number of qualifications must be made. Theories of poverty cannot be discussed with any finality. As yet it is hardly possible to compose hypotheses about the causes of social deprivation and then to prove or disprove them in a scientific manner. The following is an interpretation which makes sense to the writer in terms of his experience, limited as it is, in highly urbanized areas of great social need. In addition, all theories of poverty would appear to be value-based and the explanation put forward here is no doubt influenced by the writer's own egalitarian values. Thus the model is presented with some hesitation, but done so because the party political consensus makes it necessary that alternatives should be articulated.

The functions of poverty

The basic assumption of the alternative model is that society consists of identifiable groups whose interests are in conflict. Power—the potential ability of one group to influence another—is unevenly distributed. Indeed it rests mainly with a minority grouping. As Rex baldly puts it: 'This is the model of a society in which a ruling class, possessed of private property in the industrial means of production, capitalizes on its power base to engineer the consent of the ruled.' This minority (be it called an elite, overlapping elites or ruling class) uses its power to maintain its interests and will not willingly make substantial concessions to other sections of the population in terms of resources, position or power.

These 'structural principles on which a capitalist society is built' are used by Rex to discuss the means by which this minority controls the resources awarded to workers. They have equal relevance to that section of the population considered poor, for in such a society poverty is to be regarded not as an unfortunate mishap but as functional in helping to preserve the existing divisions of society and thereby the disproportionate distribution of resources. The existence, even the creation, of a group identifiable as the poor serves to set them apart from the rest of the population. The result is not just, as Jordan says, that the working class is divided and thereby weakened. Rather, the use of the poor as a reference group persuades those sections of society (which are neither wealthy nor poor) that their lot in terms of status, resources and power is acceptable. Consequently, the possibility that they will strive to change the position of the elite is reduced. Further, the poor act as a warning. They demonstrate the fate of those who do not conform to prevailing work and social standards. Their plight is needed to reinforce the will of others to work for low returns in unpleasant and even degrading conditions from which the economic output gives a disproportionate financial reward to a minority of existing resource holders. Not least, those in poverty act as scapegoats, a vulnerable group on whom the blame for social problems can be placed, so diverting attention away from that minority which has some control over social affairs.

Mechanisms to preserve poverty

Poverty, then, is to be regarded as an enforced condition. It contributes to the stratified divisions in society which are the channels for an unequal distribution of resources. Hence the continuation of poverty is essential to the continuation of wealth. In turn, certain social mechanisms operate to preserve poverty or social deprivation. Here only three of the mechanisms can be mentioned. First, there are the institutions which select and train recruits for the elite positions, those posts which control the economy, run the apparatus of Government and so on. Most obvious are the public schools and Oxbridge which serve to socialize a very small section of society who are then channelled into positions of influence. Rex has commented: 'So far as the administrative apparatus is concerned, the astonishing thing in Britain is the resilience of the system of recruitment and socialization through Oxbridge.' He could have made the same observations about higher posts in university administration, the armed forces, the city, and both political parties. There is no evidence that ability is confined to this minority yet their insularity and homogeneity mean that groups with different attitudes, assumptions and views have little prospect of gaining ground. In other words, the possibility of alternatives is minimized. The institutions thus function to restrict recruitment from below (although, of course, some individuals are allowed in on condition of conforming to the institution's values) and to confirm in society the principle and practice that the means to position, power, and resources should be grossly unequally distributed throughout the population. Clearly, the mechanisms which promote power or wealth and preserve poverty are closely related so that policies which aim merely to change the latter are unlikely to be effective.

Secondly, persons from this same minority tend to dominate another mechanism—the means of mass communication. It is sadly amusing to examine the names which dominate the newspaper and television discussions about poverty. A balance is maintained between Conservative and Labour, right or left, yet both sides frequently are drawn from the homogeneous minority to which reference has been made. Discussions, therefore, have all the trimmings of a debate between two houses at the same public school. Points are made about the minutiae of poverty policies but the speakers share the same assumptions and interests. Rarely, if ever, will they question their own privileged position or suggest that poverty is dependent upon the hierarchical structure of society. Hence no radical challenge to the existing distribution of resources can be communicated. Simultaneously, the very fact that the poverty case is put by those from an elitist background reinforces the belief that the poor are inadequate—they cannot speak for themselves.

Thirdly, the social services themselves are partially used to maintain poverty and deprivation. Obviously, the low levels of social security benefits and cash transfer schemes limit any major redistribution of income and so preserve the financial distance between different groupings. Noticeably, the recent Green Paper on the proposed tax credit system gives examples showing high-income families gaining more than low-income ones. Similarly, the Government's new dual pension scheme will increase the gap between those dependent upon the State reserve pension and those able to use private occupational schemes (not to mention the windfall for those with investments in insurance companies). At the same time, by making small but periodic increases in levels of benefits, the impression can be given of helping the poor and so diverting attention away from the need for radical structural reforms.

The social services may further perpetuate poverty by being the means by which the poor are sharply distinguished from the rest of society and thence treated in ways which reinforce the gap between them and others. Recently, Jordan has pointed out that not only does the receipt of Supplementary Benefit mark out the non-working poor but the introduction of Family Incomes Supplement makes clear who are the working poor. Once identified as the poor, the title bearers can expect inferior treatment from society's institutions. For instance, Kay has explained how those forced to accept means-tested welfare benefits also accept a stigma. The stigma conveys a message to others and so lowers the school's expectation of their children's performance, reduces the chances that employers will offer them well-paid jobs and even makes the police more suspicious of them. In general, the recipients of state assistance are regarded with caution, given help only after careful scutiny and expected to behave in antisocial ways. Once the label of 'poor' is imposed, it is extremely difficult to remove it.

At worst, the officials of some social services can make subjective, moralistic and stereotyped judgements about clients which serve to condemn them to inferior treatment from the social services themselves. Those assessed as 'inadequate', 'feckless', 'deadlegs', 'spongers' and 'irresponsible' receive services and attitudes considered apt for the dregs of society. Applicants for council houses with children who swear, whose house smells, whose decorations are not in good order, who are simply not 'suitable' may re-

ceive a low grading which qualifies them only for substandard council housing. Thereafter, no matter how hard the tenants try, it is impossible to keep such property in good order and so impossible to change their grading. They will be shunted from one condemned property to another until, at last, they refuse to pay rent and so confirm, in the eyes of officials, that they are not worthy of decent accommodation. This mechanism of using moralistic judgements to identify those who should receive the worst resources is even found in the Government's White Paper on pensions which stated that 'personal enterprise and foresight' would be rewarded by higher pensions. Conversely, those lacking such qualities, that is, people with low incomes, would be awarded only the lowest pension. Whether in regard to welfare benefits, housing or income, the consequences are the same. Whatever the individuals' needs and capacities, once defined as 'undeserving' or 'unworthy' they are awarded service inferior to those of others. Other social agencies accept the classification and continue the process so that the possibility of any alternative way of life is minimized. As Minns summed up his careful study of the treatment of the homeless,

a borough which based its policies on assumptions of reprehensible behaviour on the part of homeless families established a control mechanism which narrowed the options the homeless could take in dealing with complicated problems and compelled them to act in accordance with the assumptions on which help was based.

In these ways the social services can ascribe the poor with certain stereotyped characteristics and, by so doing, prevent them from ever throwing off their poverty. Social deprivation is maintained.

Finally, the condemnatory fashion with which some clients are treated will affect the latter's own image of themselves. Haggstrom has explained how extreme dependency is destructive of personal self-respect and draws particular attention to the condition of those fully dependent upon state sources for their income. When the dependency is linked with the impossibility of change and condemnation from others then the recipients may react by withdrawal, by apathy or even by an acceptance of their lot and treatment as deserved and justified. Such responses explain why some deprived persons refuse to take up their welfare entitlements or even shape their behaviour to meet the expectations of outsiders. No doubt their children will be placed in similar situations and will respond like their parents, being set aside and setting themselves aside from the rest of society. In this sense poverty is transmitted, but less by the families concerned and more by outside structural and organizational influences.

So far little reference has been made to professional social workers. Probably most would regret the use of such terms as 'feckless', 'spongers', etc., and are only too aware how often the social services fail to provide

sufficient resources for clients. Yet consideration must
also be given as to whether the casework relationship,
so central to professional social work practice, when
applied to people in poverty, only serves to maintain
their depriving situation. The casework relationship,
like all professional relationships, is an unequal one.
The social worker is cast as an expert possessing skills
and knowledge which the client lacks but needs. The
client is cast as a deviant whose difference from other
people marks him out as in need of the professional's
treatment in order to restore him. He is seen as a person who receives help not as one who can give it.
Relevant as this approach is to individuals with problems of a psychological or emotional origin, it is of
doubtful validity to those whose poverty arises from
structural factors in society. On the contrary, the client
is marked out as being in need of treatment yet put in
a relationship which fails to remove his problem and
which conveys the implication that therefore something is wrong with his character, motivation, child-
rearing practices, or whatever. In effect, the client finds
himself in a structured relationship which only emphasizes his inadequacy and powerlessness. Thus attention is directed at the client's internal deficiencies
with the result that attention is turned away from the
external causes of poverty. The social workers find
themselves, unwittingly, in a double-bind situation.
They want to relieve poverty but the powers of their
departments and their present skills are not sufficient
to help in any significant way. The limited role they
can perform may bring some comfort to the poor, but
at the same time they function to humanize poverty,
making it more acceptable to the deprived and to the
rest of society.

Some qualifications must be added to the above
interpretation of the role of the social services and
social workers. It refers to the function of poverty
and it is not implied that the forces of society are unwilling to use the social services to tackle the problems
of, say, the mentally handicapped and the physically ill.
Moreover, the officials and social workers concerned
are not regarded as consciously plotting to create
poverty. They, too, must be placed within a context of
social and economic structures which shape and con-
strain their practices. Further, this article should not
be used to support any outright attack on casework.
In the writer's opinion, the development of casework
has been a major humanizing influence and is a valid
method of social work help. It is a valuable means of
therapy and emotional support to children in care,
foster parents, the mentally disordered and so on.
Instead, the argument is that when applied to persons
in poverty this particular method may worsen rather
than improve the overall situation. One of the great
unanswered, even unposed, questions of social work
is how to distinguish when the therapeutic casework
relationship should or should not be used. Within
these limitations, it has been argued that the social
services can function to uphold poverty and thereby
the existing divisions within our society.

Proposals for change

Poverty, then, remains not because the poor are the
grit in the social machine, not because of self-perpetu-
ating 'problem families', but because certain social
mechanisms require poverty to fulfil the function of
maintaining inequalities. If this analysis has any validity, then it follows that policies based on the Joseph–
Jenkins model are unlikely to promote radical changes
in the poverty situation. Their proposed packages aim
to improve the socialization of the poor without altering the societal structures which require them to be
poor. They want to increase the skills of the poor without transforming the mechanisms which promote
inequality. They want to expand the social services without questioning their part in maintaining deprivation.

Given that poverty should be abolished, what can
be done? It can be hoped that a spread of idealism
and altruism will persuade powerful groupings to make
radical concessions. The writer's own position as a
Christian and a socialist makes him believe that this
should happen. Unfortunately, there is little evidence
of even the beginnings of such action. Some would
advocate profound structural changes via physical
revolution. But this cannot be accepted by those who
reject physical violence on grounds of principle. An
alternative is to attempt to deduce how change is
possible given the structural nature of poverty as
described in this article. Only a brief outline can be
offered in a short space but the analysis does lead to
three major points. First, as wealth and poverty are
closely related then the latter cannot be changed unless the powers of the resource-holding minority are
reduced. Secondly, profound institutional changes are
required in the social mechanisms which at present
uphold poverty. Thirdly, the major impetus for reform
is unlikely to come from those who benefit from the
present system but rather from its victims—the poor.
Indeed, any action which excludes the poor will serve
to bolster their inadequacy and ensure that they
remain powerless in regard to the distribution of
resources.

If power resides in a minority who use it unjustly to
maintain extremes of wealth and deprivation then
clearly it is not enough to centre anti-poverty policies
on poor families. Instead a direct reduction in the
power and resources of the privileged minority is
required which, in turn, would entail an attack on the
mechanisms by which power is maintained, in particular educational institutions and the vehicles of
communication. No doubt the familiar argument that
a redistribution of wealth amongst the population
would mean comparatively little gain *per capita* will be
raised. But the point is that structural changes in the
mechanisms would enlarge access to resources and
positions of influence to other groupings in society.
The breaking of the social hold of a small homogeneous minority would have important implications for
poverty: the cycle of deprivation could be broken because changes in the opportunity structure would give

it something to break into while the entry of groupings with different assumptions and values would lead
to a different distribution of resources; the focus of
attack on to the minority elite would serve to counter
the reinforcing process by which the poor are blamed
for their poverty; and the need for poverty to function
as a means of preserving rigid social divisions would
be reduced.

The social services, as one of the societal mechanisms of control, must also be subjected to change. As
will be mentioned, pressure from the poor themselves
can be anticipated but Government policies should
also be directed towards institutional reform. In particular, the agency processes by which clients are
evaluated in moral terms and subsequently condemned
to inferior treatment must be eradicated. Only when
such persons are protected against poverty discrimination (just as black people need protection against
racial discrimination) can the tendency of social
services to promote social deprivation be said to be in
check.

As the social services need to serve the poor rather
than the powerful, so too the role of social work in
relation to social deprivation requires rethinking. It
must suffice briefly to suggest three objectives for
social workers. First, to promote institutional reform
within their own agencies. Social workers are well
placed to identify the selection, delivery and rationing
systems which can operate against the poor. Secondly,
to enable the poor to maximize their use of the social
services and to become as adept at handling bureaucracy as are members of higher income groups. Thirdly, to politicize clients in the sense of encouraging them
to perceive their condition as the result of societal
forces rather than individual inadequacies.

It may well be objected that the very strength and
sophistication of the present structural system will
operate to prevent any radical changes being made.
Precisely for this reason the major drive will need to
originate outside of that system. Just as in the nineteenth century skilled workers had to organize a new
collective grouping—the trade unions—in order to
have weight in society's conflict of interests, so too will
the poor have to develop collective action. Already
there is a noticeable growth of community action
amongst residents of deprived areas and of organizations of client groupings. Amongst the latter, some
Claimants' Unions have a prepared plan for collective
action through which it is envisaged that they can
bring about changes in the nature of the social security
system, in the attitudes with which the poor are regarded and a total reorganization of the wages structure.

Despite the growth in collective action, it is generally

conceded that at some stage the groupings of the poor
will need alignments with other power forces such as
a major political party or trade unions. Further, it is
argued that community groups need the stimulus of
Government funds. Here then is a major dilemma, for
the two major parties can also be regarded as part of
the mechanisms by which poverty is maintained. Even
the Labour Party's composition at a parliamentary
level is drawn heavily from the elite minority and
powerful arguments can declare that it no longer
represents the interests of the working class, let alone
the poor. So why should Government be expected to
take steps which would reduce the power of that minority? Radical concessions will be made only if considered politically expedient or unavoidable. Jordan
believes that the polarization between rich and poor
in our society is leading to increasing violence and the
disruption of a stable political system. Possibly radical
reforms will be made in favour of the organized poor
in order to forestall such trends. Moreover, there is
some suggestion that community action and the social
involvement of the poor lead to a decrease in delinquency, a lessening of the possibility of racial violence
and the promotion of a stable community. Interesting-
ly, Midwinter in his study of urban education concludes
that 'the threat of urban breakdown is that much nearer and more apparent, and yet there is no doubt that
the potential for community education and community
development exists even in the most disadvantaged
districts'. Following his historical and contemporary
analysis, Midwinter argues that only the full and meaningful involvement of the poor can prevent that breakdown. Thus the desire to avoid social dislocation may
persuade a Government to financially support local
movements of poor residents and clients although
such steps may also lead to greater political strength
for the latter. Not least, mention must be made that
the rapid growth of the new and well-organized claiming class could carry political weight simply through
the number of votes it would control. But regardless of
Government support, the developing grassroots movements are already involving some of the very people
written off as the casualties of society and are so providing for them an alternative which neither political
party offers. The question is whether they can win the
resources, support and organization which will lead to
significant changes; to a society without extremes of
wealth and poverty; to a society where poverty does
not have to function in order to maintain social divisions; to a society where balancing interests allow the
development of qualities of caring and attitudes of
mutual respect.

References

DHSS, 1971, *Strategy for Pensions*, Cmnd 4755, HMSO.

Haggstrom, W., 1964, 'The power of the poor', in F. Riessman (ed.), *Mental Health of the Poor*, Collier-Macmillan.

Hindess, B., 1971, *The Decline of Working-class Politics*, MacGibbon & Kee.

HM Treasury, 1972, *Proposals for a Tax-credit System*, Cmnd 5116, HMSO.

Holman, R. (ed.), 1970, *Socially Deprived Families in Britain*, Bedford Square Press, pp. 144–53.

Hurry, J., 1921, *Poverty and its Vicious Circle*, Churchill.

Jenkins, R., 1972, *What Matters Now*, Fontana.

Jordan, B., 1973, *Paupers: the Making of the New Claiming Class*, Routledge & Kegan Paul.

Kay, S., 1971, 'Means-tested benefits', *Social Work Today*, 2(15).

Midwinter, E., 1973, *Patterns of Community Development*, Ward Lock.

Minns, R., 1972, 'Organizational causes of homelessness', *Policy & Politics*, 1(1).

Rex, J., 1972, 'Power', *New Society*, 22, no. 522.

V. 2 Up against the Welfare State: the Claimant Unions

Hilary Rose

The late 1960s saw the upsurge of a new form of political action, called variously community politics or community action: organizing around the neighbourhood and the home became a significant political activity. Yet to grasp the significance of community politics, embracing squatting, tenant associations, anti-urban-renewal groups, community workshops and claimant unions—to name some of the more permanent groupings is extraordinarily difficult, not least because of the ambiguity of the word community.[1] A notoriously Humpty Dumpty word, 'community is as likely to be found on the lips of Edward Heath as on those of the Angry Brigade or the Young Liberals; at times it threatens to replace with a populist woolliness the unambiguous concept of 'class'. For these reasons it is important to relate this widespread if often fragmented activity to the working-class movement as a whole.

Because the Claimant Union movement has represented one of the most durable and coherent strands within community politics it is their history which is discussed here. A history which in its turn has to be seen in the context of the working out of the Welfare State, and the changing consciousness of its inadequacies during the 1960s. [. . .]

The Birmingham model

The first Claimant Union, which became the model for the Claimant Unions up and down the country that were together to form the National Federation, arose out of the radicalization of the university campuses in 1968. Small groups of Birmingham students had set up action committees whose brief was to plan and initiate socialist activity. One of these groups included five students, all working-class in origin, who had had direct personal experience of the Welfare State and social security. The two women members

Source: J. Saville and R. Miliband (eds), *The Socialist Register*, Merlin, 1973, pp. 179, 183–7, 188–92, 193, 201, 202, 203.

were training to become social workers and one was currently taking the professional case-work course at Birmingham. One had had a fieldwork placement with Tony Lynes, the first director of CPAG. Another was a law student taught by Robert Coleman, one of the few UK lawyers then actively researching and advising on Supplementary Benefit Tribunal proceedings. In the early stages of the movement, the geographical mobility of these original activists was of direct importance for the growth and spread of the Unions.

The original union in Sparkhill, set up in January 1969, grew very slowly. There was friendly help from the students from the Socialist Society in leafleting the social security offices, and from the Law Department at Birmingham in developing the relevant social security expertise, but gradually the Unions' need for independence moved them beyond this stage. In a way it is still true that Claimant Unions' emphasis on self-management makes it difficult for them publicly to be seen to be aided by organizations or individuals such as CPAG; consequently they tend to deny that expertise or resources are tapped from outside. Most Unions which have offices have them on a rent-free basis from settlement houses, voluntary social work agencies or the local authority rather than from the organized labour movement, a situation which points to some of the contradictions involved in even the more militant sectors of community politics.[2]

Gradually a philosophy emerged which stressed that claimants had rights under social security provision, that supplementary benefits were not a matter of charity and discretion but of human rights. In this their approach is not ostensibly different from, for example, the Child Poverty Action Group who, with their Citizens Rights Office, very energetically press the demands of individuals who are getting less than their entitlements. The crucial difference is that despite an early flirtation with a more radical conception, CPAG has never seen itself as working *with* the poor, only *for* the poor. The possibility T. Lynes raised in

1968 of 'pressure groups for the poor becoming super-seded by organizations of the poor' was firmly pre-cluded by CPAG's regard for the poverty 'expert'.[3]

'Getting your rights', very early on in the life of the first Birmingham group, then became a collective activity. Individual cases were and are brought before the entire weekly meeting and a strategy decided upon by the whole group, the one-to-one relationship of helper and helped being rejected. An important organizing principle emerged, stressing people's ability to do things together for themselves, which has become central to the movement's ideology. An early paper, 'Democracy for the Poorest', presented at the Institute of Workers Control in 1969, was to spell out some of these objectives.[4]

'Self-management', a principle closely related to this self-activity of people 'doing their own thing', was also enunciated early on as a long-term goal. While it was possible to organize people into securing their rights with self-activity, self-management (that is, the control of the social services by the people who use them) has remained at the level of rhetoric, little serious work and thought having been given to the problem. Together with a commitment to an adequate income being available to all, without a means test, and an opposition to any distinction being made between the deserving and the undeserving, the minimum agreed programme which was eventually to become the Charter of the Claimant Unions at the First Federation Meeting on 21 March 1970 took shape.

The internal structure of the Union was modelled—initially—very much on the lines of any trade union or labour organization. A model agenda circulated by BCU[5] thus speaks of a committee, a quorum of four, the election of chairman and officers, itemizes the business of reading correspondence, maintaining accounts, deciding the tactics for claims and appeals, reporting back from liaison committees and concluding with political education. Decisions and recommendations for action were to be carefully noted down. This procedural clarity, so typical of the labour movement, was gradually blurred over, the whole concept of a committee and office-holders became anathema, and the Unions moved their practice into a highly participatory democracy much more in accordance with their increasingly libertarian ideas.

Not only was the Union trying to develop coherent internal forms of organization: it was simultaneously experiencing practical difficulties with one of its main tactics—the appeal. As with large sections of administrative law from, for example, planning to industrial injuries, the citizen may appeal against the relevant administrative body, in this case the Supplementary Benefits Commission, to an independent Tribunal. Because the system of benefit is profoundly discretionary, there is in principle much to be gained by querying decisions, yet for precisely the same reason the Tribunal is a very frail court to which to appeal for justice. The Supplementary Benefits tribunal is the linear descendant of the old Unemployment Assistance Board—hated for good reason—and, because it is dealing with people lacking middle-class resources to pay for expert representation, or trade union strength it is in many ways the slum among tribunals.[6] Despite its formal claim to independence, its officers are seconded from the DHSS, and the Department itself is responsible for approving nominations to Tribunal membership. The exposure of the inadequacy of the Tribunals by the Unions and CPAG has led to substantial pressure for their reform.[7] As a tactic, however, making an appeal was both a means of ensuring that claimants received their full entitlements, and simultaneously of exposing the iniquities of the supplementary benefit system. Winning, while important for maintaining membership, was not necessarily crucial, as revealing the true nature of the 'Welfare State' was of educational significance.

The kinds of complaints Birmingham Claimant Union made about the experience of their first appeal in their first year, August 1969, are the same in substance if not in detail today. Thus the first appeal was made on an issue of mortgage arrears, and the failure of the social security office to grant the automatic addition of 50 pence per week for a long-term claimant. The Union's representatives attended and reported 'gross bias and incompetence'. They claimed that[8]

> from the outset the Tribunal and Clerk were
> hostile, and not neutral. The chairman
> misrepresented the statutes—until our well-briefed
> representative corrected him . . . There was much
> hostility shown, and the appellant appeared to be
> 'on trial' instead of the question of her welfare
> being under discussion.

Eventually BCU complained to the Council of Tribunals at their treatment, arguing that the Tribunal was not independent of the DHSS and the Supplementary Benefits Commission. The Birmingham Appeal Tribunal resented the number of members coming to support a particular claimant and tried to limit the number of representatives to one. The first time that this limitation of the representatives to one took place was in December 1969 in Wolverhampton, where the appellant being ill and depressed, the representative was unable to make many notes, and, according to BCU, 'found great difficulty in being allowed to speak for Mr G. at all'. BCU argued that like the Supplementary Benefits Commission they needed to train people to represent, and that one person was the advocate and the other the trainee. They were also conscious that with well-kept notes, they were gathering further ammunition for any subsequent appeal. Angered by the slow process of the Council, the Union refused to return either with the adjourned cases, or with new cases until the Tribunal's impartiality was assured. Simultaneously with this struggle in Birmingham over the right of representation, CPAG was putting pressure on Lord Collison (chairman of the SBC) for similar rights, and an unplanned coalition operated between the Unions and CPAG which was subsequently to operate on other occasions and issues.

The Unemployed Workers' and Claimants' Union

During the same year that Birmingham Claimant Union was set up, a parallel grouping—the Unemployed Workers' and Claimants' Union—was established in Barnsley chiefly by Joe Kenyon, a disabled ex-miner. Because Kenyon was willing to be interviewed on television and generally to act as a spokesman for the Claimant Unions, the media credited Kenyon with being general secretary to one large Union with different branches, as if he were a Wal Hannington of the 1970s. In fact partly because of the libertarian influence within the Union movement, and partly because of the practical difficulties entailed in a more centralized grouping, the Unions which were to emerge after Birmingham were not branches but autonomous Unions linked together loosely through the National Federation of Claimant Unions, whose development is discussed below. Gradually even those which had been initially associated with Kenyon moved over to the Federation.

Not only did the media exacerbate the problem of spokesmen and leaders, but so did one of the Marxist groups and CPAG. Both, the former because of its involvement with the unemployment question, and the latter because of its concern with poverty, sought a spokesman for the unemployed and the poor to lend legitimacy to their own political activities.

None the less right up to 1971, Kenyon's public position stated on endless platforms up and down the country was extremely close to that of the Federation. Apart from the spate of good pamphlets[9] on how to get your welfare rights that were produced from his Barnsley home, Kenyon's most subtle contribution to the claimants' struggle was his argument linking the battle against unemployment, the right to work, with the argument linking the right not to work at an unspeakable job. Some of the more libertarian Unions have such a passionate loathing of the work ethic that they often offend working-class common sense which knows that a whole society cannot live on air and also directly offend unemployed people desperately seeking work and who loathe being dependent. [. . .]

Centralization—an organizational crisis

Without doubt Birmingham quickly built an effective relatively traditional working-class organization. It had built coalitions with the tenants' association and with the women's movement, established itself as a political entity and had acquired a substantial expertise of social security statutes and administrative instruments. While the Union continued to advocate making alliances with the labour movement, some of the tactics it advocated, such as bugging interviews

between social security officers and claimants, generated trade-union hostility. The Civil Service Union, in response to BCU's statement of intention, rapidly advised its members not to take part in interviews they thought were bugged. None the less the BCU's stance was still in favour of co-operation— although the attitude of claimants to counter clerks is fraught with the same sort of complexities as that between say, strike pickets and policemen. The Union, for example, tried to obtain a joint statement with the Civil Service Union to make it clear that 'the last thing we want is for the clerical workers to close their ranks behind the ministry. They form an exploited, overworked and underpaid class, suffering heavily from bureaucracy and the squeeze'. While the Civil Service Union remained at the official level[10] unimpressed by this statement of claimant/clerical worker solidarity, the work of individual militants in passing over to claimants the various secret rules of social security embodied in the A and the AX Codes—defying the Official Secrets Act—has contributed substantially to the Union's success.

In practice Birmingham probably gained more practical help from a community-based organization, the Tenants' Action Group, than from organized labour. And, despite its grandiloquent language of potentially organizing four million claimants, it saw as a solid achievement that in Balsall Heath, the Union was now (early 1970) able to rival the Tenants' Action Group as a second political force in the area.[11] Some success was had by working with strikers to help secure benefits for the strikers' families, and gradually, for single strikers by using Section 13 of the 1966 Social Security Act. Good personal contacts were made with the Trades Council, but influencing the choice of the workers' representatives in Tribunals continued to be a remote goal. The most blatantly anti-claimant attitudes were felt by the Claimant Union to be displayed by the Tribunal's trade-unionist member, who seemed to regard all claimants except the manifestly sick and elderly as work-shy and scroungers.[12]

The Union put out a considerable literature on how to get benefits, explaining its actions and conducting running self-analyses. Indeed its very success—securing for example no less than £3,000 for its members during the first twelve months—meant that new Unions looked to Birmingham for guidance, a practice which shifted only as other Unions began to feel their strength.

At the same time that these new Unions began to emerge in 1970, criticism in Birmingham developed concerning the centralization of the Union, focused on a single office in Camphill. The price of developing the necessary expertise and establishing an identity for the organization meant that, despite their goal of self-activity, the Union had produced alternative experts. A kind of anti-social work had developed and people became 'cases'; 'cases' were represented at appeals. Experts were referred to. The media abetted this process by identifying leaders. Thus in what appeared to be their success, by the criteria of a growing membership and economic gains for the membership, a strong vein of criticism emerged that this was the antithesis of their goals of mobilizing the claimants to act for themselves. They were ceasing to work with the community and were becoming expert individuals working for individual people who themselves were being depersonalized. BCU literature speaks angrily of being in the same position as the man from the social security or the lady social worker, 'people are grateful to us', 'we appear as angels of mercy, ugh!'—a vein of self-criticism which appears not only in BCU's discussions but also in those of other Unions, as they find themselves slipping into individual social work. This whole debate which constantly recurs in Union writing and discussion argues that social-work advocates who help claimants get the benefits to which they are entitled still do this within a framework which isolates claimants and confirms them in their dependency. Thus from Joe Kenyon[13] to Barbara Wootton,[14] Adrian Sinfield[15] or the radical social workers, whether active in CPAG and even in the Union movement itself, all are seen, even if helpful to individuals, to provide 'help' at the expense of claimants increasing the control they have over their own lives.

Decentralization and change

Almost certainly the fact that the Claimant Unions emerged in the provinces rather than the metropolis made it possible for the Unions to change deliberately their organizational model from centralized to a decentralized and federal structure. Thus they were spared the problem of the centripetal forces which focus political and media attention on London and which have not infrequently distorted the structure of organizations and of movements.

While Birmingham was slowly struggling towards a more democratic form of organizing, where there was homogeneity of role with little or no distinction between helper and helped and where there were either no officers or rapidly rotating officers, other Unions were beginning to emerge. Because the chief activists were students, the original group had a built-in geographical mobility, and as they graduated or left the Birmingham campus they tended to establish new Claimant Unions in the cities where they found themselves. In addition, the economic situation was itself rapidly deteriorating, facilitating the expansion and growth of the movement.

The National Federation

After Birmingham some of the earliest CUs to emerge were Brighton, Manchester, East, North and West London and North Staffs. By April 1970, these seven Unions met at Birmingham and agreed to set up and join the National Federation of Claimant Unions. They agreed a minimum four-point charter and defined the nature of a bona fide Claimant Union eligible to join the Federation. They saw it as a Union of people claiming, or who have claimed, supplementary benefits together with those people whose incomes were low enough to entitle them to means-tested benefits such as free school dinners or rent and rate rebates. Each Union was to be run entirely by its members, the elderly, the sick, unsupported single parents, the disabled, etc. Every claimant who joins a Union was to be represented without condition or reservation.[16]

The Charter itself was brief enough:

1. The right to adequate income without means test for all people.
2. A free Welfare State for all, with its services controlled by the people who use it.
3. No secrets and the right to full information.
4. No distinction made between so-called 'deserving' and 'undeserving'.

In addition to the seven who agreed to join and establish the Federation, another ten were in existence, some present at the meeting and others with whom Birmingham, still acting as a central co-ordinator, was in touch. These other Unions included Leeds, Tyneside, York, Plymouth, Lancaster and Morecambe, Barnsley, Bristol, South London, Edinburgh and Liverpool.

Some of the earliest Unions arose as a spontaneous response to the idea of a Claimant Union. Brighton, for example, was primarily organized by a disabled woman active in local left politics. The concept of a Claimant Union for her, and for others like her who were increasingly to appear as the movement grew, made obvious sense, pulling together hitherto disparate aspects of a personal and political existence. But while the growth of the unions partly had this spontaneous quality, which typically brought in an older tradition of political organizing, for the most part the spread of the Unions was associated with the fluid network of the ex-students, who were drawn increasingly from the colleges and universities, in particular from Cambridge and Essex. The fluidity embraced not only actual ex-students but also working-class youth unemployed or dropped out from the work situation; the distinctions between them—the students—were felt to be unimportant; they shared the same culture and life-style. These were and are highly mobile. They hitch up and down the country, stop down with friends and rapidly dig into the local community and start organizing. The ease with which this happens speaks less of the skills which they bring—which can be widely varied—than the acute material and personal needs, the emptiness and routine hopelessness of life on the Welfare State.

The conditions for growth

The three years between the first Federation meeting in March 1970 in Birmingham and the most recent in 1973 have been in themselves years favouring the growth of the Unions. Unemployment has sharply risen and, when even conservative estimates have topped the million, reality bears in its wake substantial numbers of concealed unemployed, particularly women. Economic depression, inherently uneven in its impact, has not, despite Crossman's claim, distributed unemployment 'equitably'; areas of old social and environmental privation are among the first to suffer, with the inner city a second casualty where traditional working-class areas have been invaded by the middle classes and by urban planning disasters. Prices, particularly of housing, rose rapidly, and with the new Finance Bill will rise even more in the local authority sector. Welfare benefits have been cut and a greater emphasis on selectivity has widened the social experience of means testing. Industrial unrest has not merely grown during these years, it has significantly changed its character. At Upper Clyde the men did not withdraw their labour as a response to the threatened closure of the yards, instead they conducted a work-in. The debate often became, not whether to strike, but whether a 'work-in' or a 'sit-in' was the best way of occupying a factory. The Postal Workers' strike, Rolls Royce, Coventry, Fine Tubes, and lastly the Miners' strike,[17] made men and women, who despite their working-class origins had not seen themselves as being dependent on anyone, into claimants. The economic crisis of the last two years gave birth— potentially at least—to a new sympathy between the unemployed and the unemployable.

A pauper class?

These were important shifts as the Claimant Unions, instead of organizing the long-term dispossessed and the possibly transient youth group, received a sudden infusion of workers, with often substantial union-organizing experience. Their presence was greatest in the areas most drastically affected by unemployment, but ripples spread out all over the country.[18] Inevitably this led to some of the various Marxist groups increasing their work with the Claimant Unions. The degree and nature of this involvement varied from area to area, very much determined by the local conditions and the possibilities for working-class action. Thus in Scotland, despite an officially lukewarm attitude by the Communist Party to the Claimant Unions, the Glasgow Claimant Union had active Communist members and strong trade-union connections. In Cumbernauld when a well-unionized factory was closed, the unionists now out of work simply translated themselves into an effective Claimant Union. Such Unions emerged not in response to the needs of the long-term claimant but in response to those of the unemployed. As such they tended to have a predominantly male membership and to reflect this in their political concerns, tending to put the claim of the 'right to work' as a higher priority than the interest of long-term claimants. While this distinction between temporary claimants—the unemployed—and long-term claimants affected all long-term claimants, in-

cluding the chronic sick and the elderly, it was the women who were actively to resent the assumption that the only work that was to be done was in the workplace. The various Marxist groups tended to support the unemployed workers' position at the expense of the long-term claimant and earned for themselves considerable hostility, particularly from the women, as the Marxists were felt to be using the movement in pursuit of partial and sexist ends.[19]

Certain Unions in the south, while less immediately affected, none the less sought to relate themselves to the situation of growing unemployment. North London for example, despite the fact that it was only briefly able to recruit unemployed workers, and in the main organized people who were essentially long-term claimants, retitled itself as North London Unemployed Workers' and Claimants' Union. [. . .]

Growth and its problems

With such diverse strands within the movement, nationwide Federation meetings grew correspondingly more difficult as the number of Unions increased. The criticisms which had been expressed within Birmingham of overcentralization and the making of experts came to be expressed more widely within the whole movement. Birmingham had, through being host at early Federation meetings and publishing the *Organization Bulletin*,[20] maintained the network and become something of a nerve centre to the Unions. It also published the first edition of the *Strikers' Handbook*[21] and the *Federation Journal*.[22] The idea of the handbooks—and the *Strikers' Handbook* was to play a key role in the subsequent period of widespread industrial action—was to aid the internal development of the movement, that of the journal to explain the movement to the outside world. However, when Birmingham ceased to play this central network maintenance role, it did prevent the domination of one particular Union but at the price of losing a certain coherence and integration between the Unions. Knowledge about the Unions became more limited to an oral network, which meant that new Unions starting up without being on this friendship network were unlikely to be well knitted into the movement. None the less there were certain gains associated with Birmingham's retreat from its co-ordinating role, in that the ensuing looseness facilitated the dramatic expansion of 1971 and 1972. By the end of this period the Unions were beginning to take stock of themselves as a now considerable nationwide movement, yet despite a profusion of locally sponsored activities with little national thrust.

The most dramatic period of growth did not start until the summer and early autumn of 1970. Up to that point there were seven Unions, some still fragile, but which had taken two years to build. Suddenly by November the idea of the Unions had taken hold and there were no less than eighteen. They had broken out of the relatively tight Midlands, London and Brighton network to Edinburgh in the north, to Cardiff and Plymouth in the west. Some seven months later the network began to thicken with thirty-one unions, of which seven were in London, three in Birmingham, one as far north as Aberdeen and two or three in East Anglia. In a further three months there were an additional twenty-one Unions, so by September 1971 there were sixty-four Unions all told. Between this time and the present (1973) the number has fluctuated between seventy and ninety. Some of these are large, organizing several hundreds of claimants, others are tiny, organizing a mere handful. Many claimants are, of course, active only for a few weeks or a few months, because to some extent participation is participation in crisis, and eventually all but the most dedicated are reclaimed by the demands of their life situation. The continuity structurally possible in organizing around a stable work situation—archetypally mining or docking where a shared work situation is reinforced by living in close-knit communities—means that trade unions have a better likelihood of achieving a stable membership. The claimants have to make the first step and go to the Union, it cannot come to them. But while Claimant Unions lack stable membership, it is important to understand that a once organized member does not become completely *un*organized merely because he or she can no longer take part in meetings. They become instead a reserve force, a quasi-organized group, who can be relied upon to go on gently advising and organizing claimants in the social security offices both as to their rights and as to the potentiality of the Union for helping them. To make a fairly arbitrary estimate of the numbers of claimants and their families who have been reached by the movement, if we assume that each Union has organized some 200 members, that each household has, say, 2.5 people, then the movement has reached 38,000 people.

The significance of the Federation

Unions subscribed to the belief of the importance of belonging to the Federation, and were prepared to modify their internal arrangements if the three-monthly Federation meeting which considered new applicants rejected their proposed affiliation. For example, Grimsby applied to the Bristol Federation meeting in January 1972, and was rejected when members present admitted that non-claimants were members. When the Union reported at the subsequent meeting that these were now excluded, the Federation accepted their affiliation. None the less, despite the significance of being accepted by the Federation, in many ways this marked a ritual of maturation and acceptance as a bona fide Claimant Union, rather than helping the development of the Union itself. Despite the persistent attendance at Federation by key Unions and key activists within them, not a few Unions, once having established contact and successfully affiliated, ceased to attend, finding meetings themselves unproductive and being able to get literature through the skeletal

but crucial library service which Birmingham was continuing to provide.

Where the earlier meetings of the Federation had been extremely small, they were highly effective and organizationally held together by a strong friendship network, little thought was given to the problems entailed when the number of participants moved from 20 to 250 plus young children. Eventually after a Bristol Federation meeting in early 1972, widely regarded as the nadir of disorganization, workshops with some general sessions were adopted and meetings rapidly improved. One further structural problem which Federation meetings showed themselves to be increasingly incapable of overcoming was the disproportionately large percentage of young activists attending who, being highly mobile, tended to be the dominating group at Federation meetings. As one Union member put it, 'we always had some freaks at the Federation meeting; now they are all freaks.' Thus the style of Federation meetings tended to be rather different from the Unions at the local level, the mass of whose membership were and are working-class people organizing to defend themselves against the social security system.

Non-hierarchical methods of co-ordination

When the trend towards centralism in the movement had been checked, three methods were tried as alternative non-hierarchical means to secure a co-ordinated nationwide movement. The three methods were: (1) mutual interdependence through different experiences; (2) nationwide campaigns; and (3) regional integration. Thus the first was to use the natural differences in the membership constituency of the various Unions to secure interdependency through specialist publications. The idea was to draw on, for example, East London's experiences of chronically sick members, North London's of their homeless, Birmingham's strikers, Newton Abbot's unemployed workers, Highbury and Islington's strong connections with the women's movement and their ensuing pamphlet for unsupported mothers, to South Shields' and West London's work with unemployed school-leavers and other young claimants. With some exceptions this strategy paid off; Unions were writing out of their own experiences and drawing on experiences of Unions with similar problems and, by helping themselves clarify the issues, helping, almost incidentally, the movement. What was more difficult to secure was the commitment to the publication of national publications such as a national newsletter or the journal originally started by Birmingham. Allocated to one of the London Unions as a responsibility, it assumed a lower priority than either day-to-day organizing or publications written for their own needs. The material was eventually rescued from this Union by a member of another London Union and eventually published with the aid of a CPAG grant. This issue of the journal was of considerable importance as it contained the reply from the Claimant Unions to the Fisher Committee on Abuses.[23] Because harassment by both the local social security office and by the special investigators needed exposing, to fail this responsibility was to fail in the defence of all claimants. The importance of the friendship network in keeping to the fore issues which affected all claimants, rather than issues affecting a specific local Union, is underlined by this particular episode as the actual member rescuing the journal was in fact one of the original Birmingham activists, even though subsequently it was sponsored and published by the Union of which she was a member.

The second method of achieving co-ordination was through national campaigns on specific issues. The first was the Winter Heating and Christmas Present Campaign of 1971. This was relatively ineffectual in practical terms although it served to raise claimants' consciousness. The only technique was to put in for a special needs grant, which was automatically refused. Consequently even where a Union was energetic and appealed against these refusals, all that happened was that the appeal system was choked. The pressure on the social security system was therefore not a collective pressure, but a series of individual cases each requiring representation and work by the Union—and as such easily contained within social security. The campaign was also criticizable on the grounds that it afforded the officers a means of attacking the Unions as harming claimants through misusing the appeal system with no concrete advantage for claimants. At this stage little or no effort was made to use the media to bring about other pressures on social security. Basically this first nationwide campaign was little more than local action, which had in fact been tried the previous year in Birmingham, writ large.

The next nationwide campaign was the Guaranteed Adequate Income Campaign. More ambitious in scope, this was seen as both a goal in its own right and as a means of pulling the Unions together. The media was used and the *Morning Star*, *Freedom* and *Time Out*, together with many local papers, were to cover the campaign. Yet despite the verbal support the campaign itself failed to get very far off the ground. Probably because it was everyone's issue, like the Fisher Report, it was no one's issue, whereas the third campaign, which was specifically directed towards women, was much more successful. Launched in the summer of 1972, again from North London like the Guaranteed Adequate Income Campaign, the cohabitation campaign met with much wider support. Most Unions had been involved in at least one struggle against the cohabitation rule, whose ruthless application had meant the cutting off of all benefit, sometimes merely on the strength of gossip of a malicious neighbour. Already in 1972, sufficient public opinion had been generated on this issue to gain an important concession through a surprising coalition extending from Joan Vickers, Conservative MP in the House of Commons, and CPAG at an establishment level, to the Women's Liberation Movement and the Claimant Union de-

monstrations in the streets and in social security offices.[24] The concession was that any woman accused of cohabiting could not be cut off immediately from benefit if she chose to appeal, until the hearing.[25] Despite the success particularly of this last campaign in relating the women claimants to the women's movement, thus increasing Unions' grass-root strength, in terms of co-ordinating the Unions the campaigns were only partially successful.

The third method of achieving greater co-ordination gave up the immediate target of nationwide co-ordination, and instead sought to build a closer integration at a regional level. In certain areas, notably the Midlands and London, this was much more successful, a greater frequency of meeting led to a greater continuity both of people and discussion; it also served to pool information and resources. London, for example, was able to organize regular monthly meetings, which facilitated both joint action and the emergence of new Unions. It enabled problems which were difficult for a single Union to handle, such as continued police harassment which troubled both South London and Hackney, to be dealt with on an all-London basis. Deputations to Lord Collison as Chairman of the Supplementary Benefits Commission to complain about the treatment for example of allegedly cohabiting women were able to draw on Unions who for one reason or another still eschewed the Federation.[26]

None of these methods, the shared-out responsibility for publications, the nationwide campaigns or the regional meetings, solved the question of how to knit the movement together. While all three helped, their overall effect was to make the Unions strong in a particular area and for them to be well meshed into a broad spectrum of activities at the local level, ranging from working with local strikers to help secure social security benefits—support which can be particularly valuable with ill-paid and fragilely organized groups such as the hospital workers—to working with squatting groups, women's groups, to local tenants' organizations. Thus each of these three methods of co-ordination reflect both the strengths and limitations of the libertarian ideology which has guided the movement.

Lessons and prospects

What can be learnt from the experience of the Claimant Union movement? No one on the left who has worked with the Claimant Unions can fail to respond to the sheer elan which they have brought to organizing working-class men and women around issues of the home and the street. In the brief five years since the Claimant Unions began, they have developed from the activities of a handful of students and ex-students at Birmingham to a movement which has mobilized thousands of people. The core of this strength lies in the way that the Unions have shown how it is possible to create a collective organization in opposition not merely to the meagre hand-outs of the Welfare State, but to its increasingly intense individuation. What appear to be very simple—and rather slow—ways of collectively discussing a claimant's social security problems, and planning together the best course of action, serve to recreate the collectivist decision-making distinctive to working-class culture and movements.[27] Social security, in capitalist society in general, and particularly in Britain with its extensive reliance on discretion, means that each claimant is judged by unseen rules on the merits of his or her case. The arbitrariness of this sets claimant against claimant, divided by their jealousy, for a miserable but critical number of pence. Each claimant is isolated, so that at every stage in the process of claiming social security the claimant is at once more profoundly individuated and gradually depersonalized into a total dependency as more decisions which pertain to the conduct of his or her life are taken over by the officials.

No leaflets the Unions produce show this as graphically and decisively as the cartoons.[28] These advise the claimant: 'Never see the SS alone, they never see you alone', and show the claimant on one side of the counter with a social security officer as a mere puppet in the arms of senior bureaucrats, the police and the judges. The non-neutrality of the Welfare State and its functionaries is the clear message.

Although this article has suggested that the individual Unions are often very small with a transient membership, the movement as a whole is widely recognized by the bourgeois press and the courts as 'subversive'. It was necessary in both the trials of Jake Prescott and Ian Purdie and the 'Angry Brigade' for the defence to demonstrate that despite the hysteria the Unions provoked on the part of the establishment, they were a legal and open activity and not a nursery school for insurgency, which was the prosecution's argument. (Though it is not without interest that R. Clutterbuck's book[29] on counterinsurgency features a photograph of Claimant Unions on a demonstration on the jacket.)

Claimant Unions are thus one vital strand within a nexus of activities focused on the home and the street. Like the black and the women's movement, their critique is cultural rather than merely economistic and contains an edge of anger which a regular tenants' association primarily focused on the economic questions of rent and conditions will only rarely display. This burgeoning of neighbourhood activities arises, as we have shown, partly in response to changing economic conditions, but also in response to the failure of the Labour Party and the neglect by many—if not most—Marxist groups of those not directly engaged 'at the point of production'. A wide range of attitudes to community action are expressed on the left, ranging from an open view that such activities are a petit-bourgeois irrelevancy or (worse) a diversion, to an apparently cordial regard which on closer examination sees sommunity action as a useful handmaiden to serve industrial action. Very few Marxist groups locate community action as an integral and necessary part of the class struggle.[30]

The kind of question that is posed by Marxist writers within the women's movement is strikingly similar to that posed by the claimants' movement. (Nor is this by chance; women, particularly the unsupported mothers, are one of the most militant sections within the Claimant Union, and, even when claimants are not women, they share the home as the only workplace.) Recently Dalla Costa[31] in her discussion of the liberation of women, reminds us of Gramsci's view that women should be organized that they may be 'neutralized', in order that they should not 'hold back' the revolutionary potential of the male working class. Transferred to the claimants' movement, the question must be whether community action is merely a way of neutralizing backward sections such as pensioners, women, the sick and the unemployed, or whether it offers a richer dimension to the theory and practice of human liberation.

As we have argued, most Marxist groups stand to one side of the claimants' movement: for example, SLL, despite the fact that it has published one of the best pamphlets on social security,[32] plays no part in the Union; the Communist Party has a few active members in those areas with a strong working-class membership; IS has relatively few members active in the Unions, being more committed to industrial and tenant work, though some IS women are claimant members; even IMG, which has a serious commitment to working with the Unions and is active in a number of them, does so with the handmaiden theory of the Unions, seeing them as a means of organizing the unemployed—if necessary at the expense of the interests of other kinds of claimant. Scarcely surprisingly such views have not endeared these Marxist groups, as groups, to the movement, however respected individual members may be.

The tyranny of structurelessness

The tragedy is that while the movement has defended itself and its autonomous development from becoming the mere handmaiden to the interests of the industrial worker through the exposure of the manipulative intentions of the Marxist groups, it has fallen into what 'Joreen'[33] has analysed as the 'tyranny of structurelessness'. Although she is discussing the women's movement, much of her analysis is applicable to the claimants' movement. In the desire of these new movements to break with rigidly bureaucratic and deadening organizational structures, they have turned to structurelessness. Friendship networks lie at the core of the movement. In the women's movement as in the Unions, there are no leaders, no spokespeople. Consequently the media, battening on the movement and needing such figures, seizes on its writers and those who are good on television and creates leaders, as with Kenyon and earlier some of the Birmingham activists, or at present, for that matter, Bill Jordan. Because the movements have not chosen these people to speak for them, they cannot control what they say, and therefore bitterly and futilely criticize them. In the process, as

'Joreen' points out, they exclude the very people who potentially could be of help to the movement.

But more serious than the issue of the question of the phoney leadership of the Unions created by the press, is the question of the real leadership. The rhetoric of the movement denies that leadership as such does exist, yet the reality is that it is concealed in the friendship networks which serve to link the disparate Unions both geographically and over time. While the Unions were right to reject the situation whereby office-holding becomes the privatized property of the office-holders, they have moved to the other extreme where, instead of an at least visible tyranny of office-holders, they have created the invisible tyranny of the network. The network is defended on the grounds of its fluidity and openness, yet in fact the criteria by which claimant members are accepted or excluded from the network are such that what were described earlier as the young activists virtually form the network.

Not only is this form of organization bad in itself, in that it contradicts the living democracy of the Union at the local level, but that it denies the movement the possibility of developing more complex forms of organization with which to meet the increasing oppression of the Welfare State. It is predictable that with the double combination of a Heath government and a Joseph at the DHSS, the situation of claimants will continue to be worsened as part of the general attack on the working class, yet the movement has no mode of making a co-ordinated and sustained response to any specific attack.[34] The positive contribution of the Marxists which should be to create a centralized and openly democratic structure has to date failed because such attempts have been attached to the handmaiden view of the movement. This view is linked to a concept of revolution which is predominantly economic and lacks a cultural perspective. Consequently if the Claimant Unions are to meet and surmount the present threat, both the hidden tyranny of the network and the manipulative tactics of economizing must be brought into the open and replaced by a political perspective which provides both sensitivity to the cultural issues and a coherent and democratic organizational structure. The contribution of the Claimant Unions to the working-class movement in revealing the nature of the Welfare State and in resisting its oppression is precious and must not be lost in networks or economism.

Notes

1 Not only would it be true to say that most writing on 'community' from Tönnies onwards has looked back nostalgically to past ways of living, but also that nineteenth-century social policy makers such as Thomas Chalmers specifically recommend the 'creation of parochialism' as a means of 'preventing people from forming into a combined army of hostile feeling and prejudice'. Community as a local loyalty is thus historically set in antagonism to the universality of class, and casts some light on the government's new enthusiasm for community development, etc.

2 No such generosity by voluntary social work agencies was demonstrated to the National Unemployed Workers' Movement. The funds given by the government to the Councils of Social Service to provide main halls for the unemployed were seen as subsidizing hostile and diversionary measures against the NUWM (W. Hannington, *Ten Lean Years*, Gollancz, 1940).

3 *Peace News*, 26 April 1968. Also when J. Radford of Lewisham squatters were known to be looking for funds to publish the A Code, CPAG director F. Field leaked the story to *The Times*, ostensibly on the grounds that 'publication might awaken the Tories from their appalling ignorance and lead them to cutting discretionary payments', but in practice quite appalled at the intervention of working-class direct action politics (i.e. Deptford CU) with less respect for bourgeois legality than CPAG (*The Times*, 7 December 1970).

4 BCU, 'Democracy for the poorest', *Monthly Digest*, Institute for Workers Control, Notts, March 1969.

5 Business Meeting, Standing Agenda and Sheet for Notes, BCU, 1970.

6 The quality of decision-making in Supplementary Benefit Tribunals is lower than for similar tribunals. This is particularly apparent when the same case is presented to two different Tribunals, as in 'Cohabitation: Supplementary Benefit and National Insurance Appeal Tribunals', *Welfare Law Report*, CPAG, May 1972.

7 Both research studies such as those of M. Herman, *Administrative Justice and Supplementary Benefits*, Bell, 1972, and the experience of lawyers as reported by CPAG's *Law Reports* and the LAG *Bulletin* contribute to this pressure.

8 *Journal* of the National Federation of Claimant Unions, no. 1, August 1970.

9 Such as *Outline Guide One: Social Security Supplementary Benefits*, CUWU, Barnsley, January 1971 or *Outline Guide: Strikers*, CUWU, Barnsley, January 1972.

10 *Support the Birmingham Claimant Union Campaign for a New Welfare State* (pamphlet), BCU, 1970.

11 *National Federation Organizational Bulletin*, August 1970.

12 The anti-claimant attitude or indifference of the trade union tribunal member has been widely reported: NFCU *Journal*, no. 1; Herman, op. cit; H. Rose, *Social Work Today*, 4, 1973, 409–14.

13 *The Dole Queue*, Temple-Smith 1972, especially the last chapter advocating alternative social workers.

14 'Daddy Knows Best', *Twentieth Century*, winter 1959.

15 *Which Way for Social Work?*, Fabian Tract 393, 1969.

16 In fact a position modified by Birmingham, who were to point out that the Claimant Union supported members on the basis that their claims were genuine, not fraudulent.

17 At Fine Tubes the length of the strike was such that the strikers formed their own claimant union. At the beginning of the 1972 strike a special issue of the *Miner* gave guidance as to getting SB for strikers' families. The

CU's contribution was to point out how the single striker could also secure benefit.

18 The impact of skilled men entering the unemployed movement in the interwar years was also noted, not without ambivalence; see W. Hannington, *Never on Our Knees*, Lawrence & Wishart, 1967.

19 An internal paper circulated by one of the Marxist groups urging concentration on unemployed workers was found by women at the Bristol conference (1972) precipitating sharp conflict: 'Our work in a CU should be to orientate the CU away from the unsupported mother, sick, old, etc., towards unemployed workers'.

20 The first claimants' newspaper (duplicated) was the *United Claimant News*, January 1969–December 1970 (ten issues). Birmingham in parallel with this developed the *Organization Bulletin* first produced by Birmingham, then by Birmingham for the Federation, November 1969 to July 1970.

21 *Supplementary Benefit and Industrial Disputes*, BCU, November 1969; 'On Strike', information sheet, BCU, January 1971; *Claimants' Handbook for Strikers*, Newtown, Birmingham CU, 1971.

22 *Journal* of the NFCU, no. 1, August 1970; *Journal* of the NFCU, no. 2, West London CU, December 1970; *Journal* of the NFCU, no. 3, East London CU, March 1973.

23 This issue of the journal was originally entrusted to Camden in September 1971, and contained the Unions' reply to the Fisher Committee of Enquiry into allegations of fraud and abuse of supplementary benefits. A report which when it was made refuted the possibility of widespread abuse, only to be met by Sir Keith Joseph expanding the numbers of special investigators.

24 The Cohabitation Campaign specifically planned to work with the women's lib workshops, the other allies were self-nominating. Report from the first meeting of the Cohabitation Campaign Working Party, York Conference, NFLU, 1972.

25 Reply by Sir Keith Joseph to a parliamentary question reported in *The Times*, 3 May 1972.

26 The deputation of Friday 3 December 1971 to the DHSS contained representatives from Unions from all over London, both federated and unfederated.

27 'AC', 'Bourgeois and proletarian decision-making process', *Marxist-Leninist Quarterly*, no. 4, spring 1973.

28 It is a pity that no article in the *Socialist Register*, or elsewhere, has discussed the important contribution of cartoons and street theatre to political education over recent years.

29 *Protest and the Urban Guerrilla*, Cassell, 1973.

30 The failure of most Marxist groups, particularly orthodox Communist and Trotskyite, to find an adequate theoretical perspective for movements based on the community is very marked.

31 M. Dalla Costa, 'The Power of 1', *Women and the Subversion of the Community*, Falling Wall Press, 1972.

32 *Tories Attack the Unemployed: the Social Security Swindle*, Socialist Labour League, Pocket Library, no. 3, 1972.

33 'The Tyranny of Structurelessness', *Second Wave*, 2(1), 1973.

34 The weakness of the highly decentralized structure linked chiefly through the network was demonstrated by the movement's total incapacity to respond as a movement to Stormont's attack on all social security claimants in the autumn of 1972. In order to break the rent strike, Stormont ordered that all social security benefits of debtors were to be withheld. Despite the fact that many of the key activists, members of the network, were also active on the Irish question, the Claimant Unions could not be mobilized into any significant action of solidarity. (On this issue without doubt CPAG made a much greater contribution.)

V. 3 Compulsory psychiatry

Paul Harrison

Eric Irwin has been in seventeen different mental hospitals over the last twenty years. He began to think critically about the mental health system in 1966 when he went into a hospital as a voluntary patient suffering from the acute anxiety that has been his recurrent problem. He found the hospital surroundings were making him worse and wanted to leave. He says he was then put on Section 30 of the Mental Health Act, 1959 (which allows a voluntary patient to be made a compulsory one), sat on by several nurses, and forcibly injected. After three days, while still heavily sedated, he was examined by two doctors who put him on 'Section 26—twenty-eight days' detention for treatment. For the next four weeks he was kept in a darkened room with three peepholes in the door, and released at the end of the period. He maintained he made no threats or violence that could have accounted for the treatment.

Irwin was one of the founder members, in early 1973, of the Mental Patients' Union, one of the most interesting groups in the latest wave of the anti-psychiatry movement. But where the first wave in Britain, like R. D. Laing and David Cooper, left the National Health Service altogether to set up their own alternative therapeutic communities, the newer groups feel that the abuses inside the NHS are too serious to be ignored. Their attacks centre on the Mental Health Act, 1959, still regarded by most people as a liberal piece of legislation. Concern about abuses in mental hospitals has focused almost entirely on the occasional cases of brutality by nurses against patients, and about the problems of treating and releasing mentally abnormal offenders. Yet if the radical groups are right, the Act's provisions about compulsory admission, and the practice of compulsory treatment, will also have to come under close scrutiny.

The Mental Health Act, 1959, allows compulsory admission for three days on the application of a social

worker or relative (or if the patient is brought in by a police officer) with the medical recommendation of only one psychiatrist; for twenty-eight days with two concurring medical recommendations; and, with the additional approval of the hospital managers—usually given automatically—for further periods of a year. The patient can, after twenty-eight days, appeal to a Mental Health Review Tribunal. But there were only 563 such appeals in England in 1973, and only 94 resulted in discharge. Though the law does not say so specifically, compulsory patients are not considered to have the right to refuse treatment, nor can they sue NHS staff in civil or criminal proceedings for anything done under the act, unless it was done 'in bad faith or without reasonable care'—i.e., out of malice or negligence.

The profession's usual pride in the low percentage of compulsory admissions seems misplaced. Although they have declined proportionally—from 20 per cent of all admissions in 1962 to 17 per cent in 1970, they have risen in absolute numbers from 31,874 to 32,761 over the same period. In 1958, under the old legislation, only 15 per cent were under some form of compulsory detention.

The movement to organise mental patients themselves is well developed in North America. But the most thoroughgoing experiment along these lines was the Socialist Patients' Collective in West Germany, where patients acted as their own therapists. All mental illness was held to stem from the repression and frustration of capitalist society. 'Therapy' consisted of helping people to see the social causes of their illness and turning the anger, which they had directed inward, into protest and revolutionary action. However, the SPC was thrown out of its premises at Heidelberg University; eleven members were jailed, accused of connections with the violently revolutionary Baader–Meinhof group.

The British Mental Patients' Union is conservative by comparison. But many of its members blame mental

Source: *New Society*, 16 May 1974, pp. 377–9.

hospitals and psychiatrists, if not for creating, then at least for considerably aggravating, their problems in life. For some of them, organised action for reform has been a kind of self-therapy. The founding group came together during the patients' demonstrations against the proposed closure (later revoked) of the Paddington Day Hospital in 1972. Their original pamphlet on the need for a patients' union offered a class analysis of the social origins of mental illness, very much like the SPC's. For the working class, mental illness was an escape route from poverty and frustration. For the middle class, it stemmed from an attempt to maintain distance from the working class (those who offend against middle-class values become 'deviant'). For both men and women it could come from the squeeze between economic and family roles. Finally, the pamphlet described psychiatry as 'one of the tools that capitalism uses to ensure that frustration and anger against the oppressive system is internalised' —that is, psychiatry cons the patient into believing that there is something wrong with *him*, not with the society.

The MPU dissolved itself as a centralised body at its general meeting last month. Now there are fourteen separate mental patients' unions scattered around the country, with about 1,000 members. The ultimate aim is to have branches in all the largest mental hospitals negotiating with 'management' on conditions, treatment and pay; but there are problems setting up branches. In one hospital, the organiser was allegedly threatened with compulsory detention, then discharged prematurely. The most capable patients rarely stay long. Branches may be disrupted or discredited by difficult patients.

The MPU has drawn up its own charter of demands, including the abolition of irreversible treatments; the right to be told what treatment is being given, and what the long-term effects are; the abolition of isolation treatment in locked side-rooms; the abolition of compulsory work, and the introduction of trade-union rates of pay for work done inside hospitals; and the right of the MPU to inspect all parts of hospitals including the 'back wards'. The MPU also calls for the abolition of compulsory hospitalisation.

Most of these demands are based on the individual experiences of MPU members. Although they are difficult to substantiate or refute, some of their stories show there is cause for concern.

In 1956, Eric Irwin says he narrowly escaped a leucotomy. At the time he was a voluntary patient, and he claims a doctor told him: 'I wish you were psychotic so I could do it.' Irwin is convinced that under the 'liberal' 1959 Act, he would have been 'put on a Section' and operated on. In 1960, he says, another psychiatrist told him he was a psychopath, and that psychopathy was inborn and incurable. 'I was shattered by that. But when I came out I looked it up in every textbook I could find, and found it meant so many different things that anyone could be one.' Irwin also suffers from recurrent enuresis, which some doctors

have attributed to the electro-convulsive therapy he received.

Derek Dallimore was committed on a court order. The 1959 Act allows courts to order offenders to be treated, even without trying them for the offence they are there for. He says that, while a voluntary patient, he was threatened with being 'put on a Section' if he tried to discharge himself. He was on Modecate, a drug given once monthly. 'For the first three or four days it knocks all the energy out of you, and you become a zombie. Then you're so much on edge you can't stay still. It's like having a toothache inside your bones, that you can't get at.' He is cynical about psychiatrists' ability to help: 'If you go to them saying there's something wrong with you, they'll tell you you're quite sane, but if you say you're normal, they'll do everything they can to find something wrong with you.'

Brigid O'Sullivan actually likes it in the hospital she has been in voluntarily, diagnosed as schizophrenic. 'You meet some nice and interesting people' she says. 'But the doctor only sees you every six months. Otherwise you're completely left on your own to lead your own subnormal life by yourself. The nurses take notes on you all the time, and treat you like an object.' She does occupational therapy for about thirty hours a week—making things like Christmas crackers—for £2.25. 'You don't have to work, but if you don't you only get 50p a week pocket money.'

All the patients I spoke to—some in their hospital, some at the Mental Patients' Union—were extremely sceptical about the usefulness of their treatment. On ECT: 'It's hit and miss if you feel better or worse'; 'I can't remember my childhood any more.' On drugs: 'Whatever else they do to you, they don't do any good'; 'They can't do anything for me so they give me drugs to keep me quiet.' All claimed to have seen or undergone forcible injections. Most of them know a great deal about drugs and discuss them like connoisseurs of wine. They have their own vocabulary, like prisoners: 'shrinks' are psychiatrists, 'bins' are mental hospitals, and so on.

The longest established organised group in the fight against the 1959 Act, other than the National Council for Civil Liberties, are the Scientologists. As the head of Scientology in Britain, David Gaiman, told me, the mutual critique of psychiatrists and Scientologists has been a self-reinforcing process. In the sixties, Scientologists made an increasingly radical critique of the mental health system in this country, out of a policy of hitting back at psychiatrists' criticisms of Scientology. The Scientologists blame the mental health establishment for their 'persecution' under the measures brought in by Kenneth Robinson while Minister of Health. Though the standard of proof is not always very high, the Scientologists have often been the first to make allegations which lead to official inquiries— for example, with South Ockenden. They were the first to draw up, in 1970, a declaration of human rights for mental patients, including the right to a jury trial before compulsory hospitalisation; the right to refuse treatment, particularly electric shock, brain surgery, aversion therapy, and drugs producing unwanted side-effects; the right to make official complaints without reprisal; the right to see hospital records and challenge any false information in them; and the right to sue for unlawful commitment, false reports or damaging treatment.

The Scientologists now do a cavalcade, every six months, round all the main mental hospitals in Britain, asking hospital administrators which of the rights are practised in their hospital. In 1969 they set up the Citizens' Commission for Human Rights to carry on their mental health work, collecting evidence of abuses under the 1959 Act, and taking up individual cases. The commission has secured the release of two long-term patients from Carstairs, the Scottish Broadmoor, and is preparing a full report on psychiatric abuses which it hopes to publish during [1975].

The Citizens' Commission on Human Rights is, theoretically, an independent body. Though it is sponsored by the Church of Scientology and has a Scientologist chairman, Tom Minchin, it has some non-Scientologist members. It is widely regarded as a 'front' organisation. But, whatever their underlying motives, the Scientologists do not overtly use their criticisms of psychiatry for direct propaganda. David Gaiman points out:

There is no other field where the consumer has no status at all. Psychiatry is largely a matter of value judgments, with personal opinions passed off as diagnosis. It's quite unlike any other profession, like architecture, where you have to show a level of competence or your building will fall down. There is no public judgment of the effectiveness of psychiatry. Even that wouldn't be so bad without the element of coercion.
But you can't vote with your feet or your pocket if [hospital] psychiatry does you no good.

The more recent International Commission for Human Rights—no relation—approaches the 1959 Act more from a legal and ethical than from a medical viewpoint. It was set up in Britain in 1972. The board includes eminent academics and practising psychiatrists. The commission takes up individual cases such as that of D. T. who alleged that his psychiatrist had made homosexual approaches to him. Other specialists to whom he was then referred allegedly made no attempt to check his story but took his complaints as symptoms of paranoid schizophrenia and had him compulsorily admitted. The commission's secretary, David Webster, says, 'It would seem that a person who tells an inadmissible story . . . which seems to damage the reputation of professional colleagues, is a person who is "mentally disordered".'[. . .]

Webster has reached some provisional conclusions about the 1959 Act in the course of his investigations. 'The Act contains no definition of mental illness. Basically it's not a medical act, but a social one aimed at ridding people of individuals who are a bit of a nuisance. Patients' knowledge of their rights is practically non-existent.' The commission has plans to bring a private action for assault against hospital staff for forcible injection of a voluntary patient. Like the Scientologists, Webster's commission favours some sort of lay trial, with advocates defending the patient against an application for his compulsory admission.

Even the normally staid National Association of Mental Health now shows signs of being affected by the more radical thinking. In July [1973] it produced a fairly mild document on patients' rights, demonstrating the regional variation in the use of compulsory admission (from 143 per 1,000 to 215 per 1,000 admissions, and up to 330 per 1,000 in some hospitals), and raising doubts as to whether all such admissions were necessary. However, it simply recommended hospitals and social workers to make sure that compulsory admissions were limited to the 'strictly necessary'. On the question of compulsory treatment, it pointed out that over-riding the patient's will might in itself prevent effective treatment, and recommended that a second independent psychiatric opinion should be required whenever patients objected to serious or controversial treatment.

Since Tony Smythe took over the directorship in January [1974] the NAMH is likely to be more critical. Smythe now believes that a full-scale revaluation and revision of the Mental Health Act, 1959, is necessary. His previous experience of Mental Health Review Tribunals, as secretary of the National Council for Civil Liberties, has taught him that representation doubles the chances of a patient being discharged. He is also convinced that compulsory admission procedures and the renewal of detention orders often amount to rubber-stamping. 'Mind' is, therefore, collecting evidence of potential abuses for a report on the working of the Act. Smythe now believes that one answer may lie in extending the work of the Mental Health Review Tribunals. These might be asked to adjudicate where patients refused treatment, to provide a more thorough review of detention orders than hospital management committees do at present, and possibly to hear appeals against compulsory admission.

The Butler committee, now sitting, may recommend some changes in the 1959 Act as it relates to the mentally abnormal offender and arrangements for his release. But there is no official review of the rest of the Act, and no central monitoring of the reasons for compulsory detention. There is little dissatisfaction among psychiatrists about the Act.

Consultant psychiatrists like Peter Noble, at the Maudsley Hospital, concede that abuses such as those experienced by the patients I spoke to, could well occur:

But only 1 per cent of them are due to infringements of human rights. The other 99 per cent are due to bad psychiatry and poor resources. The problem is not that we treat people against their will—in a sense they have a right to treatment even when they're too insane to want it—but that we don't treat them enough. Far from locking people up unnecessarily, we're turning out hordes of people in need of help with no proper follow-up.

But he concedes that 'effective treatment requires time, training and commitment—and those requirements are not commonly met in the present state of affairs.' He blames the poor quality of junior staff—mostly foreign graduates, some of them with poor English, using psychiatric work simply as a job while they get their qualifications to do physical medicine. At consultant level, many of the posts outside the south east are unfilled. And there are difficulties over recruiting nurses, especially at current rates of pay.

Certainly, many of the abuses complained of could stem from insensitive treatment. Consultants with an estimated average of one hour per year to spend on each patient are unlikely to prescribe for unwanted side-effects without a distressing delay, nor indeed to assess patients soon enough to ensure their prompt discharge. But the rights issue is also crucial. For without the largely unsupervised powers of compulsory treatment and admission, many of the abuses could not occur.

Only a very large-scale investigation could reveal the extent of abuses, and its conclusions would have to be tentative because of the absence of any objective records other than those of the contending parties. Nevertheless, I am convinced that compulsory powers of commitment are widely used where there is no danger to society or even to the patient himself, other than simply nuisance. And voluntary status is often illusory. The extent to which treatment is 'voluntary' is also in doubt. Besides being threatened with compulsory detention, patients can also face transfer to a locked ward or, most commonly, premature discharge. Worst of all, his complaints may be dismissed as 'symptoms' of his illness. All the standard texts cite 'delusions' of persecution as signs of paranoid schizophrenia.

I believe this dismissal is the principal reason why abuses can occur, and why they often build up unnoticed until some dramatic event makes a full-scale inquiry necessary. It is the combination of many factors: poor resources in hospital and community; a psychiatric approach to diagnosis and treatment based on the view that the patient hardly ever knows best; and a law that contains no effective checks for the 'consumer'. Given these conditions, the mental patient may emerge from mental hospital *less* able to cope with his personal problems than before—having acquired an extra set of difficulties from the very process designed to cure him.

V. 4 Magistrates' courts: a game theoretic analysis

Pat Carlen

Probation officer: 'There are so many vested interests in the court—police, probation-officers, magistrates, solicitors, social workers. It's a matter of them all fighting over one carcass.'

Both in popular discourse and in learned treatises, court appearances, hearings and trials are repeatedly referred to as 'games' or battles'. Lyman and Scott categorized social games into four types: relationship games, face games, exploitation games, and information games.[1] The first and last types have been those used most often to depict legal battles. [. . .]

[. . .] The substantive findings of [research into such games] concerning the relationship between the observed and accounted for social interaction of court personnel, the interlocking logics of such strategic interactions, and the texture and context of knowledge thereby informing judicial decisions, suggest that the use of a game framework can be explicitly utilized to demonstrate the nature of these relationships within specified and temporal boundaries. The bulk of this [article], therefore, will be directed at a game theoretic analysis of inter-professional communication in a magistrates' court, though I will put forward three arguments concerning the social meanings of magistrates justice which might suggest that, *for the defendant*, the law game is no game at all. These three arguments are:

1. that the notion of due process is a euphemistic gloss on the articulated play which occurs between representatives of adjacent legal teams;
2. that, in relation to 'due process', the defendant stands as a dummy player absorbing both the gains and losses of all contestants; and
3. that the resort to legal compromise in order to safeguard courtroom efficiency when organizational interests are in conflict, creates a situation where defendants are both victims and informed critics of an organizational game whose constitutive elements are only *ex post facto* and contingently given legal staus. [. . .]

Source: *Sociological Review*, 23 (2), May 1975, pp. 347, 348, 349, 350–1, 352–4, 355, 358–64, 368–76.

Strategies for maintaining credibility

[. . .] In very complex organizations where people operating under opposed professional hierarchies interact both formally and informally, the hierarchies of credibility are maintained by the individuals developing situated moralities which allow them to 'do their best' within the organization concerned. The tension between the demands of the absolute morality of their professional ethic and the situated morality which is shaped by their bounded professional activities, is reduced by the conviction of court and legal personnel that 'this is what any reasonable man would do in this situation'. Aware, however, that their formal rule violations are often visible to other participants; aware, too, that other team members have information essential to furthering their own goals, all participants make alliances with each other, trying to appear as if they are operating under the auspices of their professional ethic, whilst simultaneously managing inter-professional alliances whose very existence demonstrates that they are doing no such thing.

Whenever an informal alliance is made between representatives of two teams, at least a double gamble is involved. First, the other teams may perceive the informal alliance to be contrary to their interests and may invoke formal rules to sanction it; in this event parties to the alliance will have queered rather than cleared their pitch. Second, one party to the alliance may, upon receiving further information, himself perceive the alliance to be queering rather than clearing his pitch and thereupon may invoke rules in order to sanction the other party to it. This formal rule-invocation by a former informal ally is often referred to in courts as another instance of the 'stab in the back'. Because of the fear of the 'stab in the back', much of the information concerning informal alliances was given me by way of innuendo.

Pat Carlen: 'How much interaction is there between solicitors and police?'

Court Inspector(A): 'Quite a lot. The solicitor is put in the picture before the case starts if he is helpful. If he asks for anything—like a remand—the police are helpful, that is, if he is a good solicitor. If one tries to be funny, thinks he knows more than he does—then—'(shrugs shoulders)

Court Inspector (B): 'Some counsel, most of them, are honourable men. But others—you say something to them off the record and they bring it out in court. You learn not to make any more off the record remarks to them.'

Yet even when, for situational reasons, the police are prepared to adjust the formal rules so that an 'honourable' solicitor might be accommodated, they cannot afford to 'queer their pitch' and lose credibility with the magistrates.

Where police and solicitors are mutually perceived as 'honourable men' there is a two-way flow of certain items of information. Police can acquiesce in a solicitor's requests concerning remands and the timing of the case, they can facilitate his access to his client in the cells, and they can put business in his way. Solicitors can aid court administration by not obstructing the smooth flow of cases through the court and by informally (i.e. without having received instructions from a client but at the request of a policeman or magistrate) straightening out what, owing to either a defendant's lack of courtroom competence or his deliberate strategy, threatens to be a 'messy case'.

The unease associated with *actual* police/solicitor alliances is less acute than is that associated with *potential* police/probation-officer alliances. Any alliance with the police is threatening to a probation-officer's self-definition. Probation-officers, unlike solicitors, are less willing to *compromise with* the police and more aware of the dangers of being *compromised by* them. Most importantly they fear that if people in the neighbourhood suspect that police/probation-officer alliances occur, then probation-officers will queer their pitch with present and future clients.

How, then, do these potentially divisive factors infuse police/probation-officer interactions in court? At Metropolitan Court[2] all probation-officers had easy access to the cells and court papers but they were also aware of their need for diplomacy in their dealings with the police. Ultimately their mandate to maintain security in the court gives the police the edge when (in the event of the breakdown of informal negotiations) either side attempts to invoke formal rules.

Pat Carlen: 'Can you apply to the magistrate for permission to go to the cells?'

Mr M. (Probation-officer): 'Yes. He can give us *permission*, but the gaoler can always say he's concerned with security and hasn't time to talk. Eventually he *will* let us in, but he'll keep us waiting, and that, to me, sums up our position in the court.'

Despite the disclaimers of probation-officers concerning their police-imputed role of 'defence-counsellors', most of them feel more at ease with solicitors than they do with the police. *Vis-à-vis* solicitors, probation-officers feel in a position of power. Probation-officers 'have the magistrate's ear', know that 'we can always support *our* recommendations outside the court', and that, just as the probation-officer is dependent upon the policeman to give him information 'by courtesy', so is the solicitor dependent upon the probation-officer. If the probation-officer's recommendation is not the one that is considered the least of all possible penal evils known to the defendant, then the solicitor needs to ascertain what evidence or logic is going to be used to support the recommendation in time to prepare his argument against it. Solicitors are entitled to see the Social Enquiry Report at the court stage and most probation-officers will tell *some* solicitors ('Ones I trust!' 'Ones with a social conscience') what the recommendation is going to be, even *before* the report is presented to the court. Solicitors find Social Enquiry Reports very useful and will always encourage a client to have one done. For the probation-officer, however, there is still some unease associated with contact with solicitors.

All the probation-officers expressed fears that the solicitors would keep Social Enquiry Reports in order to use them again if a client should re-appear in court months, or maybe years, later, when the information would be out of date. These particular fears of probation-officers were recognized by solicitors and they were not completely groundless.

Solicitor: 'They are very jealous of their reports. They are scared that if the reports get into your hands you will keep them. And, of course, they would be useful if the case comes up again. But I don't want to fight the probation-officers or the police. If my client's on bail, and the prosecution want a remand, I'm not going to create a tension, and sometimes a fight, by being awkward about *that*.'

This diplomacy, however, is viewed with suspicion by probation-officers and leads to a second area of unease between them and solicitors; namely, the feeling on the part of the probation-officers that the solicitor puts his profits, his relations with court officials and his court performance as 'a solicitor who gets people off' *before* the best interests of the clients as they have been defined by the probation-officer. A further cause of uneasy irritation is the conviction held by probation-officers that many solicitors see Social Enquiry Reports as scripting pleas of mitigation. It was widely claimed that some barristers do *no* work in advance and merely 'stand up in court, mumble our Social Enquiry Reports and collect ten quid.'

At Metropolitan Court, however, solicitor/probation-officer relations are not very tense. Probation-officers feel strongly enough about the dearth of legal representation in magistrate's courts to break the formal rule forbidding them to recommend a solicitor to a defendant.

> *Mrs W.* (*Probation-officer*): 'Um . . . y'know, if clients are wanting solicitors, then we've got one or two tame solicitors that we recommend that they go along and see—which I'm not sure that we're supposed to do—but we give them a list and then, uh, sort of say, "Well, look, uh, I suggest that if you get in touch with this one, or this one".'

The bargains remain implicit, but probation-officers make it clear that they recommend only 'responsible' solicitors to their clients. The 'responsible' solicitor does *not* try to perform in court in order to further his client's interest as defined by his client. The 'responsible' solicitor 'takes his instructions' from the probation-officer. Mrs N., a probation-officer, spelt this out in full:

> 'Some firms, I think, are very responsible, and use the information I'm giving them correctly. And will tend to work with me rather than against me. Like, if I say, "I want to keep him in a couple of weeks"—I'm not recommending prison but I want to see if I can get him a hostel place— they will go along with me to persuade the guy that this is a good idea, rather than doing what may be in the guy's short-term interest.'

Thus, despite their awareness of areas of unease between them, alliances, which are to their mutual advantage, are made between probation-officers and solicitors. One probation-officer had a reservation about such alliances which was not related to probation-officer/solicitor relationships: 'One problem is, that the client can be left out a bit.'

Two teams of professionals have low credibility in the courts: store-detectives and social workers. In each case their credibility is low because all other participants perceive them to be inept in the management of formal and informal rule usage; they are not competent in the rules of the game. [. . .]

The potential allies of social workers are probation-officers. Indeed most probation-officers made a distinction between social workers and policemen when they were discussing *which* 'confidential' information they would pass on to '*whom*', saying that they would pass on information to social workers because 'they are in the same caring profession.' Yet whenever I asked probation-officers if they and social workers had access to each other's files, there was a pause followed by a remark like, 'We swap information, we don't actually see the files, usually.' When I further asked what kind of informal contact there was with social workers, regret was usually expressed that there 'is not so much as there should be', but that 'Where the areas *do* overlap there's usually conflict.'

The ambivalent nature of the probation-officers' relationships to the court results in a certain antagonism in their relationships with social workers just as it does in their relationships with policemen and solicitors. This is not because they fear the stab in the back (i.e. they are not afraid of social workers using items of information to discredit the probation-service) but because they feel that social workers' general lack of 'know-how' about the workings of the court can result in them queering the pitch for the client.

Again and again when talking about the presentation of Social Enquiry Reports probation-officers referred to social workers' reports in order to demonstrate how *not* to write a report.

> *Miss S.* (*Probation-officer*): 'The magistrate gets really annoyed when social workers are what he calls "chummy". They write reports and refer to "little Johnny this . . ." and "little Johnny that", not "Smith this and Smith that", and the magistrates can't stand it. I sometimes say to a social worker, "When you do the report, do refer to the person by his surname otherwise the magistrate won't like it," but they can't get into the way.'

Then the social workers' court performance leaves much to be desired:

> 'At the moment there's still a prejudice towards social workers. Yeh . . . I think it's difficult for social workers because they've not been trained in court procedure—this is not included in their training—so that they really don't know anything about the court procedure when they come in. This then robs the magistrate of having any confidence in them, 'coz they sort of see them dithering about in the court situation.'

Other probation-officers attributed the social workers' lack of courtroom competence to their self-definition: 'They like to see themselves as different— they won't recognise that basically they're social controllers too, agents of social control, just as much as we are.' Certainly the social workers to whom I spoke said that they 'hate courts', 'never know what's going on in court' and 'are *not* after all, probation-officers'. For many magistrates, however, the only reliable social worker is the one whose major source of authority is the court, that is, the probation-officer.

Performances in court

Although all teams in court need to make alliances with each other in order either to maximize their gains *or* to minimize their losses, the paramount need of all of them is to maintain credibility with the magistrate. One performance lacking in credibility may mean that future performances will be played with a handicap. Therefore all items of information that are presented to the magistrate as either evidence, facts, diagnoses or expertise have to be plausible. Police, solicitors and probation-officers give various accounts as to what magistrates find 'plausible', but, in each case, plausibility is situationally defined as meeting the demands of a justice situationally defined by particular magistrates.

Pat Carlen: 'Do you have discretion to drop cases? I noticed you dropped the charge of drunkenness against the seventy-five-year-old woman.'
Court Inspector: (Laughs) 'Yes. I dropped that. I don't know about its *legality*. You get to know what the magistrate wants. There was this "Left Turn" and it was made "No Left Turn". It was ridiculous. Any stranger just didn't know where to go. One week we had about seventy in for turning left. Well, the magistrate, he knew that turning and he didn't agree with it either. It got to the stage where he was fining them half-a-crown, then a shilling. I got on the phone to the station, I said "For God's sake send no more up. He won't stand for it".'

Likewise, the solicitor who does most of the defending in Metropolitan Court feels that he can do much better for defendants than can a solicitor unused to the vagaries of these particular magistrates.

Solicitor: 'I know exactly what the magistrate is looking for and a lot depends on presentations. This particular magistrate, he forces me to be a judge, because he takes it as an insult if I put a story to him which he sees as a whole made-up load of hotch-potch. So I have to question the client over here and I can lose the clients' sympathy because they think I don't believe them.'

At Metropolitan Court thirteen of the thirty probation-officers said that different types of Social Enquiry Reports were presented to different magistrates, although they each stressed that this practical differentiation was against Home Office ruling.

Mrs B. (*Probation-officer*): 'You *must* think who you're writing the report for. It's easier when you're writing for one of your own magistrates. You know what the magistrate wants you to put in and you *have* to think of that if you want to do the best for your client and yourself.'

Knowledge of the magistrate was said to affect, amongst other things, the length of the report, the kind of language used, the manner of referring to the client, whether or not the early history of the defendant was given (at Metropolitan Court one magistrate wanted such information to be included, the other did not), the types of argument (psychological, sociological, social-common-sensical) presented, and whether or not a *firm* recommendation was made at the end of the report. The six probation-officers who said that they would not necessarily include in the report some item of information just because the client wanted it put in, gave as their reason that they would lose credit with the magistrate if they began to write 'rubbish' in their reports. [. . .]

Manoeuvres, coaching and out-of-court play

In a *manoeuvre*, one player acts in such a way that either he forces another player to give a bad performance and thereby discredits him (called '*putting on the spot*'), or he puts forward an argument that, if rejected, would detract from another's performance (called '*cornering*').

A Court Inspector told me how a counsel had put him 'on the spot':

'Some times in court, you have a sleep. Once a counsel was addressing the magistrate, and she finished up, "Perhaps the Court Inspector would like to answer me?" I was writing a letter at the time, so I said, "I'd like a little time to consider it." I rush out and said, "What the hell is this all about?" After that I realized I should take more notice.'

Manoeuvres of the second kind are the essence of the counsel's job.

Solicitor: 'I often make a suggestion and try to get the magistrate into a corner where he can only get out by appearing to go over to the penalty-punishment side.'

Manoeuvres by one player will not succeed if those he is temporarily allied with have been insufficiently *coached* for their parts. Defendants, for instance, are seen by other players as being notoriously inept in their performances. The nervousness which makes many defendants 'deaf' (the 'court deafness' referred to by many probation-officers) can also make many of them laugh and giggle. These latter antics are not conducive to maximizing the symbolic sanctity of the law. Rather they come perilously close to mirroring its situationally absurd elements. Several defendants prime each other outside the court, 'For God's sake, don't get in there and start laughing like you did last time', and every probation-officer is familiar with the giggly defendant:

'Like there's one chap I have, he just can't stop laughing in court. Well, of course, this is like a red rag to a bull. It's partly nerves, and he's irresponsible anyway. So I told him—"Look for goodness sake, Jack, don't laugh. Pinch yourself —look up at the ceiling—anything—because they don't understand that you can't help it, and to them it seems . . ." I even told him to apologise in advance—because at one court he really came a cropper—he was given quite a stiff sentence, and his attitude in court was mentioned.'

In the courts of the lay magistrates coaching can even take place in the court whilst the magistrates are in the retiring room considering their verdict or sentence. At Inner London Court a probation-officer rushed across to a young lad as soon as the magistrates had left the court.

Probation-officer: 'You must sound as if you mean

it when he asks you if you want probation.'
Defendant: 'I *did* mean it.'
Probation-officer: 'But you've got to sound as if you do.'

Most of the coaching, however, has to be done before the performance. Solicitors cannot afford *not* to coach defendants.

Solicitor: 'I do something—and really this shouldn't be done—I prepare them for cross-questioning. You need a trained defendant like you need a trained policeman. I say "If they say to you 'did you take it?', the answer is 'Yes' or 'No' not 'I had twenty pounds in my purse, why should I take it?'." '

Court policemen feel contempt for their colleagues who underestimate the importance of the performance.

Court Inspector, Metropolitan Court: 'We who work in the courts see things a bit differently. I'm sometimes a bit pleased when they throw something out. A young policeman comes out of court and says, "What's wrong with your bloody magistrate? Threw my case out." And I say, "You come to court, you prepare your case properly".'

And where individual players let down the side they have to be coached so as not to repeat their mistakes:

Magistrate, Metropolitan Court: 'One probation-officer made reference to capitalism and Marxism —you know, capitalist society, that sort of thing, you know. And I had to say, "This won't do." I don't care about the politics of a probation-officer, but the defendant has to see that report and that kind of thing isn't appropriate to a relationship of—uh—treatment.'

Some players are not content with manoeuvres and pre-performance coaching. They resort to *fouls*. A foul is such a blatant breaking of formal rules that, when behaviour constituting such an infraction is seen, it is always defined as such by all participants. The problem for the courts, however, is that acknow-ledgment of a foul having been committed by one of the professionals is likely to detract from the display of absolutism upon which the law-game depends. Therefore, there is a tendency for fouls to be dealt with out of court. The players most commonly accused of committing fouls are the police. The accuser is usually the defendant, and magistrates have routine strategies for remedying such threats to inter-term morale. When, however, the magistrate himself perceives a foul he is in a dilemma.

Magistrate: 'When I was once certain that an officer had come in and perjured himself I got on the blower to his superior officer and gave him the word. But that's me—not the court; I can only do it because I know them—the usual thing.

But I should think it's the wrong way, and would not be approved of by those above me. The other time it happened, an officer was giving antecedents of a defendant and I became suspicious and asked if the defendant had any previous convictions, and he said "No". And I remanded the case— which again was something I shouldn't have done —because I wanted to check myself on his previous convictions. I was suspicious the officer had taken a backhander not to mention them. So I got on the blower again, and in this case the officer had even presented a blank photocopy from CRO—and his superior thought it might have happened before!'

The officer was penalized and the magistrate felt that his bypassing of the formal rules was justified by his knowledge that the *purpose* of formal rules (i.e. the safeguarding of justice) had been achieved. So, in the case of penalties for fouls committed by the *professionals* in the law-game it is considered best that justice be done *without* being seen to be done. As is demonstrated in the last section of this paper, the defendant, as dummy player, is kept sufficiently in the dark as to the exact nature of the procedural rules that usually he cannot act to prove whether formal justice has been done or not.

Making, breaking and interpreting the rules

In the multi-team game marked by inter-term alliances and manouevres, it is very difficult for any individual player to know the strategic rules of the game except *ex post facto*. The mark of the *professional* in court is that he should know the informal rules; the mark of the *competent* professional in court is that he should know the informal rules both explicit and implicit. The *strategic* rules, however, are those embedded in interpretive actions which combine knowledge of written rules with situational rules (such interpretive actions often popularly called rules-of-thumb). Hence they are difficult to isolate and identify. It can be demonstrated, however, that there are at least two routine court activities which mould rule-usage; they are described here as *playing to rule* and *making the rule fit*.

Situational alliances prevent constant open conflict between the overtly opposed professional teams within the courts, yet sometimes one side can feel that the other side needs disciplining. At such times they can invoke those formal rules which are usually held in abeyance by all sides. The tacit knowledge among all players that strict adherence to the formal rules would slow down and probably stop play altogether, puts those who are prepared to put the game at risk in this way in a very strong position. That they also put them-selves at risk, in so far as there is always the strong likelihood that those so penalized will respond with the countermove of the stab in the back, accounts for the comparatively rare use of this tactic. It is, however, similar to the type of rule-usage noted several years ago by Gouldner,[3] and its efficacy has long been recognized by workers who 'work to rule' during industrial disputes. As demonstrated below, all players can arbitrarily invoke formal rules when they feel that a player's behaviour constitutes a threat to the very existence of the game as it is normally and situationally constituted. Thus the player who situationally invokes a formal rule in order to justify his infraction of an organizationally routinized rule is seen as 'trying to be funny'. On such occasions a member of one team threatens the credibility of another team without any perceived or understandable motive. An example of this was seen at Inner London Court, where the Chief Clerk often stressed to me that he did not *break* the rules but tried to interpret them in such a way as to benefit the defendant. The police, however, saw him as always playing the rule against them, and, worse, that in so doing he was merely 'trying to be funny'.

Two other types of situation were identified where the playing to rule tactic might be operationalized; first, when some participants felt that the game, as being played, was not conducive to their own team's interests (i.e. the 'game's not worth the candle' definition of the situation) and therefore *had* to be risked in order to reinforce or reconstitute it according to the old rules. Second, when individual team members felt threatened by internecine battles concerning the interpretation and usage of their own procedural rules (i.e. when the organizational meaning of their own team-membership was being renegotiated).

Magistrates and police are often in conflict as to what the law-game should be about. Magistrates who suspect that policemen are being over-strenuous in their surveillance of a particular section of the community can repeatedly find that defendants are either Not Guilty or that they have no case to answer. A magistrate at Metropolitan Court described a routine practice which he thought that the police had established *vis-à-vis* young West Indians.

Magistrate: 'The other magistrate and myself stopped the police from bringing in West Indians for loitering. Usually they'd pick them up about three in the morning, search them, find nothing and bring them in for loitering. We stopped that.'

Police can retaliate. Formal measures can be used by policemen when they feel that the magistrates are not supporting them in the courts for the performance of duty which is demanded by the public. A policeman told me how a magistrate had been sanctioned for attempting to change the policy of the court towards vagrants.

Police sergeant, Court B: 'It was funny here yesterday. The magistrates don't want to enforce the Vagrancy Act and the police do. So they brought in seventeen cases. The magistrate was fuming, you could see it.'

The police see themselves at the centre of information control in the courts. They decide the wording of the charge; they decide the order in which cases will be called; they alone can contact Criminal Records Office in order to check a person's previous convictions; they, as prosecutors, have first chance to present their information; they have first chance to 'coach' the defendant on how he should play it in court. At every stage of the proceedings they are aware of the strategic utility of differential rule-usage. This is the essence of their organizational power—that their competent use of all the rules can blight the otherwise formally competent performers of other participants.

So the law-game is played in and out of the court; manoeuvres, coaching and alliances all facilitate the speedy administration of justice. Only momentarily does the defendant in court see the full inter-team display, and even then he is often in ignorance of the nature of the other, subsidiary games diachronically incorporated into that game-supreme—although he usually knows that 'there is *something* going on'. Sometimes, however, all participants are confronted by a new formal rule of procedure. It had to be interpreted in a way which is perceived as 'common-sense' by all professionals attempting an adequate performance in that court. It has to be made to fit.

The activity of making the rule fit is an inter-team activity, usually involving magistrates, clerks and police. The substantive Criminal Law always has to be interpreted by the magistrate with the advice of his clerk and related to the facts of the case as suggested by the evidence. The procedural rules are usually expected to be less complicated. Where, however, new procedural rules do not cover all the exigencies of court administration as perceived by all parties to it, the rules' meaning has to be situationally negotiated. An example of this occurred at Metropolitan Court early in 1973 as soon as the 1972 Criminal Justice Act became operative. On 4 January the magistrate made the following address to a defendant:

Magistrate: 'I am going to use some new powers that Parliament has given me. I'm going to defer sentence for three months, then when you come back here there'll be no further action taken regarding this offence.'
Inspector (as defendant leaves court): 'What about bail, Sir?'
Magistrate: 'There's no provision for that.' (shrugs his shoulders)

When the court had risen, the magistrate came into the gaoler's office. The inspector had meanwhile been reading the Act.

Inspector: 'I quite agree with you, Sir, about bail. What do we do, though, if she doesn't come back?'
Magistrate: 'Well that's it, the Act makes no provision for that. Send out a warrant, I suppose.'
Inspector: 'What—just to bring her back and say

"Yes you've been a good girl"?' (all policemen laugh)
Magistrate: 'Does seem ridiculous doesn't it?'
Inspector: 'So it will just go down "No Order" will it?'
Magistrate: 'Yes—if she's not in trouble—just "No Order".'

On 8 January the other magistrate was sitting. The following address was made to a defendant:

Magistrate: 'I'm going to take a chance on you. I'll defer your sentence for three months—I'll see what you do then. I'll bail you in your own recognisance of twenty-five pounds.'

At the end of the court list the clerk remonstrated with the magistrate about bailing defendants whose sentences had been deferred. The officer who had been calling the cases had often expressed admiration for this magistrate for 'knowing his own mind'. Now he turned to me, saying gleefully,

Policeman: 'He's making his own laws now.'
Pat Carlen: 'Did he *bail* him?'
Policeman: 'Yes—he's not supposed to.'
Pat Carlen: 'What about if he doesn't turn up?'
Policeman: 'That's it. We can bring him *back*. But can we take his money? He's not supposed to have done that at all.'

In the gaoler's room the Court Inspector brought out the 1972 Act and read out the significant passage. The formal rule gave little indication as how to choose between conflicting situational interpretations.

Inspector (reading): '. . . Notwithstanding Section, blah, blah, blah—a magistrates' court shall not be obliged to remand an offender in whose case it defers the passing of sentence under this section. Depends how you interpret "obliged" doesn't it.'

The magistrate and clerk, however, reached interpretive agreement by bringing into play the principal of contextual determination of meaning. The CDM principle is always accounted for by challenging anyone who implies that situational interpretation should have been more overtly congruent with a formal rule. The challenge is usually incorporated in some phrase like 'Well, what would *you* have done in the circumstances?' 'What else could we have done?' 'There was no alternative.' On 16 January I asked the magistrate who had bailed the defendant if he thought that the wording of the Act was 'ambiguous'.

Magistrate: 'We've been bailing them. I knew perfectly well that I shouldn't and I had a difference of opinion with the Chief Clerk about it. But now he's come round to my way of thinking. He's agreed that there's little else we can do. It's always like this in the first two months of a new Act, until things settle down.'

After this date both magistrates bailed defendants whose sentences had been deferred. The police said

that 'although we shouldn't do it, it makes things easier', and the *written* rules on bailing in cases of deferred sentences were not referred to again. What seemed to be an adequate situational improvisation was to gain, in future cases, the authority of a rule. This new organizational rule was, in the future, to provide the grounds for further inferences and reformulations concerning the possibility of *judicial* behaviour. Such reformulations, however, would only be given absolute status for the time being. As I have argued elsewhere, the presented rules of correspondence are both victims and authors of several capricious logics.[4] [. . .]

The dummy player
[. . .]

Going through the motions (applying the formal rules)

Warrant-officer, Metropolitan Court: 'Some bits they understand—or think they do. They never understand all of it.'

Everyone in court is aware that the defendant's information concerning what is happening is not in line with everyone else's. This is not to say defendants do not assign meaning to what is happening. They do. Many of what Emerson[5] has called their 'pitches', however, are repressed by what (in the language of games) is a call of 'off-side'. Innovatory ploys by defendants are often treated as being out of time ('Your turn will come. Not now'), out of place ('I can't deal with that here'), out of order ('These kinds of allegations cannot be made') and sometimes out of mind ('I hope you know what you're saying'). What defendants find hard to follow is the strategic intermeshing of logics which somehow achieves their objectivation. The Chief Clerk at Metropolitan Court knew from bitter experience the difficulties inherent in communicating with the 97 per cent of defendants who find their way through magistrates' courts without legal counsel, though he accounted for these difficulties by attributing them to defendants' legal incompetence. Such legal incompetence was seen to stem from an intellectual inability to grasp the legal meanings of what at first might appear to the defendant as being 'everyday' language. Even those court officials who tried hardest to make sense of legal language found that they so often 'drew a blank' that they concluded that 'The majority of people in our courts are pretty dim.'

I asked thirty probation-officers, 'When a person has appeared in court for the first time, what impression do you get as to the quality of his understanding of what's happened?' Fifty-seven per cent of the probation-officers claimed that at first appearance defendants 'understood nothing at all.' Thirty-seven per cent said that defendants understood 'very little', 3 per cent that defendants understood 'very well' and 3 per cent said that 'one cannot tell'. Yet although some of the probation-officers mentioned that their clients 'are not too bright', this was not given as a main reason for their lack of comprehension of the court proceedings. The major reasons given for defendants' non-comprehension were bad acoustics, and the stage-fright which most defendants appeared to experience in court.

In most courts it is very difficult to hear. One result of this communicative breakdown is that often magistrates act as if the defendant is stupid—or awkward—or both.

> *Mr L.* (*Probation-officer*): 'How many times does one know of cases where a defendant in court gets so tied up—if one saw him outside—one suddenly finds that he knows exactly what he wants to say—it's not all jumbled up. He *knows* what he wants to say—it—but the circumstances of the court are that he can't. If I can name one name—you know him (I laugh)—right!—Mr . . . at (Metropolitan) Court. If a client doesn't immediately catch on, doesn't know what is happening . . . he has very little understanding, in my opinion that the client may be confused or may be in a difficult state, or may be very nervous. And he immediately gets very angry with the client or appears to do so—whether he actually is or not doesn't matter. The way in which he then shouts—right? (I nod)—communicates to the client that the magistrate is angry and that he, the client—is a bit of an idiot.'

Many probation-officers made a direct link between the bad acoustics, and 'desperate fear' experienced by many defendants and the oft observed phenomenon of 'court deafness'. Certainly from the probation-box defendants can be seen shaking and moistening their lips, and a probation-officer claimed:

> 'They're terrified. That's why they can't listen to what's said to them—it's just words. Most people are desperately frightened when they're in court. I think the mind is just crippled for those few minutes. They just can't.'

Given these two general circumstances, of courts with bad acoustics and defendants already made fearful by an unfamiliar, ritualistic (i.e. the out-of-everyday) setting, it is situationally impossible for most defendants to participate in the information games of which they are both subject and object. Yet persistent attempts are made to explain the formal rules to them, it being taken-for-granted that improved communication in court will make the proceedings more just. Close consideration of the verbatim records of actual court hearings, and the negotiations which occur in and around courts, however, suggest that 'going through the motions' of explaining legal procedures and meanings to defendants adds confusion to confusion. Indeed, defendants often manifest a sense of mounting absurdity as they learn that, situationally, the logic of law is opposed to a common-sense interpretation of formal rules. This was particularly noticeable in cases where magistrates made it plain that they wanted to help defendants. These defendants often expressed particular chagrin in the gaoler's office when the magistrate, perceiving a possible defence to a charge to which they the defendants, had already pleaded Guilty, directed them to get Legal Aid or to change their plea. 'But I wanted to get it over today', they would protest as the warrant-officer explained why the case had been remanded. The case given below is typical of a not-often-quoted sequence of events which frequently occurs in the courts.

> (A man stands in the dock charged with exposing his penis with intent to insult a female. The police give evidence that the defendant was seen by a passing lady who saw him with his flies open. He was masturbating.)
> *Magistrate*: 'But the charge is that he was exposing himself with intent to insult a lady. It's a different matter if he was quietly masturbating and this lady came along.'
> *Policeman*: 'The lady says, Sir, that she was in a phone-box and she saw the bushes moving and went along there and saw him . . .'
> *Magistrate*: 'And he still had his flies open?'
> *Policeman*: 'Yes Sir.'
> *Magistrate*: (shaking his head and emphasizing each word): '*But there is a difference* between his *approaching* a lady, and him standing there masturbating himself, and this lady happened to come along. (To defendant) Do you wish to change your plea?'
> *Defendant*: 'No.'
> *Magistrate*: 'So you *were* trying to insult this lady?'
> *Defendant*: 'No. But I was doing it and she came along and saw me. So I am guilty. That's just the way I look at it.'
> *Magistrate* (to Clerk): 'Plea of Not Guilty. Look, Mr Dobbin, I'm going to adjourn this case for two weeks (the defendant looks at the ceiling and sighs) because I think you have a defence. There's no reason why you should plead Guilty to something you haven't done. (Defendant looks at magistrate very hard, sighs and shakes his head.) You'll be given Legal Aid papers to fill in, and if you can't afford a lawyer you'll be given one.'

The progress of this case shows that 'going through the motions' of due process does not always convince defendants that the law is just. The rate of play in the courts is too fast for defendants to understand the legal niceties of meaning concerning words like 'intent' and 'guilty'. Instead they find that a chop-logic is at work which defeats even their honest admissions of (what they see as) guilt. The foregoing case also demonstrates how the defendant is often verbally excluded from playing the information game. For much of the time the defendants in magistrates' courts are seen but not heard. For instance a policeman stands up and reads out a convicted person's antecedents. Often the magistrate will query something; for example, 'Why did he leave that job?', and the policeman says, 'I do not know, Sir!' He does not ask the subject of his enquiry, who stands there silently. Instead, the other authoritative sources—the reports and the records are turned to—and they are not always legible. Often defendants stand waiting while a clerk or magistrate deciphers a colleague's written record of a previous hearing!

Clerks of Court are under statutory obligation to state the specific offence with which the accused is charged in 'ordinary language avoiding as far as possible the use of technical terms'[6] and many of them do. But there are some outstanding instances of courtroom verbal exchanges where, even if the defendant understands the wording of the question, he seldom understands its procedural or juristic significance to his answers. The two *outstanding* instances are when the defendant is on an indictable charge and is asked whether he wishes his case to be heard by the magistrate or at a higher court before a jury; and when the magistrate asks the defendant if he wishes to speak from the dock, make a statement on oath, or remain silent.

> 'After all the evidence, the magistrate, if he is in a good mood says "You can either go to the witness box and make a statement, or you can stay where you are and speak from there, or you can say nothing." And most of them stay where they are and start off—and never realise that no one in the court is taking a blind bit of notice of them as they are not speaking on oath. Even when they understand all the words used in court, it doesn't mean that they understand what's going on.'

Other probation-officers, and policemen too, commented on their observations that defendants do not always know what it is they have been charged with or, even, of how the magistrate has disposed of the case. This was apparent in the courts. Some defendants would plead Guilty and then when the evidence was given, say 'oh *no*, I didn't do that.' Others, as they left the courtroom, turned to a policeman and asked him what the sentence had been. Resort to professional aid does not always reduce defendants' confusion.

Fighting over the carcass

Despite the unease which surrounds their interaction with each other, police, probation-officers and solicitors have little doubt as to the state of their own knowledge about the defendants. This is not to deny that each group is continuously pausing to reflect on the meanings of their jobs, the aims and meanings of legal processes, etc. My point here is that when they *act*, they act as professionals often do, as if they are in a state of perfect knowledge, and as if this 'perfect knowledge' has fairly stable constitutive elements within in the court setting.

For the police, 'defendant', 'prisoner' and 'criminal' are synonyms. Sixty per cent of the thirty probation-officers spontaneously mentioned their belief that the police advise people to plead Guilty. Certainly the Guilty plea is considered by the police to be the normal plea, the action appropriate for anyone in the position of defendant. For most of the police the guilt of the defendant is part of their taken-for-granted commonsensical knowledge of the courts. Just as they were exasperated if I would not agree that West Indians were 'obviously different', so were they impatient if I did not share their cynicism about the efficacy of the courts in meting out their just deserts to offenders.

> *Police sergeant, Court A*: 'You sit there, you listen to it all. *You* know what they are doing. 'Course you do! (Laughs) *I know* that many people who're sent to prison are acquitted, but that doesn't mean they're Not Guilty' (his emphases)

The police have a well-developed justification for telling people to plead Guilty and it was often explained to me with some heat:

> *Inspector, Court A*: 'It's not a matter of whether they are guilty or not—I'm not saying that's not important—but a lot of them—it's a matter of time. Take a woman on a shoplifting charge— they want to get it over. They plead guilty because they can't stand it on their minds (taps forehead). They *want* to get it over.'

The idea that any normal person on a minor charge would plead Guilty in order to 'get it over' was so taken-for-granted in the courts by the policeman that those defendants who did not acquiesce in this convention were seen as working to rule and 'trying to be funny'.

Whether a person pleads Guilty or not is contingent upon many things. Most defendants in magistrates' courts do not come into direct contact with solicitors and probation-officers. Their own defences are often very weak and do not withstand the initial emotional onslaught of the police, who rely heavily on the defendants' ignorance of their rights when they give the 'fatherly' advice as to how they should plead. It was indeed a common complaint of police that the other professionals, far from helping defendants, did them harm, and probation-officers expressed the same sentiments about solicitors:

> *Miss H (Probation-officer)*: 'The legal profession are not geared to reading probation-officers' reports properly because they want to be seen as successful people with their clients. And to be successful is to get someone out of an awkward situation, whereas, in reality, it would be better if that person went away.'

Each professional acts as if he knows what is best for the defendant, defines his reality for him and then, in order to realize that reality, tries to 'make something' of his client. Below I discuss the professional 'servicing' of defendants between court appearances, so that in court individual professional teams might claim him for their own.

Making something of the defendant

> *Miss G.* (*Probation-officer*): 'They're usually engrossed in their Social Enquiry Reports, you know. They think they are reading about somebody else. It's like an obituary. Their whole life is there.'

> *Solicitor, Metropolitan Court*: 'This is a sad case. Father killed in Dunkirk, mother killed in an air-raid two years later. He did serve in the army, and left in the normal way—with honour. Since then he's had several jobs but needs to sort himself out. It would seem worth trying to see if Probation can present him as a more worthwhile man when he attends this court again.'

In 1972 the gaoler at Metropolitan Court dealt with 8,613 prisoners of whom 1,289 applied for Legal Aid, 1,099 of these applications being granted. Some defendants had the services of a probation-officer. Apart from a handful of defendants who were represented privately, had a friend or a representative of some voluntary group, for example the Claimants' Union, the rest found their way through the courts alone. Whether or not defendants had professional help, they were always victims of a secretive, collusive but creative information-game whose rules were forever being adapted to further the interests of the professional contestants.

Faced with contradictory information from opposed professionals, many defendants yet sensed that the 'in-group' of court and enforcement personnel closed ranks at times when the whole game was threatened by any defendant who stepped out of his role of dummy player. As a result, many defendants, especially 'first-timers', acquiesce in being 'serviced' by professionals, in the hope that they will thereby propitiate those who construct and dispense justice. Victims of several capricious logics, they learn at the initial hearing that they are prevented from speaking when they want to, invited or pressed to change their pleas when they don't want to, and always regarded as people who must be spoken *for* rather than spoken *to*. The prevailing attitude towards defendants in Metropolitan Court was that they were 'pretty dim', 'rather pathetic creatures' who had 'never had a chance'. Generally, however, it was thought that the majority of them could be 'made something of', even though each professional team had its own idea of what that something was. Strategic to the representation of a defendant in court are the police, probation-officers and solicitors, each with their panoply of files, forms, records and reports.

Technically those who choose to be represented by a solicitor and those who agree to having a probation-

officer's report done are supposed to do so freely and without constraint. Technically too, the solicitor is supposed to represent the interests of his client in court. These two suppositions are mythical. Many defendants who are directed to apply for Legal Aid find that they are subjected to an outside-court training on what they *have* to say inside, such training often being given in the last ten minutes before the case is heard and often by a young solicitor whom they have never seen before. They discover that the solicitor who works regularly in one court is often more prepared to accept the police version of events than their own and that the *best* the solicitor is prepared to do in court is not to represent their own views but instead to represent *them* as characters worthy of clemency, treatment or second chances.

Theoretically defendants are free to refuse to cooperate with a probation-officer but magistrates usually *direct* reports to be done, eventually remanding in custody those convicted defendants who refuse to co-operate. The defendants' awareness of the control element in the situation was thought by probation-officers to nullify the technical gloss which presents probation as a period of voluntary supervision. Once they agree to co-operate in the construction of a Social Enquiry Report some defendants (at this stage they become 'clients') find that many things they tell the probation-officers are not considered 'relevant'. On the grounds that 'you know what the magistrate wants', six of the probation-officers told me that they would not include in the report 'just anything', even if the defendant specifically requested them to. Of the eight who said that the very fact that a defendant asked them to include it would make an item of information relevant, three said that they would write between the lines so that the magistrate would know what they were repeating *only* what the defendant had told them.

Unknown to most defendants, the majority of probation-officers at Metropolitan Court discussed their reports with the magistrates prior to the court hearing, both magistrates and probation-officers claiming that usually one can 'read between the lines of a probation-report', thereby 'seeing' things in it which remain unrevealed to the defendant. Out of court, and in front of probation-officers, magistrates referred to defendants as 'nuts' or 'psychiatric cases'; a probation-officer's reference to Marxism and capitalist society was not considered appropriate reading material for his client!

The objectification of people as defendants begins when they are charged with an offence. Thereafter objectification processes are systematically crystallized throughout the court hearing, so that by the time the magistrate asks for reports the defendant has already been transformed into client, prisoner or patient. Court officials are obliged to account for such transformations in writing. Often the court official who fills in the form which accompanies a person to prison has not been present during the court hearing. Often, as one warrant officer said, even those officials who have been in the court 'don't hear what the magistrate wants done'. But the formal rule requires that the form accompany the prisoner to prison. Court officials perceive that form to be a reflection of their competence. The Warrant-Officer at Inner London Court explained to me how difficult it can be to make observable in written form what was 'obvious' to those in the court.

'Now when the prison doctor gets someone, he doesn't want to have to ask them, "Why did the court request a medical mental report?" This is the form we fill in "Reasons which led to the court . . . " Now sometimes this is very difficult— I mean to say—there's a whisper between the magistrate and the Clerk of Court and they say "He'll be remanded for probation and medical reports." Well, some people stand there and they couldn't care less. Or they stand there and they just don't understand what's going on. They're mentally ill and if you can show it was due to the prisoner's attitude so that's why they put that there. (Reading from form) If demeanour etc. . . . If you was to stand there looking at the Public, taking not the slightest notice of court proceedings—did not seem to understand what was going on—that kind of thing.'

The defendant, bereft of any relevant rubric giving guidance on how to elude the judicial objectification processes which engulf him, struggles to tell each new and overtly sympathetic report-writer, form-filler and record-keeper how *he* defines himself and his situation. On each occasion he finds that his court records, prison records, medical records, employment records, school records and those of any other agency of which he has been client, patient, worker or prisoner have preceded him. The living obituaries actualize a social structure in which the defendants in magistrates' courts have lost the information game before it even starts. Most of them know all along that it is not a game anyway.

Not all defendants give in. Some, in choosing to go to a higher court, believe that with the benefit of a jury they will stand more equally before those whose information-state is similar to their own. Others, who have seen this game played in schools, work-places and social security offices, employ innovative strategies designed to change the run of play or even the game itself. This paper has attempted to demonstrate why so few of them succeed. [. . .]

Notes

1 Stanford M. Lyman and Marvin Scott, *A Sociology of the Absurd*, New York, Appleton-Century Crofts, 1970.
2 Reference in the text to 'Metropolitan Court' is to the stipendiary magistrates' court where I did six months of observation in the courtroom and gaoler's office. Reference to 'Inner London Court' is to the lay magistrates' court where I similarly observed for two months. Over a period of twelve months, I regularly visited six other Metropolitan magistrates' courts.
3 Alvin Gouldner, *Patterns of Industrial Bureaucracy*, New York, Free Press, 1954.
4 See Pat Carlen, 'Remedial routines for the maintenance of control in magistrates' courts', *British Journal of Law and Society*, 1(2), winter 1974, pp. 101–17.
5 R. M. Emerson, *Judging Delinquents*, Chicago, Aldine, 1967.
6 *Stone's Justices' Manual*, Butterworth, 1972.

V. 5 Prisons and the future of control systems: from concentration to dispersal

Stanley Cohen

This article is an attempt at prediction—an enterprise which social scientists (compared with our colleagues in the natural sciences) are very reluctant to undertake. The reasons for such reluctance are understandable: our information is imprecise and open to multiple interpretations; past trends are not always a reliable guide to the future; forecasts on the basis of comparing societies at different 'stages' are highly fallible. Such debates as those on the 'inevitability' of revolution, 'post-industrial society', the 'end of ideology' are littered with the corpses of failed predictions.

The problems are only marginally less intimidating when one looks at a specific and so apparently limited and special an institution as the prison rather than a whole society. Could anyone in the golden days of the triumph of the asylum—say the 1830s in America when the penitentiary was being hailed as a Utopian experiment—have predicted that, within a few decades, the whole belief in reformatory imprisonment would be under sustained attack? And during the period of attack, who could have known that the rehabilitative ideal would receive a new lease of life, through the psychiatric ideology? And who, during the halcyon era of 'treatment' which lasted right up to the 1960s could have told us that today, the notion of imprisonment as reform is greeted with profound scepticism and that (if my predictions are correct) we are witnessing the decline of the asylum as such and its supplementation by new forms of social control?

Aware, though, of the risks of the enterprise, and the unsatisfactory nature of much of my data, I would like to construct a scenario based on extrapolations from current developments in the prison systems of the advanced industrial societies of the West, particularly America and Britain. All these predictions

Source: Previously unpublished in this form. (Adapted from a paper (in Italian) in Franco Basaglia (ed.), *Crimini di Pace* (*The Crimes of Peace*), Turin, Einaudi, 1974; an abbreviated form appeared in *New Society*, 14 November 1974, pp. 407–11.) The author is Professor of Sociology, University of Essex.

assume that we can learn from the past, and I'm going to try all along to keep an eye open for historical continuities and discontinuities.

Noise from off the prison stage

In more senses than the obvious one, the prison is the ultimate depository of changes that happen elsewhere. We have only recently begun to locate the development of the prison in its proper historical context. This is the emergence in the first half of the nineteenth century of a new kind of social structure: the asylum, the prison, the workhouse, the poorhouse, the orphanage, as places designed to take care or dispose of deviant groups in an orderly way (a practice later legitimised by a common ideology of welfare and rehabilitation). The point here is not so much that such institutions might—as Goffman and others suggest—share common internal features, but that their roots are to be found in common external social developments and values.[1] Thus for Rothman, the asylum in America arose during the Jacksonian period as a response to the deviant and dependent to promote social stability when traditional ideas and practices appeared outmoded: 'The well-ordered asylum would exemplify the proper principles of social organisation and thus ensure the safety of the public to promote its glory.'

The prison specifically and the whole notion of *moral architecture* in general embodies the ideology of redemption and obedience which, in turn, served as the testing-ground for particular theories of human nature: that evil communication can corrupt and contaminate, that behaviour is totally a function of environment, that defects in social and community life could be remedied by a purpose-built agency of change. These institutions were not to be kept hidden, they were not places of the last resort when all else had failed, but the preferred solution, the pride of the nation. The asylum was conceived as a Utopian experiment.

It is difficult to exaggerate the profound changes in

deviance control which were heralded by the early-nineteenth-century asylum movement. If we just look at the difference in prison architecture, we read the story.[2] These innovations in prison design with the profound belief in the powers of architecture that came with them, were part of an effort by the state to stem vice, control passion and eliminate violence. The new technologies of pacification, isolation and control that were developed were to spread beyond the prison walls; first to encompass other types of abnormality in lunatic asylums and poor-law buildings and eventually to everyday life via the school, the factory and public housing.

We have to turn to writers like Michel Foucault for an appreciation of the broader implications of the Great Incarcerations of the nineteenth century.[3] For Foucault, taking a much broader historical canvas, these Incarcerations—lunatics into asylums, thieves into prisons, conscripts into barracks, workers into factories, children into school, were all part of a grand design intimately connected with the Industrial Revolution and the spirit of capitalism. Property had to be protected; production had to be standardised by regulations; the young had to be segregated in purpose-built institutions to be inculcated with the ideology of thrift and success. Whether or not we accept the Grand Design argument—and it contains historical flaws such as the existence of prisons in other pre-industrial societies—we cannot but see the prison of today as a very small—and not necessarily permanent—terminal point of a much larger process of social change.

According to Foucault, the power–knowledge spiral (power aiding the accumulation of information which in turn aids and reinforces power) cannot be localised within the framework of state versus citizen or ruling class versus the others, but penetrates the whole fabric of society and can easily survive the mere destruction of political institutions. With the so-called age of enlightenment, punishment becomes 'reasonable', no longer public mutilation and intense physical suffering, but the more politically and economically discreet prison sentence. Interest is transformed from punishment to surveillance, from the body to the mind; it is the beginning of a whole 'technology of subtle powers, effective and economical, in opposition to the sumptuous expenditure of the power of sovereigns' and in which 'the body becomes the prisoner of the mind'. The lawless and colourful, dangerous but tolerant (because inefficient) world of seventeenth-century social control becomes the centralised, disciplined, floodlit, all-seeing world of Bentham's Panopticon—the architectural form of the knowledge–power spiral symbolised by a circular building with a transparent watchtower in the centre. No more grilles, chains or heavy locks, but the inhibiting awareness in the prisoner's mind of a ubiquitous presence. No more instruments of torture, but the glass cages of a menagerie open to the public gaze. No more autocratic, fortress dungeon, but the laboratory and the zoo, serving also as a data-gathering centre.

The prison is the purest form of the panopticon but its application is far wider than that. Applied to schools it becomes a means of control providing the excuse to question the parents on life-style, resources, customs, piety, affiliations, and—later—child-rearing practices. Hospitals and charities gather information in the same way. Barracks, military academies, asylums, workhouses and fortress-factories are all a part of the panoptic world, articulated by a centralised and increasingly sophisticated law-enforcement network, whose main characteristic is its intangibility and invulnerability. 'We are less Greek than we think,' says Foucault. 'We are neither on the [spectators'] benches nor on the stage, but in the panopticon machine itself'—an integral part of the works.

The threefold aim of this disciplinarian system Foucault describes as making the exercise of power as cheap as possible (economically by low costs, politically by discretion and relative invisibility); ascertaining that results are carried to their maximum intensity and are drawn out as long as possible; and that knowledge–power is well linked to all its institutional apparatus (school, army, industry, medicine), thus ensuring in every field of life the docility and usefulness of the individual.

He traces this development not only to the 'enlightened' philosophy of the eighteenth century but to massive population growth (and hence, the potential threat to state security of a restless floating population) and to increasingly complex and expensive industrial production with its consequent interest in profitability. Thus the economic take-off and accumulation of capital parallels a form of political take-off—the accumulation of power–knowledge and management of human beings in as cheap a way as possible.

Of course it was soon realised that imprisonment as a Utopian vision of reform had failed; Rothman and others have shown how disillusionment set in within a few decades of the asylum's triumph. But to talk about 'failure' in this limited sense is to miss the more successful functions of the prison. Prisons remained useful in answering the needs of the control mechanism itself with its multitude of dependants. Certain political and economic demands of the working classes could be disguised as criminal attacks on law and order. The penal instrument as a whole served to maintain 'a state of permanent conflict' as well as to invent whole areas of illegality.

Let us now move a long way ahead—to today's prison scene.

Warehouses and showplaces

What seems to me beyond dispute is that in the last decade or so the disillusionment about the whole notion of imprisonment as rehabilitation—voiced, of course, for the first time a century ago—became widespread, was found in different ranges of political opinion, and was reflected in policy. From the most radical abolitionist groups to the most conservative hardliners, there occurred a profound disenchantment about the whole treatment idea in particular and imprisonment in general.

At the end of the eighteenth century the asylums and prisons were institutions of the *last* resort; by the mid-nineteenth century they became institutions of the *first* resort: the preferred solutions to problems of deviance and dependency. By the end of the 1960s they looked like not only again becoming places of the *last* resort but even being virtually abolished.

When we look at juveniles, we find that although the care/treatment model is more durable than for adults, the belief in institutions was subject to similar scepticism. In a collection of papers on development in Massachusetts (where all conventional institutions were closed down over the 1970s) one commentator compares with total certainty today's training schools with the original juvenile institutions set up in the 1820s.[4]

> Today, 125 years later, these places . . . continue to receive youngsters and subject them to programs of restraint, brutality and futility. Such institutions differ little from their original models, with one exception. Today the conviction has become almost universal that if they ever served any purpose other than as temporary places of restraint, their consistently high rates of failure to rehabilitate strongly suggest that the time has come to close them and replace them with more humane and effective measures of care, protection and treatment for young people. Nothing succeeds like an idea whose time has come. The institution as a means of coping with the problems of specific sectors of our population seems at this point to have run its course.

The movement to shift control from the cell block to the community began in the United States in the mid-1960s and was the key theme in the research and policy reflected in official government commissions from 1967 onwards. The assumption that community-based corrections—probation, parole, halfway houses, group homes, pre-trial release programmes, various 'diversion' schemes—were preferable to any prison programme became part of the official rhetoric. It was widely believed that prisons did not deter crime, and that community alternatives are more effective, less costly and more humane. By 1973—the peak of the deinstitutionalisation movement—the National Advisory Commission could recommend:

> States should refrain from building any more State institutions for juveniles; States should phase out present institutions over a five year period. They should also refrain from building more State institutions for adults for the next ten years, except where total institution planning shows that the need is imperative.

Quotations like this could be multiplied. It was clear that some consensus was emerging and that it was *partially* reflected in actual policy changes. Besides the much-cited closing of the Massachusetts reformatories, prison-building plans elsewhere were shelved and the proportions of offenders sent to conventional institutions decreased. In Britain, the changes were less dramatic but in the same direction; the *rate* of increase of the prison population began to tail off; all sorts of community alternatives, such as parole and intermediate treatment, were established. The *actual* prison populations in some European countries dropped. And all this happened despite increases in the populations and the overall crime-rate. The evidence was not unambiguous everywhere, but there did seem a clear, if uneven, trend towards the abolition or at least the reduction of imprisonment. (In the case of mental hospitals rather than prison, the drop in the institutional population was quite clear and dramatic from the 1960s onwards.)

Now the reasons for all this are complex; a mixture of humanitarianism, pragmatism and expediency—which appealed right across the political spectrum. As John Conrad writes:[5]

> The revulsion felt by liberal humanists for the degradation imposed by the prison coincided with the realization by fiscal conservatives that the costs of custody, even without the attempts at programmes, were escalating to levels of absurdity. Penal reform was a rare case in the annals of social change, in which agreement seemed to extend across the entire span of political ideology. The empiricist had established the futility of rehabilitation; the prison reformer had documented its essential inhumanity; and the cost benefit analyst had worked out the per capita costs showing that the alternatives to custody produced at least as satisfactory aggregated results at far less cost to the taxpayer. No wonder that the futurists of penology thought that a millenium was at hand.

Not only did successive Governments become committed (verbally) to what penal reformers had always asked—clearing the prisons of short-termers and setting up community care and control schemes—but certain legal changes moved towards the abolition of imprisonment and criminalisation for whole categories of offenders.

In the case of so-called 'crimes without victims', for example, drugs, abortion or homosexuality, respectable voices were raised during the 1960s not only to end imprisonment, but to decriminalise these offences; that is, to treat them in terms of some welfare or rehabilitation model. Again these voices were by no means being confined to liberals and penal reformers. All this, plus the gradual development of sustaining and supportive networks in the outside community, must be seen as part of a growing reaction against the triumph of the asylum I described earlier. The movements to get the mentally ill, infants without families, the physically maladjusted, the sub-normal and the aged out of their institutions and back into the community, while by no means successful, do not just represent the isolated voices of a few reformist cranks. And—given of course the major limitations set by the demands of retribution, general deterrence and protection—there seemed no reason to suppose that prisons would remain wholly immune from this trend.

But there *are* limits to the abolition movement and, while it is still continuing elsewhere (and I believe it to be unstoppable for most institutions other than prisons), the American experience of the last few years has provided a sobering influence on the millenarian thinking behind the deinstitutionalisation movement. It just hasn't happened: no other State followed the Massachusetts lead, no adult penitentiaries remained closed, most penalties stayed the same. In fact, by 1975, prison populations once again started keeping pace with the rapidly increased crime-rates. Disused units were opened and overcrowding started again. Parallel developments took place in British prisons between 1973 and 1976.

In the USA, this was partly because the recession increased the amount of crime, but also because of a more clearly punitive and angry ideology about crime, a type of backlash to the deinstitutionalisation movement. A hard-line-deterrent view—for example expressed in proposals for *mandatory prison sentences for first offenders*—became more respectable.

The other problem, almost forgotten by penal reforms in their euphoric mood about the decreasing prison rates, is to understand what has happened to those who *are* left behind in the institutions. There has been, and in the conceivable future will be, obvious impediments to decarceration because of the existence of a small number of criminals who 'have' to be sent away.

We have to talk about this group that *does* remain behind. The current trend in Britain—and most countries for which comparable figures are available— is to send people to prison for longer periods. (The abolition of capital punishment is an obvious cause for more prisoners to be serving life sentences. In Britain, some 900 prisoners are now serving life sentences for murder, compared with 120 in 1957.)

What all this means is that we entered into a new era of penal policy: one in which the 'problem' will become not the short-termers, the pathetic men who go in and out of our overcrowded prisons, but the existence of an increasing number of long-term, 'dangerous' men who pose entirely new difficulties of control, security and discipline. And the paradox is that because of the liberals' success, this group will be defined in even more negative and destructive terms. They will be the hard core, the bottom of the barrel, the recalcitrants, the incorrigibles: those for whom one can do nothing more than shunt them away in dispersal prisons or security wings. Prisons for this group of offenders are destined to become *human warehouses*: places where people are stored until society can think of something else to do with them.

A slightly less offensive concept than 'warehousing' is contained in what is now an official shift in policy in countries like Britain: from rehabilitative aims to what is known as *humane containment*. We are still in a transitional period: in the immediate future prisons will still be used as the ultimate form of punishment and deterrence for the existing very wide range of offenders. Indeed increasing crime-rates and some legal changes might in the short run *add* to the numbers in prison. Short sentences will continue to be served as long as non-custodial methods remain at the experimental stage or are unacceptable in terms of protection, deterrence and retribution. The prisons in which such offenders find themselves will continue to become more 'advanced' along a quasi-rehabilitative model. There will be more benefits such as group therapy, work conditions will become better, the staff will be more sophisticated—all of which, of course, does not mean that the daily indignities and deprivations of prison life will in any way diminish. A characteristic development—paralleled in mental hospitals—will be the industrial prison, where inmates are exploited as sources of cheap labour.

But in this transitional period the warehouses will exist alongside these showplaces and will force themselves onto the public consciousness (as they did throughout Europe and America in the late 1960s and Britain in the riots at Parkhurst in 1969 and Hull in 1976) in the form of riots, disturbances and escape attempts. Whatever the overall historical trend against institutionalisation might be, prisons are never able to be selective. They will continue taking those at the end of the line, the terminal cases who must be removed from society.

Segregation: a Chinese box on stage

The regimented and orderly prisons of the early nineteenth century rested on a particular view of human nature: moral order could be imposed by architecture and planning.[6] Central to these blueprints are notions we could variously call compartmentalisation, isolation, segregation, classification, separation. Walls were used as tools for the human control of human beings: not only should the prisoner be cut off from outside contamination, but the walls inside (the separate cells, exercise yards, chapels) should prevent one type of prisoner from contaminating the others. The complex geometry of nineteenth-century prisons created byzantine systems of classification: in these 'atlases of vice' one could sometimes find as many as forty categories of prisoners. These complex systems broke down because they were unpracticable and also because of the rediscovery (from America) of the reforming power of solitude. Classification promised to prevent moral contamination, but solitude promised reform as well: there were so many categories that the answer was to put everyone in his own category, and to try reforming him through prolonged self-reflection.

On the one hand, walls were raised of ever greater

solidity, at an ever-increasing frequency and with ever more cunning to compartmentalise and separate criminals and make them into reflective individuals. The cell became all important. On the other hand, great tunnels of space lined with a dense network of sophisticated services were stretched throughout the prison to give each cell an exactly equal status and to re-unify them under the gaze of the governor who was put in the very centre. Each inmate was thus cut off from every other, yet the entire population was placed under the scrutiny and jurisdiction of a dutiful servant of the state.

These novel institutions with their centrifugal vistas, their overwhelming repetition of units, their gadgets and paraphernalia for pervasive surveillance and intimate measurement, contained no accidents. Everything was arranged to eliminate the unknown, to regulate, to time and to choreograph down to the last detail every move and every thought of warders as well as convicts, all to prevent the genesis and spread of evil. In Newgate corruption and profanity were simply contained; in Pentonville they were abolished. All forms of communication—singing, whispering, winking—were magnified into crimes and then ruthlessly suppressed.

The Age of Reason gave rise to a new kind of utilitarian architecture, exemplified by the reformed prisons, in which society was to be purified by dividing man from man. This same architecture welded its cellular compartments together again with a network of alien processes, services and functions that belonged to no one but the state.

Gradually this Utopian vision went sour: custodial and management goals transcended reformative ones; isolation did not work and came to be seen as inhumane; separation and classification broke down *within* the walls. The late-nineteenth century 'seminaries of vice' became the 'inmate subcultures' of today's closed prisons.

But the impulse to classify remained. Sophisticated theories, both of management and containment on the one hand, and treatment on the other, led to a greater diversity of institutions: minimum, medium and maximum security; closed, semi-closed and open prisons, intermittent imprisonment and half-way houses. The magic wand of classification is still waved: rehabilitation and correction are believed to be possible only if the prison population is separated out into those who might benefit from a particular regime, those who would impede such a regime, those who would be 'bad risks'. Long-termers, high security risks, violent offenders, persistent escapers and the psychologically disturbed are all groups singled out as possible sources of contamination. If only they could be removed into separate institutions, then the system could go along with its business. There is as near as one could find to perfect unanimity among prison reformers, official policy-makers and prison staff at all levels in the belief that segregation is one of the master keys to a 'successful' system. (There is the same impulse to classify in other control institutions: for example, the elaborate hierarchy of 'admission' wards, 'chronic' wards, 'acute' wards and 'indeterminate' wards in mental hospitals.)

Most prison systems already contain, of course, a fair amount of classification: long-termers, sex offenders, domestic murderers, first offenders, are all segregated in different institutions or within the same institution. Over the last decade, the rationale for segregation has been strengthened by invoking the needs of control and discipline. Whenever there is a riot, a disturbance or an escape plot, the argument is produced that the trouble is all the work of a hard core of trouble-makers. If only they could be identified and segregated, then the other prisoners and staff could go along quietly with their business. The characteristic societal mode of responding to deviance is to see it as a property of a small group of specially disposed persons, who must somehow be identified and segregated. Hence the prestige and importance attached to research aimed at developing a new technology to locate 'potential' or 'predisposed' deviants before they have actually broken any rules.

In the prison setting the only question at dispute is the mode of segregation. In the British system over the last decade, for example, the choice was presented in terms of *concentration*—placement of high-risk offenders in a single Alcatraz-like maximum security institution—versus *dispersal* throughout the system. The government's eventual rejection of *single* concentration, though, should not hide the fact that considerable concentration is already a feature of the system. This takes place in at least three ways: first, through the formal categorisation of types of prisoners in terms of danger and security risk, and the particular existence of the Category A group who are subject to severe and special restrictions and deprivations; second, through the setting up of concentrated separate institutions; and third, the segregation of offenders *within* the institution: in punishment blocks, isolation cells, etc.

A closer examination of the nature of imprisonment reveals that such arrangements are by no means fortuitous: in fact they reveal the essence of the penal system. For whatever the ultimate aims of imprisonment—as discussed in conferences, newspaper editorials, Parliament, the judiciary—the daily task of the managers of the system is to maintain security through the prevention of escapes and disturbances. Because of the incompatible demands society has placed on them, the nightmare of the officials is that there should be trouble; to quote one Home Office administrator: 'If I get to the end of the day and the telephone hasn't rung, it's been a good day.' From a managerial position his problem was real: how does one maintain a quiet life, given the presence of so many forces that make for trouble and so few ways of ensuring conformity among one's charges?

The answer is management by segregation. In his study of what he terms the 'strategies of control' developed in the Californian prison system of the last fifteen years, Sheldon Messinger argues that this answer is, in fact, the *logic* of control.[7] The potential or actual trouble-makers ('security risks') are concentrated or segregated in one place to protect the special character of the systems they are prevented from entering (or expelled from) and in the hope that some means may be found for dealing with them collectively. In California this was achieved by both concentrating the high risks in one prison and in addition creating separate units within prisons: adjustment centres, segregation units, isolation blocks. This strategy of segregation leads to an elaboration of various levels of deprivation, supervision and restrictions: there are 'honour units' and 'non-honour units', isolation cells involving temporary segregation, adjustment centres with more permanent segregation and even 'indeterminate segregation' units. One adjustment centre in which disruptive inmates were segregated ended up by spawning its own segregation unit to deal with those beyond its reach.

The 'complicated Chinese box effect' which results 'with inmates in the innermost box ideally required to traverse each enclosing one on the way to relative freedom' is very much the way most prison systems are developing. As Messinger notes, the 'logic' of the segregation strategy is simple enough: 'identify potential troublemakers as early as possible, try to bring them to heel, if you fail, segregate them.' Whether this works or not in minimising disruption, what is clear is that 'the strategy of segregation leads to more segregation'. Given the organisational imperative of control, officials point out quite plausibly that other strategies are ineffective: force can only sometimes be used (in riots or disturbances) and anyway cannot make inmates want to do things: motivation through punishments and rewards are limited and one cannot freely select into or reject from the institution. With restrictions on the legitimate use of force, the control issue—which dominates the daily routine of prison officials at all levels—resolves itself into motivating prisoners to do things the management wants or else neutralising the recalcitrants. Segregation is the solution the California correctional system evolved and there is no reason to suppose that other prison managers will hit upon anything very different in the next few decades. A significant development which will facilitate such new forms of social control is the increasing power of the lower grades of prison staff. This power is capable of neutralising any liberalisation in the upper levels of the hierarchy and—in an unholy alliance with psychiatric personnel—has led to the creation of coercive forms of behaviour modification, using, for example, operant conditioning programmes. Inmates are subjected to base levels of deprivation and programmes, and then rewarded for good behaviour by successive moves towards less restrictive environments.

Out of a combination of internal system demands and external pressures, then, the Chinese box effect will slowly develop. The prisoner in the innermost box —the segregation wing, the isolation block—can look forward not to release, but, if he satisfies the staff that he is 'prepared to co-operate', transfer to the next box.

What else is happening in these prisons?

The medical model: enter the doctor

To point to the way punishment is called treatment, punishment blocks called adjustment centres, prison warders called correctional counsellors is not just standard sociological cynicism. It shows up the continuous way in which the prison system has been disguised through the euphemisms it has used to justify itself and how liberal prison reform has supplied the rhetoric as well as the means for the system to be unwittingly perpetuated. As Rothman shows for the period of exactly one hundred years ago: the original concepts of the Utopian penitentiary promoted and disguised the shift to custody; the management was persuaded that whatever it did, it would be justified.

We have only just begun to face the paradox that prison reform is as old as prison itself. The main obstacle to change became the treatment ideology and the whole medical rhetoric. This generated its own vested interests, the whole apparatus of progressive penology. Any reforming impetus becomes absorbed by the very institution it attacks. So, for example, when there is a chorus of demands to relieve overcrowding, the hard-liners will ask for more space, and so will the liberals. The architects, if there is money, will oblige. Jessica Mitford quotes a Public Relations Officer of the American Correctional Association who tells his colleagues to welcome the do-gooders and soft liberals into the prison: they're the best possible lobbyists for funds.[8]

The diffusion of a liberal reform rhetoric has overlapped in this century with the diffusion of the psychiatric ideology. Each one has sustained the other. In prisons and other such institutions of social control, this convergence reached its apotheosis in the ideology of rehabilitation. No longer have such institutions to be justified purely in terms of vengeance and punishment but as agencies of positive change: the prison becomes a 'correctional' institution. At hand to expound and administer the new ideology is a growing army of psychiatrists and their adjuncts of lesser professional groups, such as clinical psychologists and group counsellors. These groups have joined the older custodians in the jostle for power in the infrastructure of the prison world. And the scientists and technicians are beginning to win, not because of some inherent superiority in their paradigm of crime, but merely by showing that they have the power to be more effective custodians.

Prison reformers fell too easily for the rhetoric of therapy instead of treating it with caution and accepting the unpalatable consequences of recognising the prison for what it is. They were lured by such notions as the therapeutic community into thinking that the same sacrifices can service the gods of both punishment and treatment.

As the anti-psychiatry school and others have made clear about psychiatry in general, one's fears are directed not towards the possibility of a genuine helping and healing profession, but at the abuses that might occur in the development of forms of social control under the guise of benevolent treatment. The worst of these fears have been confirmed in the overt use of psychiatric manipulation to deal with political dissenters (in well-documented recent Russian cases, for example) and such fears are obviously well grounded when psychiatrists actually appear as part of the penal system. The nature of the setting lends itself to these abuses (and allied ones such as the use of prisoners as 'volunteers' for psychological and medical experimentation), while at the same time considerations of finance and 'less eligibility' ensure that prisoners are *less* likely to receive help if they voluntarily request it.

In trying to understand what is happening—and what might happen—to the medical model of imprisonment, there is a paradox I find difficult to resolve. On the one hand it is clear that much of the disenchantment with prisons I discussed earlier is due precisely to a recognition of the inappropriateness of the medical model. Again, John Conrad expresses this nicely:[9]

We promised a hospital and by the time we delivered the complex network of services and control, which comprise contemporary corrections, we found that we had put together a non-rational, intuitive structure of discretionary control containing impersonally obsessive elements unlike anything to be found in the kind of hospital we had in mind. The purpose of the hospital is to facilitate cure but there is no disease for the prison professionals to treat, as we have discovered to our embarrassment.

But, on the other hand, there is a great deal of evidence to suggest that little has stopped the penetration of prison by the medical rhetoric and indeed that new forms of 'treatment' are increasingly being used, perhaps in the last desperate throw to show that therapy is, after all, possible. The increasingly offensive nature of these treatments, though, shows that behind the paradox lies the same rationale of the late-nineteenth-century prisons: the appeal to the once Utopian ideology of reformation to buttress up a system that has already moved far away from its original aims.

The actual-present functions of psychiatry in prison —both here and in more advanced systems—are at best obscure. They might involve little more than a cooling-out function in which the therapy is used to help the inmate to adjust to the regime or else they might be consciously manipulated by the prisoner as a form of making out in the institution: therapy sessions are attended in the promise of goodies from the doctor in the form of cigarettes and a pleasant chat or—more importantly—a ticket to parole and early release on

the grounds of showing 'insight' into his problem.

Other developments, though, go somewhat beyond the mere propping up of the regime or the providing of a medical rhetoric to salve the consciences of the tender-minded. Whatever can be said against group and individual psychotherapy, vocational therapy, counselling, therapeutic-community-type experiments —and the main thing to be said against them is that they have not been shown to work very well—at least they are relatively innocuous: it is difficult to force prisoners completely into such programmes and such effects as they have are unlikely to be irreversible. All this cannot be said for the newer technological advances in behaviour control which are now being tried in prison and are certain to increase. With the general disillusionment in the 1960s in America about psycho-therapeutic methods, liberal treatment policies began to be replaced by physical methods derived primarily from behaviouristic psychology. The parallels between these methods and the principles and technology of Bentham's Panopticon are very close: the way in which the Panopticon replaced Christian redemption by materialist/behaviourist psychology is similar to the replacement of Freudianism (change through insight) by Behaviourism (change through external compliance). For both Bentham and Skinner, pleasure and pain are the driving forces to be manipulated by the environment; both have the same vision of a completely synchronised social system.

I only have space to classify these techniques: they include (1) behaviour therapy on specific offence types: positive (operant) or negative conditioning (aversion therapy); for example drugs such as Anectine (which induces pain and fear through sensations of dying or drowning) are already widely used to modify specific forms of behaviour particularly involving sexual offences; (2) chemotherapy of one sort or another—hormone transplants, chemical castration, or even psycho-surgery; (3) experiments and clinical trials of new drugs on prisoners—including injections with live cancer cells and blood from leukaemia patients, controlled diets to introduce scurvy, and the administration of bacteria to cause typhoid fever; (4) the development of pacification programmes: drugs used not to change specific criminal behaviour but to control actual or potential violence in prison. Experiments have also been carried out using such powerful tranquillisers as Prolixin which produces a zombie-like effect. Both heavy sedation and mind-altering drugs are being extensively used to control actual or potential violence in prisons. And even further: brain surgery was advocated (in such institutions as the MPDU—the Maximum Psychiatric Diagnostic Unit), in California to reduce trouble-makers to a state referred to by the California Department of Corrections as 'temporarily dormant'; and (5) the development most explicitly bringing prisons back into line with the nineteenth-century dream of total behavioural control: the introduction of total behaviour-modification programmes. These are systematic regimes based on operant conditioning—in which torture and deprivation are the 'negative reinforcements'.

Take, for example, Patuxent Institution, the unique 'total treatment facility' in Maryland with 425 convicts and headed by a psychiatrist with a treatment staff of 89 given complete autonomy over treatment and release. The behaviour modification programme, consists of promotion from filthy roach-infested punishment cells, through various levels of 'reinforcement', up to the final luxury of TV and family picnics. Some of the advocates of these policies, such as James McConnell, are committed ideologues who believe that there is no limit to the change the system can seek to achieve: 'Criminals had no right to commit crime, therefore they have no right to resist being given a new personality.' Others are pragmatic: liberal treatment hasn't worked, so why not try this?

Even such techniques, though, look innocuous in the light of the most recent technological breakthrough in behaviour control: namely, the use of electronics in the observation and control of offenders. It is beyond my scope to review the complex technical and ethical debate about these methods which—far from being in the area of science fiction—have been used and experimented with on prisoners and parolees for at least a decade. The following paragraph—taken, it should be noted, not from the writings of some 'Mad Scientists' but from a sober assessment written by two liberal criminologists—conveys some impression of what is being considered:[10]

> In the very near future, a computer technology will make possible alternatives to imprisonment. The development of systems for telemetering information from sensors implanted in or on the body will soon make possible the observation and control of human behaviour without actual physical contact. Through such telemetric devices, it will be possible to maintain twenty-four-hour-a-day surveillance over the subject and to intervene electronically or physically to influence and control selected behavior. It will thus be possible to exercise control over human behavior and from a distance without physical contact. The possible implications for criminology and corrections of such telemetric systems is tremendously significant.

This last sentence *must* be an understatement. Without reviewing all such implications, it is important to mention one aspect of the debate: if the reformist and social scientific arguments against the prison are correct, then the case for adopting these new methods looks altogether plausible. Prisons could be virtually abolished because even dangerous poor-risk or non-parolable prisoners would go into the community— with their telemetric transmitters swallowed or implanted internally—and society could still be protected and defended from them. Moreover—the clinching argument in our society—they would be tax-paying workers rather than economic liabilities. Here is an advocate of this technique quoted by Ingraham and Smith:

> A parolee thus released would probably be less likely than usual to commit offences if a record of his location were kept as the base station. If two-way communication were included in this system, a therapeutic relationship might be established in which the parolee could be rewarded, warned or otherwise signalled in accordance with the plan for therapy.

It is beyond my scope here to analyse the extension of such surveillance and control techniques outside the immediate prison setting. But such institutions as prisons and mental hospitals may be merely the embryonic locations for the developments of new forms of social control not just for those who have manifestly offended or threatened society, but for those judged— by scientific authority—to be of potential danger. As present methods of law enforcement and punishment continue to decline in effectiveness—and even orthodox criminologists such as Leslie Wilkins predict a total breakdown in the present criminal justice system before the end of the century if the same methods are used[11]—then cybernetic and psychiatric experts will be recruited. The development of national data banks and other forms of computerised and centralised recording of surveillance systems is only the beginning. As the electronics industry shifts some of its budget allocations from defence research to what is euphemistically termed 'feasibility studies in the public sector', a new law enforcement technology will develop with as little public scrutiny as could be expected with weapons of war. The depersonalised value-free language of technology is continually used. R. K. Schwitzgebel and other advocates of coercive behaviour modification (including the compulsive implantation of devices in the brain) note blandly that 'gradually a new field of study may be emerging, variously known as behavioral engineering or behavioral instrumentation'.[12] The intellectual thinks, others do the dirty work, and then the intellectual converts it all into a 'field of study'. Foucault's 'power–knowledge spiral' closes up.

Let me now return to inside the prison to another corollary of the medical model.

The curtain doesn't fall: the indeterminate sentence

A trend towards *longer* prison sentences became apparent at the same time as the deinstitutionalisation movement peaked. The demands for life sentences to mean 'just that' became strident and respectable, especially in countries which abolished or were on the way to abolishing the death penalty.

My warehouse prediction depicts the major consequence of this tendency. But—with the aid of the ideology of rehabilitation—there is another direction which medium- to long-term sentences might take which will add a wholly new element into the prisons. It has long been argued by some penal reformers that sentencing on a *fixed* time scale according to the gravity of the offence makes no sense in deciding when an offender should be allowed his liberty. The court at the time of sentence cannot know for how long a man should be imprisoned in terms of the supposed benefit of the experience; only the prison management knows when he is ready for release. Already, of course, in such matters as the remission of part of a sentence for good conduct and, more importantly, the introduction of a parole system, these principles have percolated into the system. The extreme and logical extension of the principle, though, involves setting aside the fairly rigid judicial limits within which good conduct, release on licence or parole systems operate and moving towards a degree of indeterminancy in the original setence.

A full indeterminate sentence means that the authority of the court is limited to directing the prospective prisoner to custody for a more or less indefinite period: after a stipulated period (which may be just a day), the institution or another authority may release him outright or conditionally (e.g. subject to supervision). Given all the criticism of current sentencing policy and a belief in the rehabilitative idea, this policy looks attractive to many reformers. Indeed it appears as the only logical one to adopt. As Martin Miller shows in tracing the evolution of the indeterminate sentence paradigm in America, it has long been held out as a penal panacea.[13] He quotes a penal reformer writing in 1847:

> You ask me for how long a time he should be sentenced to such confinement? Obviously, it seems to me, until the evil disposition is removed from his heart, until disqualification to go at large no longer exists; that is until he is a reformed man.

In the context of nineteenth-century reform movements and their contemporary counterparts, one can see why the notion of keeping people on ice until they could give some proof that they could be released without repeating their offence is an attractive one. It appeals to those who call for society to be protected from the dangers of further criminal depradations, but it also fits in nicely to any extension of the medical model into the area of crime and prisons. As in a hospital, the inmate can be released only when he is 'cured'. Miller again quotes an early (1905) and explicit statement of this position:

> To sentence a burglar at the time of his conviction to imprisonment for a term of five years is as irrational as it would be to send the lunatic to an asylum for the preordained time of five years or the small-pox patient to a hospital for exactly three weeks. The lunatic and the person afflicted with contagious disease must be confined until they are cured—until it is safe for the public that they be discharged. The same course is the only rational one to adopt for the criminal.

I cannot review here the full ramifications of how the Indeterminate Sentence model—used in the majority of American States—has worked out. A few points emerge, though, from the way it was implemented in California, where the system because of the wide temporal span between minimum and maximum sentence plus the employment of professional assessment personnel, acquired the reputation of the most progressive treatment-oriented model of American penal practice. There are two key criticisms: (1) the indeterminate sentence can, in fact, become an *indefinite* sentence, with men who do not conform to the norms of the releasing authority simply being stored in prison; (2) the treatment principle might become little more than a facade behind which prison administrators have available a powerful new form of social control. The inmate's uncertainty and inability to work out a temporal strategy can be used to manipulate passive obedience and conformity to the regime. Moreover dangerous or embarrassing prisoners can be held inside without the necessity of justifying this decision in a public or open hearing.

While I am not suggesting that this system will necessarily catch on in Britain and Europe, it seems likely that modified forms of the indeterminancy principle will evolve, which, together with the increasing tendency to remove clearly short-termers from the prison population, will mean that more prisoners will be indefinitely warehoused.

Conclusion: the prison into the community

So far, my predictions have been made with an odd sense of historical inevitability; as if prisons are running along some predestined path of their own and that knowledge—by criminologists, penal reformers, prisoners, politicians—cannot modify this direction. I'd partly support this pessimistic view by pointing to the ways in which outside critics have unwittingly lent credibility to the very developments they are opposed to.

But there is of course a chance for modification. As the evidence about the futility of correctional treatment becomes more widely known, the 'profound scepticism' and 'pessimism' now expressed by the experts might shift more groups towards an abolitionist direction. And even if 'tearing the walls down' is clearly not a viable political programme, some important reforms will be campaigned for. Take, for example, Jessica Mitford's radical reform package: (1) decriminalise all crimes without victims; (2) reduce all sentences; (3) provide educational, medical, psychiatric and vocational services in the prison, but make them completely independent of prison authorities with no coercion attached, nor affecting release: not part of any rehabilitative programme but to prevent damage; and (4) abolish parole and all elements of indeterminancy.

Such reforms are probably desirable both in themselves and because they will facilitate the gradual run down of imprisonment that I have assumed as a background to this whole discussion. But three warnings: first, it will be a long time before Mitford's type of programme is acceptable to orthodox prison reformers, let alone any government; second, these are *reforms* in the dictionary meaning of the term 'to make an institution better by removal or abandonment of imperfections, faults and errors'. Even if accepted fully—which is unlikely—the prison will remain. Finally: simply to cite disillusionment, cynicism, scepticism or pessimism about institutions and to produce statistics showing their relative decline doesn't mean that sociologists or activists can be at all complacent about what might replace the prison. Quite the reverse—and as a brief conclusion to this paper we must go outside the walls of the prison again to see what forms are being taken by social control in the community.

Not only are some of these community programmes themselves highly suspect but their stated rationales are often simply a matter of faith. As one excellent recent warning about the nature of so-called 'community correction' notes:[14]

> The wide acceptability of the rhetoric of
> rehabilitation used to promote community
> corrections, lingering attachment to the concept of
> community involvement or control among War
> on Poverty liberals and many segments of the
> left, a certain vagueness as to what community
> corrections actually means and a growing
> conviction among a substantial part of the
> population that prisons are needlessly cruel and
> more likely to corrupt than cure, have allowed
> programmes to proliferate largely free from
> critical scrutiny.

There was, a few years ago, an interesting phrase in the annual report for 1973 of the Howard League, the main British prison reform group:

> As we move out into the community away from
> the strict confines of institutional methods, we
> must simultaneously find new ways of using our
> traditional institutions. To polarize the situation
> by creating an artificial dichotomy between the
> prison and the community is a way of not seeing
> the real problems, which is to restore the prison
> to the community and the community to the
> prison and, in doing so, to transform them both.

I'm not sure if the author knew quite what he meant. If by 'restoring the community to the prison' is meant something like opening the prison up to outside scrutiny and accountability, clearly the tendency is quite the reverse.[15] What I want to emphasise, though, are the somewhat worrying ways in which the prison is being restored into the community, in which the cracks in the solid walls of the nineteenth-century prisons are allowing new forms of social control to percolate into the community with little scrutiny or public accountability.

There is, of course, one political sense in which the abolitionist case is quite correct in merely arguing *against* prisons and refusing to play the game of specifying 'what will you put in its place'.[16] The expectation that once custodial institutions are closed down, innovatory alternatives will then be stimulated, has been partly vindicated by the American experience. In the wake of the Massachusetts experiment, for example, all sorts of unpredictable new opportunities for care and control did develop. But despite all the optimistic hopes for community corrections—hopes as millenarian as those behind the asylum movement 150 years ago—there is no unambiguous evidence yet to prove that these programmes are more effective than conventional imprisonment. Indeed some evidence—on the questions of cost and effectiveness in reducing recidivism—is already pointing the other way.[17]

But—leaving the chimerical criterion of 'effectiveness' aside—there are other more significant consequences of restoring the prison to the community which need examination. We have to anticipate the ways in which these new measures might become increasingly coercive, how they might reproduce, under new disguises and euphemisms, the same attitudes and practices of the institutions they replaced.

The community programmes being now set up in America[18]—particularly for juveniles—have created a complicated new superstructure of social control. Visualise someone being shunted through this maze of agencies: hot-line emergency service—school counsellor—community social worker—day-care programme—probation—clinic—information and referral centre—diagnostic centre—half-way house—work release programme—hostel—parole—multi-service centre—human services network—group house—community home—youth service bureau . . .

There are two problems to which a close examination of this network should alert us. The first is that somewhere in this maze there are still 'residential agencies' which look suspiciously like the old bins. 'Closing down' has not been all that it seems. Because of the need to reassure the community that the real troublemakers are still being kept off the streets, such places as half-way houses or community homes emerge simply as the replacement of one sort of institution by another. As one enthusiastic advocate of community control explains:[19]

> A viable community service system must in
> advance prepare its *24-hour residential alternatives*
> in custodial institutions for the relatively small but
> real proportion of youngsters who need residential
> care, specialized services and controlled conditions.

Lerman's research on the Californian experience has already shown that youths diverted into the new community programme actually spent *more* time under closed supervision ('the 24-hour residential alternative') than those allocated to the control group, that is the old-style programme. The continued existence of these so-called 'alternatives' will ensure—as the warehouse scenario suggests—a more sustained moral outrage against their inmates. They will be punished more severely while more resources will go into the more glamorous, constructive part of the system. Who would want to work with people which this benign community care system has itself already labelled as hopeless?

The second problem—more worrying and more opaque—is that the very existence of this new hierarchy of control, care and treatment—with its consequent creation of new agencies, professional skills, specialist theories and vested interests—will allow more rather than fewer deviants to be swept up into the formal control system. As critics of 'community corrections' are already pointing out, the introduction of new alternatives considered more humane than the old, might simply increase their use. 'Offenders previously given probation or a suspended sentence because judges were unwilling to send them to the jungle of a prison or reformatory might be more willing to send them to a group home or foster home . . .'[20] And it is not just that *more* offenders might be caught up in the system, but that the criteria and procedures legitimated by justice and due process will become even more eroded in a system which draws its rationale from medicine and social work rather than law.

One might extrapolate from these and other developments a series of predictions even more global than I have already made in this paper: the development of new technologies of surveillance and behaviour modification, the extension of these outside the prison setting, the general tendency towards giving more discretion to non-legal administrative agencies controlling deviance.

The overall point is that although imprisonment is declining, both the *number* of persons under some form of criminal justice enterprise supervision at a given time (and the number who have ever been under such supervision) *and* the *proportion* of the population under supervision (or who have ever been under supervision) have grown greatly in the past fifty years rather than decreased (leaving aside the numbers under surveillance). And once people get into this web—the *correctional continuum*, as Americans are already calling it—they will find it more and more difficult to get out of it. The capacity to track persons is being rapidly developed and will surely be expanded.

In general then we can predict new levels of scrutiny and administrative disposition in the 'community'. Overtly or covertly, more of our lives will be under central surveillance and control.

Foucault described one historical take-off in terms of the move from 'simple' punishment to the concentrated surveillance of the asylum. We are living through another change: from the *concentration* to the *dispersal* of social control. Not only is there the formal correctional continuum as such, but (a point that obviously needs much more development) institutions such as the family and the school are being increasingly involved in the professional control apparatus through such services as school counsellors and special educational units. The highly specialised classification systems *inside* the nineteenth-century prison—the atlases of vice—are being replaced by an equally complex system of social control outside with fine gradations and levels of intervention—and all explained and justified by professional experts.

Perhaps it is already not too far-fetched to envisage a critique of these developments which looks back nostalgically to earlier models of social control.

Notes

1 The key study here—one which has revolutionised our thinking about the history of institutions—is David Rothman, *The Discovery of the Asylum: Social Order and Disorder in the New Republic*, Boston, Little, Brown, 1971.

2 Here—and throughout the paper—I am greatly indebted to the analysis of the history of prison architecture in Robin Evans: 'Prison design 1750–1842' (unpublished, Ph.D. thesis, University of Essex, 1975).

3 *Madness and Civilisation*, Tavistock, 1965; *Surveiller et punir*, Paris, Gallimard, 1975.

4 Benedict Alper, Foreword to Y. Bakal (ed.), *Closing Correctional Institutions*, Heath, 1973. For further specific comment on this experiment, see Andrew Rutherford, 'The dissolution of the training schools in Massachusetts', in Calvert Dodge (ed.), *A Nation Without Prisons*, Heath, 1975.

5 'We should never have promised a hospital', *Federal Probation*, 39(4), December 1975, pp. 3–9.

6 Much of what follows about nineteenth-century prison architecture is a summary of Evans (op. cit.).

7 'Strategies of Control', unpublished MS., Center for the Study of Law and Society, University of California, Berkeley, 1969.

8 *The American Prison Business*, Allen & Unwin, 1974.

9 op. cit., p. 8.

10 Barton L. Ingraham and Gerald W. Smith, 'The use of electronics in the observation and control of human behavior and its possible use in rehabilitation and parole', *Issues in Criminology*, 7(2), Fall 1972, pp. 35–53. A critique of this article—Michael H. Shapiro, 'The use of behavior control techniques: a response'—which concentrates particularly on the moral and ethical problems, follows in the same journal (pp. 55–93).

11 Leslie Wilkins, 'Crime and criminal justice at the turn of the century', *Annals of the American Academy of Political and Social Science*, 408, July 1973, pp. 13–20.

12 *Development and Legal Regulation of Coercive Behavior Modification Techniques with Offenders*, National Institute of Mental Health Monograph, Washington, 1971. See also the papers collected in R. L. and R. K. Schwitzgebel (eds), *Psychotechnology: Electronic Control of Mind and Behavior*, New York, Holt, Rinehart & Winston, 1973.

13 'The indeterminate sentence paradigm: resocialisation or social control?', *Issues in Criminology*, 7(2), Fall 1972, pp. 101–24.

228 *Stanley Cohen*

14 David F. Greenberg, 'Problems in community corrections', *Issues in Criminology*, 10(1), spring 1975, p. 2.

15 I am referring to the continued attempt in Britain by the Home Office—through such blanket provisions as the Official Secrets Acts—to keep prisons insulated from any outside scrutiny. For a case study of how this was used to block a research project, see S. Cohen and L. Taylor, 'Talking about prison blues', in C. Bell and H. Newby (eds), *Doing Sociological Research*, Allen & Unwin, 1977.

16 The case is convincingly made in Thomas Mathiessen, *The Politics of Abolition*, Martin Robertson, 1974.

17 Most notably, in Paul Lerman's devasting evaluation of various diversion, community service and probation subsidy programmes in California: *Community Treatment and Social Control* (University of Chicago Press, 1975). Too late for consideration in this article is Andrew Scull's much more fundamental critique of the whole decarceration movement. He shows: (1) the political and economic connections between decarceration and the changing exigencies of welfare capitalism and (2) what 'community treatment' actually involves and the likely effects of abandoning institutional controls. He paints a horrifying picture of how the decarcerated deviants—particularly the mentally ill—are dumped on communities unwilling and unable to care or cope with them. See *Decarceration: Community Treatment and the Deviant: a Radical View*, Englewood Cliffs, Prentice-Hall, 1977.

18 For an assessment of a wide selection of such programmes, see Gary R. Perlstein and Thomas Phelps (eds), *Alternatives to Prison: Community-Based Corrections*, Pacific Palisades, Cal., Goodyear, 1975.

19 Martin Gula, 'Community services and residential institutions for children', in Bakal, op. cit., p. 16 (my emphasis).

20 Greenberg, op. cit., p. 21.

Index